Deconstruction
and the
'Unfinished Project of Modernity'

Deconstruction
and the
'Unfinished Project of Modernity'

CHRISTOPHER NORRIS

THE ATHLONE PRESS
LONDON

First published in 2000 by
THE ATHLONE PRESS
1 Park Drive, London NW11 7SG

© Christopher Norris 2000

Christopher Norris has asserted his right under the Copyright, Designs and Patents
Act, 1988, to be identified as the author of this work

British Library Cataloguing in Publication Data
A catalogue record record for this book is available
from the British Library

ISBN 0 485 11564 6 HB
ISBN 0 485 12159 X PB

Typeset by Aarontype Limited, Easton, Bristol
Printed and bound in Great Britain by
Bookcraft (Bath) Ltd

For Alison

Contents

Introduction 1

Chapter 1   Deconstruction *versus* Postmodernism:
epistemology, ethics, aesthetics 6

Chapter 2   Postmodern Ethics and the Trouble with Relativism 25

Chapter 3   Deconstruction and the 'Unfinished Project of
Modernity' 48

Chapter 4   Deconstruction, Postmodernism and Philosophy
of Science 75

Chapter 5   'The Idea of the University': some interdisciplinary
soundings 103

Chapter 6   Ethics, Autonomy and Self-Invention: debating
Foucault 119

Chapter 7   'The Night in which All Cows are Black':
Paul de Man, 'mere reading' and indifference to
philosophy 136

Chapter 8   Conflict, Compromise or Complementarity: ideas
of science in modern literary theory 153

Chapter 9   Sexed Equations and Vexed Physicists: the 'two
cultures' revisited 175

Notes 202

Bibliography 223

Index 236

Introduction

I should say straight off that this book is not intended for academic specialists but for a wider readership with interests in philosophy and critical theory. It grew out of various lecture courses and seminars that I have been teaching over the past few years in the Philosophy Section at Cardiff University. Among the topics were 'Modern French Philosophy (Sartre to Derrida)', 'Philosophy of Science and Critical Theory', 'Deconstruction', and 'Literary Theory and Analytic Philosophy'. These were upper level (second- and third-year) undergraduate courses intended mainly for philosophy students but also attracting a brave handful from Literary and Cultural Studies who came along – I suspect – out of mild curiosity as to what a philosopher might have to say about postmodernism, deconstruction, and suchlike topics. In the event they gave rise to a good deal of lively seminar discussion and I hope went some way toward breaking down certain prejudices on both sides.

The book has a broadly similar aim and is pitched for the most part at much the same level. That is to say, it is intended on the one hand for those who want a more 'philosophical' approach to issues in present-day literary theory, and on the other for philosophy students who find themselves intrigued or baffled by the sorts of discussion that typically occur in literary seminars. My own background can best be described as a twenty-year passage from 'theory' to 'philosophy', one that has left me with deep reservations about much that goes on under the first rubric, but also with a strong sense that intellectual horizons are artificially narrowed by a too strict policing of this boundary-line. At any rate there is nothing to be gained by the attitude of blanket hostility that has so far prevented many analytic (i.e., mainstream Anglo-American) philosophers from engaging with various 'continental' developments – deconstruction chief among them – on the pretext that these could be of interest only to literary theorists who lack an adequate philosophical training.

I therefore spend a lot of time in the first three chapters attempting to clear up some of the misconceptions about Derrida's work that have gained wide currency among detractors and disciples alike. More specifically, I put the case that his writings are indeed 'analytic' in the proper sense of that term which applies to all good philosophy and not just to those approaches adopted by thinkers in the recent (post-1920) Anglophone line of descent.

On this non-parochial definition it denotes the virtues of logical rigour, conceptual precision, and attentiveness to details of the text in hand, even (or especially) where these turn out to involve unexpected or hitherto unnoticed complications. In short, deconstruction cannot be viewed as just a more specialised sub-branch of that wider socio-cultural phenomenon that goes under the name of 'postmodernism' and whose manifestations range all the way from fashionable styles in art, architecture, fiction and music to the 'post-philosophical' writings of Richard Rorty. Nor can it be annexed to that movement of counter-Enlightenment thought which runs from Nietzsche – or a certain reading of Nietzsche – to latterday irrationalists such as Jean Baudrillard and 'strong' cultural relativists who find inspiration in the work of Michel Foucault.

In Chapter Three I offer an account of deconstruction which brings out its deep (though problematical) affinity with the project of enlightened critique set forth by Kant and taken up – albeit with significant modifica- tions – by Jürgen Habermas. The continuing relevance of that project to present-day issues in epistemology, ethics and politics is the main ground of dispute between Derrida and postmodernist thinkers such as Jean-François Lyotard. My chief purpose here is to clarify some basic terms and distinctions which provide a firmer sense of historical perspective as well as a handle for grasping some important philosophic differences of view. I also discuss these issues in relation to the modern university, again with particular reference to Kant since his political writings – especially 'The Conflict of the Faculties' – have provided a context for recent debate about the role of philosophy as a critical voice both within and beyond the disciplinary framework of univer- sity teaching and research. In this early part of the book – especially Chapter One – I have tried to preserve a fairly informal, at times even conversational style as I think best befits an introductory discussion for readers compara- tively new to the field.

Chapter Four addresses related issues in the context of epistemology and philosophy of science. Here I examine the close affinity between Derrida's writings on the role of metaphor in scientific thought and the distinctive mode of epistemo-critical reflection (or *rationalisme appliqué*) whose chief representatives are Gaston Bachelard and Georges Canguilhem. Bachelard's work has been highly influential in recent French thought – e.g., through the notion of 'epistemological breaks' developed in different ways by Althusser and Foucault – though its distinctive character has often been obscured in readings that fall far short of Derrida's in point of concep- tual rigour and philosophic acuity. In Chapter Five I offer some critical reflections on the topic of 'interdisciplinarity', or the way that increas- ing specialisation in various disciplines has gone along with calls to redefine, renegotiate, or – at the postmodern-textualist limit – to abolish all boundaries between them. Here again I suggest that the 'radical' appeal of such arguments is compromised through the lack of any adequate standards (scientific, philosophical, or ethico-political) by which one might assess the results of this strong-revisionist enterprise were it actually carried through.

Chapter Six ('Ethics, Autonomy and Self-Invention') was written in reply to an article by Patrick Shaw that took issue with my reading of Foucault's various texts on Kant, Nietzsche and the 'philosophic discourse of modernity'. This exchange helped to focus my thoughts on a number of issues – some of them developed at length in this book – so I thought it worthwhile to revise and expand the original essay for inclusion here. I should like to thank Patrick Shaw for his continuing readiness to discuss these issues in a spirit of constructive disagreement and also Wolfe Mays – editor of *The Journal of the British Society for Phenomenology* – who offered me far more space for my response than I had any right to expect.

The issue of relevant disciplinary standards resurfaces in Chapter Seven where I discuss the work of Paul de Man and his 'indifference to philosophy' or studious flouting of the protocols that normally decide what shall count as an adequate, responsible, or competent reading of philosophic texts. Having written a book about de Man some ten years ago I found myself struck once again by the exorbitant strangeness of his thinking and the problem of deciding at just what point an attitude of principled resistance to orthodox or mainstream interpretive conventions leans over into one of perverse disregard for basic values of logic, consistency, and truth. If I am now less inclined to give de Man the benefit of the doubt – that is to say, less convinced that this strangeness results (as he would claim) from the sheer deconstructive necessity of reading against the canonical grain – then that conclusion has itself been forced upon me by long experience of teaching these texts at undergraduate and graduate level. That is to say, I have ignored the storm kicked up over de Man's wartime journalism by commentators whose stance of high-toned moral indignation very often went along with a low-minded taste for academic scandal-mongering. Whatever the connections between 'early' and 'late' de Man they can only be obscured by an attitude of prosecuting zeal which fails to respect the most elementary standards of critical-interpretive debate. At least one may hope that discussion has now moved on to the point where these questions can be raised without the resort to blanket attacks on deconstruction as a nihilist enterprise or a covert technique for assuaging the war-guilt of collaborationist intellectuals.

The following two chapters mark a shift of ground although they do address a number of closely related themes. These include (once again) the issue of disciplinarity and the kinds of boundary-dispute that often arise when thinkers venture into specialist fields where they possess no authorized or accredited expertise. Chapter Eight is basically a critical review of the various ways in which literary theorists – from I.A. Richards to the present day – have responded to the challenge of scientific knowledge in relation to their own disciplinary methods and values. Thus it traces the century-long pattern of reactive attitudes whereby science has alternately figured as a threat to those values or as a source of suggestive metaphors, models and analogies for development in the literary domain, often on the basis of a partial or a highly selective understanding. Chapter Nine started out as a review of *Intellectual Impostures*, a book by two physicists (Alan Sokal and Jean Bricmont) which appeared in the wake of Sokal's notorious *Social Text* hoax essay. I argue that the episode cannot be dismissed as just a passing salvo in the 'science wars' but should be read against the background of present-day debates about science, cultural studies, and the 'strong programme' in sociology of knowledge. Beyond that, it reveals some genuine problems with the kinds of anti-realist, cultural-relativist, or social-constructivist approach that Sokal/Bricmont take as their prime targets.

However I suggest that some physicists – quantum theorists especially – have themselves helped to encourage this trend by advancing a range of dubious speculative arguments or by declaring scientific realism no longer tenable on the basis of far-from decisive experimental evidence. This helps to explain why Sokal's article manifests all the signs of 'unstable' irony, and perhaps why the *Social Text* editors were taken in by its motley parade of citations from cultural theorists and 'respectable' scientific sources alike. My discussion covers some basic issues in the interpretation of quantum mechanics by way of showing how they have influenced debate not only in post-Kuhnian history/philosophy of science but also in various quarters of postmodernist cultural theory. What limits the effectiveness of Sokal/Bricmont's critique is their failure to acknowledge this further irony and their blanket attack on a range of (mainly French-influenced) movements of thought which require more discriminate treatment. Their case might also have gained additional force had it taken account of other – e.g., Wittgensteinian – sources for this widespread turn toward cultural-relativist thinking. By now it will be clear that I share their disquiet at the ease with which large sections of the arts-and-humanities and social-sciences community have been won over to a range of broadly 'postmodernist' positions whose chief common feature is a will to deny the values of reasoned critical debate and truth-seeking enquiry. However those values will scarcely be promoted or advanced by a flat refusal to pursue such debate across real (yet by no means unbridgeable) differences of cultural, intellectual, and disciplinary standpoint.

At any rate my work on this book has been made a great deal more rewarding and pleasurable through various meetings and exchanges over the past two years. I am happy to acknowledge some large debts of gratitude as well as permissions to reprint material in more or less extensively revised form. Chapters One and Two derive in part from some lectures I gave at the University of Santiago de Compostela in Spain on the occasion of a conference organised by my good friend Manuel Barbeito Varela. I should also like to thank Margarita Estevez Saa who produced a transcript from the often barely audible tape and who thus enabled this exercise in creative reconstruction. Frank Webster of Oxford Brookes University encouraged me to focus my thoughts on postmodernism for an essay in his volume *Understanding Contemporary Society*, published by Sage. I am grateful to Martin McQuillan and Edinburgh University Press for permission with regard to Chapter Three, reprinted from McQuillan (ed.), *Post-Theory: new directions in criticism*; to the editors and Basil Blackwell, publisher of *Cultural Values*, for Chapter Four which first appeared in that journal; to Taieb Belghazi who invited me to Rabat, Morocco for a conference on 'The Idea of the University' (whence Chapter Five); to John Hartley and Sage Publications for allowing me to ruminate at length on the Sokal affair; and to Jonathan Hart and co-editors of the *Canadian Review of Comparative Literature* for commissioning the article on de Man. Let me also – once again – thank my colleagues in the Philosophy Section at Cardiff who have offered so much in the way of intellectual stimulus, support and companionship.

Cardiff, May 1999

CHAPTER 1

Deconstruction versus *Postmodernism:* epistemology, ethics, aesthetics

I

First I want to raise some matters of definition, since these terms – 'Modernism', 'Postmodernism' and 'Deconstruction' – are used with very different senses in a range of different contexts so there is a need for clarification. Many years ago, in the 1920s, Arthur Lovejoy suggested a moratorium on use of the term 'Romanticism' because this word had been applied to so many periods, genres, styles, or movements of thought that it was now causing great confusion.[1] I think there may likewise be a case for ceasing to talk about 'Postmodernism' and even, perhaps, about 'Modernism' until we can sort out the different historical, philosophical, and more broadly socio-cultural senses that get attached to those terms. So what I want to do now is introduce a few distinctions that will perhaps make it possible to discuss these matters more usefully.

Part of the problem is that we cannot begin to define 'Postmodernism' until we have some reasonably clear working notion of what 'Modernism' means, and this term is itself subject to just as many variant usages, depending on one's scope of historical perspective or range of disciplinary interests. Literary critics and theorists have a fairly good idea of what they mean by Modernism: it is a movement that began in the early twentieth century, more particularly during the years just after the First World War. It applies to certain fictional and poetic devices, modes of writing, experimental procedures, the use of spatial form, stream-of-consciousness, the predominance of metaphor, striking juxtapositions of image and style as in *Ulysses* or 'The Waste Land', techniques of multiple narrative consciousness, the unreliable narrator, all kinds of highly self-conscious formal and aesthetic innovation.[2] Music critics also have a pretty fair idea of what they mean by musical Modernism. In brief, it would include the early expressionist and the later atonal, serial or twelve-note music of Schoenberg and his Viennese disciples; middle-period (neoclassical) Stravinsky and other such gestures of revolt against nineteenth-century Romanticism; more complex or challenging techniques of development, formal structure, harmonic progression, etc.; in other words, as Ezra Pound famously said, the desire to 'make it new' at all costs and throw off the dead weight of inherited tradition.[3] So, to this extent, musical and literary critics have a good working grasp of what 'Modernism' means for their particular descriptive or classificatory purposes. Much the same can be said of those movements in painting and the visual arts – from Cubism to Abstract Expressionism – which marked a very conscious and deliberate break with previous generic conventions, and to which the term 'modernist' is routinely applied by art-historians and critics.

However, if you look at how philosophers and intellectual historians use that term, you will find a very different range of meanings and associations. For some, the emergence of a 'philosophic discourse of modernity' dates back to the seventeenth century and Descartes's attempt to provide a new foundation for philosophy in his famous declaration 'cogito ergo sum' ('I think, therefore I am'), conceived as an absolute, indubitable ground of knowledge.[4] This was the upshot of his famous experiment in self-imposed radical doubt. Thus I might try to call everything into question by systematically doubting the existence of an external world, or of other minds, or the difference between waking and dreaming 'reality', or that between a sane (undeluded) knowledge of my own physical constitution and the mad idea that my head is made of glass. Perhaps I am the victim of an evil demiurge – Descartes' *malin genie* – who enjoys nothing more than fooling me in just such ways. (Present-day philosophers have updated Descartes's thought-experiment by asking how I can possibly *know* that I am not a brain in a vat kept alive with a constant supply of chemical nutrients and induced to believe in all the details of my 'real-world', everyday existence through a range of artificial stimuli programmed by a mad but super-intelligent computer scientist.) Yet one thing of which I can be certain – since to deny it would be plainly absurd – is that *I* must exist as thinker of the thought 'I think, therefore I am'. And from this point – so Descartes maintained – one could proceed to rebuild the foundations of an objectively-existent (mind-independent) world whose reality could no longer be taken for granted in a straightforward, commonsense way.

Thus modernity in this sense – philosophical modernity – begins with the idea that knowledge stands in need of some grounding principle or bedrock assurance proof against the challenge of sceptical doubt. Then again, moving on a couple of centuries, one might date the emergence of 'true' philosophical modernity with Kant and his hugely ambitious attempt to provide a transcendentally justified account of the various human faculties, that is to say, cognitive understanding, practical reason, aesthetic judgement, and reason in its 'pure' or speculative modes.[5] Indeed it can be argued that a great many subsequent debates – about truth, knowledge, ethics, aesthetics, the status of the human or social *vis-á-vis* the natural sciences – have their origin in various readings of Kant. So Modernism, in this context, is an attempt to define the scope, the powers and the limits of the various human faculties of knowledge, reason, and judgement. For many philosophers, at least those working in the broadly continental tradition, this would be one of the defining moments of modernity, the philosophic discourse of modernity, a discourse that has continued (though some might wish to reject or deny it) right down to the present day.

One of the most resourceful defenders of that tradition is the German philosopher Jürgen Habermas who stands directly in the line of descent from Kant. Habermas continues to distinguish the various modalities of understanding, practical reason, aesthetic judgement, etc., since he thinks it very important – not least on ethico-political grounds – to avoid mixing them up in the typical 'postmodernist' fashion.[6] However he does not entirely endorse Kant's way of thinking about these issues but in stead seeks to give them a more pragmatic, discursive, or linguistic turn. Thus Habermas talks about the 'ideal speech-situation' as a kind of implicit understanding or regulative idea that is built into all our communicative acts, our social life-forms and structures of political representation.[7] Nevertheless, in his writing there is still a strong commitment to Kantian or Enlightenment values, to what he calls 'the unfinished project of modernity'. Habermas thinks it vital to conserve that critical impulse because the only way that we can work towards a more just, equitable, truly democratic society is by keeping our sights fixed upon the possibility of achieving an enlightened consensus, in Kant's phrase a *sensus communis*. This is *not* just common sense under a fancy name, not just a kind of *de facto*, pragmatic agreement on certain matters of belief or value commitments. Rather, it is the idea of agreement arrived at through an enlightened, democratic, participant exchange on issues of shared concern for humanity. Whence Habermas's firmly-held belief that we can indeed communicate across cultural differences or conflicting ideas of moral, social, and political good; moreover, that despite those differences we can at least hope to achieve a broad consensus that may eventually resolve such localised disputes. This is a deeply Kantian viewpoint: enlightened, critical, progressive, aimed toward extending the 'public sphere' as far and as wide as possible.

So, to repeat: we need to keep in mind this distinction between, on the one hand, the cultural-aesthetic Modernist movement which emerged at a certain time, the early twentieth century, and was characterised by certain innovations of a chiefly formal and stylistic kind, and, on the other hand, the philosophic discourse of modernity which goes further back and which involves much larger claims.[8] Now, I think we can draw some related distinctions between various uses of the term 'Postmodernism'. There is a sense of the term in which it figures as a broad, rather fuzzy, ill-defined cultural phenomenon. Such is Postmodernism as described by a culture-critic like Fredric Jameson who sees signs of it everywhere and who mostly – not always – likes what he sees.[9] Jameson speaks as a Marxist, but a Marxist with distinctly postmodernist leanings. Even though these developments must be viewed as belonging to the 'cultural logic of late capitalism' – as revealing a thoroughly commodified system of cultural production/consumption – still they are the best (most representative) expressions of the stage now reached in that process. Thus, on Jameson's account, there is no point criticising, or rejecting, or deploring Postmodernism, as if one had some choice in the matter or as if one could simply opt out of it and adopt some alternative outlook. Jameson views postmodernism as a defining aspect of the way we live now: it affects our life-styles, our reading habits, our architectural surroundings, the way we listen to music, watch television, absorb the latest news of world events, respond to advertising. It is the element we inhabit, the sea we swim in, the very air we breath. It affects and pervades so many aspects of our life that it would be futile for us to declare ourselves 'against Postmodernism'. Jameson thinks that basically all we can do is say that there are some bits we like and some bits we don't like so much, or perhaps not at all. Thus, speaking for himself, he quite likes the architecture and some of the music, isn't so keen on a lot of the fiction that gets itself called 'postmodernist', but in the end thinks that these are matters of personal taste or individual predilection. After all, the whole idea of aesthetic judgement as appealing to shared (i.e., intersubjective or transindividual) criteria is just the sort of Kantian universalist argument that postmodernism has left far behind.

II

Clearly there is a measure of truth in all this. If you happen to enjoy postmodernist fiction, then I could not hope to persuade you otherwise, and indeed wouldn't want to since I disagree with Jameson in finding it (for the most part) witty, inventive, and intellectually rewarding. I might try a bit harder to change your mind if you profess to enjoy 'postmodern' music, or the sorts of music that often get described that way: for instance, the music of minimalist composers such as Philip Glass, Steve Reich, Michael Nyman, and the 'holy minimalists' Arvo Pärt and John Tavener. Perhaps I would not really hope to dissuade you or to spoil your enjoyment by coming up with good reasons to think it bad music! On the other hand, I *would* want to say that the argument does not stop there. One can go beyond the stage of just saying 'I like it' or 'I don't like it', as for instance by remarking that much of this music is mind-numbingly banal and repetitive, that it offers no aural or intellectual challenge, requires no effort of structural grasp or ability to follow a complex pattern of harmonic, tonal, or rhythmic development. In other words, it does not do what music ought to do, that is, provoke and stimulate the listener by putting up resistance to facile or habitual, quasi-automated habits of response. Still, as I have said, Jameson has a point – though a limited point – when he adopts his take-it-or-leave-it line on the varieties of postmodern cultural taste. For eventually such arguments must have an end and give way to statements of individual preference, even if that stage comes later than Jameson thinks and allows for some worth-while discussion along the way.

However, this is not the aspect of Postmodernism that I am chiefly concerned with here. There is another aspect, besides the broadly cultural-aesthetic, which I think is more open to criticism and which can be stated in the form of a few fairly basic propositions. This is 'philosophical' Postmodernism and it extends into ethics and politics, as well as into other areas like epistemology and philosophy of language. The position is set out by Jean-François Lyotard whose book *The Postmodern Condition* has been undoubtedly the single most widely read text on this topic.[10] Lyotard argues that the philosophic discourse of modernity is now historically redundant since it has long been been overtaken by so many social, political, and cultural developments. Once upon a time, no doubt, it was possible to believe in all those splendid Enlightenment values: in truth, progress, universal justice, perpetual peace, the 'sensus communis', and so forth. Perhaps one could even believe, like Kant, that all the diverse human cultures were destined to transcend their parochial conflicts of interest and achieve some sort of federal world-state – the United Nations as an Idea of Reason, if you like. Such was at any rate the 'grand narrative' of Enlightenment thinking as Lyotard reads it. This narrative of course took different forms and emphasised different details of the story from one thinker to the next. There was the Kantian grand narrative of reason, democracy, the universal 'kingdom of ends' as an ethical and socio-political ideal. After that came Hegel's dialectical conception of history as moving ever onward and up through stages of successive conflict and resolution to the point where *Geist* (Spirit or Mind) attained Absolute Knowledge and could thus write the book-to-end-all-books that was Hegel's *Phenomenology of Spirit*.[11] Hegel is actually a better example than Kant of the kind of grand-narrative (or 'metanarrative') thinking that Lyotard hopes we have now left behind with the passage to our present 'postmodern condition'. A meta-narrative is a story that wants to be more than just a story, that is to say, one which claims to have achieved an omniscient standpoint above and beyond all the other stories that people have told so far. There is also a Marxist metanarrative (or was until recently, Lyotard would say) which seeks to out-Hegel Hegel by inverting his idealist dialectic and introducing such ideas as economic determination 'in the last instance', 'forces and rela-tions of production', the base/superstructure metaphor, and class-conflict as the driving force in history. Again, this argument is manifestly con-structed on grand-narrative lines, since again it involves the assumption of an endpoint – following the short-term 'dictatorship of the proletariat' – at which time all conflicts of class-interest will somehow be transcended or resolved.

However, Lyotard says, we have to let go of these consoling illusions. We can no longer believe in the values that once characterized the Enlightenment project because, quite simply, we cannot ignore all the contrary evidence to date. That is, we have now been witness to so many wars, pogroms, bloody revolutions, counter-revolutions, post-revolutionary terrors, or resurgences of ethnic conflict that the old metanarratives (along with all their values of truth, progress, and universal justice) cannot be sustained unless through ignorance or sheer bad faith. We have seen the suppression of 'workers' democracy', of 'socialism with a human face', and of every attempt to carry such principles into practice. We have seen what happened in East Germany (1953), in Hungary (1956), and in Czechoslovakia (1968); also what occurred in the Soviet Union during seven decades of (nominally) Communist rule. In other words, there are too many melancholy instances of failed revolutionary hope for us to believe any longer in those old grand narratives – whether Kantian, Hegelian, or Marxist – that placed their faith in the power of reason to extrapolate reliably from past to future events. So we should now abandon that faith, Lyotard thinks, and instead take the tolerant postmodern-pluralist view that there exist any number of 'first-order natural pragmatic narratives', each of them having a right to express its own distinctive values, belief-system, or criteria for what should count as a 'truthful' or 'valid' statement. Moreover, we now have to recognize – as the one remaining principle of justice in a postmodern epoch – that these narratives are strictly incommensurable, that we should never presume to judge between them on grounds of justice or truth. For we are sure to commit an ethical wrong – an infraction of the narrative 'differend' – if we apply one set of criteria (i.e., our own) in order to criticize the practices or beliefs of others, or in order to adjudicate the issue between parties who may not (one or either of them) accept our terms of reference.[12] We have to accept the 'postmodern condition', that is, the fact (as Lyotard sees it) that we nowadays need to make sense of our lives in a context of multiple, open-ended, ever proliferating narratives and language-games. We tell many stories about ourselves, about history, philosophy, the human and the natural sciences, and of course about politics and the various lessons to be drawn from past and present political events. But the problem, Lyotard says, is that we have to respect the narrative *differend* and not make the error – the typical 'Enlightenment' error – of believing any one such story to possess superior truth-telling warrant.

Now, I take it that this is what 'Postmodernism' means in the more specific (philosophically articulated) sense of that term. At any rate it is useful, as a kind of preliminary ground-clearing exercise, to distinguish this from the other sense of the term which applies to such a range of otherwise disparate social and cultural phenomena that it becomes just a vague, all-purpose descriptor for 'the way we live now'. Up to a point I would agree with Jameson when he argues that one cannot reject or deplore post-modernism in this latter sense because, quite simply, there is too much of it around; it affects too many aspects of our lives. However one can, I think, mount a strong case against the kind of postmodernist thinking to be found in Lyotard and others of a similar doctrinal persuasion. One can argue that it is philosophically confused, that it carries some dubious ethical and socio-political implications, and moreover that it gives a very partial (at times a demonstrably false or distorted) account of so-called 'Enlightenment' thought.

III

Such is the case that I wish to defend in the rest of this chapter, having tried to establish some basic (albeit much-disputed) terms of reference. There are three main aspects of postmodernism, and they have to do with epistemology, ethics and aesthetics. These areas of concern were also central to Kant's critical enterprise, as likewise for the critical tradition in philosophy that has come down from Kant to present-day thinkers like Habermas and Karl-Otto Apel.[13] Epistemology has to do with knowledge, with the scope, that is to say, the powers and the limits of humanly attainable knowledge. This is the realm of cognitive *understanding* – in Kant's very specific sense of that term – and its rule is that intuitions (sensuous or phenomenal intuitions) must be brought under adequate concepts. 'Intuitions without concepts are blind; concepts without intuitions are empty.'[14] It is a question of what we can know or what we can legitimately claim to know. For Kant there were certain kinds of knowledge that were just unattainable: knowledge concerning such matters as freedom of will, the immortality of the soul, or the existence of God, along with certain speculative questions about cosmology, time, and the origins of the universe. If understanding tried to get a hold on these matters, then it would overreach itself, it would run into paradoxes, contradictions and antinomies. So in the First Critique, the *Critique of Pure Reason*, Kant is trying to define the proper scope of understanding (or epistemology) in both senses of the word 'define': to specify precisely what it *can* achieve and also to delimit its sphere of operation. Thus if we wish to achieve scientific knowledge, or if we want to understand those objects and events that make up the furniture of our everyday world, then it is the rule in such cases that intuitions be brought under adequate or corresponding concepts. Of course this is a 'rule' in the constitutive sense that it defines the precondition for possessing such knowledge, and not in the other (regulative) sense of a 'rule' that normally or standardly applies, but which we might just choose to ignore on certain occasions. So what Kant is setting out in the First *Critique* is a theory of knowledge that also involves a strict delimitation of its scope or proper remit.

For there are regions of enquiry where, if we try to achieve such knowledge, then we straight away run into all sorts of problem. If we seek to *understand* the nature of the soul, or of God, or certain issues in speculative cosmology ('Is the universe finite or infinite?' 'Did time have a beginning?', and so forth), then we strain understanding to a point where it creates insoluble antinomies. Here we possess neither adequate (determinate) concepts nor intuitions of space or time that could possibly serve to ground such knowledge. Kant has a striking metaphor at this point, one of his few really vivid and suggestive metaphors. Imagine a dove that thinks to itself: if only I could soar to a greater altitude where the air is much thinner then my wings would encounter much less resistance and who knows how fast and how high I could climb? But of course, at the limit, those wings would be flapping in a void and hence quite incapable of providing lift or forward motion. So what Kant tries to do in the First *Critique* is demonstrate the sorts of illusion that arise when when reason (pure or speculative reason) mistakenly thinks to give itself the rule that intuitions must be brought under adequate concepts. Such thinking is perfectly legitimate – indeed, cannot be dispensed with – when it comes to questions of ultimate import for the conduct of our lives in the ethical, political or religious spheres. We can indeed think about God, about the soul, about freewill, immortality and other such matters; also – when concerned with the prospects for human moral and political advancement – about ideas of progress, democracy, justice or even 'perpetual peace'. However, these are Ideas of Reason for which there exists no cognitive or factual evidence and which therefore cannot be grounded in the union of concepts with sensuous intuitions. In other words, they involve speculative uses of Reason that go far beyond the limits of cognitive understanding. So for Kant it is a matter of some urgency to establish those limits and thus to draw a line between the spheres of understanding and speculative reason.

In the Second Critique, the *Critique of Practical Reason*, Kant is concerned chiefly with ethical issues and with such questions as: how ought we to behave? in accordance with what kinds of guiding maxim or generalized principles of conduct? and how can we apply such universal rules to the various specific situations and complicated issues of choice that we confront in our everyday lives as moral agents?[15] I shall have more to say about Kantian ethics in relation to the reading of Kant proposed by Lyotard and other postmodernist thinkers. Just now, what I wish to emphasise is the problematic gap that opens up between, on the one hand, those high-level maxims (subject to the ultimate Categorical Imperative: act always on that maxim such that you could consistently will it to be adopted by every-one in a like situation) and, on the other hand, the detailed practicalities of real-world moral conduct. For it is a problem often noted by Kant's critics – those who reject his universalising approach to ethical issues – that the maxims don't provide much useful guidance when one has to choose between different (maybe conflicting) ethical priorities, or where no such rule seems to fit the particular case in hand. That is to say, there is a gap between rule and application, universal and particular, moral judgement as derived from abstract prescriptions and moral judgement as it is actually brought to bear in situations that are often more complex and difficult than anything allowed for on the strong universalist view. Among Kant's critics in this regard are communitarian thinkers who urge that we should drop all that high-level talk of rules, maxims, or categorical imperatives, and recog-nise that it is only within certain contexts – cultures, traditions, communal life-forms, language-games, shared social practices and so forth – that moral judgements make any kind of sense.[16] Moreover, there is an obvious connection here with Lyotard's call for an end to meta-narratives and for a 'postmodern' ethics whose watchword would be: let us multiply language-games as far as possible and accept no restriction on the range and variety of first-order, natural, pragmatic narratives.

In Lyotard's case this goes along with a marked shift of emphasis to the Third Critique, the *Critique of Judgement*, where Kant is concerned mainly with issues of aesthetics, though in a sense of that term much broader than its normal present-day usage.[17] For Kant, the aesthetic had to do not only with our appreciation and evaluation of works of art. Rather, it involved a whole range of issues that included, crucially, the linking-up between sensuous intuitions and concepts, a topic which Kant had first broached in the section entitled 'Transcendental Aesthetic' in the First *Critique* but had left somewhat obscure and under-explained. As we have seen, it is a condition of all understanding that intuitions be 'brought under' adequate concepts in the act of cognitive grasp. But the question remains: by what faculty or power of judgement do we manage to achieve this remarkable though everyday feat? After all, an intuition, a sensuous intuition, the phenomenal experience I can have of (say) this table in front of me is a very different thing from my concept of a table. In order to understand what a table is – and perceive this object *as* a table – I have to bring together my concept of a table and my sensuous intuition of it. But there is a real problem for Kant in negotiating this passage, in explaining how it is that the two distinct orders of perceptual experience and conceptual judgement can possibly be bridged or reconciled. This is the point at which *imagination* comes in, and imagination, for Kant in the First *Critique*, is a very obscure thing, a 'blind but indispensable function of the soul, without which we should have no knowledge whatsoever, but of which we are scarcely ever conscious'[18]. Kant usually strives for precision in defining his terms, but on this point he becomes notably obscure and even, one feels, somewhat shuffling and evasive. Anyway the issue is one that is held over for further, more elaborate treatment in the Third *Critique*. There Kant will take up the question of judgement – aesthetic judgement in the broad sense of that term – as playing a vital intermediary role in the passage from intuitions to concepts.

As we have seen, there is a similar problem in the Second *Critique* concerning the gap between high-level maxims or imperatives (which aspire to an order of universality remote from everyday experience) and what goes on in particular contexts of ethically-motivated conduct and choice. How is it, one may ask, that we are supposed to bridge that seemingly unbridgeable gap? How should we negotiate the Kantian gulf between universal precepts ('act always on that maxim . . .', etc.) and the various commonplace though difficult moral predicaments in which we may find ourselves? Again, this requires an exercise of judgement, of *imaginative* judgement in so far as it cannot be merely a matter of linking up maxims with cases on a one-to-one correspondence principle. In other words, there is always something more involved than a straightforward matching of precepts with practice, just as there is always something more to the act of bringing intuitions under concepts. In each case that 'something more' has to do with the exercise of judgement and the human capacity to seek out possible ways of deploying our faculties that are not laid down in advance or, so to speak, algorith-mically derivable from fixed procedures and guidelines.

So there are crucial issues of epistemology and ethics that Kant raises in the first two *Critiques* and which he takes up again for more extensive treatment in the *Critique of Judgement*. As I have said, the Third *Critique* is about aesthetics, but not narrowly, not just about issues concerning art or our appreciation of artworks. It is about judgement in a far more general sense: how it is that we can form judgements of nature, how it is that we achieve a knowledge of natural objects, processes, and events, given that these are not known to us directly but always *via* our various faculties of sensuous intuition, conceptual understanding, and 'imagination' as the synthesising power that makes all this possible? So the Third *Critique*, where Kant discusses aesthetics, is in fact much wider, more ambitious in scope, a cornerstone of his entire critical philosophy. He is trying to explain how the human mind understands nature, not only under its aesthetic (contemplative or 'disinterested') aspect, but also as regards the very possibility of other, more scientifically or cognitively oriented modes of knowledge. Then again, Kant resumes certain themes from the Second *Critique*, those having to do with the exercise of practical reason as belonging to a 'suprasensible' realm where it is no longer the rule that intuitions should be brought under adequate concepts. For aesthetic judgements are *indeterminate* (or 'reflective') in the sense that they are always open-ended with respect to the various possible particulars, or items of aesthetic experience, that may fall within their compass. And conversely, those particulars are not so much in quest of an 'adequate' concept as apt, through their very uniqueness and singularity, to evoke novel modes of judgement that apply to one instance and perhaps to no other.

So aesthetics – in Kant's philosophy – is the place where all sorts of problems are raised and receive not so much a definitive solution as a far-reachingly suggestive and speculative treatment. It is also in the *Critique of Judgement* that his discussion broadens out to encompass aspects of Nature – the beautiful and the sublime – that involve some particularly complex orders of aesthetic and reflective response. That is to say, the 'aesthetic' is no longer chiefly defined (as per the First *Critique*) in terms of a relationship – albeit obscure or 'buried in the depths of the soul' – between sensuous intuitions and concepts. Rather, it is conceived in teleological terms, that is, as reflecting a certain purposiveness in nature which is intelligible to us in virtue of the kindred teleology that guides our faculties and the relations between them when we respond to nature under its aesthetic (whether beautiful or sublime) aspect. In the case of the beautiful this involves a state of harmonious adjustment between *imagination and understanding*, such that we enjoy a 'free play' of the faculties as they seek for some indeterminate (reflective) mode of judgement that would do justice to some given particular. In the case of the sublime matters are more complex since here it is a question of our coming up against awesome, overwhelming, or terrifying kinds of experience, or again, of our trying to entertain ideas (like that of infinity or the mathematical sublime) to which no intuition or concept is remotely adequate. Yet even here there is a positive moment, so to speak, when the mind overcomes its initial state of abjection and acknowledges that there must be something in its own nature – its 'suprasensible' nature – that allows thought to transcend the limiting conditions of perceptual or phenomenal experience. What makes this possible, in the case of the sublime, is a complex interplay between *imagination and reason*, such that we attain to an inward awareness of all that lies beyond the sensory domain, including (most importantly for Kant) the dictates of moral conscience. Where the beautiful assures us of a harmonious relation between the faculties, as likewise between mind and nature, the sublime takes effect rather by disrupting that harmony, forcing us sharply – even painfully – up against the limits of adequate representation. Yet we can still take pleasure in the sublime, albeit a pleasure very different – more complex and ambivalent – than that provided by the beautiful. We can do so, Kant argues, precisely because the sublime points toward a realm transcending the limits of phenomenal or cognitive grasp. Thus nature presents aspects that we can somehow comprehend, although it is very obscure to us, very hard to explain just how we comprehend them.

IV

The general point I am making here is that some large issues hang on our interpretation of Kant's doctrine of the faculties. That is to say, it is not just a matter of 'academic' debate, or of mainstream *versus* postmodernist readings of this or that passage in Kant. Rather, what we make of those passages – and their place within the overall 'architectonic' of Kant's critical philosophy – has a bearing on issues far beyond that specialized domain. Kant was, for his time, a very progressive thinker, a great advocate of progressive social and political values. Of course one needs to qualify this claim in certain respects. After all, Kant was writing at a time (and in a place) when liberal thought could only go so far, when revolutionary views were better expressed under cover of a mildly reformist rhetoric, and when Kant was himself – in his later years – often subject to tight conditions of censorship by church and state.[19] I should also acknowledge (since the point has been made with considerable force by recent scholars) that Kant held some pretty repugnant views on issues of racial, ethnic, and gender difference in relation to intellectual powers.[20] Nevertheless, I think that one can draw a distinction – an eminently Kantian distinction, no doubt – between these expressions of illiberal sentiment on Kant's part and, on the other hand, the social bearing of Kant's critical philosophy. He is raising extremely important questions which thereafter became central to the whole tradition of critical-emancipatory thought. He is also arguing a strong case for the close relationship – indeed one of mutual dependence – between the values of Enlightenment critique and the interests of social, political, and humanitarian progress.

I think that those values are open to us still, and moreover that the currently fashionable strain of anti-Enlightenment rhetoric, such as we find in Lyotard, is both ethically disastrous and politically retrograde. But of course it is not enough to put the case in these terms. I am not just saying that I think postmodernism is a bad thing, ethically and politically, but also that it is based on very dubious philosophical arguments. Let me offer some evidence in support of this claim, since otherwise it will seem just as sweeping and facile as the sorts of claim I am rejecting. Epistemologically speaking, postmodernism works out as a deep-laid scepticism about the possibility of knowledge and truth, the possibility of a constructive, cooperative enterprise aimed toward truth at the end of enquiry. This scepticism takes various forms: in Lyotard's case it takes the form of an emphasis on diverse incommensurable language-games, narrative 'differends', conflicting ideologies, rival conceptions of truth, justice, progress and so forth. Lyotard would say that we are never in a position to judge between them, because if we try to adjudicate the issue and to say one is right and the other wrong, or that both are wrong, or if we impose our own interpretation, we are thereby suppressing the narrative differend and inflicting an injury on one or on both parties.[21] So, for Lyotard, the sole remaining principle of justice is to maximize the range of admissible narratives and strive so far as possible not to judge between them.

Now, on the face of it, this seems a good liberal prescription. It is obviously good to lend a willing ear to as many as possible of the various narratives (arguments, truth-claims, beliefs etc.) that make up the ongoing cultural dialogue. Just as clearly it is dogmatic and doctrinaire to reject other (from our point of view) false, partial, or prejudiced beliefs just because they happen not to fit in with our own way of thinking. So in a sense, in a very basic sense, there is a good liberal pluralist principle behind Lyotard's thinking. We should be tolerant, we should not force our views on other people, and therefore we should always be ready to acknowledge that ours is not the only possible valid or morally justified viewpoint. All the same there are problems when one tries to follow this programme through to its ultimate (postmodernist) conclusion. What are we to say, for instance, when confronted with Holocaust deniers who claim either that the Holocaust never happened or that reports of it were greatly exaggerated? Or even when confronted with the 'moderate' version of this argument which says that we shouldn't treat the Holocaust as something uniquely appalling and barbaric because there have been other comparable atrocities past and present? Are we simply to say, with Lyotard, that there is no deciding the issue here since the parties to this particular dispute are applying utterly disparate criteria of truth and historical (or narrative) accountability?

Lyotard comes very close to adopting that line when he writes about the French Holocaust-denier Robert Faurisson.[22] Thus we may wish to say that Faurisson is lying, that he is suppressing evidence, that he has a deeply repugnant ideological agenda, and that this is his motive for denying that the Holocaust occurred. Nevertheless, Lyotard says, we should be wrong or at least ill-advised to adopt that position in response to Faurisson's claims. For Faurisson is working with different criteria, he is simply not beholden to the historian's usual standards of truth, accuracy and factual warrant; nor does he subscribe to anything like the liberal consensus-view of what constitutes a decent, morally responsible approach to such matters. In other words, there is a radical incommensurability – a full-scale narrative 'differend' – between Faurisson's strong-revisionist claims and the kinds of factual and ethical objection voiced by his right-thinking liberal opponents. So when Faurisson says: 'Show me one person, one first-hand witness, who can vouch for what actually happened inside the gas-chambers at Auschwicz', then we may well be tempted to treat this demand as based on utterly fallacious reasoning from downright absurd premises. That is to say, Faurisson makes his revisionist case by adopting a wholly inappropriate criterion ('truth = only what we can know on first-hand evidential warrant'), and then using this to re-write history in accordance with his own ideological agenda. But if we take this line, Lyotard warns, we are falling straight into Faurisson's trap. For he can then turn around and accuse us – his high-toned liberal critics – of ignoring or suppressing the narrative 'differend' and thus casting him (Faurisson) in the victim's role.

It seems to me that Lyotard's argument amounts to a wholesale collapse of moral and intellectual nerve. Of course there are different historical narratives, of course historians have different approaches and, very often, widely divergent ideological perspectives. Nevertheless, there is such a thing as historical truth; not Truth with a capital T, not some kind of ultimate, transcendent, all-encompassing Truth, but the sorts of truth that historians find out through patient research, through careful sifting of the evidence, through criticism of source-texts, archival scholarship and so forth. This debate very often gets skewed because sceptics (postmodernists especially) tend to suppose that anyone who talks about truth must be upholding Capital-T truth, a discourse that is repressive, monological, authoritarian, or bent upon suppressing the narrative differend. All the same there are standards, principles, validity-conditions, ways of interpreting, criticising, comparing and contrasting the evidence which, if consistently applied, will give the historian a fair claim to be dealing in matters of truth. It is this claim that we have to abandon if we endorse Lyotard's deeply sceptical Nietzsche-derived postmodernist idea that historical 'truth' is indeed nothing more than a product of the various conflicting narratives, language-games, or 'phrase-genres' that map out the ideological field.

V

Such ideas find support from numerous quarters of present-day 'advanced' thinking in the social and human sciences. Thus, for instance, similar conclusions are drawn by postmodern historiographers such as Hayden White who argue – on the basis of notions derived from post-structuralist literary theory – that historical discourse is best viewed as a narrative or rhetorical construct.[23] Now, of course these theorists are right up to a point. There is always a narrative dimension to historical writing, at least to any history that does something more than simply list dates and events in a chronicle-like fashion. Once it passes beyond that stage history-writing indeed becomes a narrative: it has form, it has a sense-making purpose, it involves a certain way of plotting or ordering historical events, and that ordering will surely involve a certain interpretive or ideological slant. Moreover, as White observes, there are many features in common between historical and fictive discourse, among them generic conventions (tragedy, comedy, romance, satire) and the famous four master-tropes (metaphor, metonymy, synecdoche, irony) which can be shown to characterize different sorts of historical writing. All these points are well taken and worth consideration by 'positivist' historians, if indeed there are any of the latter still around. But very often they are pushed much further than this, to the point where it is claimed that historical truth is *entirely a product* of those various discourses, narratives, modes of rhetorical emplotment, and so forth.

Roland Barthes, in his essay 'The Discourse of History', was among the first to advance this idea that realism is just a discursive effect, the product of certain culture-specific (mainly nineteenth-century) codes, conventions, or narrative devices.[24] It is the same line of argument that White picks up and elaborates into a full-scale poetics of historical narrative. But these ideas are not so far from the strain of anti-realist thinking that has emerged as a prominent trend within present-day Anglo-American 'analytic' philosophy. This is the argument – to put it very briefly – that there are not and cannot be 'verification-transcendent' truths, i.e., truths that exist quite apart from our current best knowledge or beliefs, or independently of whether we possess some method or means of finding them out. Here also – in the work of philosophers such as Michael Dummett – there is the notion that history cannot be 'objective' in the sense of involving an object-domain, a realm of real-world actions and events which occurred in the past and are therefore unaffected by whatever we now happen to believe concerning them.[25] Rather, we cannot make sense of the idea that there might be truths for which we possessed no evidence, no means of verification or adequate proof-procedure. In this respect statements concerning the past are on a par with mathematical truth-claims and theories or hypotheses in the physical sciences. For 'truth' we should do better to substitute the notion of 'warranted assertability', since this makes it clear that nothing could count as a *real* entity, an *actual* past event, or a *valid* mathematical theorem except in so far as we can bear it out by applying the relevant methods of proof or verification.

In mathematics (where the case looks most plausible) this means rejecting the Platonist view according to which there exist abstract entities – numbers, sets, classes, truth-functional properties, etc. – that are somehow objectively *there* to be discovered, quite apart from whether we have yet devized (or perhaps could ever devize) an adequate proof-procedure. On the contrary, Dummett argues: such items 'exist' solely by virtue of our knowing some rule, some appropriate method of proof for arriving at a definite (decidable) result in any given case.[26] Where we possess no such method – as for instance with certain speculative theorems in pure mathematics – then the logical Principle of Bivalence fails. That is to say, these theorems are neither true nor false, nor even (as the realist would have it) 'true-or-false' in some ultimate, objective sense that may lie beyond our capacities for deciding the issue. For if the meaning of a sentence, a theorem or a statement, is given by its truth-conditions, and if those conditions are themselves fixed by what counts as an adequate proof-procedure, then clearly there is no appeal open to a realm of objective truth-values that would obtain quite apart from our current best methods of proof or verification.

Dummett's chief sources for this argument are Wittgenstein's contextualist doctrine of meaning-as-use and Frege's dictum that 'sense determines reference'.[27] On this latter view, properly referring expressions are those by which we pick out various items (objects, events, persons, numbers, etc.) in virtue of our knowing just what those expressions mean, their range of senses, semantic attributes, contexts of usage, criteria for correct application, and so forth. Whence Dummett's anti-realist position: that truth-talk is redundant, indeed nonsensical with respect to any item for which we possess no such definite criteria. At this point the realist will most likely reply: no, Dummett has got it wrong; if there is one thing we know for sure it is that there are many things we *don't* know for sure, matters whose truth is quite independent of our existing state of knowledge (or ignorance), things that we might perhaps find out in the long run, or again perhaps not, depending on whether they are ultimately knowable to creatures with our particular range of cognitive or intellectual powers. Of course there is the standard sceptical meta-induction (or 'argument from error') which holds that since we have turned out in the past to be wrong about so many things – scientific truth-claims included – therefore it is a pretty safe bet that we are wrong about most of what we claim to know now. However, the realist will then come back and remark (1) that we are able to *recognise and explain* at least some of those past errors; (2) that the sceptic is willy-nilly invoking criteria of truth and falsehood, among them the long-range criterion of progress or truth at the end of enquiry; and (3) that the argument from error can thus be turned around and used to support the realist's case for our knowledge of the growth of knowledge. What it shows is not so much the non-existence of truths beyond our (past or present) best powers of understanding but, on the contrary, the fact that there will always (now and in the future) be matters as to which we can form no judgement but whose truth-value is wholly unaffected thereby. After all, as the realist may further wish to say, the universe – together with its physical laws – existed long before there were human beings around to observe it and will most likely continue to exist long after those beings have departed.

VI

Now I don't for one moment want to suggest that Dummett's case for anti-realism is directly comparable with those other (e.g., post-structuralist or postmodernist) doctrines that I have been discussing so far. It is argued with a far greater degree of logical precision and also – especially where truth-claims about the past are concerned – with a much keener sense of the *ethical* dilemmas that arise in this context. As one who has played a prominent role in campaigns against racial prejudice and violence Dummett is unlikely to treat these matters to the kind of facile paradox-mongering that typifies Lyotard's treatment of Faurisson and the issue of Holocaust revisionism. My point is, rather, that anti-realist arguments have a currency – and also a range of conceptual resources – well beyond the sphere of present-day fashion in literary or cultural theory. Where Dummett worries (justifiably so) about their extension to issues of historical knowledge, no such anxieties seem to afflict the purveyors of current postmodernist wisdom.[28] Yet it is here that the counter-argument needs stating with maximum clarity and force. For there is a difference – one that is often blurred in the writing of theorists like Hayden White – between saying that history is narrative and saying that history is fiction. Narrative and fiction are not the same thing, although they are often (of course) aspects or attributes of one and the same text. In the etymological sense 'fiction' means something that is made or contructed. In that sense, yes, history is fictive. But it is *not* fictive in the more familiar and widespread present-day sense of being imaginary, having no reference to real-world characters and events, or being *made up* as distinct from constructed out of various sources, documentary records, eye-witness accounts, and so forth. I think that Hayden White and other postmodern historiographers tend to confuse these two things. There are differences between fictive narrative and historical narrative, different constraints in writing history, constraints having to do with matters of causality, agency, chronology, temporality, narrative sequence, a whole range of specifiable criteria which distinguish history from fiction.[29]

Of course this is not to deny the existence of what might be called 'postmodern' hybrid or cross-over genres. That is to say, there is a certain kind of transgeneric writing practised by historians like Simon Schama, for instance, which exploits fictional techniques such as flashbacks, anticipations, proleptic devices or forms of multiple narrative consciousnesses. When Hayden White reproaches historians for being so 'conservative' and behind-the times – when he wonders why they haven't caught up with Joyce and the modernists let alone with postmodern writers such as Barth or Vonnegut or Calvino – then one can see why this is felt as a challenge. Historians like Schama want to accept that challenge and produce something more adventurous than the standard modes of historical discourse: something that mixes in fictive techniques and tries to liven things up. After all, Roland Barthes was making this point many years ago: that historians were still turning out texts ('classic bourgeois-realist' texts) that traded on all the old narrative conventions and might just as well have been written before Proust came along. So one can see why some historians have become very keen – maybe a bit too keen – to cast off this irksome image of themselves as old-fashioned realists ('positivists' is the usual bugbear term) who haven't yet learned the new rules of the game.

Nevertheless, even in Schama's work – and I am thinking chiefly of his recent book *Dead Certainties*, whose punning title catches the drift very well – even here there is a marked difference between the passages of well-researched, solid, historical investigation and other sections which are more inventive, where he is trying to get inside the characters' minds, or sometimes filling in background detail for which there is no evidence.[30] Also I think that most readers are quite aware when he crosses the line between history and fiction, or those parts of the narrative that claim factual warrant and those that are implicitly making no such claim. On the other hand there are novels – or texts standardly classified as novels – which incorporate large chunks of often quite detailed and well-researched history, 'real-life' characters, socio-documentary material, and so forth. Linda Hutcheon has coined a useful term for such texts – she calls them 'pseudo-historiographic metafictions' – though they are often lumped together with other sorts of writing under the not-so-useful cover term 'postmodernist'.[31] Take, for instance, Kurt Vonnegut's *Slaughter-House Five*, which contains, among other things, a graphic description of the fire-bombing of Dresden, an event that Vonnegut knew quite a bit about, having actually been there at the time and (remarkably) survived to tell the tale. Other episodes in the novel take place on a planet called Tralfamadore and involve all sorts of surreal or fantastic fictive contrivance such as telepathy, teletransportation, and time-warps. In other words, it is an excellent example of the hybrid genre that Hutcheon is talking about. But again we are aware of the cross-over points, the points at which certain generic constraints (those applying to the narrative reconstruction of historical events) give way to other, recognisably fictive or non-truth-evaluable modes of writing. Most readers are quite good at telling the difference, even in cases like *Slaughter-House Five* or, to take some other well-known examples, Thomas Pynchon's *V* or E.L. Doctorow's *Ragtime* where novelists have gone out of their way to complicate (if not erase) the boundary-line between fact and fiction.

So we are not, as many postmodernists would have it, now moving into a phase of cultural development when it is no longer possible to make such distinctions, or where 'reality' has given way to what Baudrillard calls the 'precession of the simulacrum', that is to say, the stage at which everything becomes an effect of hyperinduced media simulation.[32] Most readers are still capable of distinguishing between fact and fiction, or between historical and fictional narrative discourse, even if some postmodernists appear to have lost that basic ability. One problem is perhaps that they are working with a theory of language and representation – a broadly post-structuralist theory – which takes Saussurean linguistics (or its own very partial and dogmatic reading of Saussure[33]) as a licence for wholesale pronouncements of the sort:

'everything is constructed in (or by) language', 'there is nothing outside the text', 'narrative realism is a bourgeois illusion' and suchlike. If you start out from that sort of doctrinaire anti-realist stance then most likely you won't have anything very helpful to say when it comes to more subtle generic distinctions. Some theorists have recognised this problem and have looked elsewhere – for instance, to developments in modal or 'possible-worlds' logic – as a means of explaining just what is involved in the kinds of intuitive adjustment we make when reading various types of texts, whether fictive, historical, mixed-genre, or whatever.[34] Thus it is a matter of epistemic access, of the degree to which such narrative 'worlds' are accessible from (or compatible with) the world that we actually inhabit along with all its objects, events, past history, laws of nature, time-space coordinates, etc. In which case the different narrative genres can be ranked on a scale that extends, roughly speaking, from documentary realism at the one end (where any departures from this-world correspondence will most likely be categorized as errors concerning matters of contingent fact) to science-fiction fantasy at the opposite extreme (where even laws of nature and space-time frameworks may be subject to controlled violation at the author's whim). This approach seems to me much better – more 'philosophical', if you like, but also more sensitive to important distinctions in narrative theory and historiography – than anything available from post-structuralism or its current postmodernist spin-off doctrines. At any rate there is good reason to reject any argument (such as Baudrillard's) which would treat those distinctions as so many figments of a 'discourse' still nostalgically attached to superannuated notions of truth, reality, and critical reason. Terry Eagleton seems much nearer the mark – in his book *The Illusions of Postmodernism* – when he excoriates the bad faith of intellectuals who raise their own evasion of social and ethical responsibility into a high point of fashionable doctrine.[35]

CHAPTER 2

Postmodern Ethics and the Trouble with Relativism

I

Up to now I have mainly been discussing some epistemological aspects of the issue between modernism and postmodernism, that is, questions having to do with the scope and limits of attainable knowledge in various fields of enquiry. Historical understanding is a crucial test-case – as I suggested at the end of Chapter One – since it seems to offer a strong point of purchase for sceptical or relativist arguments. Such arguments mostly start out by attacking the typecast 'positivist' belief that we can gain objective knowledge of past events through methods of empirical research that should ideally involve no interpretive or ideological slant. Once having skewered this naive belief – as for instance by remarking that 'facts' are themselves linguistic or discursive constructs, or that history writing always involves some form of narrative-rhetorical emplotment – the sceptic can then move on to assert a more wholesale version of the doctrine such as those put forward by post-structuralists, postmodernists, and 'strong' textualists.[1] What they standardly ignore is the basic distinction (basic at least to any realist counter-argument) between *res gestae* and *historia rerum gestarum*, or 'history' as that which actually occurred quite apart from our current best state of knowledge concerning it and 'history' as that which historians recount from their various (no doubt partial and prejudiced) viewpoints.

Nor is such thinking by any means confined to the furthermost reaches of postmodern literary academe. It is also present in the work of anti-realist philosophers such as Michael Dummett, those who maintain – on logico-semantic grounds – that since we cannot have access to objective (or 'verification-transcendent') truths, therefore quite simply it makes no sense to posit the existence of historical facts for which we possess no documentary evidence or reliable means of ascertainment.[2] Thus, according to Dummett, '[t]he only notion of truth for past-tense statements which we could have acquired from our training in their use is that which coincides with the justifiability of the assertions of such statements, i.e., with the existence of situations which we are capable of recognising as obtaining and which justify such assertions'.[3] Of course there is a great difference between

Dummett's philosophical position – hedged about as it is with understandable worries about the kinds of unscrupulous historical revisionism
to which such an argument might lead – and the typically insouciant
postmodernist outlook which finds no cause for concern in the notion of
history as a text that can always be rewritten in accordance with present-day
interests and values. All the same Dummett can see no way of avoiding the
anti-realist upshot that follows from a joint application of the Fregean logico-
semantic doctrine that 'sense determines reference' and the Wittgenstein-
derived communitarian theory of meaning-as-use.[4] 'Of course', he writes,
'like everyone else, I feel a strong undertow towards the realist view; but then,
there are certain errors of thought to which the human mind seems naturally
prone'.[5] In which case – it appears – the best one can do is adopt Hume's
advice, keep those sceptical doubts for the study, and otherwise continue
one's day-to-day life with no thought for such matters.

However that advice is not so easily taken if one believes that
philosophical issues have a bearing outside and beyond the more specialised
spheres of academic debate. It will then seem all the more urgent to show
(*contra* Quine) that the Humean predicament is not the human predicament, or that realism does have conceptual resources that can meet the kinds
of challenge currently posed by anti-realists and sceptics of various
persuasion. For it is clear that such doubts cannot be confined to the
range of well-worn epistemological questions that Hume famously despaired
of answering and that philosophers have none the less continued to discuss,
often with great ingenuity though without (one suspects) much hope of
producing an argument-to-end-all-arguments.[6] Rather they are doubts
which – if valid at all – must affect every aspect of human knowledge and
experience, including (as I have said) the way that we think about ethical
issues in relation to questions of justificatory warrant. And this applies even
in the case of arguments which make a point of stressing the fact/value
distinction or the absolute and principled impossibility of deriving a moral-
evaluative 'ought' from a constative, descriptive, or assertoric 'is'. That is to
say, such arguments – from Hume to Lyotard – partake of a strong anti-
realist bias which disposes them toward a sceptical view not only as concerns
the cognitive grounding of ethical judgements but also with regard to factual
or empirical truth-claims. So one way of looking at postmodernism is to
view it as the sceptical *ne plus ultra* of an outlook which raises the incommensurability of constative and evaluative judgements to a point where any
notion of shared or intersubjectively valid truth must appear just an authoritarian ploy for enforcing some particular (quasi-universalist) set of values
and beliefs. In which case the only ethical attitude with a genuine claim to
that title is one that makes allowance for the sheer multiplicity of 'first-order
natural narrative pragmatics' and which therefore – on principle – rejects
the idea that moral judgements can themselves be assessed (approved or

found wanting) in terms of their responsiveness to salient aspects of a knowable human reality.

The realist about ethics will often respond by denying the fact/value dichotomy or – in Lyotard's broadly equivalent terms – the cognitive/evaluative or constative/performative dualisms.[7] She will typically argue that a judgement such as 'Apartheid was wrong' or 'Slavery was an unjust institution' is one that derives its ethico-political force from a knowledge of the way those systems worked in practice, their effect on the people (victims and oppressors) directly involved, and their real-world character as practices which led to great human suffering.[8] Moreover, she will view such suffering as itself just the kind of moral consideration that can and should be reckoned into any realist assessment of Apartheid or slavery, along with the various beneficial effects – for human wellbeing and social justice – that resulted from abolishing such practices. So when Nelson Mandela or Abraham Lincoln took their stand on these issues, they were not (or not only) appealing to some realm of transcendent moral values divorced from the grinding day-to-day misery of life in the black South African townships or in antebellum US slave plantations. Rather, they were reaching an evaluative judgement ('these practices are bad!') based on an *accurate realist assessment* of (1) the factual-historical situation, (2) its consequences for large numbers of victimized human beings, and (3) the likelihood of radically transforming their lives, prospects, and entitlements if the system could be overthrown. Moderate anti-realists about ethics could probably accept most of this with the caveat that there remain certain problems – logical problems at least – about the passage from factual claims to evaluative judgements. But the case is much worse with postmodernists like Lyotard who raise the fact/value disjunction to a high point of ethical principle. For on this view there is no way of bridging the gulf except by an infraction of the narrative 'differend' – that between diverse incommensurable language-games or 'phrase-genres' – which would itself then constitute an ethical injustice toward all parties concerned.

I started out in Chapter One with some lessons from Kant because he, more than anyone, set the agenda for a good deal of modern and, indeed, postmodern debate about just what constitutes knowledge and how it relates to other (e.g., ethical or aesthetic) modes of judgement. This also seemed a good starting-point since the postmodern 'turn' in thinkers like Lyotard can be seen as both a turn *back to* Kant – about whom Lyotard has written on numerous occasions – and a turn *away from* (or decisively against) certain crucial Kantian arguments and distinctions. These latter have to do with the precise relationship between the various orders of cognitive understanding, practical reason, and judgement in its reflective and aesthetic modes. What Kant seeks to do – and here I am summarizing with brutal rapidity – is bring them into a complex interconnected system (Gilles Deleuze, in his excellent early book on Kant, calls it a system of constantly 'rotating chairmanship') such that their priorities remain distinct, and the boundaries between them sufficiently well-marked, while allowing for at least some degree of mutual interdependence and exchange.[9] Thus, for instance, it is important not to confuse the domain of cognitive understanding (where the ruling criterion is, to repeat, that intuitions be 'brought under' adequate concepts) with the domain of ethics or practical reason where no such criterion properly applies, where reflective judgement has much greater scope, and where there is no straightforward or one-to-one match between high-level maxims and particular cases. Any confusion here can only have bad philosophical (and moral) consequences since it will tend toward a determinist view in matters where this would leave no room for the exercise of human choice, agency, and ethical responsibility. It would thus undermine Kant's double-aspect theory, his idea of human beings as, on the one hand, physical creatures subject to the laws of natural or causal necessity, but also, on the other, as autonomous agents subject only to those maxims and imperatives that issue from the sovereign voice of moral conscience. However, it is just as wrong to deny that cognitive judgements (or determinate concepts) can or should play a significant role in matters of ethico-evaluative judgement and choice. For this is just the opposite kind of error, one that flees the bugbear of determinism only to cut moral reasoning off from any possible justification in terms of real-world situated human experience.

Lyotard is not alone among recent French commentators in pushing this antinomy so hard that it becomes something like a deconstructive lever for prising apart the entire Kantian system or 'doctrine' of the faculties. For instance, there are some well-known passages from Foucault's early book *The Order of Things* [*Les mots et les choses*] where he talks about the discourse of nineteenth-century humanism as having taken rise from Kant's idea of man as a curious 'empirico-transcendental doublet', a hybrid creature impossibly torn between rival (naturalistic and non-naturalistic) conceptions of his own defining attributes.[10] Lyotard is a much better reader of Kant in the sense that he does stick closely to the texts, albeit with a practised eye for just those sections – especially the 'Analytic of the Sublime' in the Third *Critique* – which are fruitful of paradox and whose 'lessons' can then be read back into Kantian epistemology and ethics.[11] However the chief point I wish to make here is that postmodernism does have a definite philosophical agenda, one that involves, among other things, a desire to displace or discredit the 'philosophic discourse of modernity' by discovering (or inventing) all manner of problems at its very heart. I should mention also that some of the best recent commentaries on Kant – by scholars such as Onora O'Neill – are devoted to answering just the kinds of criticism that are levelled against him by readers of a postmodernist or anti-Enlightenment persuasion.[12]

Hence one main area of dispute between modernist and postmodernist thinkers, namely the issue of ethics in relation to questions of knowledge and truth. The work of the Jewish-Lithuanian thinker Emmanuel Levinas has been most widely influential in this regard.[13] Levinas believes that the entirety of Western (post-Hellenic) philosophical thought has been premised on the notion of epistemology – or theory of knowledge – as philosophy's primary concern. From the ancient Greeks down – from Plato and Aristotle to Descartes, Kant, and Husserl – epistemology has been conceived as 'first philosophy' or as that which constitutes the basis and starting-point for other (e.g., ethical) interests and concerns. For Levinas, on the contrary, ethics is where all philosophy ought to begin, and ethics in a sense that radically exceeds or transcends the sorts of question that philosophers have hitherto asked even when talking about ethical issues. So what Levinas seeks to do is reverse that traditional order of priority between epistemological and ethical questions. For him, it is the demand of the other person – her or his absolute, intransigent demand upon me – which takes priority over every other consideration. It must therefore assign second place to issues of epistemology, confined as these are (on Levinas's account) to the sphere of a narrowly 'egological' or first-person subject-centred conception of knowledge and truth. This demand of the other person upon me is the demand of radical otherness or alterity. I should never start out from the assumption that the other person is pretty much like me in her experiences, needs, desires, values, commitments, or priorities. The most basic ethical principle for Levinas is to treat the other person as *absolutely* other, non-negotiably other, in the sense of not sharing – or not being known to share – any of my own ideas of the common good. We should never assume that there exists any commonality between our own most deeply-felt needs and concerns and those of the other person.

So the other exerts a kind of intransitive summons, a call to relinquish all our own interests and priorities, along with our 'egological' ideas of the other as a mirror-image of ourselves. This, then, for Levinas, is the guiding principle – more than that, the absolute precondition – for any ethics worthy of the name. And here, for the first time explicitly, I shall complicate matters in some degree by introducing the topic of deconstruction. In fact it has figured tacitly, as a kind of running comparison, in everything I have said so far about postmodernism, but now I want to bring this contrast out into the open. There is an early essay by Jacques Derrida – 'Violence and Metaphysics' – where Derrida engages with Levinas in a critical but none the less respectful and admiring way.[14] This is perhaps a good place to remark that Derrida, in his criticism of other thinkers, is never polemical or destructive, never out to represent them as merely mistaken or deluded. He is not claiming to see through Levinas's arguments or to show them up as hopelessly in thrall to some naive 'logocentric' or 'metaphysical' prejudice.

On the contrary: he says that Levinas is a very important, indeed an 'indispensable' thinker. Yet Derrida finds certain problems with Levinas, especially with this notion of radical alterity (or otherness) as the starting-point of any authentically ethical relation. Thus he raises the crucial question: how could it be possible for me to establish relations with the other, to treat them with friendship, tolerance, sympathy, a due regard for their differences of outlook, of values, interests, concerns, and so forth, if I started out – as Levinas requires – by abjuring any claim to understand the other as a person recognisably *like myself* in at least certain basic respects? For if the other were indeed radically other, then we could have no reason – no grounds in common humanity – to think her a suitable candidate for that kind of treatment. Certainly I could have no ethical relationship with her, since this presupposes – at very least – that she and I inhabit a human sphere (an intersubjective lifeworld) of shared knowledge, communal experience, and mutual understanding. If I didn't suppose her to have at least that much in common with myself then, quite simply, she would figure as one more object in my cognitive-perceptual field. This is Derrida's point – briefly summarised – when he says that Levinasian ethics runs the risk of reducing to a kind of empiricism, a view of the self-other relation as strangely devoid of interpersonal content and even as resembling the process by which (on the empiricist account) we acquire knowledge through exposure to the stream of incoming sensory data. For what calls upon us to recognise others as persons – persons having a genuine claim on our ethical concern – is precisely the range of fundamental respects in which they, like us, are sentient beings with kindred capacities for certain kinds of humanly distinctive knowledge and experience.

I am putting all this in very simple terms, as you will know if you have read 'Violence and Metaphysics', where Derrida goes some lengthy and complicated ways around in making his point against Levinas's ethic of absolute or radical alterity. However, it is not distorting his argument – or one important aspect of his argument – if we interpret him as saying that there must be some degree of mutual *rapport*, some basis of shared understanding or common humanity, in order for us to acknowledge the very real differences that exist between human individuals, their needs, preferences, interests, and concerns. In short, the other person is an *alter ego*, and Derrida puts equal emphasis on both words: 'alter' (other) and 'ego' (I, first person singular). The other person is other, irreducibly other, in the sense that we cannot ever claim to know them – to get 'inside' their experience – so as to remove all barriers to perfect understanding. But they are also – like us – human beings with a first-person perspective on the world, a perspective that we can none the less enter into through modes of shared understanding, just as various observers can perceive the same object from different angles while agreeing to describe it as the same object. This we can do, as Husserl makes clear, on the basis of inhabiting a shared spatio-temporal lifeworld and possessing a shared cognitive-conceptual frame-work.[15] It is also why, without seeking to impose our viewpoint, we can none the less claim to comprehend how things appear to others, not only as concerns objects in the field of sensory perception but also with respect to differing perspectives on the lifeworld of humanly significant meanings, values, and beliefs. This does not mean (as Levinas would have it) that we thereby reduce them to the confines of our own 'egological' knowledge and experience, or that we treat them merely as passive projections of our own all-constituting ego. We can and must take due account of their differences, but we can do so only by analogy with the kinds of knowledge and experience that we possess in virtue of our shared humanity.

This is Husserl's main topic in Section Five of his book *Cartesian Meditations*.[16] If we are always in some sense interpreting the world from our own first-person perspective, then how can we claim to have an insight (a genuine, non-self-centred insight) into other people's thoughts, experiences, feelings, or modes of being-in-the-world? Now Husserl's answer, and also Derrida's – since he is, after all, here defending Husserl against Levinas's strictures – is that, yes, we must understand other people to a very large extent on the basis of our own experience. Yet this is precisely what gives us the capacity to *put ourselves in their place* so far as possible, and hence to comprehend those other respects in which they differ from ourselves. Moreover, Levinas does an injustice to Husserl when he claims that Husserlian phenomenology is merely another, more sophisticated version of the old epistemological drive to subjugate ethics (the realm of absolute alterity) to the sphere of the 'self-same' or self-identical in thought, the ideal of knowledge pursued by philosophers from Plato to Descartes, Kant, and beyond. For this is to ignore a crucial aspect of Husserl's thinking, one that is also present in Kant though not developed to anything like the same level of refinement and self-critical awareness. It is his point, briefly put, that the interests of knowledge *cannot* be severed from ethical concerns (or placed in radical opposition to them) since both involve the exercise of judgement in one or another of its complex modalities. After all, the most distinctive aspect of Kantian epistemology – as compared with Cartesian rationalism on the one hand and Lockean or Humean empiricism on the other – is precisely the role that it assigns to judgement as a normative dimension prerequisite to all forms of knowledge or acts of understanding. This is what constitutes his chief claim to have achieved a decisive advance beyond Descartes' starkly dualist theory of mental representation (his appeal to a disembodied realm of 'clear and distinct ideas'), and the rival empiricist conception of knowledge as resulting from the mind's largely passive registration of incoming sensory data. For Kant, these were merely opposite sides of the same dilemma, one that arose through the failure to allow for judgement as a mediating term or activity between the otherwise disparate realms of sensuous intuition and conceptual grasp.

As we have seen already, there are problems with interpreting just how this process occurs, or with construing the role of Kantian 'productive imagination' as a further (albeit 'dark' and 'obscure') faculty that somehow accomplishes the problematic passage from sense-data to concepts *via* the schematisms of understanding.[17] It is here – in these passages where Kant's argument seems threatened by a vicious explanatory regress – that later philosophers (from Fichte and Hegel to Schopenhauer, Nietzsche and Heidegger) have proposed various strong-revisionist or depth-hermeneutical readings.[18] They have also offered a point of leverage for postmodernist interpreters of Kant (such as Lyotard) who are likewise intent upon recasting Kant's philosophy in the image of their own distinctly aestheticized ethico-political concerns. Yet there is a different way of viewing the centrality of judgement to Kant's philosophy as a whole, that is, the extent to which it serves as a bridge between the various faculties or their various modes of complex relationship and reciprocal dependence. As I have said, it is a view that credits Kant with having taken the decisive step beyond those inertly representational theories of knowledge – whether rationalist or empiricist – which failed to offer any adequate account of the mind's active or synthesising power in the process of interpreting experience. For the most part this understanding of Kant has been pursued by thinkers in the broadly 'continental' (i.e., mainland-European) tradition, especially those – Husserl among them – who have sought to develop and refine Kant's account of knowledge, experience and judgement. But there are also clear signs that thinkers in the 'other' (analytic or mainstream Anglophone) tradition are currently in process of rediscovering this aspect of Kantian philosophy. Thus, for instance, two recent books – by Robert Brandom and John McDowell – have both looked to Kant as the first philosopher who accorded judgement this central role not only as regards the knowledge-constitutive link between sensuous intuitions and concepts of understanding, but also with respect to the relationship between cognitive interests and the ethical sphere of shared (intersubjectively-validated) principles of reason and conduct.[19] That is to say, we shall not get very far along the way to an other-regarding ethics unless we start out from the idea of a common lifeworld, some of whose basic features – those that provide the very conditions of possibility for human knowledge and experience – are also what enable mutual understanding to occur across differences of cultural perspective or ethical viewpoint.

Nevertheless, as I have said, there are problems with Kant's way of arguing for this all-important connection between the realm of cognitive or epistemological interests and the value-sphere of ethical, interpersonal, or socio-political judgements. Thus opponents could claim – as indeed they still do – that Kantian ethics inhabits a realm of wholly abstract imperatives or formal maxims quite apart from the detailed (often messy) practicalities of real-world, situated moral choice.[20] And there is likewise a problem, as Husserl sees it, with the Kantian epistemological requirement which holds that intuitions must be somehow 'brought under' adequate concepts while on the one hand failing to account for that process with adequate critical rigour, and on the other paying insufficient attention to the lifeworld – the shared horizon of communal beliefs – that constitutes the necessary background condition for any understanding of our own or other people's experience. How far these two demands could be jointly satisfied, or whether they give rise to an unresolved tension throughout Husserl's work, is a question that Derrida himself addresses in a number of important early texts.[21] At any rate they offer a strong counter-argument – on ethical as well as epistemological grounds – to the idea of ethics as 'first philosophy' in the absolute, intransigent sense of that claim proposed by Levinas and lately taken up (in a variety of contexts and idioms) by postmodernist thinkers.

Thus, for instance, his idea of the ethical relation as one of radical 'alterity' very easily translates into Lyotard's idea of the *differend*, that is, the idea of justice as involving an acceptance that there exist any number of diverse 'incommensurable' narratives or language-games, each of them justified by its own (strictly immanent) criteria, and none of them affording a privileged vantage-point from which to adjudicate the issue. I have remarked already on the problems with this kind of ultra-relativist thinking when transposed from the linguistic to the epistemological and thence to the historical, ethical, or socio-political spheres. What I have also maintained, here and elsewhere, is the case for viewing deconstruction – contrary to received opinion – as *not* just another, more sophisticated version of the present-day postmodern-sceptical turn against Enlightenment values and beliefs.[22]

II

Let me now develop this point by examining some versions of the currently widespread talk about otherness, alterity, heterogeneity, difference, incommensurability, and so forth. In postmodern ethics – in the work of thinkers like Zygmunt Bauman – it is the idea that other people, other cultures, traditions, or historical periods are so different from ours, for all that we can know, so *radically* different from ours, that we can never be justified in presuming to interpret their beliefs according to our own criteria of truth or justice.[23] But this is surely a counsel of despair, or would be if its implications were followed right through. For in that case we could never lay claim to the least understanding of past historical periods, other cultures, other systems of belief or ethico-evaluative viewpoints. If indeed it were true that language-games, narratives or discourses differed so fundamentally, then of course there could be no possibility of translation or mutual understanding between them. One finds this idea in many quarters of postmodern debate, and also – albeit less dramatically expressed – in various 'post-analytic' schools of Anglo-American philosophy.

The best-known source is Quine's argument – in his essay 'Two Dogmas of Empiricism' – to the effect that what counts as a 'real' (as opposed to a fictive, mythic, or non-existent) object is entirely a matter of our choice between various referential frameworks or ontological schemes.[24] Thus Quine may prefer (*qua* 'lay physicist') to accept what present-day science has to say about the furniture of the universe or the ultimate constituents of matter. Nevertheless – *qua* philosopher with strongly pragmatist leanings – Quine takes it that there is ultimately no reason (in the nature of things or the nature of human understanding) to come out in favour of this or any other candidate scheme. Thus what counts as real – be it centaurs, Homer's gods, numbers, mathematical classes, or brick houses on Elm Street – will always depend upon our chosen ontology and the sorts of object that it picks out or quantifies over. In Quine's pithy statement, 'to be is to be the value of a variable'.

This goes along with three further arguments, all tending to support the idea of wholesale ontological relativity. Two of them – the 'under-determination of theory by evidence' and the 'theory-laden character of observation-statements' – are often deployed jointly to make the same point. That is, they are taken to demolish the case for any epistemology that banks on the standard (more specifically: the standard logical-empiricist) distinction between matters-of-fact and truths-of-reason.[25] In Quine's view this is just a bad legacy of the old Kantian idea that one can draw a firm line between analytic and synthetic statements, on the one hand those that are trivially true just in virtue of their logical structure (of their predicate's being somehow 'contained in' their subject), and on the other hand those that possess empirical content and which therefore involve something more than sheerly tautological self-evidence. On the contrary, according to Quine: it is always possible that we might have to revise the so-called 'laws' or ground-rules of logical reasoning in response to some anomaly or discrepant result thrown up in the course of scientific investigation, such as (for instance) the wave/particle dualism in quantum physics. Far better, he urges, to think of human knowledge as a 'fabric' or 'web' of interconnected observations, beliefs, theories, logical axioms, and so forth, some of which (those at the observational periphery) we may think of as always revisable in response to new sensory inputs, while others (those at the logical core) we tend to treat as fixed and immutable whatever the pressures exerted upon them by conflicting experiential data. For this image helps us to grasp Quine's point that *nothing* – not even the best-entrenched logical 'law' – is in principle immune from change or revision should the weight of empirical evidence count decisively against it.

Whence the third main argument that Quine brings forward, namely that of meaning-holism. This is the contextualist thesis according to which statements cannot be assessed for truth or falsehood on a one-for-one correspondence principle but only in so far as they occupy a place in the total fabric of knowledge or belief at some given time. Thus, for observation-sentences and theories alike, it is always a question of our claims being tested against the 'incoming barrage' of sensory stimuli on the one hand, and the entire existing framework of currently accredited scientific knowledge on the other. From which it follows, on Quine's pragmatist account, that it will always be possible to save the phenomena – or preserve some cherished theory – by redistributing predicates, redefining certain crucial terms, or (at the limit) admitting some revision to logical 'laws' such as those of bivalent truth/falsehood or excluded middle.[26] No doubt this is very much a strategy of last resort, and one that Quine elsewhere seems more reluctant to endorse. Thus in his textbook treatment of the issue, one finds him arguing that it could *never* be rational to suspend those laws (at any rate the law of non-contradiction) or to interpret other people – 'native informants' – as applying a radically different, non-standard or deviant logic.[27] Still it is the position that he takes in 'Two Dogmas', an essay whose influence has extended far beyond the specialized philosophical domain. For it is not hard to see how Quine's doctrines of meaning-holism and ontological relativity fit in with a range of current ideas that are often advanced – albeit with different ends in view – by postmodernist, post-structuralist and kindred schools of thought.

Then again, take Thomas Kuhn's celebrated book *The Structure of Scientific Revolutions*, where he claims (very much in agreement with Quine) that different scientific theories – those on either side of a major paradigm-shift – commit their believers to different ('incommensurable') worldviews, conceptual schemes, or ontologies.[28] So, for instance, when Aristotle watched a swinging stone, he saw a piece of matter seeking out its proper place in the cosmos or the order of the elements. Galileo, on the other hand, saw it as a pendulum – subject to the laws of gravitationally-induced motion – because he had a different theory to explain what caused that particular phenomenon. Now, according to Kuhn, we had better not say that Galileo's theory marked an advance over Aristotle's in terms of correctness, explanatory power, or predictive-observational warrant. For there is just no point in making such comparisons where theories diverge so radically that we lack any means – any neutral language – for translating or adjudicating between them. That is to say, these theories are strictly incommensurable in so far as they assign a different meaning or reference to every term in their respective observation-languages. Thus Aristotle and

Galileo (like Newton and Einstein after them) quite literally 'lived in different worlds', worlds that contained different objects behaving in accordance
with different laws.

The best short answer to this is given by Hilary Putnam. 'Suppose', he
invites us,

> a terrestrial rock were transported to the moon and released. Aristotle's
> physics clearly implies that it would fall to the earth, while Newton's
> physics gives the correct prediction (that it would stay on the moon, or
> fall to the surface of the moon if lifted and released). There is a certain
> magnificent indifference to *detail* in saying grandly that Aristotle's physics
> and Newton's are 'incommensurable'.[29]

I call Putnam to witness here mainly because, although once a robust scientific realist, he has now come round (retreated, I would say) to a theory of
'internal realism' that effectively concedes all the main points at issue.[30] Still,
he is clear enough about the kinds of absurdity that result from pushing anti-
realism through to its logical conclusion. And the same can be said – as I have
argued elsewhere – about a good many compromise settlements or half-way
stations on the road to anti-realism.[31]

It is not surprising that Kuhn cites Quine as a source for his idea of radical
meaning-variance between scientific paradigms, as likewise for his closely-
connected claim with regard to ontological relativity. For it is only on this
Quinean-holistic account – if the reference of terms is fixed solely by their
meaning in this or that context, and the context in question expanded to
embrace the entire 'web' or 'fabric' of currently accepted beliefs – it is only
then, as I say, that Kuhn's ultra-relativist argument begins to look remotely
plausible. Thus, to take another instance, we should have to conclude that
there is no question of our now knowing more about atoms than those
ancient speculative thinkers (like Democritus, Leucippus and Epicurus) who
happened to hit on this idea for no better reason – or with no better
evidence – than an *a priori* conviction that there must come a point beyond
which matter is no longer divisible into smaller and smaller particles. Now
we might want to say (I do!) that this was a piece of inspired proto-scientific
guesswork, and that later thinkers – from Dalton to Rutherford, Einstein
and Bohr – worked out the theory in much more detail and with increasing powers of assisted observation, descriptive accuracy, or experimental
proof.[32] But if one accepts Kuhn's argument then this is a wrong and a
naively realist (as well as a smugly progressivist) way of putting it. Rather,
those thinkers were all of them talking about different things, from Epicurus's metaphysical doctrine of 'atoms and the void' to Dalton's concept of
atomic weight as a means of explaining certain chemical properties and,

beyond that, Bohr's early notion of the atom as kind of miniature solar system with electrons orbiting the nucleus. And, in so far as they were talking about different things, there can be no common ground – no shared or fixed points of reference – whereby to compare their theories in terms of progressively more adequate knowledge.

The same applies to Priestley's and Lavoisier's rival (phlogiston- and oxygen-based) theories of combustion. That each performed a series of crucial experiments which appeared to bear out his own theory – to generate results perfectly in accord with its predictions – is yet further grist for Kuhn's relativist mill. Thus Priestley showed combustion to produce a quantity of 'dephlogistated air', while Lavoisier accounted for the same experimental phenomena in terms of his preferred oxygen-hypothesis. So we are wrong to suppose, in the wisdom of hindsight, that Priestley was working with a false theory – one that involved the positing of a non-existent substance – while Lavoisier came up with the correct explanation. Rather we should say, here as in the previous cases, that what is involved is a wholesale difference of paradigms, along with their various regional ontologies, causal-explanatory schemes, frameworks of meaning and reference, etc. In which case we won't be so tempted to talk about 'progress' or the advancement of scientific knowledge in a way that presumptively neglects or overrides the *differend* between them. I am reverting to Lyotard's idiom here because I think it catches the main point at issue in Kuhn's relativistic philosophy of science as well as in Lyotard's postmodernist conception of justice as an imperative always to maximize the range of 'incommensurable' language-games, narratives, or phrase-genres. For they have both done much to encourage the view that any talk of truth – or of progress toward truth at the end of enquiry – is by its very nature authoritarian and aimed toward suppressing freedom of enquiry.

There is also, I would suggest, a comparison to be drawn with Levinasian ethics and its invocation of a radical 'otherness' – a realm of absolute alterity – that exists altogether outside and beyond the resources of Western (epistemologically-fixated) thought. For this again drives a wedge between ethical judgements and the various sorts of truth-evaluable knowledge – factual, circumstantial, scientific, historical, sociological, etc. – that can otherwise be seen as closely bound up with the process of reflective thought by which we typically arrive at such judgements. Again, this seems to me a downright counsel of despair, an extreme version of the old argument that there is no passage – no logical passage – from an 'is' to an 'ought', or (in Lyotard's postmodern parlance) from constative to performative phrase-genres. In philosophy of science the doctrine works out as a Kuhnian incommensurability-thesis along with the idea – pushed hardest by Paul Feyerabend – that we should abandon all notions of truth, method, or reputable ('genuine') science, and henceforth adopt an attitude of 'anything goes' as the best, most tolerant and liberal approach.[33] However this attitude can be shown to have some far-from-liberal consequences, as when Feyerabend sides with the Catholic Church against Galileo on account of the latter's shrewdly manipulative use of scientific evidence, not to mention his presumption in challenging the mores of his time and place. My point in all this is that relativist philosophies may often turn out to place sharp limits on the freedom of thought and enquiry when it comes to questioning their own favoured kinds of argument or evidential sources. Thus Kuhn adopts a thoroughly sceptical-relativist outlook in his treatment of various episodes from the history of the physical sciences. Yet he – like the 'strong' sociologists of knowledge – seems to entertain no serious doubts as to the facts thrown up by historical research or by social-scientific methods of enquiry.[34] Indeed, he exhibits a well-nigh positivist confidence that those facts can be used to challenge (or demolish) the idea of real advancements in knowledge having been achieved in physics, chemistry, and biology. But there is – I submit – something very odd, not to say perverse, about an approach that discounts the massive self-evidence of progress in those fields only to repose on the far more dubious – at any rate, the widely contested – claims of the social and human sciences.

There is a similar case to be made against Quinean and kindred arguments to the effect that meaning-variance between the terms involved in different scientific theories is sufficient to rule out comparison in point of accuracy, scope, explanatory grasp, predictive power, etc. Or again: any preference can only have to do with a 'vaguely pragmatic' inclination to make adjustments to one or another thread in the total 'fabric' of currently-held beliefs.[35] For it would seem fairly clear – on any but the most extreme of sceptical views – that we have better reason to believe in the truth-claims of physical science (or the achievements of scientific method to date) than to believe in those various semantical theories, such as meaning-holism or the 'underdetermination' of theory by evidence, that possess nothing like the same degree of rational and evidential warrant. Anti-realist doctrines are in this sense open to the same objection that has often been brought against scepticism with regard to other minds, to the existence of an 'external' world, and other such time-honoured philosophic foibles. That is to say, these doubts cannot be dispelled by any kind of *logical* argument, any more than Hume could discover any *logical* ground for believing in the existence of a causal nexus beyond the mere fact of repeated co-occurrence or observed regularity. Still one cannot be a serious sceptic as concerns these matters without, in the process, rendering so much of one's experience wholly unintelligible that the case collapses into manifest absurdity.[36]

This argument perhaps succeeds more readily in respect of 'other minds' and the 'external world', where it takes a good deal of perverse ingenuity to maintain a thoroughgoing sceptical stance. However, the situation is not so very different with regard to scientific realism since here also the sceptic's case – whether about causality or the existence of those items that figure in our current best theories – is one that runs counter to a vast range of evidence supporting the realist interpretation.[37] Besides, there are some strong arguments even from within the 'semantic' camp that cast doubt on the Quine-Kuhn theses of radical meaning-variance, framework relativism, and paradigm-incommensurability. Hartry Field, for one, has proposed a theory of partial and overlapping reference whereby to explain how terms such as 'mass' or 'atom' have a certain stability and continuity of usage despite playing a role in very different scientific paradigms.[38] Thus Newton and Einstein were working with conceptions of 'mass' that cannot, of course, be *directly* translated one into the other or *straightforwardly* compared as referring to one and the same physical quantity. However, it is possible to analyse the term into various, more specific senses – such as 'rest-mass', 'inertial mass', or 'relativistic mass' – which can then be assigned to particular instances of usage and particular contexts of argument. In which case there is no reason to accept the 'strong' thesis with regard to meaning-variance or any of the consequences that are taken to flow from it, such as Quine's ontological-relativist argument or Kuhn's notion of radically disjunct (world-transformative) paradigm shifts. Rather, we can see that Newtonian 'mass' still has meaning, reference, and a well-defined scope of application even though it now figures – after Einstein – as valid only for certain restricted purposes or within a certain classical limit as specified by the General Theory of Relativity.

In short, Field's approach has one great virtue, as compared with the wholesale relativist view: namely, that it brings semantics into line with what science (or current-best physical theory) has to tell us concerning such matters. Likewise, if one wants to make sense of the history of modern particle-physics then one will have to assume that Dalton, Rutherford, Einstein and Bohr were *to this extent at least* talking about 'the same thing', that is say, disagreeing precisely with respect to the structure, properties, and internal constitution of 'atoms'.[39] On the alternative (Quinean-Kuhnian) view, we should have no warrant – realist prejudice aside – for supposing that science had in any way advanced toward a better, more detailed or adequate knowledge of atoms or anything else. Of course the sceptic may still want to claim that this merely begs the question against relativist, anti-realist, instrumentalist, conventionalist, or social-constructivist arguments since it takes for granted the reality – the perduring ontological status – of whatever it is that scientists have striven to describe or explain with their various theories or hypotheses. Nevertheless this manifests a strange disregard for the single most elementary truth thrown up in the course of scientific enquiry to date, a truth that was well-known to Aristotle but which has often been lost from view in later philosophical dispute. It is the fact, simply put, that what renders our beliefs true or false is the way things stand in reality, rather than – a strictly preposterous notion – reality being somehow a product of (or 'constructed by') whatever we happen to believe concerning it. For if this were the case then there could be no explaining how scientists (also historians and others) can sometimes, if rarely, step outside their inherited paradigms, language-games, discourses or conceptual schemes and make some discovery that constitutes a genuine advance in knowledge.

III

'Preposterous' in its etymological sense means 'getting things back to front', which is just what happens – or so I would suggest – when theorists take the linguistic turn toward notions of radical meaning-variance or paradigm-incommensurability. For the result of such thinking – if consistently pursued – is to render scientific progress a miracle (or a species of wishful illusion), and to leave it likewise an ultimate mystery why science should so often have managed to explain what would otherwise lack any adequate, convincing, or remotely plausible explanation. My point – to repeat – is that talk of 'difference', 'otherness', 'incommensurability' 'alterity', 'heterogeneity', etc., is by no means confined to the fashionable discourse of postmodernist cultural theory. It is also very much a leading theme in post-Kuhnian philosophy of science and in other disciplines – such as historiography and sociology of knowledge – that have taken on board some version of the generalized difference-principle. What very often goes along with this (most explicitly in Lyotard's case) is a belief that justice can best be served by promoting the greatest possible variety of language-games, narratives, phrase-genres, etc., and rejecting any notion of truth – even the Kantian-Peircean regulative idea of truth at the end of enquiry – as a power-ploy aimed at suppressing or negating the narrative-discursive 'differend'. The same applies to Foucault's Nietzschean 'genealogies' of power-knowledge, despite the clear signs in his later texts and interviews that Foucault had come to recognise the problems (chiefly the normative confusions) that resulted from the idea of truth as nothing more than a product of power/knowledge differentials.[40]

I have argued that this whole approach is radically misconceived, not only in epistemological but also in ethical and socio-political terms. As applied to philosophy of science it quickly leads on, *via* milder varieties of cultural-linguistic relativism, to arguments of the full-fledged Feyerabend type where truth *just is* whatever counts as such according to this or that belief-system, be it orthodox or non-standard ('revolutionary') science, alternative medicine, voodoo magic, or the forcibly applied dictates of Catholic orthodoxy *versus* Galileo's heliocentric hypothesis. Now this also has a crucial bearing on the way that one construes the relation between epistemology and ethics, between the cognitive and evaluative 'phrase-genres' in Lyotard's post-modernist parlance, or again – to adopt a Habermasian phrase – between knowledge and human interests.[41] That is to say, there is the risk of collapsing those distinctions and producing *either* a determinist outlook that allows no room for human agency, choice, responsibility, etc., *or* a purely notional postmodernist freedom to 'redescribe' the world in whatever way we choose as if wishing could make it so. This latter is the kind of argument to be found in the writings of a 'post-analytic' (indeed avowedly 'post-philosophical') thinker like Richard Rorty, one who counts philosophy a pointless and boring enterprise so long as it remains hung up on old-fashioned notions such as 'reality' and 'truth'.[42] However, there is also a risk – and here we return to Levinas – of construing the ethical relation in terms so remote from the human sphere of shared cognitive and intersubjective interests that the 'other' becomes *absolutely* other, and can therefore exert no distinctive claim – no claim as a human being – on my capacity for acknowledging their point of view or respecting their moral autonomy. Indeed, the Levinasian ethical imperative can often sound disturbingly close to Kierkegaard's conception of authentic Christian faith as that which at the limit transcends and cancels all merely human ties and obligations.[43]

So I think it is important to take the point of Derrida's essay on Levinas and see that there are dangers in attempting to derive an ethics from the idea of radical otherness or alterity. Moreover, there are urgent political and social reasons for resisting this counter-Enlightenment attack on the values of truth, of mutual understanding, of shared human interests and values across otherwise large differences of language, culture, or belief. After all, it is far from clear that what the world needs now is a heightened sense of the various factors that divide human beings and cultures one from another, and which prevent them from perceiving their common humanity. If you think about the lethal conflicts that are raging in many parts of the world at this moment then you may find reason to reject such a view. Very often these conflicts come about because human beings are successfully indoctrinated with a notion of radical otherness, that is, an incapacity to recognise other people *as* human beings on account of some supposedly deep-laid racial, ethnic, religious, or ideological difference. It is possible, all too possible, for whole populations to be swung into this way of thinking, to simply exclude those others from the realm of shared humanity, to see them as utterly and incomprehensibly different or alien to themselves.

Of course I am not claiming, absurdly, that Levinas's thought (or that of his disciples) is some kind of disguised apologia for the current resurgence of ethnic and religious strife in various parts of the world. However I *do* want to argue that these ideas about radical otherness – so prominent in the postmodern discourse on ethical and political questions – have perhaps been too readily endorsed by thinkers of a liberal-pluralist persuasion. For the trouble with incommensurability-arguments, whether in epistemology or ethics, is that they tend to give rise to an us-and-them outlook which in effect leaves 'us' with a choice between two, equally drastic alternatives. That is, we can treat 'them' either as utterly opaque (presuming to understand nothing of their meanings, intentions, motives, interests, values, etc.), or as comprehensible only on our own terms, that is to say, in so far as we *must* willy-nilly understand them according to *our* linguistic, cultural, inter-pretive, or ethico-political lights.

The first may be called the 'Levinas option' and should, I think, be treated with caution for the reasons I have suggested above. The second is an unintended consequence of theories – pragmatist or liberal-communitarian theories – which typically maintain that meanings, values, and beliefs are 'internal' to this or that cultural form of life, and should therefore be judged by their own criteria and not by some externally-imposed set of stan-dards. This idea is very widespread nowadays, mainly in the arts and humanities sector though also – *via* the 'strong programme' in sociology of knowledge – as applied to the history and philosophy of science.[44] Its sources include late Wittgenstein (at least on one influential reading) and a range of other variants on the present-day linguistic or hermeneutic turn.[45] Where the unintended consequence strikes is through the fact that if this were *really* the case – if we and other people were talking, interpreting, reasoning, judging, making decisions, and so forth, always by our own 'internal' or culture-specific criteria – then we should always *ipso facto* be understanding others as we ourselves saw fit, or in keeping with our own (communally-sanctioned) ideas of truth and justice. Moreover, if it should so happen that we – and not they – were members of a strongly-placed community or interest-group (such as Rorty's 'North-Atlantic bourgeois liberal postmodern pragmatist' culture) then those others might not get much of a chance to make their voices heard. In which case the tolerant liberal view could well turn out to have sharp limits when it comes to deciding who qualifies for a voice in the 'cultural conversation of man-kind'.[46] In this connection consider the 1999 NATO bombing of Serbia, carried out in the name of 'liberal' and 'humanitarian' values, but deliber-ately targeted against certain sections of the Serbian civilian population – TV journalists included – who were thereby defined as possessing no claim to protection in respect of those same (purportedly 'universal') values.

Of course the Rortian pragmatist can always respond that this would be a distorted conversation and one that failed the liberal test of preserving a *genuine* open-ended multiplicity of participant voices, beliefs, values, worldviews, ideologies, etc. But he or she would then be faced with a further choice between two problematical alternatives. The first is difficult for anyone who takes this communitarian line since it must involve something like the Kantian-Habermasian appeal to an enlightened *sensus communis* (or 'ideal speech-situation') that would act as a context-transcendent regulative idea, and would hence rule against certain forms of merely *de facto*, i.e., partial or distorted consensus.[47] The second option is to grasp the other horn of this dilemma and deny that such 'external' criticism could ever be justified since it means, in effect, that we have cut ourselves off from any genuine (inward) understanding of the language-game or life-form concerned, and are hence simply not qualified to express any views on the matter. This approach is most familiar from the work of Peter Winch and other disciples of Wittgenstein in the social and human sciences.[48] However, it offers no adequate reponse to the problem about imposing our values and beliefs willy-nilly, as argued above. Worse than that, it very often tends to work out as a dogmatic statement of the full-blown cultural-relativist view, as for instance with Winch's idea that belief in witchcraft is no less 'rational' than the belief in (say) antibiotics as a cure for certain kinds of illness since witchcraft has its role within a given cultural life-form and we are simply not qualified to judge or criticize life-forms other than our own.

IV

I have perhaps said enough already – in connection with Lyotard – to indicate why I think this a wrong-headed, philosophically confused, and (not to mince words) a morally pernicious doctrine. My point is that the ethical bearing of these arguments – whether Winch's about witchcraft, Lyotard's about Holocaust revisionism, or Feyerabend's about the Catholic Church *contra* Galileo – cannot (or should not) be prescriptively divorced from their status as epistemological claims about the scope and limits of human knowledge concerning matters of scientific truth or historical fact. Any doctrine, such as Lyotard's, that raises the 'differend' between cognitive and evaluative judgements to a high point of absolute (quasi-Kantian) principle is sure to generate normative confusions of the kind that I have remarked upon here. At any rate there are several good reasons for rejecting the cultural-relativist approach both with regard to cognitive (scientific or factual) truth-claims, and with respect to differences of evaluative (ethico-political) judgement. They include, for instance, Donald Davidson's well-known argument – in his essay 'On the Very Idea of a Conceptual Scheme' – to the effect that talk of divergent language-games, discourses, life-forms, paradigms or ontological frameworks is strictly unintelligible unless it is assumed – which would seem *ex hypothesi* ruled out – that we *do* in fact possess some interlingual or trans-paradigm criteria for making comparisons between them.[49]

On Davidson's theory those criteria are supplied by the fact that, in order for anything to *count* as a language, it must exhibit certain qualifying features (devices for reference and cross-reference, for anaphora, negation, conjunction, disjunction, quantification, and so forth) in the absence of which it could simply not serve for even the most basic expressive-communicative purposes. Those devices can then be construed as providing a basic logico-syntactic framework that explains how we can (and do) most often manage to translate across large differences of belief-system, semantic field, scientific paradigm, 'conceptual scheme', or whatever. Syntax is thus 'more sociable' than semantics, Davidson maintains, in so far as it allows us a whole range of shared conceptual resources which don't fall prey to standard objections from the cultural-relativist quarter. Also it helps to make the point that truth – or the attitude of holding-true – is more basic to language (or human understanding in general) than the various localized or culture-specific 'conventions' that of course differ widely from one context to another. For since the meaning of a sentence is paradigmatically given by its truth-conditions – and in other, non-standard cases (such as metaphor, irony, or malapropism) by our allowing those conditions not to hold for some particular, context-specific reason – therefore we have no practical choice but to accept this order of priorities.[50] In short, truth-related concepts and values are so deeply built into our basic grasp of linguistic behaviour that it makes no sense to reverse that order and argue (in standard post-structuralist fashion) that meaning is purely 'conventional', that convention goes all the way down, and that 'truth' is whatever counts as such according to the local conventions.[51]

However, the more immediate context of debate – at least for our purposes here – is the present-day 'continental' tradition rather than its Anglo-American 'analytic' counterpart. In that context the issue is most sharply posed by German thinkers such as Habermas, Karl-Otto Apel, and Albrecht Wellmer who can be seen as sustaining the 'unfinished project' of enlightened critical modernity against its mainly French or French-influenced postmodernist detractors.[52] This is, I should acknowledge, a broad-brush picture that elides some salient distinctions within each camp. Still it may be helpful in suggesting that we ought perhaps to draw the line rather differently, that is, not so much between 'continental' and 'analytic' schools but rather between, on the one hand, those approaches that preserve a commitment to the values of truth-based intersubjective enquiry, and on the other those approaches that find no room for such values. I should not wish to claim that Davidsonian 'truth' – defined (after Tarski) in formal terms and non-committal on the realist issue – can be simply or straightforwardly deployed against arguments in the postmodern-sceptical-relativist vein.[53] Nor can it readily be marshalled on the side of an ethico-political project, such as that of Habermas, which requires a more detailed and nuanced account of the various human interests (cognitive, ethico-evaluative, aesthetic or 'world-disclosive') that between them constitute the philosophic discourse of modernity. For it is here, if anywhere, that the two traditions part company: in the analytic stress on technical issues about meaning, truth, and logic, as opposed to the broadly continental emphasis – deriving from Kant – on the complex relationship between those various orders of thought and judgement. All the same there is a certain alignment of interests between truth-based formal philosophies of language in the analytic mode and philosophies of meaning and interpretation that seek to conserve the Enlightenment commitment to values of truth and emancipatory critique. That is, they converge on this important point about the basic commonality of human knowledge and experience, of what makes sense – what enables mutual understanding to occur – across otherwise large differences of language, thought and culture.

If you look at things from this angle then perhaps you will decide that the real division is not so much one that falls between so-called 'analytic' and so-called 'continental' philosophy. Rather, it is what separates thinkers who seek to build on that basic commonality – who accept it as an *a priori* condition of achieving any progress in these matters – and on the other hand those who reject such thinking as a residue of bad old 'Enlightenment' beliefs, that is, a false universalism premised on obsolete (quasi-transcendental) notions of reason, validity, and truth. On this view truth-talk in whatever guise is just another means of suppressing the narrative *differend* or – as Foucault would have it – just another form of the ubiquitous will-to-power that operates all the more effectively by adopting such a high-toned rhetorical stance.[54] It should scarcely need saying – but very often does in the current, sharply polarized context of debate – that this latter typecast characterization is absurdly wide of the mark. With respect to Kant (the usual target here) it involves a massive conflation of distinct arguments, truth-claims, modes of judgement, and value-spheres. Still less can the standard rebuke be applied to present-day thinkers such as Habermas, those who have sought to uphold and defend the 'unfinished project' of modernity even while conceding its failures (or limited achievements) to date and the need for continuing refinement, elaboration, and critique.[55]

However I must now make good my promise and bring this argument back around to deconstruction and its status *vis-à-vis* the two opposed 'discourses' of modernity and postmodernity. What I wish to say – as you will no doubt have gathered by now – is that deconstruction stands very firmly apart from postmodernism. All too often it is treated as just a more specialized, more 'philosophical' sub-branch or variant of postmodernism. I think that they are two quite distinct developments, albeit with certain shared sources (from Kant, Hegel and Nietzsche to Saussure and of course Derrida), but with a quite different way of reading those source-texts and different criteria – I would say, different standards – of valid argument. Deconstruction is often viewed, by its Anglophone critics especially, as the sort of thing that postmodernists typically get up to when they acquire a smattering of philosophy and don't wish to be put down as mere cultural or literary theorists. However, as I have argued, there are crucial distinctions to be drawn between (say) Lyotard's and Derrida's approaches to Kant, or between postmodernism's wholesale rejection of Enlightenment values and the far more complex and nuanced relationship that emerges through a deconstructive reading of Enlightenment texts.[56] One problem here is that the main parties to this dispute – including, regrettably, Derrida and Habermas – have sometimes been pressured by their camp-followers to adopt an adversarial stance that obscures both the real points at issue between them and the extent of their shared interests, values, and concerns. So I shall finish by trying to spell out the issues in a way that so far as possible avoids such distracting polemics.

V

There are, I should admit, some additional problems to be faced in addressing this topic of 'deconstruction and the philosophic discourse of modernity'. In part they have to do with Habermas's reading of Derrida, a reading that is sometimes careless, that gets Derrida wrong in certain crucial respects, and which has done more than its share to encourage the recent round of hostilities.[57] Derrida has tended to respond in kind, that is, to treat Habermas with withering scorn as someone who just can't be bothered to read what is put in front of him.[58] However it would be wrong to dismiss the whole issue as just an unfortunate misunderstanding on both sides. For there are several passages in Derrida's texts where he says quite specifically that deconstruction is *not* another version of 'critique' in the Kantian or post-Kantian mode.[59] Here he seems to think of 'critique' as something destructive, polemical, perhaps even violent: an attempt to undermine or discredit opposing views. And Derrida is – with just a few exceptions, among them his responses to Habermas and Searle – an irenic and not a polemical thinker. For the result of a deconstructive reading (as witness for instance his essays on Plato, Rousseau, Husserl, or J.L. Austin) is to draw out hitherto unnoticed subtleties and complexities in the text, rather than to show the text up as merely naive or deluded.[60] This is no doubt why he has certain qualms about annexing deconstruction to the practice or the heritage of Enlightenment critique.

Nevertheless, as I have argued, that description is by no means wide of the mark if applied to Derrida's various readings of texts in the Western philosophical tradition. For there is a sense – an eminently Kantian sense – in which 'critique' is not at all a matter of polemics, not a matter of attacking or dismissing beliefs that one thinks naive or ill-founded. Rather, it is a matter of posing certain questions that have to do with the *conditions of possibility* for language and thought in general, conditions that may sometimes conflict with what an author expressly or overtly states regarding (say) the priority of speech over writing, or nature over culture, or concept over metaphor. These are *transcendental* questions, again in the strict (Kantian) sense of that term. That is, they are concerned with philosophical issues about thought, perception, language, logic, and intentionality, issues which cannot (or should not) be construed in merely polemical terms. So we can take Derrida at his word when he cautions us against the idea of deconstruction as a 'simple progressive critique in the manner of the Enlightenment'.[61] Nevertheless, it would be wrong to suppose, for that reason, that deconstruction is squarely aligned with postmodernism in its antagonism towards the philosophic discourse of modernity.

This difference comes out very clearly in his essay on Levinas where, as I have said, Derrida makes the case against an ethics of absolute 'alterity' or 'otherness', an ethics that would somehow bypass the appeal to a shared human realm of concepts, perceptions, meanings, values, or modes of experience.[62] The essay is a *critique* of Levinas's thinking in just the sense of that term that I am invoking here. While in no way polemical – indeed quite the reverse – it still draws attention to what can only be called the conditions of *im*possibility for an ethics conceived as Levinas would wish, that is to say, on a radicalized principle of difference erected into a high point of doctrine. Thus Derrida takes issue with Levinas on the twofold grounds: (1) that his notion of absolute 'otherness' is philosophically unsustainable, hence open to a form of deconstructive immanent critique; and (2) that it requires – in the name of ethics – a willed renunciation of just those capacities (of tolerance, mutual regard, sympathetic insight) that enable us to treat the other as an *alter ego*, and which thereby open a space for the ethical relationship.

In short, Derrida criticizes Levinas's thinking, and does so (moreover) through a close reading of his texts which maintains the highest standards of philosophic rigour and ethical accountability. But of course, this presupposes (as Habermas could readily agree) that in order for such criticism to proceed there must exist the basis for shared understanding across and despite the difference of views between Derrida and Levinas. Which is also to say – *pace* some of Derrida's more guarded pronounce-ments – that there is nothing inherently violent or antagonistic about the discourse of 'enlightened' critique, whatever its potential abuses when applied in a doctrinaire or un-self-critical fashion. At any rate I hope to have laid out some valid arguments for viewing deconstruction as very much a part of the 'unfinished project' of modernity. In the following chapters I shall take up these issues with respect to their bearing on current debates in philosophy of science, epistemology, ethics, and the role of philosophy as a critical voice within the modern university system.

CHAPTER 3

Deconstruction and the 'Unfinished Project of Modernity'

I

Commentaries on Derrida tend to divide very sharply when it comes to assessing the relationship between deconstruction and what Habermas calls the 'unfinished project' of post-Kantian critical thought.[1] For some – postmodernists and Rorty-style 'strong' textualists among them – this relationship is not so much a matter of continuing critical engagement as a straightforward rejection, on Derrida's part, of all those 'enlightened' truth-claims and values that once made up the philosophic discourse of modernity.[2] Thus Derrida is interpreted as taking the view that philosophy is just one voice in the 'cultural conversation of mankind', or again, just another 'kind of writing' (Rorty's phrase) whose chief merit is to move the conversation along by inventing new language-games, metaphors, narratives, modes of self-description and so forth.[3] On this account it is merely unfortunate – the last thing for which his writings should be valued – when Derrida reverts to certain forms of argument in the 'quasi-transcendental' (or conditions-of-possibilty) mode which betray a lingering Kantian influence. For others – most notably Rodophe Gasché – it is just those elements in Derrida's work that constitute its chief philosophical merit, its claim both to *conserve and to radicalize* the critical impulse of modernity.[4] The third main tendency in Derrida exegesis is that represented by thinkers such as Habermas who interpret him pretty much in Rorty's fashion – as a gadfly rhetorician bent upon levelling the 'genre-distinction' between philosophy and literature – but who draw very different conclusions as to the value and desirability of carrying that project through.[5]

Thus, according to Habermas, deconstruction can best be seen as a further stage in the history of irrationalist or counter-enlightenment thought which first took hold very soon after Kant and which harked back to an earlier (pre-Kantian) phase when thinking had not yet accomplished the passage to a critical awareness of its various constitutive powers and limits. What Rorty most likes about Derrida – his supposed indifference to the standards of 'serious', 'constructive' philosophical enquiry – is what Habermas finds most reprehensible. Indeed he takes it as evidence enough of the close link between deconstruction and the wider postmodernist retreat from any notion of progressive or emancipatory thought. And his complaint is taken up – albeit in a different (broadly 'analytic' or Anglo-American) key – by opponents of Derrida such as John Searle who profess to see nothing in deconstruction but a wilful desire to play mischievous games not only with the texts of philosophers from Plato to Austin but also with those 'ordinary-language' codes and conventions that allow philosophy its claim to treat issues of shared human concern.[6] Hence the bad name that deconstruction has acquired – whether by hearsay or (less often) through direct acquaintance with the texts – among mainstream philosophers on both sides of the notional rift between 'continental' and 'analytic' lines of descent.

That this rift may not run as deep or wide as commonly thought is a case that has been argued with considerable force by recent commentators, Michael Dummett among them.[7] Indeed Derrida himself voices some perplexity – in the course of his response to Searle – concerning the hybrid derivation of those various arguments brought against him by critics who supposedly speak for the two philosophical cultures.[8] At any rate Searle and Habermas have this much in common: that they charge deconstruction with illicitly collapsing certain cardinal distinctions, as for instance between philosophy and literature, reason and rhetoric, or language in its various (e.g. constative and performative or cognitive, ethico-evaluative and 'world-disclosive') aspects. Moreover, they both see Derrida as refusing to engage in rational debate and embracing what amounts to a nihilist outlook – or an attitude of 'anything goes' – with regard to crucial issues of truth, meaning and interpretation. For Searle, this results from Derrida's failure to grasp the basic principles of speech-act theory, or rather (more likely) his perverse desire to make trouble by wilfully misreading texts and creating all manner of pseudo-problems. For Habermas, it is more a matter of placing deconstruction in the wider present-day cultural context of philosophies that have given up too soon on the 'unfinished project' of modernity, and which continue to rehearse issues that belonged to an earlier, subject-centred discourse of epistemology and ethics.[9]

Thus Derrida's obsession (as Habermas sees it) with the predicament of 'logocentric' reason – with the aporias created by a so-called Western 'metaphysics of presence' – is one that by now should have ceased to exert such a hold with the turn toward language (or communicative action) as the best way forward from those false dilemmas. In short, Habermas agrees with Rorty when he interprets Derrida as (1) out to demolish the philosophic discourse of enlightenment, and (2) subject to a backward pull that prevents him from exploring the alternative resources now offered by a speech-act theory (a 'universal pragmatics') with strongly normative validity-conditions. Where they differ is on the question whether anything is to be gained by recasting those typically Kantian issues in a somewhat updated or

'linguistified' form. Rorty sees this as just another sad example of the way
that philosophers attempt to hang onto their old delusions of grandeur by
periodically scaling down their epistemological claims while inventing some
new technical idiom that smuggles those claims in again by the back door.[10]
This is why he treats Derrida's 'philosophical' writings as symptomatic of a
retrograde tendency which we can safely ignore once we have taken the point
of his other, more liberating 'textualist' performances. On Habermas's
reading, conversely, the trouble with deconstruction is that it skips straight
across – in typical postmodernist style – from disillusionment with that
old, subject-centred epistemological paradigm to an attitude of all-out
hermeneutic licence where there exist no constraints upon the range of interpretative options, whether in the sphere of 'ordinary language' or in various
more specialized branches of enquiry.

Searle is less concerned with these long-term genealogical issues, speaking
as he does from a briskly (not to say brusquely) 'analytic' standpoint that
assumes all genuine philosophic problems to be capable of solution simply by
applying certain straightforward speech-act precepts. Thus for him it is just a
matter of Derrida's lacking the most basic competence in these matters, rather
than a case calling for treatment in the largescale historical-philosophico-
diagnostic mode.[11] Still he concurs with Habermas in viewing deconstruction
as a product of the drive to conflate different aspects of language, aspects
which need to be distinguished not only for the sake of philosophical clarity
but also in order to explain how linguistic communication is possible in
various (standard and non-standard, e.g. fictional) contexts. Moreover, he
shares Habermas's belief that Derrida has muddied the waters by taking the
latter sorts of case – metaphor, fiction, poetry, 'deviant' utterances of various
kind – as somehow (absurdly) prior or prerequisite to language in its normal,
everyday-communicative role. As Habermas describes it this amounts to a
massive over-emphasis on the aesthetic, the rhetorical, or 'world-disclosive'
dimension of language and a consequent failure to make room for those other
(truth-related or ethico-evaluative) dimensions which are thereby consigned
to a merely derivative and ancillary status.

So it is – on this account – that Derrida betrays the unfinished project
of modernity and opens the way to a postmodern notion of endless
interpretative 'freeplay' where there is no longer any place for such typecast
Enlightenment values as truth, reason, and critique. In short, Habermas
agrees point-for-point with Rorty that the most significant aspect of
Derrida's work is its desire to have done with those antiquated values and its
idea of philosophy as just another another 'kind of writing', on a par with
other (on the whole more inventive and entertaining) kinds such as fiction,
poetry, and literary criticism. But where Rorty thoroughly approves this turn
in the present-day 'cultural conversation', Habermas views it as one more
sign of the widespread failure of moral, political, and intellectual nerve that

goes under the blanket name of postmodernism. Unlike Searle he shows some awareness of the complex and intricate character of Derrida's arguments, especially as regards their relationship to Kant and to episodes in the post-Kantian history of thought from Fichte, Schelling and Hegel to recent, sharply polarized debates in the wake of Nietzsche and Husserl. But on the main point at issue – Derrida's supposed irrationalist retreat from the sphere of intersubjective understanding or shared communicative norms – Habermas and Searle can properly be seen as making common cause.

I have written elsewhere at some length on the various distortions and misunderstandings that have given rise to this prevalent notion of Derrida as a counter-Enlightenment thinker deploying all the means at his crafty disposal to subvert or discredit the philosophic discourse of modernity.[12] What I want to do now is approach the same topic from a slightly different angle, one that takes in the question of deconstruction's bearing *vis-à-vis* the claims of Enlightenment critique, but which treats that question in a wider institutional context. For it is clear that both Derrida *and* his opponents see a strong connection at this point, that is to say, between relatively specialized questions concerning the powers, the scope and limits of critical reason in its various modes of deployment, and on the other hand primarily ethical questions concerning the comportment of critical intellectuals in the wider social sphere. Of course Derrida's writings on Kant are the obvious place to go if one wishes to grasp the issues at stake in this current, much-publicized debate about the ethics and the politics of deconstruction.[13] I shall therefore focus my discussion on two of his texts from the 1980s : '*Mochlos, or The Conflict of the Faculties*' and 'The Parergon'. (*Mochlos* and *parergon* are the Greek words meaning 'lever' and 'frame', a pair of terms whose significance will I hope become clear in the course of this chapter.) There is no denying that Derrida maintains a complex, ambivalent, at times mistrustful attitude toward the philosophic discourse of modernity. But there is also no warrant – prejudice aside – for counting him among the postmodern enemies of reason or those who (as Habermas charges) wish to revoke the unfinished project of critical-emancipatory thought.

II

In '*Mochlos* – or the Conflict of the Faculties' Derrida takes his sub-title from an an essay by Kant which addresses various issues having to to do with the intellectual division of labour between various academic disciplines and the order of priority that governs their relationship.[14] What is in question here is a certain idea of the modern University, an idea that has come down to us principally from Kant and from other philosophers (Humboldt among them) in the broadly 'Enlightenment' tradition. For it is not just a play on words to point out the link between Kant's 'system' of the faculties – pure (or speculative) reason, cognitive understanding, practical reason, aesthetic judgement, etc. – and the various faculties (i.e., university departments, disciplines or subject-areas) that we have largely taken over from that same tradition.

To be sure, the division of labour has changed in some respects, as for instance through the development of new, more specialized fields of scientific research or new interdisciplinary ventures. (These are not opposite trends, by the way, but very often go closely together, as with the emergence of molecular biology as a specialized discipline that unites physics and chemistry with the life sciences.) But essentially we are working with the same ground-plan, the same disciplinary 'map', so to speak, which one could use as a guide to find one's way around the modern university campus. So there are the sciences, the natural or physical sciences (both 'pure' and 'applied') whose different branches and sub-branches would each have its campus location. Then there are the various 'humanities' or 'social sciences' departments – history, anthropology, sociology, economics, philosophy, literature, languages ancient and modern – which would probably occupy rather less space, or perhaps (some of them nowadays) just an office with part-time secretary and a small supply of headed notepaper. In some cases – e.g., sociology and econom- ics – the exact location and amount of room might depend on their perceived standing *vis-à-vis* the natural sciences, that is, the extent to which they adopt properly 'scientific' (empirical or quantitative) methods and techniques. So there are shifts of alignment going on all the time, brought about by pressures 'internal' and 'external', in so far as one can actually distinguish those two sorts of pressure. This is indeed one of the questions that Derrida raises with regard to the modern post-Kantian idea of the university as an autonomous institution where certain intellectual pursuits – such as phi- losophy – should properly be subject to no forms of 'external' interference or control. Still there is a sense in which all these disciplines – and the various relations (not mention the rivalries) between them – have their model in Kant's seemingly rigid but in fact quite flexible schema. Here we might recall Gilles Deleuze's happy metaphor of the system of 'rotating chairmanship' whereby the different faculties (pure reason, understanding, practical reason, and judgement) take up a prominent or subsidiary role according to the case in hand.[15]

What interests Derrida, in his writings on Kant, is the extent to which this can still be thought of as a model – albeit an idealized model, a regulative 'idea of reason' in the Kantian sense – for the conduct of debate in or upon the modern university. Up to a point he shares the postmodernist outlook of scepticism with regard to its continuing relevance or validity. Thus, as might be expected, Derrida sets out to deconstruct the various oppositions between 'pure' and 'applied' research, between (on the one hand) disinterested, speculative, or purely truth-seeking disciplines, and (on the other) areas of research whose interests are dictated by 'external' incentives such as commercial funding or government contracts. For Kant, in his essay 'The Conflict of the Faculties', it is important – indeed a vital condition for academic freedom in the modern university – that these distinctions be constantly borne in mind.[16] Moreover, Philosophy is the subject-area where reason asserts its right to pursue such enquiries without hindrance, restraint, or the threat of censorship. It can legitimately assert that right, Kant argues, since it does not (or should not) exert any claim to influence people – people outside the university – in matters of political, moral, or religious belief, as distinct from raising speculative issues in politics, ethics, and theology. There are other disciplines (law, theology, medicine – the so-called 'higher' faculties) which do have that kind of extramural influence on account of their closer relationship with the State and with the offices of state-administered power. These are the disciplines that possess some *leverage* in matters of executive decision-taking and policy-formation – whence one meaning of the 'mochlos' metaphor, as Derrida deploys it. In exchange for this privilege they can and should be held accountable for upholding whatever the State rightly decrees with regard to political, social, and religious obligations. And if they overstep the limit in this respect – as, for instance, by pursuing speculative questions that might have a dangerous (subversive) impact on the beliefs or conduct of people outside the university – then their published opinions may properly be subject to censorship.

Philosophy is therefore a 'lower' faculty in the sense that it lays no claim to executive power. Furthermore, Kant says, it is very important that philosophers should not seek to arrogate such power, because if they did then they could have no legitimate complaint when their writings and teachings were censored or suppressed. Thus 'the freedom of the lower faculty, though *absolute*, is a freedom of judgement and intra-university speech, a freedom to speak out on *that which is*, through judgements essentially theoretical'.[17] And again, in Derrida's words:

> [t]his freedom of judgement Kant takes to be the unconditioned condition of university autonomy, and that unconditioned condition is nothing other than philosophy. Autonomy is philosophical reason insofar as it grants itself its own law, namely the truth. Which is why the lower faculty is called the philosophy faculty; and without a philosophy department in a university, there is no university.[18]

However that prerogative is granted only on certain mutually agreed terms and conditions. If philosophers presumed to tell people what they should believe or how they should act – setting up, in effect, as an arm of the executive – then they would be breaking the contract (or the unwritten concordat) that guarantees their freedom of thought and expression. For philosophy has to do with the exercise of reason in a mode quite distinct, or in a sphere quite separate, from the interests of church and state. It can discuss theology but it must not instruct people as to just what religious beliefs they should hold; it can raise important issues about God, about the immortality of the soul, about the possibility (or impossibility) of proving God's existence, but should exercise a due caution lest those issues stir up public controversy. In the realm of politics likewise, philosophers may question all manner of received (or state-sanctioned) beliefs with regard to freedom, democracy, human rights, or the scope and limits of legitimate state power. However, it should do so always in its proper ('theoretical') mode, and without seeking an influence beyond the sphere of 'disinterested' philosophical enquiry. For these are issues that could have quite explosive or incendiary effects upon the population at large if they were discussed, say, in the popular press or in books of wide public appeal. However, Kant advises, there is a bargain to be struck, or – to put it less crudely – an 'enlightened' compromise solution. This will help to prevent any damage either to the interests of philosophy (through unwarranted restrictions on its freedom of thought and speech) or to the interests of legitimate state power (through forcing it to act beyond its proper remit in such delicate matters). Philosophers will not tell people what to think, they will not stray beyond their appointed domain, they will confine their speculation to the learned (not-too-accessible) books and journals. And in return for that agreement the politicians, theologians, and guardians of the public peace will refrain from intervening in issues that should scarcely be cause for official concern.

No doubt we have to do some charitable reading-between-the-lines in order to avoid the impression of hypocrisy or moral cowardice. At this time Kant had serious problems with state and church censorship, after a fairly long period of relative freedom.[19] Certainly he is making (or implying) some much higher claims for philosophy – for its bearing on matters of moral, religious, and political conscience – than he can safely express straight out. He is *not* just taking a line of least resistance, caving in under pressure, and requesting that philosophers be left free to pursue their harmless speculations, just so long as they treat of religious questions 'within the limits of reason alone' (another of his nicely-judged titles) and agree not to meddle with politics.[20] On the contrary, it is hard to imagine any reader of Kant – except perhaps the most gullible of state censors – who would fail to perceive the ironic subtext of a work like 'The Conflict of the Faculties'. For if there is one Kantian precept that demands to be heard – not only in these occasional writings but also throughout the three *Critiques* – it is the principle enshrined in his famous watchword 'Sapere aude!', that is, 'have the courage to think for yourself!'. In other words, it is Kant's paramount belief that human beings achieve autonomy (or 'maturity') in matters of scientific, intellectual, ethical, and religious judgement only to the extent that they accept nothing on trust – or in blind faith – and hence claim the freedom to exercise their powers of enlightened critical reason.

Now Derrida is sceptical about all this, though only up to a point. He thinks it an illusion – though also, one might say, a vital and necessary illusion – that philosophy can somehow rise above the various interests that bear in upon it from 'outside' the university, or from other disciplines 'inside' the university which more or less directly represent those interests. Thus it is no longer possible in good faith – or in good intellectual conscience – to accept this idea of the Philosophy faculty as representing in itself, by some special dispensation, the good conscience of the modern (enlightened) university system. For there is, as Derrida pointedly remarks elsewhere, no discipline or subject-area nowadays that is so remote from the interests of state power or the imperatives of 'applied' research that it might not receive government support or funding by the US Navy.[21] After all, it is hard to tell what might be the pay-off – the long-term strategic yield – of a research-programme in (say) translation studies, or in literary theory, or even in the deconstructive reading of texts. Deconstruction might just turn out to be useful in devizing some new and well-nigh unbreakable code for the communication of military secrets, or perhaps for cracking such a code should the need arise. At this point, Derrida says, we can no longer have much faith in the Kantian distinction between 'pure' and 'applied' research, or the interests of knowledge and the interests of power, or those disciplines (philosophy chief among them) that pursue truth 'for its own sake' and those that adopt a pragmatic, instrumentalist approach.

Kant considered it vital to preserve this distinction since only thus, he believed, could philosophy be saved from the threat of state-sponsored interference. In Austinian terms, it is the distinction between *constative* and *performative* modes of utterance, that is to say, between speech-acts with assertoric force (those to which criteria of truth or falsehood apply), and speech-acts – such as promises, threats, requests, imperatives, etc. – whose truth is not at issue but rather their aptness in some given situation or context of utterance.[22] With performatives, the sole criterion is whether or not they meet the various 'felicity'-conditions that decide what shall count as a proper or genuine sample of the kind. If those conditions are met – if it is the right form of words, uttered in the right context, and by a speaker with due authority or qualifications – then the speech-act carries the intended performative (or 'illocutionary') force. Beyond that, it may also have 'perlocutionary' effects, as for instance by securing the desired result when an order has been issued or a request properly made and duly acted upon. Hence the analogy that Derrida draws between speech-act theory and the Kantian division of the faculties. It is the idea of philosophy as a 'constative' discipline concerned with matters of theoretical truth (matters that lie 'within the limits of reason alone'), and claiming no right to exercise power in the 'performative' or politico-juridical domain. For there is then less danger that the censors or guardians of the public peace will take it upon themselves to cross that line (so to speak) in the opposite direction and pre-sume to legislate on matters of a purely philosophical or speculative nature.

In his well-known essay on Austin ('Signature Event Context') Derrida produces a variety of arguments to show that this distinction between constative and performative speech-acts is highly unstable or hard to main-tain in any rigorous, philosophically adequate way.[23] It is subject to effects of undecidability which result from the problem of defining what should count as a genuine speech-act, whether in terms of speaker's intention (sincerely meaning what one says) or with reference to various circumstantial factors (appropriate context of utterance). I shall not go further into these issues here since they have already received a good deal of critical com-mentary.[24] My point is that Derrida finds similar problems with Kant's attempt – his perhaps rather less than sincere attempt – to keep philosophy safely apart from the realm of public-political affairs. Thus:

> Kant needs, as he says, to trace, between a responsibility concerning truth and a responsibility concerning action, a linear frontier, an indivisible and rigorously uncrossable line. To do so he has to submit language to a particular treatment. Language is an element common to both spheres of responsibility, and one that deprives us of any rigorous distinction between the two spaces that Kant at all costs wanted to dissociate. ... Kant speaks only of language when he speaks about the 'manifestation of truth', or 'influence over the people', or the interpretation of sacred texts in theological terms, or, conversely, philosophical terms, etc. And yet he continually effaces something in language that scrambles the limits which a criticist critique claims to assign to the faculties, to the interior of the faculties, and, as will be seen, between the university's inside and its outside.[25]

In part this is a matter of the problems that arise with any attempt to hold the line between 'pure' and 'applied' research, or truth pursued for its own sake – in the mode of disinterested speculative reason – and knowledge pursued with certain predetermined ends in view, be they techno-scientific, military-strategic, socio-political, or whatever. This is why, as Derrida says, he has 'let himself be guided' in his reading of Kant by the discourse of speech-act theory and – more specifically – the kinds of complication that can be seen to affect the constative/performative dichotomy. The connection is brought out in the following passage which modulates between Kant's doctrine of the faculties (in both senses of that term) and Austin's approach to the classification of speech-act forms, genres, or modalities.

The pure concept of the university is constructed by Kant on the possibility and necessity of a language purely theoretical, inspired solely by an interest in truth, with a structure that one today would call purely constative. This ideal is undoubtedly guaranteed, in the Kantian proposal as such, by pure practical reason, by prescriptive utterances, by the postulate of freedom on the one hand, and, on the other, by virtue of a de facto political authority supposed in principle to let itself be guided by reason. But this in no way keeps the performative structure from being excluded, in principle, from the language whereby Kant regulates both the concept of the university and what within it is purely autonomous, namely . . . the 'lower' faculty, the faculty of philosophy.[26]

Thus the chief problem with speech-act theory – that of distinguishing clearly between constative and performative modes of utterance – is also the problem that afflicts any doctrine, like Kant's, aimed toward establishing a guaranteed space within the university for the exercise of reason in its pure speculative mode, unbeholden to the interests of executive power and laying no claim to such power on its own behalf. Besides, this doctrine goes clean against what Kant had to say elsewhere about the 'public', as opposed to the 'private' uses of reason, and the duty of enlightened intellectuals not only to 'think for themselves' but to think on behalf of humanity at large, that is, with reference to a public sphere of shared ethico-political values and concerns.[27] So there is strong *prima facie* warrant to suppose that Kant cannot really mean what he says in thus restricting philosophy – or the purest, most essential interests of philosophy – to a realm where the privilege of free thought is purchased at the price of willing acquiescence in the dictates of authorized public belief.

This reading finds additional support if one looks more closely at Kant's 'doctrine' of the faculties as developed throughout the three *Critiques*. For it then becomes clear just how many and various are the linkages, exchanges, or relations of mutual interdependence that exist between them. This applies especially to the *Critique of Judgement* where Kant addresses a number of issues that were left unresolved – or inadequately treated – in its predecessor works.[28] They include, as exegetes have often noted, the epistemological issue (taken up from the First *Critique*) of just how sensuous intuitions can be 'brought under' corresponding concepts, and – with regard to the *Critique of Practical Reason* – the question of how generalized ethical maxims apply to particular cases of situated moral judgement.[29] But there is also the problem of accounting for that exercise of free, 'disinterested' judgement which, according to Kant, transcends all merely self-motivated ('pathological') tastes and inclinations. This is why aesthetics – improbably enough – assumes so prominent a role in Kant's philosophy: as the sphere of thought where judgement attains a maximal distance from the promptings of unregenerate desire or self-interest. In the case of the beautiful this condition comes about through the harmony achieved between the two 'faculties' of understanding and imagination. In the case of the sublime it results, more paradoxically, through the failure of understanding to grasp what lies beyond its utmost scope of comprehension. That is to say, it transpires through the mind's suddenly confronting images of awesome power or violence in nature (the dynamical sublime), or ideas of reason, such as those of the infinite or the infinitesimal, which yet remain devoid of conceptual-intuitive content (the mathematical sublime). For it is precisely at this point where understanding despairs of bringing intuitions under adequate concepts that we are somehow made aware of a higher realm – a realm of 'suprasensible' ideas – which allows us the glimpse of a moral law (that of 'pure practical reason') transcending the confines of creaturely existence.[30]

So the Third *Critique* is the text where various lines of thought are taken up and developed more fully – redeemed, so to speak, like promissory notes that Kant had held over from his previous works on epistemology and ethics. Indeed, it is the text where his entire project comes under critical review, since everything depends upon Kant's being able to bring the various 'faculties' into some kind of overarching order, some system of complex yet harmonious interdependence. For it is not only in the ethical or 'suprasensible' sphere – i.e., that of practical reason – that Kant seeks to draw this suggestive analogy with aesthetic judgement in its twofold (beautiful and sublime) aspects. The analogy is also of crucial importance for his attempt to explain how our knowledge of the world (everyday or scientific knowledge) presupposes the existence of an order in nature which corresponds to the various forms or processes of human understanding and reflective enquiry. This is Kant's theme in the second part of the *Critique of Judgement*, the part where he discusses nature under its teleological aspect as a regulative idea – an Idea of Reason – in the absence of which such knowledge would be wholly unattainable. For there could then be no means of bridging the gulf between concepts and sensuous intuitions, or intuitions and the realm of natural (real-world) objects, processes and events to which those intuitions must be thought to correspond. In other words, there is a certain image of nature which is the condition of possibility for everything we can claim to know or understand concerning the natural sciences or indeed our most basic forms of perceptual and cognitive grasp.

Once again, commentators are deeply divided on the extent to which Kant is successful in carrying this argument through. In fact one could argue that the two main traditions of modern Kant commentary – 'analytic' and 'continental' – part company on just this question of whether the issues raised in his First *Critique* are in any way resolved – or need resolving – through a teleological doctrine of nature and the faculties of human judgement. Analytic philosophers mostly take the view that this whole aspect of

Kant's thinking should best be passed over in tactful silence, or treated as merely an unfortunate lapse into the kind of speculative whimsy that has got post-Kantian 'continental' philosophy its well-deserved bad name. From the latter viewpoint, conversely, there are problems left outstanding in the First *Critique* – problems such as that gulf between concepts and phenomenal intuitions – which cannot be addressed except through the turn toward a more reflective, hermeneutic, or aesthetically-oriented approach.[31] Thus the difference works out, very often, as a 'continental' tendency to read Kant backwards, starting out from ideas developed in the *Critique of Judgement*, as opposed to a broadly 'analytic' stress on the primacy of Kant's epistemo-logical concerns. The former line of argument is one that runs from Heidegger's *Kant and the Problem of Metaphysics* to Lyotard's reflections on the Kantian sublime as a mode of judgement that disrupts or disarticulates the entire 'system' of the faculties.[32] And one could also suggest – as does Pierre Bourdieu in his brilliant short study of Heidegger – that the division reaches back into treatments of the First *Critique*, with commentators tending to lay chief stress *either* on the relatively clear-cut arguments that Kant puts forward in the 'Transcendental Analytic', *or* on those problematic passages in the 'Transcendental Aesthetic' which in turn give a hold for Heideggerian reflections in the depth-hermeneutical manner.[33] At any rate there are clearly some large issues bound up with this particular 'conflict of the faculties' as it takes shape among Kant's exegetes of varying philosophical persuasion.

III

Let me now return – not before time – to Derrida's deconstructive reading of Kant on the relation between philosophy and politics, or (more precisely) between the various faculties of 'pure' and 'applied' knowledge. As I have said, he offers various reasons to doubt that any such distinction could ever be firmly maintained, whether at Kant's time (when philosophers were subject, like everyone else, to numerous 'external' pressures and incentives), or again, in the present-day university context (where this argument applies with yet greater force). Thus:

> Kant ... wanted to make a line of demarcation pass between thinkers in the university and businessmen of knowledge or agents of government power, between the inside and the outside closest to the university enclosure. But this line, Kant certainly has to recognize, not only passes along the border and around the institution. It traverses the faculties, and this is a place of conflict, of an unavoidable conflict.[34]

However this is *not* to say that we should give up altogether on the Kantian attempt to secure a space for philosophical reflection – for the free exercise of critical and speculative thought – secure from intrusions of executive power. What is notable about Derrida's reading of Kant is its focus on the notion of aesthetic 'disinterest', or on the 'free play' of the faculties that is supposedly the hallmark of aesthetic judgement when released from precisely those same pressures and incentives. For if this case can be argued convincingly – that is to say, if philosophy can establish its claim for the existence of just such a purely contemplative, disinterested state of mind – then the way is open to distinguish elsewhere (in the natural and the human sciences alike) between 'pure' and 'applied' branches of research, or enquiries pursued for their own sake 'within the limits of reason alone' and enquiries pursued with some practical end in view. Thus aesthetic 'disinterest' becomes the very touchstone of a critical philosophy – and a doctrine of the faculties – premised on the freedom to 'think for oneself' without regard to such extraneous motives.

The most relevant text here is Derrida's essay 'The Parergon', an extended reading of the Third *Critique* that raises exactly these questions concerning aesthetic judgement and its status *vis-à-vis* the other Kantian faculties.[35] What Derrida finds especially interesting – or symptomatic – is Kant's desire always to draw lines, to establish boundaries or lay down limits for their exercise in this or that context as defined by his overall system of priorities. (That 'Kant' in German is a common noun meaning 'edge', 'border', or 'dividing-line' is a nice coincidence that Derrida duly notes without pushing the point too hard.) Thus understanding has its own special interest, namely that of bringing intuitions 'under' concepts, an interest that *must not* be confused with the interests of pure (speculative) reason on pain of producing insoluble aporias such as those laid out for inspection in the 'Transcendental Dialectic' of the First *Critique*.[36] Then again, there are the interests of practical reason – and of 'pure practical reason' especially – which require an autonomous (freely-willed) choice to accept the dictates of moral law, and should therefore *on no account* suffer confusion with the interests of cognitive understanding. And so it goes on: one must always exercise the greatest care to distinguish concepts from ideas, constitutive from regulative ideas, determinate from reflective judgements, judgements of taste ('disinterested' taste) from judgements admitting some taint of self-interest, some extraneous motivation, etc. This last distinction is closely related to that between 'free' and 'adherent' beauty, the one appreciated solely in and for itself, the other at least to some degree in virtue of its function or fitness of design for the purpose in hand. Thus the attitude of pure, disinterested aesthetic contemplation, called forth by some suitable object, is for Kant the very epitome of what transpires between mind and nature when the faculties achieve that state of harmonious balance or perfected internal adjustment that his system ultimately requires.

For Derrida, conversely, these various distinctions are all of them marked by a chronic instability – or lack of conceptual rigour – which leaves them open to a critical reading in the deconstructive mode. His title for this essay ('The Parergon') refers to the Greek word for 'frame', that is to say, whatever surrounds and sets off the artwork itself (the *ergon*), and which therefore should not be considered properly a part of the work or in any way integral to it. Thus – to take the most obvious or literal case – the frame of a painting is something that can always be changed without altering the various essential qualities (of balance, composition, formal structure, the internal play of light and shade) which belong to that work and no other. And this applies even more to external factors beyond or outside the frame, such as the wall on which the painting is hung, the surrounding decor, other paintings in the same room, the architectural features of the building wherein the exhibition has been mounted, and so forth. Yet of course these factors *do* have an influence on the way that the painting is perceived or appreciated, whatever Kant's steadfast formalist refusal to accept that they *should* have any such influence. Thus it can scarcely be denied that aesthetic considerations play some considerable part in deciding what kind of frame best serves to set off or enhance the painting's qualities. (A wrong choice of frame may spoil the overall effect by distracting one's attention, obscuring certain salient details, or disturbing the 'internal' sense of perspective.) Moreover, it is impossible to draw a line at this point and decree that whatever lies *outside* the frame – wall, decor, surroundings, etc. – can safely be excluded from the realm of aesthetic judgement. For when the formalist citadel has once been breached by what Derrida calls this 'logic of parergonality', then such distinctions can only be a matter of stipulative warrant, rather than pertaining to the very nature of aesthetic judgement or experience.

Derrida finds numerous examples in the Third *Critique* which show Kant attempting to hold that line, the line that should properly fall between work and frame, or again, between the framing concepts of aesthetic philosophy and whatever should lie either definitely inside or definitely outside its proper domain. In each case the example proves somehow recalcitrant, or fails to make the point as intended. Some of them are plainly problematic – even slightly absurd – as for instance when Kant asks whether the robes or draperies adorning a statue can be considered integral to its form, or when he cites such architectural features as the flying buttress and decides that they serve a mainly functional purpose, and should therefore be counted mere outworks (or *parerga*) devoid of genuine aesthetic value. But these examples point to a deeper problem which extends beyond Kant's aesthetic philosophy to the entire project of the three *Critiques*. For that project depends, as we have seen, on the making good of certain cardinal distinctions which are held over for their most elaborate treatment in those passages of the third *Critique* where Kant seeks to justify his claim for the exercise of judgement in its strictly non-partisan, its purely 'disinterested' mode. And this claim depends in turn on his ability to show – to deduce from first principles but also with the aid of convincing illustrative cases – that one can indeed distinguish 'free' from 'adherent' beauty, or disinterested judgements from those that admit some degree of 'extrinsic' motivation. However Kant's argument breaks down on both counts: through the fact that his examples regularly fail to make the intended point, and through the *impossibility* of drawing that prescriptive line between aesthetic and other modalities of judgement.

For this is not just a matter of Kant's having spoiled an otherwise strong philosophical case by offering some inept or ill-chosen illustrations along the way. Rather, it is a question of his not being able to offer any argument in support of that case – any argument on philosophic grounds – that would respect the conditions (or remain within the boundaries) which Kant has laid down for judgements concerning the aesthetic. For it is a characterizing feature of all such judgements, according to Kant, that they cannot involve the application of determinate *concepts*, that is to say, the kind of under-standing that is properly achieved – as he argues in the First *Critique* – by bringing sensuous or phenomenal intuitions under adequate or correspond-ing concepts. If this were the case with aesthetic judgements then, quite simply, the aesthetic would cease to exist as a distinctive modality of experi-ence, one that in some sense transcends and reconciles the other 'faculties' and their various potential conflicts of interest. What enables it to do so, as Kant seeks to show, is precisely the *lack* of any governing concept – any rule of judgement laid down, so to speak, in advance of particular applications – whereby one could establish fixed criteria in matters of aesthetic taste. On the contrary: such judgements are *indeterminate* in the sense that they always start out from the particular (that is, from some unique item of experience) and only then go in search of generalized criteria or principles whereby to justify their claim. Thus with judgements of the beautiful there is always room for disagreement – for differences of view concerning what should count as a good, excellent, or paradigm example of the kind – even if those disagreements must at last be referred to the *sensus communis* of enlightened public taste or informed participant debate.

This is why the beautiful figures, for Kant, as an image of what should ideally be attainable in the ethical and socio-political spheres. It is a realm of intersubjective exchange where there exist certain widely shared criteria – of competence, good taste, expert opinion, 'disinterested' judge-ment, etc. – but where nobody can or should claim the right to silence opposing views by coming up with some argument-to-end-all-arguments, or some determinate *concept* that would finally establish what counts as a beautiful landscape, painting, symphony, poem, or whatever. It is for this reason that Kant keeps judgements of the beautiful firmly on the side of our aesthetic responses – in the 'free play' that beauty evokes between the two faculties of imagination and understanding – rather than seeking to locate it in this or that objectively existent feature of the artwork or the natural world. And it is also why he makes such a point of insisting that determinate concepts have no place in our appreciation of nature or of art under their strictly aesthetic aspects. For the result of applying (or attempting to apply) such concepts would be to close off discussion at just that point where judgements of the beautiful extend by analogy to the conduct of debate in other spheres, among them that of 'pure practical reason', or ethical judgement in its highest, most purely 'disinterested' mode. Here also it is the case – according to Kant – that these judgements can only be distorted or compromised if they suffer some admixture of desire, self-interest, or other such 'pathological' motives. Thus aesthetic 'disinterest' is a highly precarious state, threatened on the one hand by encroachments from the realm of determinate (conceptual) knowledge, and on the other by various intrusive interests – whether privately self-seeking or partisan-political – that would leave it with no sphere in which to operate. And the same applies to those fields of intellectual enquiry – like philosophy itself, as Kant describes it in 'The Conflict of the Faculties' – which can rightfully claim an unrestricted freedom of thought and speech just so long as they observe the limits laid down for the exercise of judgement in its purely disinterested, specu-lative mode.

IV

So it is not hard to see why Derrida focuses on the Third *Critique* as providing some crucial points of leverage (the Archimedean 'mochlos' metaphor again) for deconstructing Kant's doctrine of the faculties. That is to say, the idea of aesthetic 'disinterest' is one that bears a considerable burden of argument, and whose further implications extend to every aspect of Kant's philosophical endeavour. If there are problems in maintaining that idea – as indeed there are, on Derrida's showing – then those problems can scarcely be kept from affecting the entire associated Kantian system of terms, distinctions, faculty-limits, proper spheres of competence. etc. Thus, for instance, it is vital that aesthetic experience should not be confused with the philosophic discourse *on* or *of* aesthetics, since the latter necessarily employs certain *concepts* (most often binary pairs: form/content, intrinsic/extrinsic, 'free' *versus* 'adherent' beauty, etc.) whose application involves determinate judgements, and can therefore by very definition play no role in aesthetic experience. For there would otherwise be nothing distinctive or especially valuable about aesthetic experience, that is to say, nothing that could set it apart from the various theories and ideas held about it by aestheticians, philosophers, literary critics, art-historians, sociologists of taste, and so forth. Moreover, this argument would apply even to a doctrinaire formalist such as

Kant, one who wants to draw a categorical line between qualities intrinsic to the work itself – to its unique or essential form – and everything else that might somehow affect our judgement of it, whether 'ornamental' features of no aesthetic value or extraneous factors of the kind mostly instanced by historians or sociologists. For it is just as much a problem with the formalist approach that it cannot help but use a conceptual discourse – a discourse of determinate judgements – when staking these claims for the autonomy of art and the strictly *sui generis* character of aesthetic experience.

In short, as Derrida might put it, the condition of possibility for Kantian aesthetics is also its condition of *im*possibility. It is the strictly paradoxical requirement that philosophy should speak of art (or of nature under its aesthetic-contemplative aspect) in terms that achieve a sufficient degree of conceptual rigour and precision, while at the same time acknowledging the impertinence of such terms where aesthetic experience itself is concerned. For if one lets go of this cardinal distinction then aesthetics becomes – as some would have it, sociologists like Bourdieu among them – a wholly pointless or a merely self-promoting endeavour, one that might just as well be abolished forthwith or absorbed into some other, more productive and disciplined field of enquiry.[37] (For Bourdieu that field is the sociology of taste as a sub-branch of cultural studies; for others it is history, anthropology, psychology, linguistics, critical theory or literary criticism.[38]) And it is not just the aestheticians who would find themselves suddenly out of a job if the distinctive nature of aesthetic experience were subject to any such conceptual definition, their own favoured sorts included. For there would then be all manner of perfectly adequate substitutes for that experience, as for instance by reading a detailed catalogue-description rather than looking at a picture, or following a Schenker-type thematic depth-analysis rather than listening to a symphony, or perusing the various critics and commentators on 'Hamlet' rather than reading the play or attending a performance. Then again: one might conclude that a thorough knowledge – a good conceptual grasp – of the issues raised in Kant's Third *Critique* and other such works was enough to offset a very limited acquaintance with art, music, or literature.

Aesthetic 'disinterest' is thus the key idea on which Kant bases his claims for the autonomy of art and for the qualitative difference, as he sees it, between aesthetic experience and the various concepts that philosophers may use in their efforts to define or categorize that experience. It is also a crucial resource, by analogy, for his thinking about issues in ethics, politics, and the structure of the modern (enlightened) university. This latter he conceives as a sphere wherein the various 'faculties' each have their own appointed domain, and where philosophy occupies a privileged place – most closely analogous to that of pure practical reason – such that its freedom to pronounce on 'theoretical' matters is guaranteed by its self-denying ordinance in matters of executive authority and power. Thus if Kant is unable to make good his claims for the disinterested character of aesthetic judgement, then that failure can be seen to have large and highly damaging implications for his entire doctrine of the faculties. And this is precisely Derrida's point: that despite all his efforts to delimit the sphere of the aesthetic – to set it off from purposive interests on the one hand, and from determinate concepts on the other – Kant rather demonstrates the *impossibility* (the absolute and principled impossibility) of sustaining any such argument.

It is not just a matter of Kant's coming up with a range of ill-chosen examples (draperies on statues, flying buttresses, load-supporting pillars, and the like) which are meant to uphold the formalist dichotomy of 'intrinsic' *versus* 'extrinsic' features, but which in fact render that distinction untenable. Nor is it simply on account of Kant's aversion to the sensuous qualities in art, whether colour and texture in painting, metaphor and imagery in poems, or just about everything in music that belongs to the 'intensive manifold' of sensations, as opposed to its formal or structural features. No doubt this bias can be explained up to a point by Kant's pietist mistrust of the senses, his limited range of aesthetic appreciation, and – in particular – his idea of music as the lowest of the arts on account of its strong sensuous-emotional appeal and its supposed lack of intellectual content. But of course this raises a further problem with regard to Kant's insistence that aesthetic judgements should *not* be confused with determinate judgements, or subject to the same standards that apply in the realm of conceptual understanding. For if Kant has any principled (as distinct from merely personal) reason for preferring literature and the visual arts over music it must be his belief that music is the artform least amenable to treatment in precisely those terms, i.e., as pointing beyond the merely sensuous to a higher realm of articulate meanings or significant forms. But in that case one might just as well argue (with Schopenhauer and Nietzsche) that music is the purest of the arts *precisely on account* of its resisting translation into any such conceptual terms. Moreover, this claim could be seen as following – ironically enough – from Kant's own emphasis on the nonconceptual character of aesthetic experience. Against which it might in turn be argued (as by Mark DeBellis in his recent study *Music and Conceptualization*) that there is no good reason, aesthetic prejudice aside, for holding our experience of music to exist in a realm quite apart from the various descriptive or analytic concepts that we may bring to bear *in the very act or process* of educated musical response. Thus:

a trained listener, when asked to describe what she hears, is apt to respond – spontaneously, and without much ratiocination – in a way that employs theoretical terminology: she hears a piece under a certain music-theoretic description and will give that description in describing what she hears. There is simply no principled basis on which to say that trained listeners do not hear chords as tonics and dominants in as full-blooded a sense as that in which ordinary perceivers see tables and chairs.[39]

This passage indicates a central problem with Kantian aesthetics, namely its self-contradictory commitment to a theory of judgement that finds no place for conceptual understanding in our experience of art, but which none the less deploys a whole battery of elaborated concepts in order to propound that same theory.

The point can be made more simply by asking: why should it not be the case that our knowledge of a work such as the Third *Critique* may decisively affect our experience of artworks or of nature as an object of aesthetic contemplation? Then again: by what right (the classic Kantian *quid juris* question) does Kant lay it down that aesthetic experience *must* be held distinct from any concepts gained through the reading of philosophical, theoretical, or other such (presumptively) non-aesthetic works? For it can scarcely be denied that the concepts we bring to such experience – concepts like that of aesthetic 'disinterest' or of the beautiful as theorized by Kant, among others – *can and do* very often have a marked influence on our aesthetic responses and judgements. Thus, for instance, a knowledge of Kant's views might very well affect the way that we respond to such works as Picasso's 'Guernica', or Orwell's *Animal Farm*, or Beethoven's *Eroica* Symphony, or Britten's *War Requiem*. These are all of them works that, in Keats's phrase, have a 'palpable design' on the viewer/reader/listener, a didactic intent – to convince or persuade – which cannot easily be reconciled with the Kantian doctrine of aesthetic disinterest.

Now we might wish to say that Kant was wrong and that there is just no reason why we should appreciate these works any the less for their carrying a strong political or moral charge. Or again, we might take a more conciliatory line by adopting what amounts to a double-aspect theory, one that allows us to switch at will between a 'properly' aesthetic attitude and a mode of response more attuned to their suasive purpose. On this view we could have some sympathy with Orwell in his complaint that the reviewers of *Animal Farm* all latched onto its uses as a piece of Cold War propaganda and ignored its literary merits as a piece of carefully crafted allegorical fiction. At any rate there would then be no problem with the Picasso and Beethoven examples since our aesthetic valuation would in no way depend on our judgement of events during the Spanish Civil War, or our present-day (affirmative or negative) response to Beethoven's outlook of Promethean humanism. Still there is a sense in which all these responses *cannot but* be affected by our knowledge of the issues raised in Kant's Third *Critique*. And to that extent it must be the case – *contra* Kant – that conceptual

understanding is intimately involved with aesthetic experience and judgement. For clearly such notions as 'disinterest' or formal 'autonomy' are
notions that gain whatever pertinence they have from our ability to grasp
and apply them in accord with certain well-defined conceptual criteria.

It is at just this point – the point of conflict between Kant's aesthetic
principles and their governing logic – that Derrida locates all the problems
and aporias that emerge from a deconstructive reading of the Third *Critique*.
They are not the kinds of problem that could be cleared up by adopting one
or other of the above 'solutions', i.e., by simply endorsing Kant's aesthetic
philosophy, by rejecting that philosophy outright, or by adopting what I
have called the double-aspect theory and switching criteria as and when
required. Least of all can they be made to disappear – shown up as merely
illusory – if one espouses a 'strong'-sociological outlook according to which
they are just the sorts of problem that result from the invention of pseudo-
disciplines such as philosophical aesthetics. Now this is an important point
to grasp about Derrida's work in general and, more specifically, his writings
on Kant. To be sure, those texts go a long way toward deconstructing Kant's
doctrine of the faculties and showing the entire system to depend upon a
series of value-laden terms and distinctions whose status is constantly called
into question, or whose logic turns out to be everywhere subject to a
countervailing logic of 'parergonality', a logic of logical anomalies. And it is
precisely the borderline cases that cause all this trouble, whether artworks (or
details of works) that cannot be firmly located either 'inside' or 'outside' the
aesthetic frame of reference, or judgements that are not conceptually
determinate yet require an appeal to determinate concepts, or, again, that
mode (concept?) of aesthetic experience for which Kant offers the
oxymoronic phrase 'purposeless purposiveness'. All these are examples of
the 'logic of parergonality' that Derrida finds perpetually at work in Kant's
Third *Critique*, and whose effects are most pronounced whenever it is a
question of placing a frame – a conceptual frame – around that which
cannot (or should not) be subject to conceptual definition. But he is also, as
I have said, very far from adopting a pragmatic line of least resistance that
would claim to solve these problems at a stroke by treating them as mere
relics of that old philosophical 'discourse' of modernity which specialized in
producing such pseudo-dilemmas. For Derrida is no less insistent than Kant
that these are real issues, that they have a wider bearing beyond the 'strictly'
aesthetic domain, and that they need thinking through with the utmost care
and precision.

V

This claim is borne out, albeit in negative fashion, by the fact that a strong
sociologist like Bourdieu devotes a long appendix (in his book *Distinction: a*

critique of taste) to attacking Derrida's essay on Kant.[40] Bourdieu's chief complaint – academic turf-wars apart – is that Derrida perpetuates the elitist discourse of aesthetic 'values' and 'taste' by adopting a philosophical, rather than a cultural or social-diagnostic approach. He is right, it seems to me, about Derrida's refusal to yield up aesthetics (and the rest of philosophy along with it) to a generalized sociology of culture – or a theory of 'cultural capital' – which levels not only dubious distinctions of 'taste' but also genuine differences of scope, interest, method, and competence between the disciplines. However he is wrong in attributing this to an 'elitist' desire, on Derrida's part, to uphold the various structures of privilege and power that are partly maintained through the unequal distribution of cultural and intellectual capital. For it is here that Derrida – like Adorno before him, in an essay on Karl Mannheim – holds out against the strong-sociological drive to reduce every discipline of thought (philosophy included) to a reflex product of vested interests or hegemonic socio-cultural values.[41]

For Adorno, this entails a practice of 'negative-dialectical' thought which rejects any version of Hegel's appeal to a false (because premature) reconciliation between subject and object, mind and nature, concept and intuition, or things as they are and things as they might be in some different – radically transformed – order of social existence.[42] Hence his resolute critique of 'identity-thinking', the idea – prevalent among episte-mologists from Kant to Husserl – that particulars (as given through sensuous intuition) can be somehow 'brought under' adequate concepts without resistance or remainder.[43] On the contrary: it is only through a vigilant awareness of the non-identity, the gap that opens up (so to speak) between these orders of thought and cognition, that dialectics can find some purchase for resisting the pressures of commodified mass-culture and ideological control. Now Adorno has sometimes been claimed as a 'postmodern' thinker, and up to a point the description is apt enough.[44] After all, it is a constant theme in his writing – and one that sets him apart from second-generation Frankfurt theorists like Habermas – that the Enlightenment project has so far miscarried from its original aims and values that it is now complicit with the drive toward total domination of the lifeworld through the forces of instrumental reason. However this is a grossly one-sided char-acterization, as will soon become apparent to anyone who reads Adorno's texts with adequate care and attention. For his thinking could scarcely be more opposed to that strain of facile postmodernist talk which blithely announces an end to Enlightenment and its associated values of truth, reason, and critique. To be sure, Adorno questions those values and subjects them to relentless (even ruthless) criticism in the negative-dialectical mode. To some present-day defenders of Enlightenment thought – Habermas among them – this approach has seemed little short of outright rejection and betrayal.[45] Yet Adorno pursues it always with a will to redeem the 'unfinished project' of modernity by testing its limits, locating its blind-spots of prejudice, and insisting that the project live up to its own highest standards of critical thought.

There is a similar misconstrual of Derrida's work which takes deconstruction to be merely a 'destructive' or a nihilist project, one that sets out to dismantle the entire structure of (so-called) 'Western metaphysics' while having no useful alternative project to set in its place. This idea goes along with the notion of Derrida as a counter-Enlightenment or postmodern thinker whose aim is to deconstruct (for which read: subvert from within and destroy altogether) such presumptively obsolete values as truth, reason, and critique. However, as I have said, it is a false and prejudicial reading which ignores the many passages – especially in his essays on Kant – where Derrida affirms the need to keep faith with Enlightenment thought precisely by taking nothing on trust, its own more doctrinaire values and assumptions included.[46] Thus philosophy plays and should continue to play a decisive critical role. It is possible – indeed, it is a prime moral and intellectual imperative – not to accept the necessity of compromise, at least the sorts of compromise typically endorsed by postmodernist thinkers who equate truth with what is currently good (or 'performatively' valid) in the way of consensus belief.[47] Philosophy, Kant says, occupies the left bench in the parliament of the faculties, the left bench having been – since the French Revolution when this custom was established – the locus of dissent, the seat of opposition, the place from which criticism comes. Of course this is not (or not simply) a party-political distinction as between right and left, conservative and socialist, 'republican' and 'democrat', or whatever. Rather it has to do with Kant's idea of philosophy as a voice that is raised on behalf of no particular group interest or political faction, a voice of critical reason unbeholden to established structures of authority and power. Thus, according to Kant, 'in as free a system of government as must exist where truth is at issue, there must also be an opposition party (the left side), and that bench belongs to the philosophy faculty, for without its rigorous examinations and objections, the government would not be adequately informed'.[48] If we think of the Kantian system as Deleuze describes it, that is, as a system of constantly 'rotating chairmanship', then this role would be occupied in turn by those faculties with least direct involvement in the exercise of power, faculties such as pure practical reason and disinterested judgement of the kind aptly figured in aesthetic estimations of the beautiful.[49]

As we have seen, Derrida doubts very strongly whether any such line can be drawn between intra- and extra-philosophical interests, or between (on the one hand) disciplines concerned purely with the pursuit of truth 'for its own sake', and (on the other) disciplines that respond to 'outside' pressures and incentives. However he is equally far from thinking that we should let go of that Kantian distinction and embrace the current postmodernist wisdom according to which such talk is just another kind of 'performative' rhetoric, one that adopts a high moral tone (a fine-sounding language of principle, 'disinterest', etc.) as a cover for its own self-interested motives. For the left bench is the side from which criticism comes and should at least strive for some degree of autonomy, of non-compliance with the dictates of instrumental reason or executive power. After all, as Derrida describes it (paraphrasing Kant), '[t]he concept of *universitas* is more than the philo-sophical concept of a research and teaching institution; it is the concept of philosophy itself, and is Reason, or rather the principle of reason *as an institution*'.[50] So Derrida is sceptical up to a point with regard to Kant's claims for the role of philosophy as an arbiter of truth and justice in the so-called 'parliament' of the faculties. But he doesn't lean over from scepticism into downright cynicism, as may be said of postmodernists like Lyotard for whom this idea of critical disinterest (or reflective detachment from power-seeking drives and interests) must be seen as just a relic of old-style 'Enlightenment' thought.[51] On this view everything has to do with the interests of power, with the extent to which so-called 'critical' intellectuals (philosophers, sociologists, workers in the human and the natural sciences) plug themselves into various power networks, various ways of extending or enhancing their 'performative' capacity to make things happen, to convince other people, to win the most lucrative research-grants, and so forth. As I have said, Derrida accepts all this as a simply undeniable real-world aspect of the situation in which many intellectuals – philosophers included – find themselves now. Moreover it is the same sort of situation that they have always had to cope with, as can be seen very clearly from Kant's compromise 'solution' in 'The Conflict of the Faculties'. Nevertheless – and this is where he differs most sharply with Lyotard – one can take due account of these obstacles to the exercise of 'free', 'disinterested' critical thought while still seeking *so far as possible* to keep a space open for it.

Of course that space cannot be confined to the Philosophy Department of the modern (post-Kantian) university, or the Humanities Faculty, or those branches of the 'pure' sciences (e.g., mathematics or theoretical physics) that are supposedly least subject to pressures from the commercial, the military-industrial, or the political-executive centres of power. On the one hand this ignores the extent to which even those disciplines have to compete for funding, to prove their utility, establish their cost-effectiveness, their 'relevance' in terms of deferred benefits or the current job-market indicators. On the other it implies a serene indifference, on the part of comfortably tenured 'critical' intellectuals, toward whatever goes on in the world outside the philosophy seminar-room or the institute for advanced scientific research. Whence the various boundary-disputes – the conflicts of interest, internal and external – that arise as soon as one attempts to demarcate the various zones of disciplinary competence. These conflicts arise from what

Derrida calls the 'paradoxical structure' of any limits imposed *either* on the exercise of speculative, truth-seeking thought *or* on the wielders of executive power – those outside the university – in so far as they seek to curtail academic freedom by dictating programmes of 'pure' as well as 'applied' research. After all, as Kant is obliged to concede, that freedom depends upon a certain charter (written or unwritten) whose guarantor is precisely the state or some other state-sanctioned authority. Thus the modern university may indeed be founded on a Kantian idea of Reason, more precisely an idea of Pure Practical Reason, that is, the *de jure* postulate of freedom in matters of moral and intellectual conscience. However this status is ultimately granted 'by virtue of a *de facto* political authority', one that is 'supposed in principle to let itself be guided by reason', but whose power to accord (or withold) that privilege rests with the executive branch.

I shall now quote at some length so as to bring out the kind of supplementary (or 'parergonal') logic that Derrida perceives constantly at work in Kant's doctrine of the faculties.

> Though destined to separate power from knowledge and action from truth, they distinguish sets that are each time somehow in excess of themselves, covering each time the whole of which they should figure only a part or a sub-set. And so the whole forms an *invaginated pocket* on the inside of every part or sub-set. We recognised the difficulty of distinguishing the inside from the outside of the university, and then, on the inside, of distinguishing between the two classes of faculties. We are not done, however, with this intestine division and its folding partition on the inside of each space. The philosophy faculty is further divided into two 'departments': the *historical* sciences (history, geography, linguistics, humanities, etc.) and the *purely rational* sciences (pure mathematics, pure philosophy, the metaphysics of nature and morals); pure philosophy, on the inside of the so-called philosophy faculty, is therefore still just a part of the whole whose idea it nonetheless safeguards. But insofar as it is *historical*, it also covers the domain of the higher faculties. ... Due to this double overflowing, conflicts are inevitable. And they must also reappear inside each faculty, since the faculty of philosophy is itself divisible.[52]

Of course Kant is speaking of 'philosophy' in a much wider (more 'interdisciplinary') sense than one expects to find in present-day usage. However it is precisely Derrida's point that any attempt to restrict or delimit the scope of what counts as philosophical enquiry will always run up against just those problems that Kant confronts in his effort to confine such enquiry 'within the limits of reason alone'. That is to say, there is a properly philosophical aspect of any academic discipline (whether in the natural sciences, in mathematics, anthropology, jurisprudence, history, sociology, linguistics, or literary theory) where issues are raised concerning the truth or validity of certain governing precepts. 'Philosophy' in this sense is the name for that discipline of thought which has no proper disciplinary home but which represents the interest of reason – of pure practical reason – as a conscientious arbiter of justice and truth. However that interest is always tied up with various motivating pressures that come from outside the university precinct – or the sphere of pure practical reason – and which need to be taken into account by any critical discourse on the faculties, their scope and limits. Thus 'there may be no possible inside to the university, and no internal coherence to its concept'.[53] And again, in more practical terms: 'there can be very serious competition and border-conflicts between non-university centres of research and university faculties claiming at once to be doing research and transmitting knowledge, to be producing and reproducing knowledge'.[54]

So it is impossible nowadays – more so perhaps than at Kant's time – for the 'pure' disciplines (philosophy among them) to maintain their preferred self-image as a haven of disinterested truth-seeking thought. To uphold this ideal in its classical (Kantian) form would be the kind of illusion that Kant himself pinpoints in the First *Critique* when he imagines the metaphoric dove of pure reason thinking to soar high and free by escaping altogether from the earth's constrictive atmosphere. 'Is it not nowadays', Derrida rhetorically asks, 'for reasons involving the structure of knowledge, especially impossible to distinguish rigorously between scholars and technicians of science, just as it is to trace, between knowledge and power, the limit within whose shelter Kant sought to preserve the university structure?'[55] However there is another side to this question, one that turns it around so as to ask *by what right* philosophy should be prevented from raising issues of truth and justice with regard to those applied disciplines (or those extra-mural interests) that threaten to encroach on its own domain. After all,

> [t]he university is there *to tell the truth*, to judge and to criticize in the most rigorous sense of the term, namely to discern and decide between the true and the false; and when it is also entitled to decide between the just and the unjust, the moral and the immoral, this is insofar as reason and freedom of judgement are implicated there as well.[56]

In short, it is idle to maintain the idea of Philosophy as a locus of free thought *within* the University system unless it is also assumed to reach out *beyond* the university, to engage with just those conflicts of interest that exist in the wider socio-political or public-administrative sphere. For otherwise there could be no point of contact, no critical purchase (so to speak) between the exercise of reason in its 'pure speculative' or ideally 'disinterested' mode and the kinds of issue that should properly concern intellectuals in their 'public' role as thinkers committed to furthering the interests of truth and justice.

Hence (to repeat) Derrida's idea of philosophy as a *mochlos*, a lever, a critical discourse that occupies the left bench in the parliament of faculties and which uses that position to exert a force outside and beyond its apparently very limited sphere. More straightforwardly: we have to be aware of the extent to which every academic discipline is compromised by 'outside' interests, by its sources of funding (direct or indirect), its relationship with other disciplines, or its possible long-term application in fields far beyond its original research-domain. After all, Kant himself 'is in the process of justifying, in terms of reason, what was a de facto organization determined by the government of his day, as if by accident its king [i.e., Friedrich Wilhelm, who had expressed grave displeasure at certain of Kant's writings] were a philosopher'.[57] This is all the more the case nowadays when there exist so many complex relays of power or forms of indirect leverage, whether those exerted from outside the university or between its various component disciplines. Yet we still need to preserve a margin of freedom, a space where thinking can make good its claim to examine, to criticize, and (if need be) to raise a dissenting voice without the threat of censorship by those who wield executive power.

This is why Derrida goes such a long and complicated way around in deconstructing Kant's doctrine or system of the faculties. His purpose is *not* to level the difference between (say) philosophy and literary criticism, or jurisprudence and speech-act theory, or sociology and narrative poetics, or again – pushing this argument all the way – between the human and social sciences on the one hand and the natural sciences on the other.[58] Each of these claims has its present-day advocates, often citing Derrida's texts by way of notional support. Richard Rorty is perhaps the best-known exponent of the view that deconstruction is most usefully employed in debunking our idea of the various disciplines as somehow corresponding to real differences of method, approach, subject-matter, or knowledge-constitutive interest. Thus philosophy becomes, for Rorty, just another 'kind of writing' whose value is measured – as with other kinds of writing like poetry, fiction, literary criticism, ethnography, molecular biology, or nuclear physics – by its capacity to yield striking new metaphors or bold (strong-revisionist) accounts of its own history to date.[59]

However, this is not at all Derrida's intention in drawing out the complex structures of relationship and interdependence that cut across Kant's already quite complicated groundplan of the various faculty divisions. No doubt we need to recognise that the plan is incomplete or under-detailed; that there exist all manner of labyrinthine passages or short-cut routes between and within the different buildings. And the same applies to Kant's doctrine of the 'faculties' in its other, more familiar guise: to the system of self-regulating checks and limits whose function it is to prevent any conflict of interests between cognitive understanding and practical reason, or judgement in its twofold (determinate and reflective) modes. Here again there is no ques-tion – for Derrida any more than for Lyotard – of upholding this doctrine in anything like its original Kantian aprioristic form. But there is also no question, for Derrida, of taking the postmodern line of least resistance and hence denying the very possibility that reason might exert some critical leverage – some effective counter-pressure – against the weight of consensus-thinking, of conformist ideology, or of vested interests within or outside the university. For if the various divisions, internal and external, are a deal more complex than Kant allows, still it is the case – for Derrida as for Kant – that the modern 'enlightened' university (like the modern 'enlightened' polity) stands or falls on its willingness to tolerate dissenting or critical views.

CHAPTER 4

Deconstruction, Postmodernism and Philosophy of Science

I

Very often deconstruction is viewed as just an offshoot – or a somewhat more 'philosophical' sub-branch – of that wider cultural phenomenon that goes under the name of postmodernism. In what follows I propose to challenge this idea by contrasting some of Derrida's arguments with those typically advanced by postmodernist thinkers. It seems to me that one important difference between them, one reason why (to put it very simply) Derrida's work is 'modern' rather than 'postmodern', is that deconstruction is closely related to a certain tradition of thought about issues in epistemology and philosophy of science.[1] This is not – I should stress – just a preferential gloss or just one reading among the multitude that are licenced by Derrida's notion of interpretive 'freeplay', often (and wrongly) construed as *carte blanche* for inventing all manner of perverse and ingenious games with texts. Thus Derrida is routinely taken to assert that texts can be read however one likes since there is nothing – no appeal to context or authorial intent – that could possibly decide the issue or limit the range of permissible options in any given case. On the contrary, he has often been at pains to repudiate this 'anything goes' approach and to lay down stringent criteria for what properly counts as a deconstructive reading.[2] Moreover, he has provided numerous examples – for instance in his writings on Plato, Aristotle, Kant, Hegel, Husserl, J.L. Austin and others – of the way that deconstruction both respects and complicates those received (conservative but none the less essential) standards of interpretive truth.[3] I shall here look at one particular instance – his essay 'White Mythology: metaphor in the text of philosophy' (henceforth referred to as 'WM') – since it brings out very clearly the kinds of misreading to which Derrida's texts have been subject by commentators (literary theorists chiefly) who take for granted his indifference to any such standards.[4]

If you read 'White Mythology' with adequate care, and without these fixed preconceptions, then you will see that Derrida is simply not saying many of the things that postmodernists want him to say. Indeed, very often, he is saying exactly the opposite. One familiar postmodernist line on Derrida – adopted, for instance, by Richard Rorty in a well-known essay – is that there is no need to bother with all that difficult (mostly pre-1980) 'philosophical' stuff since his later writings have shown us the best way beyond such narrowly technical concerns.[5] Rather than work through the complicated arguments of texts like *Speech and Phenomena* or *Of Grammatology*, we had much better skip straight forward to those gamy productions, such as *The Post Card: from Socrates to Freud and beyond*, where Derrida throws off any lingering attachment to that old 'logocentric' discourse of reason and truth.[6] This approach tends to work out as a series of vaguely deconstructionist slogans or *idées recues*: 'truth is a fiction', 'reason is a kind of rhetorical imposture', 'all concepts are forgotten or sublimated metaphors', 'philosophy is just another "kind of writing"'. This is Rorty's postmodernist summation of Derrida and it is one that has understandably gone down well in departments of English or Comparative Literature. (It also appears to have convinced many philosophers that reading Derrida is not worth their time and effort.[7]) Traditionally, philosophy thought of itself as a specialised, exacting, intellectually rigorous discipline for evaluating truth-claims or addressing issues that lay beyond the remit of other, more regional sciences. Above all, it claimed to be a constructive or problem-solving endeavour that brought its special expertise to bear on a range of well-defined topics and problems. Rorty rejects this received self-image as one that has held philosophers captive, that has given them a sense of having something uniquely important to say at the cost of rendering their work simply dull or unintelligible to the vast majority of readers. It goes along with certain time-worn metaphors that philosophers have mistaken for concepts, like that of the mind as a 'mirror of nature', or of epistemology as first philosophy since only a theory of knowledge can provide adequate 'foundations' or indubitable 'grounds' for our diverse projects of enquiry.[8]

However this picture is now (at last) losing its hold, having more or less defined what philosophy was – or took itself to be – from Plato to Descartes, Kant, Husserl, and the mainstream 'analytic' tradition. On the contrary, Rorty urges: philosophy at its best tells us new stories, invents new metaphors, devizes new ways of enriching or enlivening the 'cultural conversation of mankind'. Of course it includes the kinds of story or metaphor that mainstream philosophers are happy with, stories like that of philosophical 'progress' as a gradual achievement of conceptual clarity over well-defined problem areas, or kindred metaphors like that of reason as a source of 'clear and distinct' ideas. However these tend to be boring, predictable, uninventive stories and metaphors which just recycle the same old themes with some occasional minor variation. Thus the great virtue of Derrida's texts, for Rorty, is that they show how philosophy can learn to live down to its status as just another 'kind of writing' along with all the others, while also living up to this new-found challenge of inventing fresh and original styles of self-description. But we shall miss the whole point of

Derrida's writing – so Rorty believes – if we take him too much at face value when he slips back into the old style of offering distinctively 'philosophical' arguments in the Kantian transcendental or 'conditions of possibility' mode. Such arguments may seem to play a large role in some of his early works, as when Derrida reads (say) Rousseau or Husserl on the relation between nature and culture, speech and writing, or the phenomenology of time-consciousness.[9] Nevertheless we should do much better to assume that these are just apprentice exercises which show Derrida still in the grip of an old philosophical fixation, a habit of thought that he will soon throw off once he sees (like Rorty) that there is just no mileage in pursuing those long superannuated questions. At which point we shall have to acknowledge – again like Rorty – that the best of Derrida is not to be found in his carefully-argued early 'analytical' texts but in texts that adopt a playful, irreverent, and 'literary' stance toward the history of earnest philosophical debate from Plato to Heidegger *et au-delà*.

Now I think it can be shown that Rorty is quite simply *wrong* about Derrida. 'White Mythology' is especially instructive in this regard since it offers a lengthy, detailed, and (above all) a meticulously argued account of the role of metaphor in various texts of the Western philosophical tradition from Aristotle to Gaston Bachelard. Up to a point, I should acknowledge, Derrida does say some of the things that Rorty wants him to say. That point is quickly reached – but thereafter subject to intensive critical analysis – in an essay which contains some of the most penetrating commentary ever written on the topic of metaphor *vis-à-vis* the discourse of logic, concept, and reason. Thus Derrida remarks (following Nietzsche and Anatole France) that philosophy is full of metaphors, figural expressions that were once – presumably – recognised as such but were then literalized, transformed into concepts, and hence became blanched or erased into a kind of subliminal 'white mythology'.[10] The very word 'concept' is a metaphor from the Latin for 'taking-together', that is to say, for comprehending various ideas (perceptions, impressions, or images) through a relatively abstract process of thought. 'Comprehension' is another such metaphor deriving from a kindred etymological root, namely, the idea of intellectual *grasp* as achieved by the mind's active synthesising power. 'Metaphor' is itself a metaphor; in present-day Greek it signifies a mode of public transport, a tram or a bus, something that carries you from one place to another, just as metaphors provide the vehicle whereby meanings are transported from one context to another. So the notion of metaphor is in some sense *literally* metaphoric. But 'literal' is also a metaphor since it derives from the Latin word for *letter*, i.e., the notion that by looking intently at the letters on a page you can figure out their literal (non-metaphoric or plain-prose) meaning. And the same applies to more abstract terms such as 'theory'. *Theory* derives from the Greek *thea* (= 'spectacle') and its verb-form *theorein* (= 'watch', 'spectate', 'witness'). So *theatre* is a place where you watch events unfolding out there, in front of you, on the stage, whereas *theory* involves a kind of inward theatre where ideas, concepts, or representations pass before the mind in a state of contemplative review.

Derrida offers a whole series of further such examples, metaphors whose original ('literal') meaning derived from the sensory or phenomenal realm, but which were then taken over – so this argument runs – by the abstract discourse of philosophy and thereafter subject to a process of attrition whereby that original meaning was progressively erased. For the most part these metaphors have do to with seeing, with the visual or ocular domain ('insight', 'theory', the Cartesian appeal to 'clear and distinct ideas'), or with tactile analogies such as 'grasp', 'comprehension', or 'concept'. In each case this passage from the sensuous to the abstract – or from image to idea – is conceived in terms of a parallel decline from the vividness of poetic language to the abstract rigours of conceptual or philosophic thought. Hence Derrida's title 'White Mythology' (*La mythologie blanche*), taken from a Nietzsche-inspired dialogue by Anatole France which arraigns the meta-physicians as a 'sorry lot of poets' whose language no longer possesses that power to express or evoke the vivid particulars of sensuous experience.[11] Such was of course Nietzsche's great complaint against philosophy from Socrates down: that it had lost the courage of its own root metaphors (the sorts of 'poetic' expression to be found in the pre-Socratics: 'everything is fire', 'everything is water', 'constant change is the principle of all things') and turned toward a language of lifeless abstraction and arid conceptual precision. For Heidegger, likewise, Socrates figured as the first philosopher of antiquity whose thinking set this unfortunate process in train and who stands behind the whole subsequent course of 'Western metaphysics' as a discourse given over to abstract conceptions of truth, justice, and beauty.[12] In short, these thinkers all take the view that the passage from metaphor to concept – or from poetry to philosophy – is a process of epochal decline, one that has worked constantly to obscure that original sense of metaphoric richness and vitality.

Now one might very well be forgiven for reading the first section of Derrida's 'White Mythology' as yet another meditation on this same sorry theme in the manner of Nietzsche, Heidegger, and Anatole France. (Indeed, this portion of the essay is largely devoted to a detailed critical commentary on France's dialogue 'The Garden of Epicurus'.) Certainly Derrida stresses the point that philosophy can never fully account for its own metaphorical resources – never survey them from outside and above – since there will always be metaphors that somehow escape its conceptual net, figures of thought so deeply ingrained in the discourse of philosophic reason that they lack any alternative means of expression. Strictly speaking, these figures are examples of the trope *catachresis*, terms for which there exists no literal counterpart, and which cannot be defined or paraphrased without falling back on some other other, equally metaphorical substitute term. Thus philosophy will always at some point encounter a limit to its powers of conceptualization, its attempt to devize a general tropology – a theory of metaphor or philosophy of rhetoric – that would properly control and delimit the field of its own metaphorical production. In Derrida's words, 'it gets "carried away" each time that one of its products – here, the concept of metaphor – attempts in vain to include under its own law the totality of the field to which the product belongs' (WM, p. 219). That is to say, there will always be at least one metaphor that necessarily escapes definition since it plays a strictly indispensable role in the process of conceptual elucidation and critique. (Consider the terms 'metaphor' and 'definition', along with the phrase 'conceptual elucidation', as deployed in the foregoing sentence.)

So one can see why some commentators – Rorty among them – have read 'White Mythology' as a wholesale assault on the concept/metaphor dichotomy, along with other cognate distinctions such as those between reason and rhetoric, constative and performative language, or – by extension – philosophy and literature. From here, very often, they have proceeded to draw the lesson that philosophy is indeed just a 'kind of writing', a kind that has up to now been distinguished mainly by its failure to acknowledge that fact, but which might yet shed its grandiose delusions and come to play a useful if scaled-down role in the ongoing cultural conversation. To be sure, this account is plausible enough if one gets no further than the early part of 'White Mythology', the part where Derrida is more or less paraphrasing Anatole France and a certain, currently fashionable reading of Nietzsche. But then, in the remainder of the essay, Derrida mounts a second line of argument which effectively turns this thesis on its head. That is to say, he points out that if we are going to think about metaphor at all, or think about it to any purpose, then we shall have to acknowledge that all our concepts, theories, or working definitions of metaphor have been based on certain *philosophical* distinctions, notably that between concept and metaphor. Moreover, they have been refined and developed throughout the centuries by thinkers – from Aristotle down – who have thought about metaphor always in the context of other philosophical concerns.

Thus, in Aristotle's case, the theory of metaphor is closely tied up with his theory of *mimesis* (or artistic representation), and this in turn with his thinking about language, logic, grammar, rhetoric, hermeneutics, natural science in its various branches, epistemology, ontology, and ultimately metaphysics as that branch of knowledge that contains and subsumes all the others.[13] In other words, the discourse on metaphor is always a discourse that takes its bearings from philosophy, even when attacking philosophy's pretension to master the field of metaphor. So we cannot simply say that 'all concepts are metaphors', or that philosophy is just another 'kind of (metaphoric) writing', because this circles back to the prior question: what is metaphor? In order to address that question we shall need to take account of those various theories of metaphor that have been advanced either by philosophers (from Aristotle to Max Black and Donald Davidson) or by literary critics (from Aristotle, again, to theorists such Coleridge, I.A. Richards, and William Empson) whose work has drawn upon a whole range of philosophically-elaborated concepts and distinctions.[14] Thus the question arises: 'can these defining tropes that are prior to all philosophical rhetoric and that produce philosophemes still be called metaphors?' (WM, p. 255). Any answer will clearly involve something more than a simple re-statement of the Nietzschean (or quasi-Nietzschean) case for inverting the traditional order of priority between concept and metaphor. That is, it will also at some point need to acknowledge that 'the criteria for a classification of philosophical metaphors are borrowed from a derivative philosophical discourse' (p. 224). And although that discourse is itself 'derivative' (i.e., dependent on certain metaphors, those of 'dependence' and 'derivation' among them) it still provides the only possible means of examining metaphor's ubiquitous role in the texts of philosophy. For, as Derrida writes, 'the general taxonomy of metaphors – so-called philosophical metaphors in particular – would presuppose the solution of important problems, and primarily of problems which constitute the entirety of philosophy in its history' (p. 228).

No doubt those problems (ontological, epistemological, and metaphysical) are as far from having been solved as philosophy is from attaining a full-scale systematic grasp of the various metaphors that make up its own discourse. But this is precisely Derrida's point: that we cannot advance a single proposition on the topic of metaphor (least of all on its role in the texts of philosophy) without redeploying a whole range of philosophical terms and arguments, among them the concept/metaphor distinction as developed by philosophers, rhetoricians, and literary theorists from Aristotle down. Thus '[t]he concept of metaphor, along with all the predicates that permit its ordered extension and comprehension, is a philosopheme' (WM, p. 228). A 'philosopheme', that is, in the sense that it belongs with those other 'fundamental and structuring' tropes which have hitherto defined the very nature and scope of genuine philosophical enquiry. These latter include 'the opposition of the proper and the nonproper, of essence and accident, of intuition and discourse, of thought and language, of the intelligible and the sensible' (p. 229). In order for those distinctions to be held in place it is necessary also that metaphor should occupy a strictly subordinate role *vis-à-vis* the discourse of philosophic reason and truth, a role wherein it can always be treated as a kind of 'detour' – a tropological swerve – on the path toward proper or literal signification. In which case one would have to suppose 'that the sense aimed at through these figures is an essence rigorously independent of that which transports it, which is an already philosophical thesis, one might even say philosophy's unique thesis, the thesis which constitutes the concept of metaphor' (p. 229). Undoubtedly Derrida – like Nietzsche before him – sees this as a strictly impossible ideal, one that ignores all the complicating factors which arise whenever philosophy attempts to bring metaphor under the rule of concept, system, or method. However, one should also take note of the numerous passages in 'White Mythology' where Derrida insists that any adequate (philosophically informed) treatment of metaphor will need to respect those traditional requirements – of rigour, clarity, conceptual precision, and logical consistency – which find no place in the postmodern-textualist view of philosophy as just another 'kind of writing'.

II

'White Mythology' is therefore a crucial text in Derrida's *oeuvre* because it shows that he is still very much engaged with distinctively philosophical interests and concerns. To be sure, he is far from endorsing the idea of philosophy as some kind of master-discourse, a discourse uniquely or exclusively aimed toward truth, and marked off from other disciplines by its ethos of pure, 'disinterested' enquiry. However, he is equally far from suggesting that we should henceforth simply abandon such 'logocentric' notions and treat philosophy as one more language-game or optional style of talk. Indeed, as can be seen in 'White Mythology', Derrida is still practising what is surely the most basic and distinctive form of philosophical argument, one that goes back to Plato's dialogues but which receives its most elaborate development in Kant. This is the transcendental mode of argument, the argument from 'conditions of possibility', that which consists in asking questions of the type: how is it possible for us to have knowledge and experience? what are the necessary conditions for such knowledge and experience? how is it that we can understand other people? how is it that we can treat other people as different from ourselves, but also as belonging to a communal realm of intersubjectively intelligible thoughts, meanings, and beliefs?[15] And again: what are the necessary conditions for any theory or concept of metaphor, given the extent to which all such theories or concepts are themselves caught up in a chain of metaphorical swerves, displacements, and substitutions which philosophy can never fully control or comprehend?

In this last case, as so often in Derrida's work, the argument takes a negative-transcendental (or 'condition-of-*im*possibility') form, where the upshot is to show that certain distinctions cannot be drawn in as clear-cut a fashion as philosophers have sometimes supposed.[16] Thus Derrida devotes a long section of 'White Mythology' to discussing the role of metaphor in science and the attempt of various thinkers – from Aristotle to Bachelard and Canguilhem – to specify the precise point at which scientific concepts emerge from a pre-scientific matrix of metaphor, analogy, image-based thinking and suchlike 'anthropomorphic' residues. Predictably enough, he raises certain doubts as to whether that point of transition can be fixed or defined, since any such attempt must assume the possibility of drawing a clear-cut distinction between metaphor and concept, and it is just this distinction which – according to Derrida – will always turn out to elude philosophy's utmost conceptual grasp. Nevertheless there is a sense (*pace* the cultural relativists and the 'strong' sociologists of knowledge) in which science does make progress, does advance – in Bachelard's phrase – from 'less efficient' to 'more efficient tropic-concepts', and does develop increasingly precise criteria for testing its various hypotheses, theories, observation-statements, etc.[17] Moreover, the result of this endeavour is most often to exclude (or at any rate to minimize) any errors brought about by the residual attachment to naive, 'commonsense', or anthropomorphic habits of thought. In short, it involves what Bachelard describes as an ongoing process of 'rectification and critique', a process whereby certain metaphors (and not others) prove themselves capable of further refinement to the point where they attain a sufficient degree of conceptual or descriptive-explanatory grasp. His examples include the tetrahedral structure of the carbon molecule, a 'tropic-concept' whose history nicely illustrates this progress from the stage of intuitive analogy or illustrative metaphor to the stage of well-supported scientific theory.

Georges Canguilhem, Bachelard's student, took a similar approach in his work on the history of biology and the life-sciences.[18] Here also he discovered some striking cases of advances that could have come about only through the 'rectification' of various images or metaphors which started life (so to speak) as borrowings from some other, roughly analogous domain, but which were then subject to the same process of conceptual elaboration and critique. Thus, to take one of Canguilhem's best-known examples: the idea of the cellular structure of organic tissue was at first a largely metaphorical notion, one whose intuitive appeal lay in its conjuring up certain anthropomorphic or 'affective' values.[19] These values had to do with cooperative labour, with the image of life at its most elementary level as involving forms of complex reciprocal reliance and support, like the patterns of activity manifested by bees in a beehive. So the cellular theory started out as a metaphor, a useful and suggestive metaphor, certainly, but as yet still tied to an image-based, affective, analogical phase of thought that must be seen as belonging to the pre-history of the modern ('mature') life-sciences. For it is a main point of Canguilhem's argument – like Bachelard's before him – that science *is* a progressive enterprise, that its progress involves the advancement through stages of 'rectification and critique', and moreover, that historians and philosophers of science have to take their bearings from the current best state of knowledge in any given field. For we should otherwise have no means of distinguishing between scientific truth and falsehood, between successful and unsuccessful theories past or present, or again (to adopt Imre Lakatos's terminology) between 'progressive' and 'degenerating' research-programmes.[20] Nor could we make any distinction, on other than pragmatic grounds, between thoroughly discredited or falsified theories (such as Priestley's phlogiston-based theory of combustion), and those – like Black's 'caloric' hypothesis – which can be seen to have contributed importantly to later scientific developments (in this case the theory of specific heat), even though they involved certain false suppositions. Thus Bachelard speaks of two kinds of history, *histoire sanctionée* and *histoire perimée*, the first concerned chiefly with episodes that have played some role in the growth of scientific knowledge to date, the second with episodes that must appear 'marginal' because they made no such contribution.

I hope it will be clear by now why I have taken this brief excursion *via* recent French philosophy of science in the critical-rationalist line of descent from Bachelard to Canguilhem. For it is a point worth making – and one seldom made by Derrida's commentators, friendly or hostile – that his work belongs very much in that line, whatever the problems he raises with regard to the concept/metaphor distinction or the idea of philosophy as a discipline equipped to survey, delimit, or control the field of its own metaphorical production. Most importantly, he shares Bachelard's concern with the *conditions of possibility* for scientific knowledge and also for the kinds of knowledge achieved through philosophical reflection on the history of science at its various stages of development. Also he insists – again like Bachelard – that these projects of enquiry, though closely related, cannot be simply run together in a way that would annul the distinction between *histoire sanctionée* and *histoire perimée*, or history of science (properly speaking) and the history of past scientific beliefs, or again, between critical philosophy of science and other (e.g. cultural-contextualist or 'strong'-sociological) approaches. For this results most often in the kind of wholesale relativist outlook that suspends all questions of truth and falsehood, or which treats all scientific theories – past and present – as products of their own cultural time and place, and hence as strictly on par with respect to their justificatory warrant.[21]

This fashionable doctrine has various sources, among them late Wittgenstein (on language-games and cultural 'forms of life'), Thomas Kuhn (on scientific truth as 'internal' to this or that historically emergent paradigm), and of course the Strong Programme in Sociology of Knowledge with its systematic drive to suspend or ignore such distinctions.[22] They also include Foucault's 'archaeologies' or 'genealogies' of knowlege, hermeneutic approaches deriving from Heidegger or Gadamer, Lyotard's idea of the 'postmodern condition' as it bears on questions of knowledge and truth, and Rorty's full-fledged 'textualist' view of science as proceeding from one revolution to the next through switches of metaphor that apparently occur for no better reason than periodic boredom with old styles of talk.[23] Now it is often assumed – sometimes on the strength of Rorty's account – that deconstruction in general, and Derrida's work in particular, is just another version of this postmodern 'turn' against the values of truth, reason, criticism, and conceptual analysis. However that reading ignores the many passages, in 'White Mythology' and other texts, where Derrida affirms the necessity – the 'absolute and principled' necessity – of thinking these issues through with the greatest possible rigour and precision. Thus he is far from rejecting Bachelard's idea of the 'epistemological break', the decisive stage of scientific advance where a vague, imprecise, or metaphorical notion gives way to an adequately theorized concept with the power to transform some given field of enquiry. To be sure, Derrida goes further than Bachelard – further (one might say) in a Nietzschean direction – toward showing how certain metaphorical residues will always inhabit the discourse of science or philosophy of science. But he also makes the case that any such argument, his own and Nietzsche's included, must itself depend on those same analytical resources that philosophy has developed and refined, among them the metaphor/concept distinction and the process of 'rectification and critique' described by Bachelard.

Thus there is no point in saying that 'all concepts are metaphors' unless it is also kept in mind that the *concept of metaphor* is one with a lengthy and complex philosophical history. That is to say, it is a concept whose structural genealogy requires both a detailed comparative treatment taking in the major theories of metaphor from Aristotle, *via* Nietzsche, to Bachelard, and a critical approach that examines those theories in terms of their implicit presuppositions, their 'unthought axiomatics', or their covert reliance on metaphor and analogy in their own conceptual formulations. To evade that task simply by proclaiming the ubiquity of metaphor – in the postmodernist or 'strong-textualist' vein – is to court the accusation that such thinking has indeed regressed to a stage of confused etymopoeic or pseudo-scientific reverie. It is just this charge that Habermas brings against Derrida: that he has set out deliberately to blur the 'genre-distinction' between concept and metaphor, reason and rhetoric, or philosophy and literature.[24] Deconstruction would then figure as just another variant of the current irrationalist drive to revoke the 'philosophic discourse of modernity' and thus revert to a pre-Enlightenment phase when that discourse had not yet separated out into its various, relatively specialized modes of cognitive, reflective, ethico-political, and aesthetic (or 'world-disclosive') thought.

However this is a false or, at any rate, a very partial and simplified reading of Derrida, as I have argued at length elsewhere.[25] For one thing it ignores those writings on Kant in which Derrida affirms the need to 'keep faith' with the unfinished project of modernity, even – or especially – where its values are threatened by just those countervailing pressures and tendencies that

Habermas calls to account.[26] For another, it fails to note the many passages (in 'White Mythology' and kindred texts) where Derrida provides rigorous arguments – arguments in the transcendental or condition-of-possibility mode – to the effect that understanding *cannot do without* the critical resources that philosophy has developed, not least through its refinement of the metaphor/concept distinction and its critique of naive, image-based, or anthropomorphic habits of thought. In Bachelard this took the form of a twofold project, one of whose branches was a 'psychoanalysis' or applied phenomenology of poetic image and metaphor, while the other had to with scientific knowledge conceived as entailing a definite break with that realm of intuitive, pre-scientific 'reverie'.[27] There was no question, for Bachelard, that science might simply replace poetry, or that philosophy of science might eventually command the whole field by showing how metaphor and sensuous imagery were the product of merely confused or indistinct ideas. Rather, these two projects should be seen as strictly complementary, as involving different methods and criteria, and hence – between them – as providing a detailed contrastive account of poetic-metaphorical and conceptual-analytic thinking. Besides, it was evident to Bachelard that science would always at some point have recourse to analogy and metaphor, especially during periods of imminent 'revolution' or drastic paradigm-change, and therefore that philosophy of science would always have a use for analyses drawn from the other (pre-scientific) domain. However, it was vital to keep that distinction in view since otherwise we should lose all sense of the difference – the knowledge-constitutive difference – between changes of metaphor that answer to changes of poetic or imaginative vision and those that portend a decisive shift in the order of scientific theory-construction.

For some – Rorty among them – we should do much better to let this distinction drop, along with all its other conversation-blocking analogues, such as (for instance) those between philosophy and literature, reason and rhetoric, or the natural and the human sciences. Indeed, one could envisage a comparative study of philosophers who have written on this topic – on the role of metaphor in science – in terms of their various positions on a scale whose end-points are the twin extremes of literalism and wholesale meta-phorico-poetic constructivism. This scale would then extend all the way from the belief that scientific theories should properly have no place for metaphor to the Rorty-style textualist persuasion that 'all concepts are metaphors', scientific concepts included, and hence that nothing can be gained by attempting to analyse or elucidate those metaphors. Derrida's point – like Bachelard's before him – is that both extremes are equally untenable, the one failing to explain how science could ever make progress through imaginative 'leaps' beyond the framework of preexistent concepts, while the other fails to provide any terms (any adequate scientific or philosophical terms) for distinguishing valid from invalid theories, or progressive from degenerating research-programmes. This is why Derrida conserves a crucial role for Bachelard's idea of the 'epistemological break', despite the impossibility – as he argues – of pressing *right through* with that idea as applied to the conceptualization of metaphor or the treatment of science (and philosophy of science) as a process of ongoing 'rectification and critique'.

III

We can best get a sense of what is distinctive about Derrida's project by comparing the mixed fortunes of Bachelard's work in other contexts of recent French philosophical and cultural debate. His phrase 'epistemological break' was taken over by various theorists, among them the 'structuralist Marxist' Louis Althusser, who deployed it with a view to distinguishing between Marx's early (Hegelian, humanist, or 'pre-Marxist') phase and his later (mature, theoretically developed, or properly 'scientific') writings.[28] It also served in a range of analogous contexts, as for instance to explain how Marxist 'science' – in this rigorously theorized sense – might relate to the realm of everyday lived experience, or to 'ideology' conceived as an imaginary projection of real (i.e., material) conditions of existence. This is not the place for a detailed account of the rise and fall of Althusserian structural Marxism. Sufficient to say that the project ran into various difficulties, some of them intrinsic and having to do with its wiredrawn conceptual structure, others the result of its reception-history at the hands of literary and cultural critics.[29] At any rate what followed was a marked reaction against such high theoreticist claims and a turn toward the notion of language, discourse, or signifying systems in general as marking the limits of knowledge and representation from one period to the next. This movement went under the broad title of post-structuralism and was much influenced by Foucault's highly sceptical (indeed ultra-nominalist) approach to issues of interpretative truth and method.

In his earlier works – such as *The Order of Things* and *The Archaeology of Knowledge* – Foucault's thinking displayed a clear indebtedness to Bachelard's philosophy of science, especially his theory of 'epistemological breaks'.[30] These latter were conceived by Foucault as marking the crucial point of transition between various historically shifting modes of discursive representation. However he deployed this theory in a manner quite alien to Bachelard's usage and with nothing like the same degree of conceptual precision. That is, it took on a massively expanded scope whereby whole epochs – the Renaissance, the 'classical age', the periods of historicism and emergent modernity – were conceived on the model of a 'discourse' (or ensemble of signifying terms and relations) that encompassed the entirety of knowledge at any given time. Needless to say, this holistic approach left little room for detailed study of the way that specific transformations came about within particular disciplines or fields of research. Nor could it make any allowance for those stages of advancement in scientific knowledge – attained through the 'rectification and critique' of anthropomorphic images or metaphors – which had been a main focus of Bachelard's and Canguilhem's work. Rather, it tended to treat such shifts in the currency of accredited belief as more like a series of large-scale seismic eruptions, affecting the entire landscape of knowledge and reaching right down to its deepest strata, but occurring for no reason other than the build-up of multiple conflicting pressures and strains. Thus if Foucault still finds a certain use for Bachelard's idea of the 'epistemological break' it is a use that effectively empties that idea of any critical or properly epistemological force.

What is thus ruled out is the idea that science – and philosophy of science – might seek to clarify the sources of its own capacity for advancing beyond the stage of naively metaphorical or image-based thought. For Foucault, such claims are merely the product of a certain phase in the history of knowledge or discursive representation, a phase that is epitomised by Kant's project of critical epistemology. This project rests on an illusory idea of 'man' as the subject-presumed-to-know, a strange 'empirical-transcendental doublet' – in Foucault's famous phrase – who is somehow both object and subject of his own cogitations. That is to say, he is a curiously bifurcated creature somehow capable *both* of achieving objective self-knowledge in the causal, anthropological, or empirically-determined mode, *and* of rising above that realm to vindicate the claims of autonomous selfhood and free-willed ethical or speculative thought. Foucault treats this as just a momentary 'fold' in the fabric of discursive representations, one that took rise at precisely the time when ruptures had emerged within the previous ('classical') order of discourse, an order wherein there was presumed to exist a one-for-one unproblematical match between signs, ideas, and objects-of-thought. Hence Kant's vaunted 'Copernican Revolution' in philosophy, with 'man' (the knowing, willing and judging subject) henceforth at the centre of all those disciplines or fields of enquiry that had hitherto found no need for such a strange and extravagant hypothesis. On the one hand this resulted in the rise of the human sciences, of anthropology, sociology, history, psychology and other such disciplines devoted to the study of human behaviour under its various empirical descriptions and classifications. On the other ('transcendental') side it produced both ethics as a discourse on the values of human free will and autonomy, and epistemology as an investigation of human understanding, its scope and limits, as deduced by a process of *a priori* reasoning from the conditions of possibility for knowledge and experience in general.

Thus 'man' is an invention of comparatively recent date and one whose image can be seen, even now, as dissolving back into the element whence he arose, 'like a face drawn in sand at the ocean's edge'.[31] For it is Foucault's claim – dramatically heightened in the typical late-60s French antihumanist vein – that this epoch is already receding from view, having suffered the successive assaults of Nietzschean epistemological scepticism, Freudian psychoanalysis, and the linguistic (or structuralist) turn across various disciplines, all of which developments have had the effect of radically 'decentering' or dethroning the subject from its erstwhile privileged role. So one can see why Foucault has no real use for Bachelard's concept of 'epistemological breaks', except in so far as the phrase continues to function as a vague pointer toward rifts and transformations in the discursive 'order of things'. For these breaks have to do with epistemology only in the sense that they concern what *once counted* as knowledge and truth, 'knowledge' according to the then-prevalent structure of signs or representations, and 'truth' as defined by conventional ideas of method or scientific discipline. There is simply no place in Foucault's approach for a normative conception of science (or philosophy of science) that would seek to distinguish true from false or progressive from non-progressive theories, paradigms, methodologies, or research-programmes. Still less is there a role for the kind of detailed epistemo-critical analysis that would claim – like Bachelard – to specify the conditions for advances in scientific knowledge.

In Foucault's case – as with so many movements in recent French thought – this seems to spring largely from a will to throw off the legacy of Cartesian rationalism, in particular the concept (or metaphor) of knowledge as consisting in the mind's having guaranteed access to 'clear and distinct ideas'. Thus when Foucault lays such emphasis on the 'decentering' of the subject by language – or its dispersal into various discursively-produced 'subject-positions' – then it seems to be Descartes, rather than Kant, whose philosophy provides the chief target. After all, Kant was at great pains to distinguish the various orders of empirical, noumenal, and transcendental subjectivity, and moreover to stress that any confusion between them – any error such as that made by Descartes in his attempt to prove the substantive existence of the first-person thinking subject through the formula *cogito, ergo sum* – must give rise to all manner of strictly unthinkable antinomies.[32] So there is a strong case for claiming that Foucault's strain of anti-epistemological thought is a product of this curious fixation on Descartes and the problems of a subject-centred discourse of reason, knowledge, and truth.

Now Bachelard likewise defines his project to a large extent against the Cartesian idea of knowledge as proceeding from *a priori* principles grounded in the absolute certainty attained through an exercise of self-reflexive critical thought. His reasons for this should be evident enough from what I have said so far. They include his argument that science makes progress precisely through *breaking* with the kinds of intuitive self-evidence that typify its early (proto-scientific) stages of enquiry, or that 'stand to reason' just so long as reason has not yet entered upon the path of more adequate conceptual analysis and critique. Thus advances come about at just the point where any *direct* appeal to Cartesian criteria – to 'clear and distinct ideas' – would constitute an obstacle to further, more productive or theoretically elaborated thought. Also there is the argument (taken up by Derrida) that this appeal is itself metaphorical and image-based, deriving from the age-old philosopic *topoi* of knowledge as the 'inner light' of reason, or truth as that to which the mind gains access through its power of accurate and focused inward reflection. In short, Bachelard rejects that whole aspect of Descartes' thinking – along with later, more refined versions, such as the project of Husserlian phenomenology – which equates knowledge with the coming-to-light of truths vouchsafed through the exercise of reason in its critical-reflective (or transcendental) mode.[33] However, he argues, there is an important distinction to be drawn between this, the more familiar Descartes, author of the *Meditations* with its subject-centred epistemological approach, and that 'other' Descartes whose thinking is represented by certain parts of the *Discourse on Method* and kindred texts aimed toward the better 'regulation' of reason in its chiefly scientific or epistemo-critical mode.[34] For in these works there is far less emphasis on the idea of reason as a self-sufficient source of indubitable truths and grounding intuitions. Rather, they are intended as a working guide to the *critical application* of reason, that is to say, the possibility of freeing thought from its adherence to naive (intuitive, commonsense, or image-based) modes of understanding. In this respect they are much closer to Bachelard's conception of *le rationalisme appliqué*, his belief that scientific advances can come about only through a constant dialectic – or process of mutual interrogative exchange – between intuitive insight and rational method.

Thus at certain times (i.e., during periods of Kuhnian 'revolutionary' science) it will often be the case that some attractive new hypothesis is put forward without, as yet, finding adequate support from observational data or from a well-established theory that can somehow be adapted or extended to cover the case in hand. Such was, for instance, the early situation of Galileo's heterodox astronomy, or of Einstein's Special Theory of Relativity when the Michelson-Morley results had appeared to disconfirm it by showing that the velocity of light was indeed affected by its direction of travel relative to an all-pervasive ether. (Subsequent tests produced a contrary [i.e., a nil-velocity-difference] result and it is now accepted in most quarters that the discrepancy was due to errors of measurement in the first experimental set-up.[35]) One could multiply examples to similar effect from various fields of scientific research, among them astrophysics, molecular biology, and the atomic theory of matter from the ancient atomists to Dalton, Rutherford, and Bohr. In each case these theories moved through a stage (or a series of stages) when their form was indeed metaphoric in the sense that it involved some complex analogical scheme or some intuitive leap to a novel hypothesis beyond their current best powers of experimental proof or adequate conceptualization. Hence Bachelard's well-known example of the tetrahedral structure of carbon, an image (or metaphor) clearly adopted for just such reasons, and one that in fact proved highly conducive to further theoretical refinement and research. So it is that some metaphors (not others) are capable of yielding genuine scientific insight through a process of critical 'rectification' that works to separate their truth-content from their origin in forms of analogical, image-based or anthropomorphic thinking.

Another good example would be Bohr's early model of the atom as a kind of miniature solar system with the nucleus surrounded by orbiting electrons whose paths (that is to say, whose position and angular momentum at any given time) could be specified in terms of just that heuristic metaphor. This idea was intuitively appealing – for obvious reasons – and proved highly fruitful of further discoveries concerning the subatomic structure of matter. However, it was quickly superseded by Bohr's conversion to a quantum-mechanical theory that denied the very possibility of assigning such values (except as a probabilistic outcome of the associated wave-function), and which thus resisted the utmost efforts of quasi-visual representation.[36] We are therefore not to think of subatomic 'particles' as possessing definite (objective) properties of location and/or momentum but should rather think of them as somehow manifesting particle-like or wave-like behaviour according to the type of experimental set-up or the kind of measurement performed upon them. Nor is this by any means a special case or an isolated instance of scientific theory getting into conflict with commonsense-intuitive modes of understanding. There is still much debate – among physicists and philosophers alike – as regards the best interpretation to be placed on those quantum-mechanical formalisms and whether they might yet be capable of a realist construal that avoids some of the more mind-wrenching paradoxes of the Bohr-derived orthodox ('Copenhagen') theory.[37] But it is also the case across a range of other fields – starting nearly two centuries ago with the development of non-Euclidean geometries – that scientific advances have most often come about through a break with the eminently Kantian idea of knowledge as a matter of bringing intuitions under adequate concepts. That is to say, they have meant abandoning not only the ground of naive sense-certainty but also the appeal to those *a priori* structures of thought and cognition which, according to Kant, were prerequisite to any science of the phenomenal world.[38]

There is no room here for a detailed account of the various closely-related developments – in physics, geometry, mathematics, epistemology, and philosophy of logic – that eventually produced this decisive turn against subject-centred or intuition-based conceptions of knowledge and truth. (Readers may wish to consult J. Alberto Coffa's recent, highly illuminating study.[39]) My point is that philosophers have responded in very different ways to what is perceived as a kind of legitimation-crisis in the discourse of science and philosophy of science. For some – postmodernists like Lyotard among them – it is a sign that we have now moved on into a phase where 'performativity' (not truth) is the name of the game, and when cultural theorists can best take a lead from those branches of science (such as quantum mechanics and chaos-theory) that have supposedly given up all ideas of objectivity or truth at the end of enquiry.[40] For others, such as Rorty, the lesson to be drawn is that scientists (like everyone else) can never get outside the various language-games, metaphors, or descriptive schemes that happen to prevail at this or that stage in the ongoing 'cultural conversation'. From which Rorty concludes that there is just no point – professional self-interest aside – in trying to come up with some theory of metaphor (or account of its role in scientific theory-formation) that would somehow distinguish 'good' or productive from 'bad' or non-productive examples of the kind. Then again, there are those – disciples of Foucault and at least a few readers of Quine – who take for granted the dissolution of that old, subject-centred epistemological paradigm, along with the impossibility of maintaining any version of the Kantian dualism between analytic and synthetic statements.[41]

What these responses have in common, despite their very mixed genealogy, is the turn toward a thoroughly holistic approach to issues of meaning and truth, one that in principle places no limit on the variety of ways in which language can 'correctly' describe the world, or – as Quine would have it – on the various options for redistributing truth-values and predicates over the total fabric of currently accepted beliefs. For it is then a short distance to Rorty's 'textualist' idea that things *just are* – for all practical purposes – the way that we represent them as being under this or that favoured range of descriptions, language-games or metaphors. In which case, clearly, it is no use seeking to uphold any version of the concept/metaphor dualism or to theorize the structure and workings of metaphor in various (scientific and other) contexts of enquiry. These efforts will always prove circular or self-defeating at the point where their own favoured terms of analysis – terms such as 'theory', 'concept' and 'analysis' – prove to be themselves metaphorical at root or so many items in a language-game (a 'kind of writing') that gives no hold for such treatment.

IV

Now, as I have said, there are passages in Derrida's 'White Mythology' where he makes just this point about the impossibility of ever producing a fully elaborated theory or concept of metaphor. 'By definition', he writes,

> there is no properly philosophical category to qualify a certain number of tropes that have conditioned the so-called 'fundamental', 'structuring',

'original' philosophical oppositions: they are so many 'metaphors' that would constitute the rubrics of such a tropology, the words 'turn' or 'trope' or 'metaphor' being no exception to the rule. (WM, p. 229)

Thus philosophy *cannot but* attempt to theorize metaphor on its own conceptual terms, terms that have defined the very nature of philosophical enquiry from its ancient Greek inception to the present. Yet in so doing it will always find itself caught up in a process of circular reappropriation, a dependence on certain metaphors ('fundamental', 'structuring', 'original' tropes) for which there exist no literal, plain-prose equivalents, and which therefore constitute the absolute limit of any such enquiry. Indeed, there is no choice for theorists of metaphor – whether philosophers, rhetoricians, or literary critics – but to work with a concept (that of 'metaphor' itself) that takes for granted the distinction between literal and metaphoric meaning. For it can readily be shown that theorists from Aristotle down have treated metaphor always as a 'detour' on the path to truth, that is to say, as a swerve from the proper or literal sense that is none the less capable of yielding knowledge through a grasp of its various kinds and structural features. But this is to beg the main point at issue: namely, that philosophy wields all the necessary concepts or instruments for analysing metaphor without, in the process, having recourse to a language that is itself radically metaphorical.

In short, as Derrida remarks, 'metaphor has been issued from a network of philosophemes which themselves correspond to tropes or to figures'. Furthermore,

[t]his stratum of 'tutelary' tropes, the layer of 'primary' philosophemes (assuming that the quotation marks will serve as a sufficient precaution here), cannot be dominated. It cannot dominate itself, cannot be dominated by what it itself has engendered, has made to grow on its own soil, supported on its own base. Therefore, it gets 'carried away' each time that one of its products – here, the concept of metaphor – attempts in vain to include under its own law the totality of the field to which the product belongs. (WM, p. 219)

So clearly there is a sense in which Derrida rejects philosophy's 'unique thesis' with regard to metaphor, i.e., the belief that it involves only a 'provisional loss of meaning', a momentary detour from the proper (literal) signification which can always be redeemed – at any rate in the case of 'good', truth-yielding metaphors – through analysis of its various compo-nent terms and structure. This claim was first made by Aristotle when he remarked that, of the various kinds of metaphor, the best are those of the Fourth Type, the sort that involves a complex or four-term structure of analogy ('as A is to B, so C is to D').[42] With this type of metaphor it is possible to achieve genuine advances in knowledge, advances that occur through the power of thought to perceive a significant relation or resemblance between hitherto unconnected domains of knowledge. 'Metaphor, thus, as an effect of *mimesis* and *homoiosis*, the manifestation of analogy, will be a means of knowledge, a means that is subordinate, but certain' (WM, p. 238). 'Subordinate' in so far as it approaches truth only by way of complex analogical transfer, that is to say, through a swerve from literal sense that would not be required if we possessed more adequate conceptual and linguistic resources. But 'certain', none the less, to the extent that good metaphors are reliably truth-conducive, working as they do in this oblique fashion to bring about a knowledge that will finally dispense with such short-term heuristic devices.

For Bachelard, likewise, it is the chief virtue of scientific metaphor – a virtue that it shares with the poetic imagination – to enable this creative passage beyond the limits of received or orthodox thinking. But still the chief test of a good scientific metaphor, for Bachelard as for Aristotle, is its ability to withstand the rigours of conceptual 'rectification and critique', that is to say, its possessing a complex analogical structure where the various terms can be applied and critically assessed in some given context of enquiry. Thus the tetrahedral structure of carbon and the planetary model of the atom were metaphors that played a significant role in the advancement of scientific knowlege, and which did so precisely through drawing attention to analogies of just this kind, even if those analogies were not yet brought to the highest (scientifically most adequate) stage of conceptual definition. For there is really no point in staging this issue – as it often tends to be staged – as a quarrel between those who maintain that science has to do with matters of strict, literal truth and those others – postmodernists and typecast deconstructionists – who claim that metaphor goes 'all the way down', and hence that truth is itself just a kind of literalized or sublimated metaphor. What is thereby obscured is the crucial difference – as Bachelard very clearly brings out – between metaphors that remain on the side of poetic or imaginative 'reverie', and metaphors which – by virtue of their structure and capacity for further development – may properly be counted among the resources of a developing scientific theory or research-programme.

Now it may well come as a surprise to many readers that the above few sentences are a fairly close close paraphrase of Derrida's argument in certain crucial passages of his essay 'White Mythology'. For as I have said, this text has acquired the reputation of pushing to the limit (and a good way beyond) with the notion that 'all concepts are metaphors', 'all truths just a product of the epistemic will-to-power', and kindred variations on that stock Nietzschean-Foucauldian theme. However this is not at all what Derrida is saying, even though it fits well enough with what many commentators – sympathetic or hostile – would undoubtedly wish him to say. In fact the main part of 'White Mythology' is given over to a rigorously argued critique of the standard postmodern (or quasi-deconstructionist) idea that scientific or philosophical concepts can be treated as *nothing more* than a repertoire of sublimated metaphors, images, or tropes. Thus, with particular reference to Bachelard: '[d]oes not a scientific critique's rectification rather proceed from an inefficient tropic-concept that is poorly constructed, to an operative tropic-concept that is more refined and more powerful in a given field and at a determined phase of the scientific process?' (WM, p. 264). Of course there are other passages – several of which I have cited above – that offer some pretext or apparent justification for readings in the postmodern-textualist vein. However it is also Derrida's contention that any worthwhile critical treatment of metaphor will have to go by way of those various philosophically-articulated theories – from Aristotle down – where that topic has always been closely related to issues of truth and knowledge.

This is why Derrida looks to philosophy of science, and to Bachelard and Canguilhem especially, for his examples of 'truth-tropic' metaphors, or figures of thought that have proved their scientific worth through a process of ongoing 'rectification and critique'. It is also what sets his discussion apart from other, more holistic or generalized claims with regard to metaphor and its role in scientific theory-construction. These would include Rorty's advice that we drop the metaphor/concept distinction and replace it with one between Kuhnian 'normal' and 'revolutionary' phases of science, the former typified by its willingness to stick with routine, literalized, or 'dead' metaphors, the latter by its seeking out new turns of thought to move the conversation along.[43] Kuhn himself had certain reservations with regard to this kind of textualist or strong-descriptivist talk.[44] All the same one can see how Rorty gets there by taking Kuhn's thesis that scientific 'revolutions' involve a wholesale paradigm-change (so that scientists before and after the event may be said to 'live in different worlds'), and grafting it onto the Nietzschean idea of language as radically metaphorical. He can then treat Kuhn's more cautious pronouncements or circumspect choices of meta-phor – such as that of scientists viewing the same world 'through differently coloured spectacles' – as unfortunate lapses which can safely be ignored by those who have abandoned that old objectivist style of thought. Much better, he advises, that we push right through with the Kuhnian argument and cease the vain effort to articulate a theory of metaphor that would somehow hold the line between 'properly' scientific and other (e.g. poetic or imaginative) modes of description.

I should not wish to claim – against the evidence of passages from 'White Mythology' like those cited above – that Derrida is altogether out of sympathy with this way of thinking about metaphor and its role in the discourse of philosophy or science. If any further such evidence were needed then the following passage explains very clearly just why he thinks it impossible that a theory of metaphor could ever dominate the field of its own metaphorical production.

> The criteria for a classification of philosophical metaphors are borrowed from a derivative philosophical discourse. Perhaps this might be legitimate if these figures were governed, consciously and calculatedly, by the identifiable author of a system, or if the issue were to describe a philosophical rhetoric in the service of an autonomous theory constituted before and outside its own language, manipulating its tropes like tools. This is an undoubtedly philosophic, and certainly Platonic, ideal, an ideal that is produced in the separation (and order) between philosophy and dialectics on the one hand and (sophistic) rhetoric on the other, the separation demanded by Plato himself. Directly or not, it is this separation and this hierarchy that we must question here. (WM, p. 224)

So there is no question but that Derrida sees immense problems confronting any theory of metaphor – or epistemology of tropes – once alerted to the kinds of metaphorical language that inhabit its own discourse. However, it is also important to remark that this passage is aimed against a certain understanding of what it would mean for philosophy to 'dominate' the field of metaphor, or for the 'author of a system' – a philosophical rhetoric – to attain that degree of lucid theoretical grasp. In fact Derrida's target is not so much 'philosophy', 'theory' or 'system' as such but rather the idea that any progress toward a more rigorous (conceptually adequate) treatment of metaphor in the texts of philosophy must go by way of a consciousness fully in possession of the requisite concepts. This point should scarcely need making for any reader acquainted with Derrida's work on (for instance) Plato, Aristotle, Rousseau, Hegel, Husserl and J.L. Austin.[45] In each case – he argues – these thinkers have been mostly been construed on just such a theory of self-present meaning or authorial intent. That is to say, it is assumed by the majority of exegetes (1) that their texts both say what they mean and properly, reliably mean what they say; (2) that the authors were themselves fully conscious of the various implications (logical and rhetorical) of the theses advanced under their name; and (3) that this provides an adequate basis for the claim that we can know what an author intended in adopting some given theoretical position or particular form of words. Moreover (4), any argument to contrary effect – such as Derrida proposes in his deconstructive readings of philosophers from Plato to Austin – can then be safely dismissed out of hand as a product of ignorance, incompetence, or wilful misinterpretation.

This is not the place for a detailed account of the arguments that Derrida brings to bear in questioning the 'logocentric' order of values and priorities which has standardly governed the reading of philosophical texts. I shall here just mention – having argued the case at much greater length elsewhere – that these issues are focused with particular clarity in his essay on Austin and speech-act theory, an essay that raises all sorts of problem with regard to the logical implications of Austin's approach, but which does so always through a close attentiveness to matters of textual detail.[46] My point is rather that there is no good reason – *pace* opponents like Searle – to suppose that deconstruction is any less rigorous, responsible, or philosophically adequate on account of its rejecting the straightforward appeal to notions such as authorial intent or normal (as opposed to deviant) contexts of speech-act utterance.[47] For there do exist other criteria by which to assess the cogency of philosophic arguments, namely those that Derrida implicitly invokes in the above-cited passage from 'White Mythology'. What that passage calls into doubt is not so much the idea that philosophy might have something useful to say about metaphor but the notion (to repeat) that any knowledge thus attained is dependent on 'these figures [being] governed, consciously and calculatedly, by the identifiable author of a system', or on their somehow being placed 'in the service of an autonomous theory constituted before and outside its own language, manipulating its tropes like tools'. (WM, p. 224) It is the same kind of metalinguistic delusion that leads some speech-act theorists – Searle among them – to pass clean over the complex, self-implicating logic of Austin's text in the hope of producing a classificatory system (a generalized theory of performatives) that would command the entire field, so to speak, from outside and above.[48] However this is not to suggest that we reject the whole enterprise of speech-act theory, any more than it endorses a Rorty-style case for just accepting that 'all concepts are metaphors' (or 'all philosophy a kind of writing'), and letting the issue go at that. Rather, it is to make the more specific point – here as in Derrida's early texts on Plato, Rousseau, and Husserl – that such gestures of command over language are often premised on the notion of a consciousness fully in command of its own expressive resources and hence able to dictate in advance what shall count as an adequate theory of metaphor or speech-act classification.

This is why, as Derrida remarks, such theories evince 'an undoubtedly philosophic, and certainly Platonic ideal', one that always refers back to 'the identifiable author of a system', and which moreover is produced 'in the separation ... between philosophy or dialectics on the one hand and (sophistic) rhetoric on the other' (WM, p. 224). Thus the claims of system and method are closely bound up with the idea of language as placing itself at the sovereign disposal of a subject whose speech-acts, meanings, and intentions should properly be construed in accordance with rules laid down on its own self-authorizing warrant. Now it is wrong to suppose (as many commentators do) that Derrida is a wholesale anti-intentionalist, one who quite simply rejects the idea – the old-fashioned fideist idea – that interpretation or textual exegesis have anything to do with respect for an author's original or governing intent. In fact he has some strong statements in *Of Grammatology* to the effect that reading cannot dispense with such 'elementary protocols' of interpretive fidelity and truth, even though these standards provide only a 'guardrail' that prevents exegesis from going off 'in any direction whatsoever'.[49] What deconstruction aims to show, on the contrary, is the precise relation in any given case between that which an author expressly intends to say, and that which the text constrains him or her to mean through effects (such as the 'logic of supplementarity' in Rousseau's writing) that cannot be reduced to any straightforward intentionalist account.

It is a similar case that Derrida is making with regard to metaphor and the various attempts – by philosophers, rhetoricians, and literary critics – to elucidate its structure and workings from a metalinguistic standpoint. What is questionable about these attempts is *not* their commitment to the highest standards of conceptual clarity, detailed analysis, or rigorous argumentation. Nor is it the fact (as Derrida points out, following Nietzsche) that even such seemingly abstract criteria are themselves derivative from a range of covert or sublimated metaphors which philosophy can never expunge from its own discourse. After all, there is no reason to conclude from this that philosophers are merely wasting their time when they try to attain a more detailed, conceptually adequate knowledge of those various 'fundamental', 'structuring', or 'original' tropes. To draw that conclusion – as Rorty does – is to mistake what is undoubtedly a complicating factor in the philosophic discourse on metaphor for a knock-down argument against the very notion (maintained by theorists from Aristotle to Bachelard) that philosophy does indeed have something to learn from the analysis of metaphor, not least as applied to the texts of its own tradition. Where this claim becomes dubious, rather, is at the point where it joins with that traditional 'logocentric' idea of knowledge as somehow vouchsafed to the thinking subject through a direct (privileged or first-person) epistemic access to meanings, intentions, or ideas. It is ironic that Searle should accuse Derrida of himself being in the grip of a typically 'French' Cartesian illusion, that is to say, the belief that if speech-act categories cannot be made absolutely rigorous (or ideally clear and distinct), then one might just as well give up altogether on the effort to distinguish constatives from performatives, or genuine from non-genuine speech-acts, or 'normal' from 'deviant' contexts of utterance.[50] For it is precisely Derrida's point against Searle's (though not, I should emphasise, Austin's) treatment of these issues that it claims the kind of proprietory warrant – or self-assured interpretive grasp – that can only come from an authorized appeal to what speakers (or writers, Austin included) properly and genuinely mean by their words. And that appeal goes along with the systematizing drive to erect a full-scale theory of speech-acts on the basis of strongly normative distinctions (such as those instanced above) which are themselves held in place by the assumed possibility of knowing how they work, so to speak, from the inside.

Now one way to understand Derrida's argument – with respect to both metaphor and speech-act theory – is to see it as part of the wider present-day shift from subject-centred epistemologies to alternative conceptions of meaning, knowledge, and truth. I have already traced a line of descent for this approach that has to do chiefly with issues in philosophy of science and which includes Bachelard's and Canguilhem's work on the role of metaphor in the process of scientific theory-construction. I have also suggested that the shift has come about in response to various developments (from non-Euclidean geometry to relativity-theory and quantum mechanics) which are counter-intuitive sometimes to the point of resisting any effort of concrete or quasi-visual representation. These developments challenged the Kantian conception of synthetic *a priori* knowledge, along with the idea – common to many schools of thought in philosophy of science – that phenomenal intuitions (or observational data) must be 'brought under' adequate or corresponding concepts. Above all they established a different, more dialectical relationship between speculative thinking (often conducted at the level of heuristic metaphor) and critical-evaluative methods for assessing the results of such thought. It is this relationship that Bachelard seeks to characterize through his studies of *le rationalisme appliqué*, and which can also be seen in Derrida's analyses of metaphor in the texts of philosophy.

V

In conclusion I should like to return briefly to some passages from 'White Mythology' where Derrida discusses Aristotle's theory of metaphor and, more specifically, the way that metaphor figures as a 'detour' on the path to a reappropriation of literal, self-present truth. What guides this theory is the idea of language as aspiring to a perfect structural homology between word, concept, and referent such that the noun (in its literal usage) would provide an anchor-point for the process of signification, and the other parts of speech then assume their proper place as elements in a well-regulated system. For the noun is (according to Aristotle) the 'first semantic entity', the 'smallest signifying element', one whose parts are without meaning but which unites in itself the two dimensions of sound and sense. It is therefore the point at which language begins, i.e., properly human language (belonging to creatures in possession of *logos*), as opposed to mere inarticulate animal noises. Moreover, it is always with implicit reference to the noun as a locus of proper (literal) meaning that Aristotle defines those other distinctively human activities – among them metaphor and *mimesis* – which offer a 'subordinate but certain' means of acquiring veridical knowledge. Thus:

> [t]he condition for metaphor (for good and true metaphor) is the condition for truth. Therefore it is to be expected that the animal, deprived of *logos* ... also would be incapable of mimesis. *Mimesis* thus determined belongs to *logos*, and is not animalistic aping, or gesticular mimicry; it is tied to the possibility of meaning and truth in discourse. ... The power of truth, as the unveiling of nature (*physis*) by *mimesis*, congenitally belongs to the physics of man, to anthropophysics ... For the same reason, pleasure, the second 'cause' of *mimesis* and metaphor, is the pleasure of knowing, of learning by resemblance, of recognizing the same. (WM, pp. 237–8)

So metaphor occupies a place in what Derrida calls the 'great immobile chain' of Aristotelian ontology, a chain whose various links include 'its theory of the analogy of Being, its logic, its epistemology, and more precisely its poetics and its rhetoric' (p. 236). But if the chain were indeed 'immobile' – if everything fitted together in this preordained fashion – then it is hard to see how knowledge could advance or how new discoveries could ever come about through fresh observation and the exercise of speculative thought.

This is of course where metaphor comes in, that is to say, the 'good' (truth-conducive) kind of metaphor that enables us to 'see resemblances', or to break with routine habits of thought and perception. Yet in order to do so, Aristotle argues, metaphor must always accept its role – its properly 'subordinate' role – with respect to those other values that determine what shall count as a 'good' metaphor. In Derrida's words:

> *Mimesis* is never without the *theoretical* perception of resemblance or similarity, that is, of that which always will be posited as the condition for metaphor. *Homoiosis* is not only constitutive of the value of truth (*aletheia*) which governs the entire chain; it is that without which the metaphorical operation is impossible. (WM, p. 237)

But again there is a problem if one asks what scope this could allow for discoveries or changes in scientific thinking, given that every link in the chain – from *aletheia* (truth), through *homoiosis* (correspondence or representation), to *mimesis* (imitation) and then metaphor (perception of likeness) – is thought to be governed by a strictly 'immobile' order of truth-preserving relations. Only if metaphor were *not* thus reduced to a properly 'subordinate' role could one explain how knowledge can at times make progress by breaking with established patterns of thought or habits of perception. For it would otherwise forever be held within the limits of an immutable paradigm extending all the way from ontology, *via* epistemology, to logic, grammar, and rhetoric. In which case one could make no sense of Aristotle's claims for the advancement of human understanding, whether through 'good' (heuristically productive) metaphors or indeed through other, more strictly regulated modes of observation, experiment, or theory-construction.

This is not to say, in postmodern-textualist fashion, that since all language is radically metaphorical – scientific language included – therefore it is impossible to theorize metaphor or distinguish its various structures or modes of operation. Rather, it is to make Bachelard's (and Derrida's) point: that although such attempts will always fall short of a full-scale systematic treatment – for reasons that Derrida explains in 'White Mythology' – nevertheless they are a part of that continuing dialectical process through which all advances in knowledge come about. What resists adequate theorization is not so much the process itself as the activity of thought that produces those advances, occurring as it does – most often – at a level inaccessible to conscious awareness or punctual reflective grasp. As I have said, this is where Bachelard marks his distance from that whole philosophical tradition that comes down from Descartes to Kant, and thence from Husserl to various schools of (mainly French) phenomemo-logical thought. It is a distance captured by Bachelard's phrase *rationalisme appliqué*, but also by Popper's idea of 'epistemology without the knowing subject' and other such ways of acknowledging the fact that modern science has entered a phase of development where intuitions can no longer be 'brought under' adequate concepts.

The following passage from 'White Mythology' – again *à propos* Aristotle's theory of metaphor – may help to make this point more clearly. 'The discourse on metaphor', Derrida writes,

> belongs to a treatise *peri lexos*. There is lexis, and within it metaphor, in the extent to which thought is not made manifest by itself, in the extent to which the meaning of what is said or thought is not a phenomenon of itself. *Dianoia* as such is not yet related to metaphor. There is metaphor only in the extent to which someone is supposed to make manifest, by means of statement, a given thought that of itself remains inapparent, hidden, or latent. Thought stumbles upon metaphor, or metaphor falls to thought, at the moment when meaning attempts to emerge from itself in order to be stated, enunciated, brought to the light of language. And yet – such is our problem – the theory of metaphor remains a theory of *meaning* and posits a certain original *naturality* of this figure. (WM, p. 233)

It is not hard to see how this passage relates to Derrida's early work on Husserl and his deconstructive readings of various texts in the Western 'logocentric' tradition. Thus his argument here concerning metaphor – that it marks the non-self-present character of thought and language in general, or the extent to which 'the meaning of what is said or thought is not a phenomenon of itself' – is also the argument that Derrida pursues in a wide range of other contexts. What is less often noticed is its bearing on those issues in epistemology and philosophy of science that were raised within the French critical-rationalist tradition by thinkers like Bachelard and Canguilhem, and which have also been central to recent Anglo-American debate. For this is precisely Derrida's case with regard to Aristotle: that his treatment of metaphor leaves open certain crucial questions concerning the limits of an 'anthropophysical' account, one that would treat all knowledge (including that produced by 'good', truth-tropic metaphors) as subject to an order of changeless, 'immobile' truth grounded in the very nature of human cognitive powers and capacities.

Thus, as Derrida remarks, '[t]his truth is not certain. There can be bad metaphors. Are the latter metaphors? Only an axiology supported by a theory of truth can answer this question; and this axiology belongs to the interior of rhetoric. It cannot be neutral' (WM, p. 241). One response – that offered by the current 'strong' textualists and promoters of so-called 'postmodern' science – is to say that truth is indeed a linguistic, a metaphorical, performative or fictive construct, and that philosophers are therefore embarked upon a hopeless endeavour when they seek to theorize its structure and workings in adequate (philosophical) terms. However this is not Derrida's response, as can be seen from his framing the above question in a sharply paradoxical but *not* a purely rhetorical or dismissive form. Rather, it is a matter – for Derrida as for Bachelard – of re-thinking the concept/metaphor relationship (or that between science, philosophy of science, and the analysis of scientific image and metaphor) so as to acknowledge those decisive transformations that have occurred in various post-1900 areas of research, theoretical physics chief among them. For it is largely as a consequence of just these changes – along with earlier developments such as the emergence of non-Euclidean geometries – that philosophy of science has been led to revise some of its most basic conceptions of truth and method. When Derrida questions such ideas it is not for one moment in order to suggest that we should henceforth abandon the 'logocentric' values of conceptual precision, logical rigour, or rational accountability. On the contrary: these remain imperative values for philosophy as well as for the physical sciences, whatever the new sorts of challenge that arise when thinking abandons the security of 'natural' (commonsense-intuitive) knowledge. Thus:

> it is indispensable to study the terrain on which the Aristotelian definition [of metaphor] could have been constructed. But this study would lose all

pertinence if it were not preceded, or in any event controlled, by the systematic and internal reconstitution of the text to be reinscribed. Even if partial and preliminary the task is not limited to a commentary on a textual surface. No transparency is granted it. The issue already is one of an active interpretation setting to work an entire system of rules and transformations. (WM, p. 231)

In which case the critical reading of philosophic texts – of Aristotle's texts on metaphor, or of Derrida's text on the theories of metaphor advanced by Aristotle and Bachelard – must itself exemplify the same kind of rigour and logical precision as applies to the assessment of scientific theories, hypotheses, or truth-claims. That is to say, it cannot rest content with simply reproducing the manifest sense (or intuitively evident purport) of whatever it is given to interpret. Rather, it must pass beyond the illusion of 'transparently' accessible meaning to a level where different, more exacting criteria come into play. 'White Mythology' is one of the very few texts on this *topos* of metaphor in the discourse of science and philosophy that manage to sustain such a high level of detailed analytic commentary.

CHAPTER 5

'The Idea of the University': some interdisciplinary soundings

I

There has been a lot of talk just lately – much of it emanating from literary and cultural theorists – about the 'idea of the university' and its lineage from Kant to the present.[1] This talk has often issued from a postmodern, sceptical-relativist viewpoint which treats the various disciplines (the natural and human sciences alike) as so many 'discourses' of recent date whose lease has now expired – not before time – with the advent of a new dispensation. Its sources will no doubt be familiar enough to anyone who has followed the fortunes of 'theory' (that ill-defined but populous genre) over the past two decades and more. I shall list them here – perforce in rather summary style – and then go on to ask just why these ideas have achieved fashionable currency at a time when universities – in Britain and elsewhere – are in a state of crisis brought about by other (more urgently practical) concerns.

They include, among others, Foucault on the archaeology of knowledge or (in his later, more Nietzschean vein) the genealogy of truth-values; Lyotard on the so-called 'postmodern condition' and on science – theoretical physics especially – as a paralogistic activity nowadays legitimized in performative, rather than constative terms; sundry post-structuralists on the 'arbitrary' char–acter of the sign and – supposedly following from this – the likewise arbitrary (discursively-constructed) character of all knowledges, truth-claims, and disciplines; Lyotard (again) on the Kantian sublime as that which exceeds and utterly disrupts all our normal, rationally accountable modes of thought; and a whole range of thinkers (ethnographic 'thick' describers, strong sociologists of knowledge, Kuhnian or Feyerabend-inspired debun-kers of scientific progress, sceptical historiographers, literary theorists with ambitions way beyond their metier) who all have an interest in breaking down that old (presumptively obsolete) idea that there might be real differ-ences between the various fields and methods of enquiry which have shaped the modern university and its faculty system.[2] To think like this – so the argu-ment goes – is merely to display one's deluded attachment to an outworn realist epistemology and a Whiggish 'metanarrative' notion of the disciplines that holds them accountable to certain standards of truth, progress, constructive criticism, cooperative enquiry and so forth.

In this chapter I shall argue conversely that the 'idea of the university' cannot be divorced from certain other regulative ideas, that is to say, 'ideas of reason' (in the Kantian sense) which may not be fully realised in any existing university – or other institution – but which all the same possess a validity transcending particular circumstances of time and place. Chief among them, I suggest, are the interconnected values of truth, criticism, mutual understanding (so far as humanly possible), and respect for differences of moral and intellectual viewpoint. Yet of course there is a certain tension here since – as cultural relativists and postmodernists are quick to point out – the ideas of truth and criticism can very easily get into conflict with the idea of tolerance for the widest variety of beliefs, attitudes, and value-commitments. In which case – they urge – we should give up those bad old 'Enlightenment' ideas and recognise that what counts as 'truth' or valid 'criticism' will vary so much across cultures, languages, historical periods, or (indeed) academic disciplines as to rule out any truth-claims or criticisms based on our own (necessarily culture-relative) habits of belief.

I think that they are wrong about this – philosophically and ethically confused – and, moreover, that any *genuinely* enlightened 'idea of the university' must balance the idea of tolerance for opposing viewpoints with the idea of truth arrived at through criticism of false, prejudicial, or misinformed beliefs. Similar issues arise with regard to the notion of inter-disciplinarity, an idea that is nowadays very often construed as a call to sink the differences between disciplines, e.g., between historiography and literary theory, or philosophy and the sociology of knowledge, or the physical sciences and 'science studies' as a sub-branch of cultural criticism. Here again it is suggested that the 'disciplines' as we know them are merely products of a certain phase in the late-modern (university-based) division of intellectual labour, a system whose structures cannot – and should not – survive the epochal shift to a postmodern polity where no such division any longer applies. Thus the case for softening up disciplinary boundaries goes along with the case for treating our beliefs – our current best ideas of truth, method and criticism – as culture-relative and hence as valid only in so far as they belong to some particular localized discourse, language-game, cultural life-form, or whatever. As against all this I shall argue (1) that such relativist doctrines are self-refuting, (2) that they cannot begin to explain how we could ever comprehend beliefs or worldviews other than our own, and (3) that they stand squarely opposed to any 'idea of the university' premised on certain shared values – of truth, criticism, free and open debate – *despite and across* all the manifest differences of aim, interest, method, and priority to be found in the various disciplines. That is to say, the university is and should remain one site where such differences can be respected while sustaining a sense of properly universal (discipline-transcendent) interests and values.

II

Let us start – for reasons I shall shortly explain – with some issues in current linguistic philosophy. On the relativist account, as Donald Davidson observes, there can be nothing to prevent us from completely misconstruing other people's intentions, ontological commitments, epistemic criteria, or notions of rational-evaluative warrant.[3] Furthermore, we should have no alternative but to understand them according to our own (admittedly culture-specific) values and beliefs. This idea may look fairly plausible if one focuses attention on the problems that arise in particular cases of semantic (word-for-word) translation between languages, or – at the opposite extreme – on the issue of 'ontological relativity' conceived as a wholesale version of the same sort of problem.[4] Among post-structuralists it has taken hold through the notion of language (Saussure's *la langue*) as a network of relationships and differences 'without positive terms', such that the 'arbitrary' link between signifier and signified becomes a high point of cultural-relativist theory.[5] Here again there is a certain preemptive narrowing of focus – to the individual 'sign' as a two-term structure conceived in isolation from its other (referential or logico-syntactic) functions – along with a hugely generalized model of language (or discourse) which takes this thesis as its pretext for declaring such concerns strictly off limits. It is then a short step to the relativist doctrine that treats all meanings, truth-claims, or validity-conditions as internal to some given language, culture or localized conceptual scheme. For on this view the attempt to translate or interpret across such schemes would at some stage encounter referential opacity, problems of conceptual or communicative grasp, or at any rate the impossibility of knowing for sure whether its own ontology matched up with that of the target language.

Davidson's basic answer to this is a form of transcendental *tu quoque* argument which simply asks how, given such beliefs, the relativist could claim to perceive or locate any particular instance of mistranslation. That is to say, if the relativist is right – whatever that might mean – then he or she could never have evidence or reason for making that claim. Thus relativism is inherently self-defeating to the extent that, by advancing these generalized statements ('all truths are relative', 'all translation merely a species of mistranslation') it undercuts the very possibility of showing how and where such obstacles occur. For if we are all floating around in a sea of ontological relativity – or (to vary the metaphor) casting about for just one among the open-ended range of interpretative options – then there is nothing that could possibly count *for us* as a demonstrable instance of failed understanding or of paradigm-incommensurability.

However Davidson also has a stronger claim, a positive version of this standard anti-relativist argument from the 'conditions of possibility' for

thought and language in general. It has to do with the tendency among relativists to rest their case on localized instances of *semantic* underdetermination, or on the fact (worked hard by post-structuralists and ethnolinguists of
a Whorfian bent) that different languages on occasion have different ways
of hooking up signifiers to signifieds. Where the fallacy enters, on Davidson's account, is in treating such examples as the norm, or in failing to see
that language has resources beyond those captured by a structural-semantic
or a purely semiotic account. More precisely: 'what forms the skeleton of
what we call a language is the pattern of inference and structure created by
the logical constants: the sentential connectives, quantifiers, and devices for
cross-reference'.[6] In which case, he argues,

> knowledge of the circumstances under which someone holds sentences
> true is central to interpretation. ... Although most thoughts are not
> beliefs, it is the pattern of beliefs that allows us to identify any thought;
> analogously, in the case of language, although most sentences are not
> concerned with truth, it is the pattern of sentences held true that gives
> utterances their meaning.[7]

There has been much debate – not least in Davidson's own later writings –
about just how far such a theory can or should go toward giving a substantive (as opposed to a 'minimalist' or, as some would have it, it a wholly
redundant) account of these truth-conditions.[8] For a while he appeared
willing to accept the idea, proposed by Rorty among others, that since the
truth of any given candidate-sentence depended on its relation to all other
sentences held true by the speaker at some given time, therefore it might just
as well be cashed out in terms of a pragmatist conception of what is
(currently and contingently) 'good in the way of belief'.[9] More recently
Davidson has revoked this large – indeed highly damaging – concession
and has sought to specify the concept of 'truth' so as to give it substantive
content and to bring out the patent inadequacy of any such purely circular
(holistic) definition.[10]

On my own reading, argued at length elsewhere, this was always the
strong implication of Davidson's work and the point which placed him
decisively at odds with any version of the widespread relativist turn in
various present-day disciplines.[11] For Davidson, truth is where we start
from – that is to say, from the attitude of holding-true as a necessary feature
of all conceivable languages – and it is on this basis that we can then
proceed to make adjustments (whether localized or far-reaching) to our sense
of what would count as an adequate truth-preserving interpretation. Thus
'we compensate for the paucity of evidence concerning the meaning of individual sentences not by trying to produce evidence for the meanings of
words but by considering the evidence for a theory of the language to which

the sentence belongs'.[12] This we are able to do because languages (and speakers) have a lot more in common than is allowed for by the kinds of theory currently in vogue, those that 'get the matter backward' – in Davidson's phrase – by viewing truth as internal (or relative) to some particular language, discourse, paradigm, or conceptual scheme. Syntax is in this sense more 'sociable' than semantics since it offers more scope for locating those various structures (of assertion, negation, entailment, cross-reference, anaphora, and so forth) in the absence of which no language could possibly function as such, and which therefore provide a strong counter-argument to the cultural-relativist case.[13] Agreement on these matters 'may take the form of widespread sharing of sentences held true by speakers of "the same language"'. Then again it may consist of 'agreement in the large mediated by a theory of truth contrived by an interpreter for speakers of another language'.[14] But in neither case – and this is Davidson's central point – can there be grounds for adopting the kind of *a priori* sceptical position that would raise local problems of communicative grasp into a wholesale doctrine of meaning-variance, referential opacity, 'ontological relativity', and the like.

Davidson puts the case most succinctly in his remarks about Whorfian ethnolinguistics and its bearing on questions of interlingual or cross-cultural understanding. According to Whorf there are languages, like Hopi Indian, whose entire 'metaphysics' – that is to say, whose organising concepts and categories, semantic resources, and logico-grammatical structures – are so utterly remote from our own (or from those to which we have cultural access) as to place them quite beyond reach of our understanding.[15] Thus Hopi science, as a product of that same (to us) wholly alien metaphysics, would likewise involve a wholly different – indeed 'incommensurable' – set of explanatory principles, space-time coordinates, causal hypotheses, obser-vation protocols, and validity-conditions. In this respect Whorf is very much in agreement with philosophers like Quine and Kuhn who argue that theories (or scientific world-views) are always underdetermined by the evidence, that the 'evidence' is always selectively construed in accordance with this or that theory, and hence – *a fortiori* – that we have no choice but to accept the thesis of ontological relativity.[16] This creates large prob-lems for Quine when he seeks nevertheless to defend an outlook of sturdy science-based physicalism, that is, when his statements cannot be squared with the notion of 'reality' as coming down to our choice of language-game, conceptual scheme, privileged ontology, Kuhnian 'paradigm', or whatever. In the end he is forced back – like Davidson on occasion – to a kind of last-ditch behaviorist account which simply cuts out all normative criteria and appeals directly to the sensory inputs (or the patterns of nerve-end stimuli) that somehow match up with observation-sentences. But then it is hard to see how these problems are resolved by renouncing what Quine calls the last 'dogma' of empiricism – the analytic/synthetic distinction – only to smuggle it back under the guise of 'stimulus-analytic' sentences (i.e., those uttered by speakers exposed to the same range of sensory inputs) and observation data assumed to possess some kind of self-validating warrant.[17]

This is, to say the least, an oddly self-defeating position and one that Davidson – at other moments – is properly anxious to avoid. His counter-argument is simple enough: that neither Quine nor Whorf can coherently maintain this ultra-relativist stance while claiming (as they must) to occupy some vantage-point in relation to which the differences between languages or paradigms could be rendered in any degree intelligible. Thus: 'Whorf, wanting to demonstrate that Hopi incorporates a metaphysics so alien to ours that Hopi and English cannot, as he puts it, be "calibrated", uses English to convey the contents of sample Hopi sentences'.[18] And in Quine's case also the relativity-thesis goes along with a simply unavoidable commitment to both the truth of his own relativist convictions and – however incompatible with those – the status of scientific observation-sentences as warranted in terms of their (presumably) stimulus-synthetic content. In short, as Davidson remarks, 'there does not seem to be much hope for a test that a conceptual scheme is radically different from ours if that test depends on the assumption that we can divorce the notion of truth from that of translation'.[19] Such is the negative – the weak-transcendental – version of Davidson's argument. But it can also be stated in the positive mode: that '[i]f we can produce a theory that reconciles charity and the formal conditions for a theory, we have done all that could be done to ensure communication. Nothing more is possible, and nothing more is needed'.[20]

It remains for me to give more substance to the claim that these technical-sounding issues in philosophy of language are closely bound up with issues of intellectual, ethical, and socio-political responsibility. The connection is perhaps most obvious when post-structuralists argue for a wholesale dissolution of the 'subject' – more specifically the knowing, reasoning, willing, and judging subject of Kantian thought – into a figment of the obsolete humanist imaginary, or a 'subject-position' thrown up by one particular (short-lived) discursive paradigm.[21] Such scepticism at least has the cautionary merit of showing what results when linguistic determinism is pushed to this strictly unthinkable extreme. For it leaves room only – as with Lyotard and Foucault – for the recourse to notions like that of judging absolutely 'without criteria', or of political ('revolutionary') justice as that which by very definition stands outside all the ground-rules, procedures, or ethical values of conventional ('bourgeois') justice and morality.[22] Nothing could more clearly illustrate the normative confusions that arise from this joint devaluation of truth and ethics to the point where they figure as mere configurations of language or discourse. For the way is then open either to a placidly consensus-based (pragmatist or communitarian) doctrine which equates truth with what is locally and contingently 'good in the way of belief', or again, to those forms of more radical scepticism whose upshot, very often, is a postmodern 'ethics' that admits of no appeal beyond the solitary voice of conscience or the decisionist dictates of spontaneous revolutionary 'justice'. This comes dangerously close to the idea of ethics as a kind of oracular or revealed truth, such as would create an insuperable gulf between judgements of the highest import for existence and other ('human, all-too-human') values and concerns. The risk is all the greater, I would maintain, when relativism takes the ethical turn toward notions of absolute 'difference' or 'alterity' which effectively legislate against the appeal to intersubjective criteria.[23] And these notions would scarcely have attained such prominence – would indeed lack any plausibility – were it not for the widespread sceptical *doxa* that treats all truth-claims (including those of the natural sciences) as valid only by the cultural lights of this or that interpretive community.

II

Paul Feyerabend's anarchist theory of knowledge in effect gives us the worst of both worlds.[24] On the one hand it renders science an impenetrable mystery in so far as we are required to view all its findings – experimental data, theoretical constructs, hypotheses, causal explanations – as so many meta-phors (or favoured language-games) devoid of veridical content. In which case there is a problem about explaining (for instance) how aircraft fly in accordance with the laws of aerodynamics; why the development of anti-biotics or inoculation techniques succeeded in halting the spread of various diseases; how developments in mathematics and modern symbolic logic brought about the present-day computer revolution; and – at the point where speculative thought turns out to have far-reaching practical conse-quences – how quantum mechanics gave rise to whole new technologies undreamt of in previous conceptual paradigms. On the other hand, as regards the issue of social responsibility, Feyerabend offers no help in dis-tinguishing good (progressive or enlightened) from bad (dogmatic or merely obscurantist) forms of intervention and control.

One might suppose, charitably, that his endorsement of Church authority *contra* Galileo is a piece of impish anarchist humour intended to scandalize the solemn custodians of scientific rigour and truth. But in fact it goes along with his general view that truth is up for grabs by whoever can mount the most impressive display of rhetorical self-justification. Like Rorty, he views 'science' – along with all notions of scientific 'truth' or 'progress' – as merely the honorific label we attach (or the compliment we standardly pay) to whatever kinds of discourse enjoy most prestige under the current rules of the game.[25] And those rules are in turn nothing more than the conventions that happen to prevail within this or that paradigm, research-programme, or wider scientific community.

Feyerabend thus draws the lesson – again in company with Rorty – that science (like philosophy) does best to abandon all notions of method, conceptual rigour, theoretical consistency, and the like. For those ideas are nothing more than the false self-image – the rhetorical stock-in-trade – of an enterprise blind to its own deep complicity with the forces of instru-mental reason. Hence his open letter to the commission of enquiry set up by the Catholic Church to determine whether or not Galileo was right to advance the heliocentric hypothesis. Since the 'truth' of such matters is neither here nor there – depending as it does on one's choice of favoured paradigm or argumentative strategy – the issue comes down to which model best promoted the interests of social stability and peace. So the cardinals should not be over-impressed by what was, in any case, hardly a textbook sample of scientific method or reasoning. Rather they should follow Feyerabend's line in discounting those old delusory appeals to the 'context of justification' – i.e., of truths supposedly arrived at through the process of disciplined scientific enquiry – as opposed to the 'context of discovery' with all its local, contingent, social, psychological, and other such 'extraneous' factors. For they will then be able to argue in good conscience that Galileo was wrong – and Bellarmine right – as regards the differing importance they attached to the question of science's wider cultural and social responsibilities. That Galileo can be shown to have fudged certain issues in squaring his theory with the observational or experimental data is yet further reason, as Feyerabend sees it, for revising the doxastic account.[26] In short, it is only their failure of nerve – or the fact that Galileo's 'truth' won out in a culture increasingly prone to a naive and unquestioning faith in science – which has led the theologians to adopt this defensive (and undignified) posture of seeking to make belated amends. Much better they should stick to their original position and argue that the Church was entirely justified (on social, moral, and doctrinal grounds) in demanding Galileo's retraction of a thesis which threatened to subvert the entire existing order of social and religious values.

It should, I suppose, be accounted a virtue in Feyerabend's work that it pushes right through with this relativist (or anarchist) debunking of scientific truth-claims and thus brings out some of the manifest absurdities to which such arguments lead. One could take a certain mischievous pleasure in listing all the items of belief – from mistaken but in their own time respectable scientific theories to the whole range of crackpot, superstitious, or 'paranormal' claims – which on his account would possess as good a title to 'truth' as anything currently accorded that status. But my purpose here is not to set Feyerabend up as an all-too-easy target. Rather, it is to show that his position follows logically enough from those other – on the face of it less 'radical' – arguments that would relativize truth to the operative norms (or the discourse-specific criteria) of some particular language-game, interpretive community, or cultural 'form of life'.[27] For these arguments likewise entail the view that there is ultimately no difference – in pragmatist terms, no difference that makes any difference – between the context of discovery for scientific truth-claims and the context of justification wherein those claims are purportedly tested (confirmed or falsified) by experiment, observation, and various forms of inductive reasoning or hypothetico-deductive inference.[28] In which case one might as well go the whole hog with Feyerabend and concede that scientific 'truth' *just is* a product of whatever convictions and beliefs happen to have captured the cultural high ground at any given time. Moreover, the way is then open to those varieties of crudely reductive psycho-biographical account that would discover the origin – the formative matrix – of a scientist's thinking in some crucial (hitherto neglected) fact about his or her childhood experience, sexual orientation, religious beliefs, or whatever. All that is needed in order to accommodate this to the conventionalist ('interpretive community') view is the argument that certain individual fixations have a kind of diffusive self-propagating power which enables them to take hold in just the same way that religious beliefs gain credence.

One of the best short answers to this whole way of thinking is to be found in William Empson's 1930 review of E.A. Burtt's book *The Metaphysical Foundations of Modern Science*.[29] It is all the more apposite since Burtt takes a line which in many ways anticipates Feyerabend on the pre-rational origins of scientific 'reason', on the ubiquity of religious preoccupations in the discourse of early modern science, and also on the claim of psycho-biography to reveal the deepest springs or motivating sources of scientific thought. On the contrary, Empson writes: 'it is unsafe to explain discovery in terms of a man's intellectual preconceptions, because the act of discovery is precisely that of stepping outside preconceptions'.[30] Like Feyerabend, Burtt sees science as enjoying a degree of institutional and cultural prestige that has led to both a harmful disenchantment of the world – through its undermining of traditional beliefs – and a range of undesirable social and ethical consequences. Thus he aims to cut this leviathan down to size by showing on the one hand how its origins lie in various sorts of neurosis, private obsession, or displaced sexual fantasy, and on the other how science has acquired a mystique – an aura of infallibility – which differs scarcely at all from that of the more dogmatic theological systems. However, as Empson points out, this analysis begs all the relevant questions as to what constitutes an adequate *explanation* for just those features of the scientific worldview that Burtt would trace back to their pre-scientific (religious or psychological) sources.

Mr Burtt hopes that the problems of materialism and determinism, that the Ice Age of the imagination which the sciences seemed to impose, will be resolved by a study of the adolescent fantasies of Kepler. Certainly this may be one front of the war, but it can hardly be an important one; the stress on history is fallacious here, because just that 'present knowledge', in the light of which he interprets his history (but which he assumes almost without recognising) is the real parent of his conclusions.[31]

In other words Burtt is claiming scientific (or at any rate rationally warranted) status for an argument that overtly impugns all the bases of science and rational warrant.

Empson is not entirely averse to such arguments – whether pyschoanalytic or sociological – just so long as they acknowledge (as Burtt fails to do) the extent to which their own understanding draws upon given explanatory models. His complaint finds an echo in Bruno Latour's recent book *We Have Never Been Modern*, where the point is made with regard to those putatively 'postmodern' sceptical debunkers of science who will always shift back – when need arises – to some favoured brand of scientific argument.[32] Hence what Latour sees as the chronic oscillation in their work between a 'hard' sociological approach to the culturally-constructed character of the natural sciences and a 'soft' inclination to exempt this approach from any question concerning its own social or cultural determinants. On this view, as he puts it, 'society has to produce everything arbitrarily including the cosmic order, biology, chemistry, and the laws of physics!'.[33] But such approaches run up against the obvious problem: that this deprives them of the necessary conceptual resources whereby to theorize the relationship between 'nature' and 'culture', or wherewith to explain (on their own 'scientific' terms) how science plays a role in the social construction of these various kinds of quasi-knowledge. Could it then be the case, Latour wonders,

> [that] social scientists have simply forgotten that before projecting itself onto things society has to be made, built, constructed? And out of what material could it be built if not out of non-social, non-human resources? But social theory is forbidden to draw this conclusion because it has no conception of objects except the one handed down by the alternative 'hard' sciences which are so strong that they simply determine social order which in turn becomes flimsy and immaterial.[34]

It is the same objection that Empson brings against reductive (sociological or psychobiographical) accounts of scientific discovery which in effect leave nothing to be discovered save the social construction – or the culture-specific character – of all sorts of knowledge, their own necessarily included. These accounts merely invert the usual, 'naive' or 'commonsense' order of priorities which attributes factual or veridical status to the truth-claims of the natural sciences and which tends to regard the humanistic disciplines (anthropology, sociology, history, psychology or literary criticism) as primarily aimed toward interpretation and therefore as possessed of no such 'hard' predictive or explanatory power. But in so doing – in emptying 'science' of its every last cognitive claim – they manage unwittingly to reveal 'how badly constructed was the social theory as well as the epistemology that went with those denunciations'.[35] For at this point the phrase (and the discipline) 'sociology of science' turns out to be wholly devoid of content, a pseudo-discipline sadly embarked upon elaborating theories of its own demise in the absence of anything that could possibly serve as an object for explanatory treatment.

Latour offers the notion of 'quasi-objects', a realm ontologically midway, so to speak, between *realia* assumed to exist independently of human social or knowledge-constitutive interests, and those objects that are otherwise construed – e.g. by the 'strong programme' in sociology of knowledge – as existing only relative to this or that research-programme or wider community of knowledge. Such entities, he writes,

> are much more social, much more fabricated, much more collective than the 'hard' parts of nature, but they are in no way the arbitrary receptacles of a full-fledged society. On the other hand they are much more real, nonhuman and objective than those shapeless screens on which society – for unknown reasons – needed to be 'projected'.[36]

This argument is all the more striking for the fact that Latour is himself best known for his essays in the sociology of science or on the localized contexts of scientific knowledge-production.[37] Empson is a good deal sturdier in his defence of scientific realism, although – as I have said – he is quite willing to acknowledge that sociology (and even psychobiography) may turn up some interesting facts about the way that scientists go about their work. Where the error takes hold – and here he agrees with Latour – is with the further move that would treat those facts as a pretext for simply collapsing the distinction between context of discovery and context of justification, and which would thus view scientific truth as a product of the various motivating interests (religious, metaphysical, private-obsessional or whatever) whose relevance is, or ought to be, wholly confined to the former sphere. 'This sort of approach', Empson writes, 'would maintain that the Newtonian system was the fantasy of a man who escaped dementia praecox only by a successful externalisation into mathematics'. But it would also need to explain 'in what way such a system is likely to be unsatisfying to normally sexed people; why, for instance, it is such an annoyance to Mr Burtt'.[38] In other words, this line of thought has the awkward (self-implicating) consequence that any 'explanations' offered will always reflect some predisposed bias, some fixed *parti pris* in the investigator's mind that results from his or her social conditioning, fantasy-repertoire, or habits of psychological projection.

The argument thus reduces to manifest absurdity for just those reasons pointed out by Latour. On the one hand it fails the most elementary test of explaining how science has actually produced a working account of certain real-world objects, processes, and events which even the sceptic can hardly treat as just a product of transient social forces or subliminal drives. (Perhaps one should modify this claim, with Feyerabend in mind, and suggest rather that where scepticism is pushed that far the reason is to be sought, not in 'science' and its socio- or psycho-pathological aspects, but in the mind-set of those who carry the crusade against science to such obsessive and implausible lengths.) On the other hand it fails *even by its own criteria* to provide any adequate explanatory account of how particular instances of scientific thought may be influenced by factors in the psychological or social realm. For in order to do this it would need to find room for the distinction between truth and falsehood, science and ideology, genuinely knowledge-constitutive interests and those other sorts of interest that deflect science from its truth-seeking aim.

Such is Latour's intention in speaking about the realm of 'quasi-objects' as the locus where a qualified realist ontology can make terms with a sociology of science that avoids these self-disabling aporias and thus still provides itself with something to explain. The case is made yet more convincingly by Roy Bhaskar when he argues for critical realism as the best – indeed the only viable – solution to these sceptical-relativist dilemmas. What is required, according to Bhaskar, is a 'stratified' ontology that makes full allowance for the range of differing relations between scientific knowledge and the object-domain that constitutes its field of enquiry.[39] On the one hand that domain exhibits aspects or properties – 'intransitive' features as Bhaskar terms them – which are characterized chiefly by their sheer *materiality*, or their obdurate resistance to alternative (e.g., sociological) modes of explana-tion. On the other it still leaves room for locating those blindspots of ideological prejudice – those illlusions brought about by dogmatic adherence to a narrowly positivist paradigm – which can then be shown up through critical treatment in the social-diagnostic mode. As Bhaskar puts it:

> facts are real, but they are historically specific social realities. . . . Fetishism, by naturalizing facts, at once collapses and so destratifies their generative or sustaining social context and the mode of their production, reproduction, and transformation in time, *ipso facto* dehistoricizing and eternalizing them. The fact form then acts so as to obscure, from scientists and non-scientists alike, the historically specific (cognitive and non-cognitive) structures and relations governing sense-experience in science.[40]

Otherwise philosophy of science is condemned perpetually to oscillate between a naive or unself-critical positivism and a fargone cultural-relativist approach that views 'reality' as nothing more than a product of the various discourses, paradigms, or social constructions which jostle for supremacy at any given time.

No doubt there is a need – an ethical and socio-political need – to demystify those false self-images of science (positivism chief among them) which have led to the various crises and dilemmas diagnosed by critics from Adorno and Horkheimer to the present.[41] However such criticism will lack any purpose (becoming, in effect, just a mirror-image of that same positivist error) if it equates 'science' with a mode of purely instrumental or means-end rationality, one that by very definition excludes all concern with issues in the ethico-political domain. Bhaskar thus agrees with Habermas in rejecting that grossly reductive view of modernity and its discontents which led Adorno and Horkheimer to interpret the so-called 'dialectic of enlightenment' as a monologic discourse irredeemably bent upon subjugating nature and humanity alike to its iron-cage technocratic rule.[42] What such arguments ignore – even more so in the case of out-and-out sceptics like Feyerabend – is the whole range of complex inter-articulated truth-claims, interests, and values that developed within that discourse and which still provide a forum (a 'public sphere') for the continued debate about science and its wider social responsibilities.

Thus Bhaskar again:

> Facts are indeed paradigmatic social institutions. They are *real*, in as much as but for them certain determinate states of the physical world, for which our intellectual agency is a necessary condition, could not occur. They are *social*, in as much as, though dependent upon human agency, they are irreducible to a purely individual production. But although all facts are social results, not every social result is a fact: facts are the results of specific cognitive, and especially empirically grounded, processes of social production.[43]

It is because they adopt such a bleakly determinist or single-track notion of scientific 'reason' that Adorno and Horkheimer find themselves compelled to denounce the heritage of Enlightenment thought even while implicitly invoking its critical resources. (Hence what Habermas shrewdly diagnoses as the 'performative contradiction' everywhere manifest in their work.) And the case is yet worse with those adepts of the postmodern turn in philosophy or sociology of science who celebrate the freedoms to be had by declaring an end to the oppressive regime of truth, reality, reason, logical consistency, and other such obsolete values. For it then becomes possible – as I have argued above – for arch-debunkers like Feyerabend to endorse the most regressive and authoritarian of irrationalist creeds just so long as they serve to deflate the image of a caricatured 'scientific' reason.

This is why Bhaskar sees a close link (or a mutually supportive relation) between the critical-realist stance in philosophy of science and the values of emancipatory critique in the socio-political sphere. On the postmodern view these positions would appear diametrically opposed, since any form of realism – no matter how nuanced or critical – necessarily figures to this way of thinking as a sell-out to the authoritarian discourse of scientific reason and truth, and hence as lending support to the current institutional status quo. In so far as such thinking operates (as most often it does) with an implicit left-to-right scale of political values, the assumption is roughly that 'right' epistemologies are sure to be realist and truth-based, while left-leaning sociologies of knowledge are marked by their willingness to abandon that entire (outmoded and inherently authoritarian) mindset. For Bhaskar, on the contrary, nothing could be less conducive to the interests of human emancipation than this attitude that counts reality a world well lost in order to assert the conventional, the arbitrary, the discursively or socially-constructed character of all scientific truth-claims. On the one hand it invites all the familiar counter-arguments – the charges of inconsistency, self-contradiction, or commitment to a range of strictly unthinkable conse-quences – which have standardly been brought against relativists of various stripe by philosophers through the ages. On the other, more specifically, it fails to acknowledge that the *precondition* for holding science accountable to ethical or socio-political values is that science should be recognised as also possessing its own criteria of truth, method, and responsible enquiry. These latter would include the requirement – rejected derisively by Feyerabend – that it should *not* cave in to the dictates of conformist (e.g. state-sponsored or theologically-sanctioned) belief. Rather it is – or it should be – committed to questioning the truth of such beliefs wherever they conflict with the best evidence to hand or the theory that best explains or accom-modates that evidence.

Of course there is the standard sceptical move at this point which consists in denying (with Feyerabend and the 'strong' sociologists of knowledge) that such theories or evidence can ever break free of their own cultural context. Otherwise the sceptic may assert, like Quine, that what counts as 'evidence' can only be construed in relation to some one of a range of possible theories, all of which 'fit the facts' as construed by their own ontological or conceptual scheme, and none of which can therefore lay exclusive claim to evidential or explanatory warrant.[44] Thus it follows – on this view – that 'facts' and 'theories' are equally underdetermined, and that philosophy of science has no choice but to relativize truth to some holistic account of how various items hang together in the framework of accredited belief. From here, it might seem, the only choice of escape-routes is one that falls out between Quine's scientifically face-saving (but epistemologically vacuous) appeal to a crude physicalist theory of meaning, perception, and knowledge-acquisition, or – on the other hand – Feyerabend's strain of free-for-all 'anarchist' licence. I have argued that both options are misconceived and that neither provides an adequate approach to the history and philosophy of science. Moreover, they leave no room for any genuine (informed and socially-responsive) criticism of science that would avoid the self-disabling relativist upshot – or the attitude of downright hostility —manifest in so much recent discussion of these topics. For if the truth-claims of science are warranted only by their social acceptability (or by their happening to fit with this or that view of what is good in the way of belief) then the same must apply to those criticisms mounted in the name of some better, more acceptable conception of the human good. In which case – witness Feyerabend's treatment of the issue between Bellarmine and Galileo –there can be no appeal beyond the authority of those best placed to enforce (or to propagate) their views.

III

My purpose here has *not* been to reject all forms of interdisciplinary endeavour, nor to recommend that we return to some narrowly orthodox view of the disciplines and their proper (knowledge-constitutive) remit. Such an argument is plainly untenable given the extent to which present-day knowledge – in the natural and human sciences alike – involves all manner of cross-disciplinary ventures and exchanges. Thus molecular biologists can scarcely manage without a fairly advanced understanding of atomic or subatomic physics, and historians would clearly do well to read up on the latest ideas in literary theory and narrative poetics, if only in order to strengthen their arguments against the more extreme and damaging forms of postmodern-sceptical-revisionist doctrine.[45] Philosophers of science have much to learn from historians of science, and both may profit – on occasion at least – from the sorts of case-history standardly adduced by 'strong' sociologists of knowledge. On the positive side they can become more aware of how scientists respond to various pressures of circumstance, social conditions, ideological belief-systems, etc. On the negative side – through a critical reading – they can observe some of the errors which result from an approach that simply conflates the two contexts of discovery and justification.[46]

What I have emphasised, rather, is the need to maintain some grasp of the specific differences between disciplines – differences of scope, method, interest, evidential criteria, explanatory warrant, and justified inference – rather than treating them as so many 'discourses' whose truth-claims can then be 'deconstructed' in accordance with the latest social-sciences or cultural-studies wisdom. Such arguments are often advanced in a spirit of progressive or liberating zeal, as if the word 'discipline' – as used in the university or scientific context – were pretty much synonymous with 'discipline' as a means of repression, surveillance, or social control. Foucault must undoubtedly take some of the blame here although his writings on the topic can better be seen as part of a much wider and deeper cultural-relativist trend. From this viewpoint 'power' and 'knowledge' are strictly indissociable terms, always and everywhere enmeshed in structures of internalized subjection to authority.[47] The effect of such thinking is to rule out the prospect that some kinds of knowledge may be oriented both toward truth and toward the interests of human wellbeing through their critical-emancipatory character.

It is this idea – sustained in the discourse of critical intellectuals from Kant to Habermas – that needs to be defended against a whole range of present-day attacks. These may come from governments anxious to restrict freedom of enquiry; from adminstrators bent upon moulding curricula to the shape of their own market-led ambitions; from adepts of the new interdisciplinarity as a matter of knowing not very much about everything in general; or again, from the proponents of a cultural-relativist agenda with its own distinctly hegemonic designs. There can be no doubt that the 'idea of the university' has nowadays fallen upon hard times. Whether or not it survives these assaults is a question closely linked to the prospects for change in a culture very largely given over to the dominance of unthinking bureaucratic rationality.

CHAPTER 6

Ethics, Autonomy and Self-Invention: debating Foucault

I

This chapter is a revised and expanded version of my response to an essay by Patrick Shaw entitled 'Whatever Happened to the French Foucault? Norris on Foucault'.[1] Shaw raised some challenging points with regard to an earlier article of mine where I had discussed – among other things – Foucault's variously angled misreadings of Kant, his aestheticised conception of ethics (Kant *avec* Baudelaire!) as a realm of private cultivation or 'care of the self', his quarrel with the values of enlightened critical modernity, and the lack of any adequate normative dimension by which to assess his more 'radical' claims in the socio-political sphere.[2] Moreover this might help to explain why Foucault's thought was itself open to so many sharply divergent readings, all of them offering a fair show of textual-interpretative warrant. These commentaries have spanned the whole range from those on the Nietzschean post-structuralist cultural left who take its self-proclaimed radicalism pretty much at face value to those of a liberal-quietist persuasion – like Richard Rorty – who play up the theme of aesthetic self-fashioning and hence play down the idea of Foucault as a significant political thinker.[3] Thus Rorty recommends that we politely ignore all that *soi-disant* 'radical' stuff and treat Foucault as a true Baudelairean aesthete at heart who sometimes displayed an unfortunate desire to interpret his private predilections as the basis for a full-scale transvaluation of ethico-political values.[4]

No doubt this reading gets Foucault wrong by all the usual standards of interpretative truth and fidelity to author's intent. Moreover, it is an ideologically-motivated reading which sins against the basic Kantian requirement that we should treat texts (like persons) as ends in themselves rather than as merely the convenient means to some overriding strategy or purpose on the strong-willed interpreter's part. Yet of course this requirement is one that Foucault himself treated with scant respect not only in his dealings with Kant but also through his generalized Nietzschean belief that such talk was merely the lip-service paid by pious exegetes whose motivating interests were pursued under cover of a specious truth-regarding rhetoric.[5] My own view – to which Shaw took exception – was that Foucault had boxed himself into a corner by adopting an all-out sceptical stance which left him in the classic relativist predicament of implicitly denying the truth or validity of each and every statement in his own work, whether as regards matters of historical fact or judgements of an ethico-political character. Such objections have often been brought against him by other critics, notably by Jürgen Habermas and Karl-Otto Apel who point out the kinds of 'performative contradiction' (i.e., the self-refuting paradoxes) that always result when such sceptical doctrines are held accountable to the basic requirement of making sense by their own methodological or interpretative lights.[6] In Foucault's case – as in Nietzsche's before him – this problem tends to escape notice through the sheer rhetorical energy of his writing and also by the fact that he maintains a certain protective distance between his Nietzsche-inspired 'genealogical' assaults on the name and nature of truth and his other, more patiently documented studies of various episodes in the history of medicine, psychiatric practice, or the human, social, and natural sciences.[7] All the same it is a genuine problem and one that clearly invites the kind of 'trans-cendental *tu quoque*' or double-standard charge levelled at him by Habermas and Apel.

I should mention that Shaw has himself written about the place of logical reasoning in everyday practical and communicative contexts, as well as about the limits of logic – at any rate the kinds of text-book logic codified by theorists from Aristotle down – when it comes to more complex (non-codifiable) matters of rational judgement or evaluative choice.[8] Indeed, having now read some of Shaw's work in this field, I am rather less sure as to just where he stands with regard to Foucault's manifest strain of Nietzsche-inspired irrationalism, his invocation of rhetoric as a counter-term to the strictures of logical argument, and his downright refusal (at least in those middle-period genealogical writings) to abide by the ground-rules – not merely the 'conventions' – of reasoned critical debate. Most likely – I conclude – Shaw was less concerned to vindicate Foucault's Nietzschean ethics and politics than to point out the kinds of logical problem that arise when commentators such as myself lay claim to a 'truth' of the Foucauldian text while none the less rejecting certain salient aspects of Foucault's thought. At any rate Shaw's essay sent me back to these issues with a renewed sense of the challenge they pose, in particular for anyone who wants to argue that some (e.g., Rorty-style) revisionist readings quite definitely get Foucault wrong whereas others (e.g., their own!) possess adequate inter-pretative warrant in virtue of perceiving the issues more clearly or correcting for certain unfortunate lapses or biases.

Such approaches in the mode of 'rational reconstruction' are common enough among philosophers in the Anglophone analytic tradition where they often take the form of a highly selective (and at times sharply dismissive) treatment of earlier thinkers' work.[9] They are often frowned upon by those in the 'other' (continental or mainland-European) tradition who adopt a more hermeneutical method of enquiry, that is to say, an approach that on principle holds itself open to ideas, beliefs, and presuppositions which fail to match up with our present-day canons of rational warrant.[10] Yet of course there are some in the 'continental' camp – Habermas preeminent among them – who would accept the hermeneutical argument up to a point while none the less maintaining (very much in the Kantian critical line of descent) that we can and should distinguish true from false beliefs, or valid from invalid modes of intersubjective agreement.[11] It seemed to me that Shaw's essay approached these issues from an interesting angle and that therefore it was worth recasting my response in a form that would make the whole discussion more accessible by including some fairly extensive quotations from his text. I have also enlarged on various points in order to clarify their relevance to other main lines of argument in this book.

II

Shaw's case can be summarised as follows, I hope without undue simpli-fication. What he chiefly objects to is my failure (as he sees it) to credit Foucault with a 'radically committed Nietzschean approach' to issues of truth, ethics, and political conduct. My argument purportedly goes off the rails by assuming that this Nietzschean stance leads to a 'private-aestheticist' conception of the self, i.e., a quest for perfection of the individual life as if it were a work of art, cut off from any active engagement with ethical or socio-political concerns.[12] Moreover I get Foucault wrong on a number of crucial points, among them (1) his relation to Kant and the discourse of 'enlightened' critical modernity; (2) his thinking of 'inhuman thoughts' which Shaw takes as evidence of Foucault's 'radicalism' as opposed to my quaint liberal attachment to humanist values; and (3) the fact that he (Foucault) rejects any version of the Rortian compromise deal whereby 'strong' self-shapers in the private realm can be safely left to their own devices just so long as they do it 'on their own time' and don't presume to legislate for other people by setting up as universal intellectuals in the bad old 'enlightenment' style.[13]

Things get rather complicated here since I criticise Rorty's version of 'liberalism' on just these grounds – that it severs the link between private and public domains – while agreeing with Shaw that it goes the wrong way around in attempting to tame or domesticate Foucault for (US-style) 'liberal' consumption. However – according to Shaw – my own argument is much closer to Rorty's than might appear since I fall back on the same false dichotomy through my talk of Foucault as a 'private-aestheticist' thinker betrayed into an outlook of ethico-political quietism by his Nietzschean idea of the strong individual as a solitary transvaluer of values who is thereby cut off from any active participation in matters of shared public concern. 'Having begun by giving weight to Foucault's radicalism, he [Norris] comes to minimize it, regarding it as an aberration, and so ends up by himself subscribing to a large extent to what he had previously regarded as a misreading.' (Shaw, p. 280)

So the charge-sheet – in sum – is that I make too much of the Kantian connection, fail to recognise the Nietzschean 'radical' strain, and fall in eventually (despite my own misgivings) with Rorty's idea of Foucault as a strong self-inventor at heart who 'occasionally succumb[s] to the temptation of trying to find a public counterpart to his private search' (cited by Shaw, p. 279). On this last point I am fully in agreement with Shaw: that 'when Rorty accuses Foucault of succumbing to temptation it is by the light of Rorty's own liberalism that the charge is made', and moreover that, 'if so, then he is clearly begging the question' (ibid). In fact I spend a good deal of time – in that article and elsewhere – explaining what I think is wrong with Rorty's liberalism and also why I think he misreads Foucault in certain significant respects.[14] However my point is that Foucault's 'radicalism' is none the less open to just such a reading since it lacks any adequate *normative* dimension – any reasoned and principled approach to these issues – that would give it a more than notional or rhetorical force. On Shaw's account I start out 'by showing due scepticism of Rorty's assimilation of Foucault to the pragmatist agenda', but then 'in the course of a few pages . . . completely switch tack, playing up the theme of aesthetic self-invention and ignoring [the] Nietzschean elements' (Shaw, p. 280). However, in my view it is just those 'Nietzschean elements' that enable Rorty to argue his case with at least some degree of plausibility. That is to say, it is the theme of self-invention (or 'care of the self'), so central to Foucault's later thought, which gives Rorty his handle for claiming that one need not worry too much about all the barnstorming rhetoric just so long as one keeps a liberal eye on the private/ public distinction and puts his occasional lapses down to moments of wayward 'temptation'. This attitude is 'quietist' in so far as it envisages self-invention as an activity that is played out *despite and against* the encroaching pressures of a public sphere conceived to exist *outside and beyond* the realm of aesthetic self-fulfilment. I do indeed think – for reasons set out elsewhere in this book – that Kant is a much better source of guidance here and that Foucault's various misreadings of Kant are indicative of problems with his own ethico-political agenda, early and late.

Now one may well agree – especially in light of Nietzsche's latterday reception history – that strong self-inventors, while often inspiring, are not the most reliable of role-models in the conduct of our everyday civic and moral lives. Thus we had better look elsewhere (as Rorty would have it, to boringly 'constructive' thinkers like Kant, Habermas or Rawls) if we want help in formulating ethical codes or advice on drawing up sound laws and constitutional principles.[15] But this is to pose yet another of those sharp dichotomies which Shaw quite rightly wants to avoid since they go along with Rorty's particular kind of liberal-pragmatist quietism, i.e., his idea of 'radical' self-invention as something that can best (most safely) be indulged in strict quarantine from the public sphere of rights, duties, and ethico-political obligations. For it is hard to see how Foucault can hope to bridge this divide, given his redefinition of 'autonomy' in terms of aesthetic self-fashioning rather than in terms of a wider responsibility to interests and values transcending those of the isolated 'private' individual.[16]

Shaw thinks that I force this dilemma on Foucault by framing the issues in a way that reflects both my Kantian assumptions and my refusal to accept the elements of Nietzschean 'radicalism' that lift his thought onto an altogether different plane. Thus I am just flat wrong (Shaw maintains) in suggesting that 'the Nietzschean elements in Foucault *rule out* political radicalism', and that 'the only way that Foucault is able to retain any sort of radical stance is through his inability fully to exorcise the ghost of Kant' (Shaw, p. 283). To which I am tempted to respond: well, it all depends on what you mean by 'radicalism'. Of course I wouldn't for a moment deny that Foucault's thinking is 'radical' in the sense that it entails a transvaluation of such basic concepts as truth, knowledge, power, agency, selfhood, and ethical responsibility. Nor would I deny that this transvaluation might have far-reaching effects if he managed to persuade a sizable proportion of his readers to adopt something like the same attitude. What I cannot accept is Shaw's idea – everywhere implicit in his article though nowhere explained or justified – that a radicalism of this sort has substantive ethico-political implications. After all there are radicals left and right, not to mention those of the self-styled 'radical' social-democratic or Blairite 'Third-Way' centre.

In this connection it is perhaps worth recalling that Foucault's record of political judgements – for instance, his enthusiasm for the Iranian Revolution – was scarcely such as to inspire great confidence in his powers of realistic assessment or evaluative grasp.[17] Also there is a fair amount of evidence – not only from the more sensationalist or prurient biographical sources – that his quest for self-knowledge through forms of extreme sexual experience was one that may well have carried large risks for others beside himself.[18] At any rate – more to the point – it is far from clear that Foucault's 'radicalism' entailed any kind of ethico-political commitment beyond a desire to challenge and subvert disciplinary regimes or institutional discourses of power/knowledge. This criticism has most often been voiced by critics of a broadly liberal or communitarian persuasion – like Michael Walzer – whom Shaw would no doubt regard as incapable of reading the radical Foucault except by their own dimly revisionist lights.[19] However it is a charge that has also been brought by those on the political left – whether Marxists, feminists, or critical theorists such as Habermas – who are likewise alert to the dangers of a sheerly reactive oppositional discourse that lacks any adequate normative or justificatory grounds.[20] For this leads to the idea of resistance or subversion as 'radical' ends in themselves, quite aside from any question as to the nature (the specific political or ethical character) of the regime, discourse, or value-system against which such efforts are directed. After all there are cases – like Spain during the 1930s or Chile during the 1970s – where the will to resist took a violently authoritarian and anti-democratic form, and where the antecedent structures of state power must surely be seen as benign in comparison.

Foucault's curious blindness in this regard goes along with his Nietzsche-derived concept of power as an all-pervasive 'capillary' force that reaches into every last crevice of our public, social, and private lives.[21] Hence his idea of liberal democracy and the welfare state as merely another, more efficient means of extending the mechanisms of social control to a point where subjects become the willing agents of their own self-imposed disciplinary regimes. Hence also his drastically levelling conception of political power, tending as it does to equate all forms of adminstered social change or governmentality with the workings of a totalitarian system whose model is that of the Gulag Archipelago. This results directly from Foucault's undiffer-entiating rhetoric of power/knowledge, a rhetoric which in turn takes its chief inspiration from Nietzsche's sceptical-relativist assault on the values of enlightenment thought as developed in Kant's critical and practical philos-ophy.[22] Thus Shaw is perfectly true to Nietzsche and Foucault in rejecting any notion of autonomous selfhood or agency that would involve an appeal to such values or to the Kantian modalities of knowledge, reason, and judgement.[23] However this leaves him hard put to explain how subjects could possibly achieve the will to resist those instituted structures of power/ knowledge which, according to Foucault, define their very sense of public and private identity. The only route left open is a recourse to the kind of quasi-ethical stance that seeks to transcend these problems by adopting a rhetoric of 'strong' self-creation with its primary sources in Nietzsche, Baudelaire, and nineteenth-century romantic-symbolist aesthetics.

In short, Foucault's Hobbesian construal of power/knowledge is such as to preclude any viable account of the complex relationship that Kant perceives between knowledge-constitutive interests and the normative dimension of practical reason or ethico-political thought.[24] This is why Foucault's 'radicalism' – like Nietzsche's before him – is so lacking in substantive content and prone to the kind of decisionist vagaries that marked his well-documented record of involvement in various (often short-lived) movements and causes.[25] It is also no doubt why his work has exerted such widespread influence across a range of political positions – left and right – all of which can plausibly lay some claim to the 'radical' Foucault. Again Nietzsche's reception-history should be enough to make the point, along with that of Heidegger who was – we may recall – a major influence on

Foucault's thinking, early and late, but who doesn't figure anywhere in Shaw's account.[26] No doubt it is the case, as Shaw says, that 'if the Nietzschean influence is really paramount', then 'Foucault is not simply endorsing liberalism when he condemns the search for a common, binding morality'; moreover, that 'his words must bear a more radical interpretation than Rorty wishes to give them, and the attack on moral obligation must be taken at face value' (Shaw, p. 277). But to interpret those words 'at face value' – i.e., in keeping with Foucault's intent – doesn't entail that *the reader* should endorse them or accept this Nietzschean doctrine of 'strong' self-creation as the only alternative to Rorty's liberal-quietist gloss. Rather one could argue that this is just another false dilemma brought about by Foucault's narrow conception of the scope for active political engagement beyond that private sphere. This is why Rorty can present his drastically dichotomised reading of Foucault – and likewise of other 'strong-revisionist' thinkers like Nietzsche and Heidegger – as the best way of keeping them from doing harm, or of making sure that these ideas about radical self-invention don't get a hold in the public sphere where they might cause all sorts of mischief.[27]

Of course this would strike the activist Foucault as a typically 'liberal' strategy of evasion, a device for maintaining that 'proper' separation of realms (aesthetic, ethical, juridical, constitutional and so forth) which has always served the interests of a repressive and conservative social order. 'On this more radical view', as Shaw writes, 'liberalism is itself part of the framework which must be overcome in the task of self-invention.' (p. 277) But again one may ask why the issue should be posed in such sharply polarised terms. After all, on the face of it, there is no good reason – temperamental bias apart – for denying that people can achieve a fair measure of authenticity in their ethical and socio-political lives while *neither* caving in to the values of consensus-based 'liberal' thought *nor* striking out on a solitary path that sets them at odds with every last precept of moral and social custom. Shaw accepts this Foucauldian view – accepts it 'at face value' – and therefore concludes that when I beg to dissent it must be because, despite all my criticisms of Rorty, I am urging something like the Rortian approach, that is to say, the idea that we should admire Foucault for his performance as a Nietzschean strong self-inventor while tactfully ignoring his political claims. Thus 'Norris thinks that Foucault is faced with a genuine problem of how self-invention is possible *and that Rorty can be read as pointing towards a promising way of solving it*' (p. 281; Shaw's italics). Well yes, sure enough, I think that there is a 'genuine problem' with Foucault's idea of radical self-invention and one with potentially dire implications for the conduct of our ethical, social, and political lives. But no, far from it: I think that Rorty's proposed 'solution' in effect gives us the worst of both worlds, offering as it does a wildly implausible account of

Foucault's beliefs while endorsing a dichotomy between private and public spheres which amounts to just a pretext for cynical disengagement on the part of those 'liberal ironists' (Rorty's phrase) who have long since abandoned any hope of achieving a better, more just and equitable state of society. It seem to me that I am here not so much being hoist with my own petard as blamed for certain problems with Foucault's project which Rorty is then plausibly able to exploit for his own *soi-disant* 'liberal' purposes.

III

Oddly enough Shaw himself subscribes to something very like the Rortian dualism of 'private' *versus* 'public' realms, or the distinction between what strong self-inventors (like Foucault) can safely be allowed to get up to 'on their own time' and what good liberals should properly regard as the limits placed upon self-cultivation by a due concern with obligations in the wider civic or ethico-political sphere. On the one hand, '[t]he assumption of an interesting connection between what matters most and one's obligations to others may not be necessary if one approaches the matter from within the liberal perspective' (Shaw, p. 277). On the other, '[s]elf-invention might require the thinking of inhuman thoughts, acting in ways which go beyond good and evil' (p. 278). So far as Shaw is concerned, following Nietzsche and Foucault, it is this latter possibility which opens up the prospect of truly 'radical' thinking, while the former (Rorty-style) compromise doctrine is both false to Foucault and devoid of such genuinely radical force. Yet here again Shaw takes it that these alternatives exhaust the field and hence that if one doesn't go along with Rorty's weak-revisionist reading of Foucault then one must surely accept the Foucauldian doctrine in its full-blown Nietzschean (strong-revisionist) form.

Thus, according to Shaw, 'there is no good reason ... to abandon the French reading of Foucault, the Foucault whose radical inspiration is Nietzsche', since 'Rorty's attempt to construe him [Foucault] as a quasi-liberal is not very cogent even on its own terms' (p. 279). However there remains the third possibility of a *critical* reading of Foucault that would fully acknowledge the inadequacy of Rorty's account, and also the fact that the 'French' (Nietzsche-inspired) construal is more faithful to Foucault's intentions, while none the less denying that Foucault is justified when he poses the issues in a way that gives rise to such a drastic choice between equally bad alternatives. As Shaw sees it, 'the Nietzsche-inspired, French Foucault precisely *must* transcend the cultural consensus which, for Rorty, provides the limit of intelligibility. He must be prepared to think inhuman thoughts. He must somehow think the unthinkable' (p. 280). I have no quarrel with this as a summary/paraphrase of Foucault's Nietzschean aspirations, any more than with Shaw's claim that the Rortian liberal-quietist reading is demonstrably way off-beam. But I don't think he makes an adequate case for counting it a strength in Foucault's work that it enables us somehow to 'think inhuman thoughts' or to push self-creation to the point of transvaluing every received ethical or socio-political value. In fact this is just the kind of pseudo-radical rhetoric that exerted such a powerful influence on the post-1968 generation of French intellectuals for whom Nietzsche and Heidegger seemed to offer a different, more exciting way forward from the political hopes that had once been invested in the 'discourse' of Marxist or left-activist thought.[28] In Foucault's case – as with many others, Lyotard among them – it produced a very marked anti-humanist reaction, that is to say, a belief that concepts of 'the human' went along with a drive to limit and contain any thought of radically alternative modes of existence or political engagement.[29] This is presumably what Shaw has in mind when he sides with the French-Nietzschean Foucault, one who has the courage to 'think inhuman thoughts' and to push right through with that transvaluation of human, all-too-human values which alone promises to bring us out 'beyond good and evil' as hitherto conceived.

However this strikes me as either just a kind of empty rhetorical posturing or, worse still, an incentive to modes of 'strong' antihumanist thought which – like Nietzsche's and Heidegger's – can easily be used to encourage or condone any kind of downright illiberal creed. So it is scarcely surprising, as I have said, that Foucault's record of political involvements includes not only his estimable work on behalf of various oppressed, marginalised, or 'deviant' minorities but also a phase of high hopes for Khomeini's Iranian Revolution and various other instances of misplaced 'radical' zeal.[30] Of course it would be wrong – exploiting the benefit of hindsight – to make too much of these lapses of political judgement or to use them (as hostile commentators often do) as a pretext for some pious disquisition on the follies committed by *engagé* intellectuals. Still there is a real problem about Foucault's idea of ethico-political commitment as somehow transpiring through an act of choice that has more to do with the project of individual self-invention than with the wider realm of shared (transindividually valid) interests, values, and concerns. Once again Shaw thinks that I am foisting this dilemma onto Foucault by taking it for granted that 'the alternative to reasoned argument and principled justification is a retreat from any sort of public engagement into private self-fashioning' (p. 284). Moreover, I under-rate the power of rhetoric as a formative influence on the way we conceive both our individual projects and our sense of their place in the wider social and political context. After all, Shaw remarks, a fifth-century BC Athenian would scarcely have taken this low view of rhetoric or considered it merely a suasive technique deployed for self-interested (private) ends and having no place in the public sphere of open participant debate. On the contrary, rhetoric was an eminently public art which allowed individuals to cultivate their personal gifts – to achieve the highest possible degree of self-fulfilment – while also promoting the welfare of the *polis*. Thus, according to Shaw, my devaluation of rhetoric goes along with my failure to grasp the relation between Foucault's emphasis on self-invention (alluding perhaps to the term *inventio* in its technical-rhetorical sense) and his equal stress on the scope this provides for active engagement in the ethico-political realm.

However this is not what I meant by 'rhetoric' as it figures in Foucault's writings. What I chiefly had in mind was the rhetorical (or linguistic-constructivist) 'turn' that has characterised a good deal of recent thinking in various disciplines and which has often drawn inspiration from Foucault's work. On this view everything is a construct of language, discourse, or representation since there is simply no access to the world or our experience of it except through discursively mediated forms of knowledge and representation.[31] Moreover, this extends to the whole range of concepts – such as choice, agency, will, commitment, rights, obligations, and so forth – that have figured in the various historically shifting configurations of ethico-political discourse which Foucault sets out to analyse in his early 'archaeologies' of knowledge and his later genealogical writings.[32] It was in this sense specifically – to pick up the point from Shaw – that I 'portray[ed] Foucault's Nietzscheanism as leading him into rhetoric rather than argument' (Shaw, p. 283). For the result of such a radically sceptical approach is to leave no room for attributing powers of reasoned and principled judgement, whether as concerns our grounds of knowledge in epistemological matters or our capacity for informed and responsible choice in the ethical-political sphere.

This is why I laid such stress on Foucault's revisionist readings of Kant, from *The Order of Things* (where he speaks of Kantian 'man' as that 'strange empirical-transcendental doublet') to late texts such as 'What Is Enlightenment' where he views Kant through a Nietzschean optic and – improbably enough – through a notion of radical autonomy derived from Baudelaire and the symbolist ethos of aesthetic self-fashioning.[33] It scarcely needs saying how remote this all is from Kant's conception of autonomous moral agency, that is, his requirement that practical reason should laid down rules for its own conduct in accordance with universal maxims and imperatives that transcend the merely 'heteronomous' promptings of individual taste or inclination.[34] Of course there are problems with this abstract-universalist conception of ethics, problems that were pointed out by Hegel and which have lately been rehearsed by proponents of alternative (e.g., virtue-based or communitarian) approaches. But they cannot be resolved by a doctrine, like Foucault's, that claims to go beyond all the vexing antinomies of Kantian moral philosophy through the appeal to a rhetoric of strong self-invention conceived – after Nietzsche and Baudelaire – as utterly transforming the scope and character of ethico-political discourse.

Thus, according to Shaw, I get Foucault wrong because I 'underestimate the resources for radicalism which are available from a Nietzschean perspective', and again, because 'as far as Norris is concerned, the Nietzschean element in Foucault rules out the thinking of inhuman thoughts, militating against radicalism rather than sustaining it' (Shaw, p. 276). This in turn goes along with my failure to recognise the power of rhetoric as a motivating force in the active transformation of moral, social, and political values. After all, as Shaw says, 'Foucault certainly engaged with public issues in his writings, presumably hoping to affect public outcomes; and this was not an unreasonable hope.' (p. 284) But the question remains as to what kinds of rhetoric might be deployed, and to what sorts of 'radical' end, if we follow Nietzsche's and Foucault's advice to give up our attachment to outmoded humanist beliefs and henceforth learn to 'think inhuman thoughts'. As I write Serbian paramilitaries are conducting a large-scale terrorist campaign against the Albanian population of Kossovo, a task to which no doubt they were enjoined by a state-sponsored rhetoric of xenophobic hatred that effectively silenced the voice of human, all-too-human ethical conscience. At the same time the citizens of the NATO member-countries are being urged by their governments through every kind of mass-media persuasion to endorse a senseless aerial bombardment of Belgrade and other Serbian cities whose only effect so far has been to worsen the whole situation by uniting the Serbs behind their hitherto unpopular leadership and creating yet more intense ethnic antagonisms. It seems to me that this example – one of many in the catalogue of man's inhumanity to man – should at least give pause to anyone tempted by the Nietzschean-Foucauldian-postmodernist rhetoric which equates 'radicalism' with the overcoming of liberal-humanist values or the capacity to 'think inhuman thoughts'.

Other critics of Foucault, Michael Walzer among them, have made the same point from a different angle when they note his curious failure to discriminate between different kinds of repressive or coercive disciplinary regime.[35] Thus, according to Foucault, it is the merest of 'liberal' illusions to suppose that that we have made any humanitarian progress from the feudal dispensation of babarous torments inflicted on the criminal's body in the name of sovereign power to those modern institutions – of community care, psychiatric medicine, remedial counselling, and so forth – which, if anything, involve a yet more brutal assault on the subject's most intimate thoughts and desires.[36] What this amounts to, again, is an levelling conception of power/knowledge which draws no distinction between the Gulag Archipelago (Foucault's favoured metaphor in this context) and the workings of internalised thought-control imposed by so-called liberal-humanist or social-democratic modes of displinary surveillance.

I cannot see that Shaw's case is much helped by his idea of rhetoric as a means of self-empowerment or an escape-route from the otherwise exitless prison of Foucault's linguistic-discursive determinism. 'Norris is surely wrong', he writes, 'to suppose that we can *choose* what to make of a piece of rhetoric. Rhetoric affects us regardless of our will. If the radical Foucault touches the right chords in us then we will come to see things differently and our framework of thought (including, perhaps, socio-political thought) will be destabilized.' (Shaw, p. 284) This passage seems to me a very striking example of the kinds of dilemma that Foucault runs into – and that he forces on his goodwilled exegetes – when attempting to carve out a space for human autonomy despite and against the ubiquitous workings of institutionalised power/knowledge. For if rhetoric is as powerful as all that – if it 'affects us regardless of our will' – then its 'destabilising' force will be something entirely beyond our control and just as likely to produce some new and unprecedented reign of terror as to move things in a different, more progressive or politically enabling direction. Indeed, the whole force of Foucault's argument is to treat such comparative value-judgements as merely a product of that old-style liberal-humanist mindset which fails to acknowledge its own hopelessly deluded and obsolescent character. However it is then hard to see what remains of Shaw's case for the power of rhetoric as a means of 'radically' transforming our sense of ethical, social, and political possibility. For it is precisely his point in the above-quoted passage that rhetoric exerts its effect quite aside from any act of deliberative 'choice' on our part or any critical-evaluative stance we might take toward it. Thus if Foucault 'touches the right chords in us' then we will be carried along by the rhetorical force of his writing and will thereafter come to 'see things differently' as if through a kind of unwilled conversion-experience.

On this account rhetoric is conceived as bypassing the powers of reflective or critical judgement and appealing direct to some preconscious level of thought, instinct, or desire. Shaw goes on to develop his case for the transvaluative power of rhetoric in distinctly irrationalist and no doubt authentically Nietzschean-Foucauldian terms. Thus: 'Norris assumes that if Foucault is not offering justifications then nothing *compels* us to share his vision of things. Foucault would accept that nothing compels agreement but, nonetheless, he hopes to recruit people to his way of seeing things. Rhetoric can still touch us and change us and bring us to share a different vision.' (Shaw, p. 284) The metaphor of recruitment is suggestive here, implying as it does that persuasion occurs not so much through sheer coercive force but through a strategy of strong-willed rhetorical imposition that leaves no room for critical dissent or for resistance on reasoned and principled grounds. It seems to me that Foucault is driven to adopt this position by his Nietzschean idea of rhetoric as a field of contending forces and counter-forces which preclude any appeal to the exercise of judgement in its various (e.g., Kantian) modes and capacities. As a result his argument swings back and forth between a form of extreme linguistic-discursive determinism where the subject exists only as a figment or illusory projection of language to a private-individualist ethos where subjects cultivate a radical autonomy conceived in terms of aesthetic self-fashioning or perfection of the life as a work of art. What leads him to this impasse – I suggest – is precisely Foucault's counter-enlightenment rhetoric, his strong-revisionist (not to say downright perverse) misreading of Kant, and his deep suspicion of the very idea that rational argument involves 'offering justifications' rather than deploying rhetorical means of enforcing or 'recruiting' assent.

IV

Hence the unwitting irony of that passage in *The Order of Things* where Foucault makes sport with Kant's idea of man as a strange 'empirical-transcendental doublet'.[37] In Foucault this antinomy is pushed to breaking-point and beyond, with the split falling out between a determinist notion of subjectivity as entirely constructed in or by language/discourse, and a starkly opposite conception where the subject is free to invent or fashion a self in accordance with his or her own most authentic desires. Indeed Shaw registers the force of this objection – or something very like it – but once again puts it down to a sheer misreading of Foucault. Thus:

> it is hard to see in general how an appeal to acts of pure poetic self-invention, whether private or public, could possibly give a solution. If capillary power is pervasive enough to render problematic a person's ordinary, mundane actions, then surely acts of pure self-invention must be at least as problematic and probably much more so. To suppose that people can invent themselves is to take it that pre-existing character and values can be replaced completely and in a short time. This is a very strong claim, even if one is not in general sceptical about free actions. (Shaw, p. 281)

But this is to misidentify the problem in a way that effectively distracts attention from its real source in Foucault's understanding of language, subjectivity, ethical agency, and the claims of authentic ('autonomous') selfhood. Of course Foucault is not suggesting – absurdly – that 'people can invent themselves' in the sense that 'pre-existing character and values can be replaced completely and in a short time'. What he *does* quite explicitly maintain is that selves can be fashioned, like works of art, through the cultivation of distinctive qualities *despite and against* the ubiquitous effects of 'capillary power', or the way in which – on his own account – techniques of internalised surveillance and control nowadays extend to the innermost depths of our 'private' thoughts, wishes, and desires.

Here again Shaw states the issue very clearly while shying away from its ultimate implications. 'The concentration in [Foucault's] middle period writings on capillary power and its subtleties makes it very hard to see how there can be any substantial freedom of action.' (p. 280) In which case, he asks:

> How, then, can there be room for the vertiginous freedom involved in radical self-invention? Having shackled us so firmly that even our thoughts and desires become permeated – 'The soul is the effect and instrument of a political anatomy; the soul is the prison of the body' – Foucault seems to have made escape through genuinely free agency next to impossible. And yet the possibility of self-invention is taken for granted in Foucault's later writings. (pp. 280–1)

Shaw's answer, as I have said, is to deny that this is really such a problem once we appreciate the 'radical' force of Foucault's Nietzscheanism and the way that he enjoins us to 'think inhuman thoughts' regardless of received (liberal-humanist) proprieties. It will also come to seem less pressing – he thinks – if one adopts a Nietzschean-Foucauldian view of rhetoric as that which enables the strong self-fashioner to transcend those irksome Kantian constraints and redefine 'autonomy' in terms more conducive to the fulfilment of his or her most cherished aims and ideals. Now, according to Shaw, this doesn't mean that such a project must be viewed as '*private-aestheticist*' in the sense of being played out (as Rorty would have it) in the life-style of dandyish aesthetes like Baudelaire whose poetic vocation has nothing to do with matters of social responsibility or ethico-political conscience. Perhaps it is the case – he concedes – that Foucault's choice of Baudelaire as an exemplary figure in this context 'encourages the view that the aesthetic is of no direct political relevance', since it 'might suggest one form of self-absorption, namely, dandyism: making of the body, one's feelings, one's very existence a work of art' (Shaw, p. 280). But we shall get Foucault wrong, Shaw believes, if we take take this example too much at face value or presume to find evidence of Foucault's 'quietism' in the fact that he cites Baudelaire – of all people! – as a source for the idea of aesthetic self-fashioning as a strategy of last resort in the face of modern disciplinary power. Rather we should see that this cannot be the gist of Foucault's argument given what he has to say elsewhere about the mechanisms by which such power reaches right down into our deepest, most intimate thoughts and desires. For in that case clearly there can no be question of the self carving out a space of 'private' freedom which would somehow be immune from its pervasive operations.

However this argument merely re-states the central problem with Foucault's whole enterprise while in no way resolving that problem or suggesting a viable alternative conception. 'Ironically', Shaw remarks, it is Foucault's own genealogical writings which ought to arouse our suspicions of any proposed solution to the problem of power along any such lines. Can the realm of artistic creation really be free from capillary power? It seems all too probable that our attempts here, as elsewhere, will be subject to subtle conditioning. If freedom is never all-or-nothing, if power regroups, one would expect it to pervade the private-aesthetic realm, too, implicitly or explicitly introducing norms of style. (p. 282)

No doubt it is the case that freedom is 'never all-or-nothing', and that any significant margins of choice – whether in the realms of ethics, politics, or aesthetics – must always be viewed against a complex background of normative rules and constraints. Were it not for those limiting (but also enabling) conditions then of course the very notion of 'freedom' would lack any meaningful content. However it is Foucault who sets things up in such a way as to present us with an all-or-nothing choice between, on the one hand, a bleakly determinist doctrine of capillary power and, on the other, a notional 'freedom' for which he can find no better example than that of the Baudelairean poet-as-dandy, one who adopts 'an ironic attitude which makes it possible to grasp an aspect of the fleeting moment' (Shaw, p. 282).

Now I take Shaw's point that this is not the whole story, that Foucault 'does not regard self-invention as necessarily confined to the private life', and moreover that 'other forms of self-invention besides dandyism are possible, some of which are more engaged with the body politic' (p. 282). However we are then confronted with a different kind of all-or-nothing choice, one that is posed very sharply by Foucault and reproduced in the various passages from Shaw's article that I have cited above. This is the choice between private-aestheticist quietism and the ethos of self-fashioning writ large as a Nietzschean will-to-persuade through sheerly affective rhetorical force. Such would be the attitude of those who (in Shaw's words) 'think that self-invention is of chief importance', who do not 'consider themselves morally bound by public conventions', and for whom therefore the highest good is the 'thinking of inhuman thoughts, acting in ways that go beyond good and evil' (p. 278). It is here that Rorty's reading of Foucault gets a hold, however implausible it might seem when judged by normative criteria of truth or fidelity to author's intent. For if one takes it (as Shaw does) 'at face value' then Foucault's prescription for a Nietzschean overcoming of liberal-humanist values is one that gives genuine grounds for disquiet, and which thus helps to justify Rorty's claim that we should treat him with a large protective measure of 'liberal-ironist' detachment. That is, such thinkers are best understood by discounting some of their more extreme and ethico-politically dubious claims, and treating them rather as strong self-fashioners – inspirational figures in their way – who once in a while become prone to delusions of legislative grandeur.

To be sure, one can sympathise with Shaw in his eloquent protest that this is a misreading of the 'radical' (i.e., Nietzschean) Foucault and one that can only be made to stick through a highly selective, not to say myopic construal of the relevant texts. Thus 'Rorty's suggestion that Foucault can continue to use "in good faith, for public purposes" the common political vocabulary seems plainly wrong, since the sincere use of that vocabulary would carry with it a commitment to liberal structures of thought which Foucault does not share' (Shaw, p. 278). I agree that there is something decidedly odd about a version of Foucault that brings him out pretty much on a wavelength with Rorty's blandly accommodating style of liberal-consensus thinking. Besides, such thinking itself has a certain rhetorically coercive aspect, as I have argued at length elsewhere and as Foucault would no doubt be quick to remark.[38] All the same one can see Rorty's point when it comes to the 'radical' (French-Nietzschean) Foucault and his project for a trans-valuation of values that would certainly extend far beyond the sphere of 'autonomous' self-invention. For that project is aimed directly against the alternative (Kantian-liberal) conception of autonomy which takes it that practical reason has to do with the human capacity for making reasoned and principled judgements quite apart from the promptings of mere self-interest or the will to assert one's own values in opposition to those of a dominant consensus. This involves an appeal both to individual conscience and also to the public sphere – the *sensus communis* of shared interests and informed participant debate – wherein any conflicts that arise must ultimately be resolved.[39] Foucault's 'radicalism' amounts to an attack on both fronts, one that reduces the Kantian subject (the reasoning, judging, and willing subject) to a mere epiphenomenon of discourse while it spurns any notion of an intersubjectively valid 'tribunal' that could place certain limits on the scope for self-creation in the strong Nietzschean mode.

According to Shaw 'there is no good reason, from anything Rorty offers, to abandon the French reading of Foucault, the Foucault whose radical inspiration is Nietzsche' (p. 279). But this is once again to pose the issue in highly questionable terms. If Rorty's were indeed the sole alternative to Foucault's approach then one might perhaps be hard put to choose between the 'radical' allure of a rhetoric that enjoins us to 'think inhuman thoughts' and the anodyne prescription of a liberal irony which treats that rhetoric with fond indulgence by confining it safely to the 'private' sphere' while counselling an attitude of wise acquiescence in prevailing consensus beliefs. However this is not how the choice works out unless one endorses the view – common to Foucault and Rorty, as well as to sundry post-structuralists, postmodernists, and counter-enlightenment thinkers – that there is no longer any mileage in the Kantian 'discourse' of ethical universalism and critical-emancipatory values. It seems to me, conversely, that this whole way of thinking marks a break with the 'unfinished project of modernity' – to borrow Habermas's resonant phrase[40] – and a consequent failure to envisage any option besides those of a 'weak' (consensus-based) Rortian liberalism or a 'strong' Foucauldian will to overcome all the values that have characterised that project.

This false antithesis is neatly exemplified in the final paragraph of Shaw's essay where he appears to let the main issue go by default while none the less sticking to his case for Foucault as a radical transvaluer of values, one to whom conventional standards of consistency just don't apply. Thus:

> Even if there is no escape along these lines, even if Norris is right and ultimately the dilemma – Kantianism or quietism – holds, it cannot be concluded that Foucault himself ever accepted this. He thought that Nietzsche's was a tenable approach. Even in his final interview Foucault emphatically asserts, 'I am simply Nietzschean'. (Shaw, p. 289)

In my view the issue is not so much this pseudo-dilemma – 'Kantianism or quietism' – nor again the choice as Shaw poses it, i.e., the moribund discourse of liberal humanism *versus* the 'radical' thinking of inhuman thoughts. Rather it is a question of deciding between Rorty's liberal quietism, Foucault's illiberal (Nietzschean) persuasion, and lastly an approach – e.g., that of Habermas – which conserves the most important aspects of Kantian thought while subjecting them to further refinement and critique from a modern (post-foundationalist) standpoint. No doubt Shaw's Foucault – the strong rhetorician – would reject my claim that we have any scope for deliberative choice in such matters. After all, to repeat, 'Norris is surely wrong to suppose that we can *choose* what to make of a piece of rhetoric', [since] '[r]hetoric affects us regardless of our will' (Shaw, p. 284). But then there is the question – nowhere adequately answered by Foucault – as to how those strong-willed self-fashioning types could ever break free of the dominant rhetorics or discourses which must presumably affect their every last thought, wish, and desire. Nothing, I submit, could more clearly illustrate the self-contradictions that characterise Foucault's thought and which emerge to striking effect in Shaw's (on its own terms) admirably faithful rendition.

CHAPTER 7

'The Night in which All Cows are Black': Paul de Man, 'mere reading' and indifference to philosophy

I

In the previous chapter I raised what I took to be some crucial problems with Foucault's thinking about ethics and politics, in particular his 'strong' revisionist account of Kantian ethical themes. This led me to question the kinds of *soi-disant* 'radical' rhetoric that often find their chief inspiration in Foucault and which just as often go along with current post-structuralist and postmodernist claims to have achieved a wholesale Nietzschean transvaluation of values, not least with respect to those values enshrined in the old-style enlightenment 'discourse' of truth, reason, and critique. What results – I suggest – is an ethics and a politics devoid of any genuine normative content and hence liable to appropriation by radicalisms left or right, that is to say, by any discourse which defines itself solely in opposition to prevailing (e.g., 'liberal') modes of thought. Foucault's work thus stands in sharp contrast to the writings of Paul de Man, a literary theorist whose deconstructive approach to the texts of (among others) Rousseau, Kant, and Nietzsche is as far as possible from lending itself to any direct political extrapolation or any straightforward endorsement in the name of this or that programme for radical change. Indeed, it is the sheer *resistance* of de Man's writings – their intransigent refusal to yield up intelligible meanings or arguments – which has led to charges of obscurantism, political evasiveness, or even (in the light of his recently discovered wartime journalism) a crypto-fascist desire to subvert or destroy the very bases of ethical decision and responsibility.

In this chapter I discuss some of the issues raised by de Man's extraordinary project. While rejecting the above sorts of claim – inspired as they are, most often, by a blanket hostility to 'deconstruction' and all its works – I also warn against any too ready acceptance of a mode of thought which gains its uncanny (for some, its almost spellbinding) power from a professed disregard for basic standards of philosophical, interpretive, or textual-expository truth. Thus it makes little sense to speak of a generalised 'politics of deconstruction' that would somehow find significant common ground between (on the one hand) Derrida's writings on Kant, the modern university, or the critical role of philosophy *vis-à-vis* the interests of state authority and power, and (on the other) de Man's dark broodings on the capacity of language to 'disarticulate' every such claim through its relentless deconstruction of the meanings and values that we deludedly project upon it. So my purpose here is to enter some large caveats with respect to de Man's work – in particular its raising 'indifference to philosophy' into a high point of deconstructive principle – while also explaining just why that work has been able to exert such a singular force of fascination on some extremely acute and philosophically well-equipped commentators, Rodolphe Gasché preeminent among them. I shall then proceed to offer suggestions as to how we might engage in a critique of de Man's thought that takes full measure of that disconcerting force yet resists its more dogmatic or rhetorically coercive aspects. This chapter is therefore very much a part of my aim to put the case for deconstruction as a critical discourse which continues the 'unfinished project of modernity' while pursuing that project – true to its spirit – in some new and challenging directions.

II

Since the appearance of his first book on Derrida in 1986 Rodolphe Gasché has acquired a well-deserved reputation as one of the most astute and philosophically informed commentators on deconstruction.[1] During that time he has published a number of essays about Paul de Man – among them, most notably, ' "Setzung" and "Übersetzung" ' and 'In-Difference to Philosophy' – which have a strong claim to be the best things yet written on this strange, disconcerting, utterly distinctive and (at times) perversely idiosyncratic thinker. The present volume collects these previously published texts together with a good deal of new or extensively reworked material.[2] Of course this involves a degree of repetition between chapters, or some passages where Gasché returns to aspects of de Man's work that have received fairly extensive commentary at earlier points in his book. However, these passages are far from redundant since he is always reengaging with unresolved issues, or attempting to find some different (more adequate) approach to arguments that have so far eluded, baffled, or defied his best efforts of critical exegesis. Indeed the chief merit of Gasché's book – and one that sets it decidedly apart from the general run of commentaries – is its determination to take full measure of de Man's claims as a thinker whose work cannot be categorised according to any conventional understanding of 'philosophy' or 'literary theory'. At times he is over-prone to endorse the view that de Man's thought is *so* original – so utterly unbeholden to conventional standards of truth, textual warrant, logical consistency, argumentative coherence, etc. – that those standards can simply have no place in any reckoning with its implications. Still Gasché very rightly rejects the idea promoted by some literary theorists that deconstruction represents the final undoing of 'philosophy' at the hands of rhetoric, or that a reading in the deconstructive mode is one that *de facto* subverts or discredits all the concepts and truth-claims of Western 'logocentric' reason.

Indeed, a good portion of his book is devoted to showing just how far de Man's writings depart from any normative idea of what counts as a valid philosophic argument or a duly accountable reading of texts in line with received scholarly-interpretive protocols. Nevertheless he very strongly contests the claim that de Man was just a crafty rhetorician and perverter of truth whose work can be dismissed – now that we know about the notorious wartime journalism – as the product of a deeply corrupt intelligence anxious to invent sophistical ploys for covering its own intellectual and moral tracks.[3] In this latter connection Gasché has a long closing chapter which steers an admirably clear-headed path among all the swirling claims and counter-claims provoked by the discovery of de Man's articles in *Le Soir* and *Het Vlaamsche Land*. That is to say, it comes closest to achieving the right balance between frank admission of their often morally repugnant (at best opportunist and unprincipled) character and refusal to adopt the kind of high-handed approach that takes no account of their cultural-historical context, their resistance to cooption for the purposes of straightforward Nazi propaganda, and – most of all – the complete lack of warrant for treating his later 'deconstructionist' work as in any way continuous or subtly collusive with those none the less deeply compromised early productions.[4] One may feel that Gasché is somewhat over-stating his case for the defence when he asserts that '[t]hey are not even sympathetic to the Nazi cause [but] are, primarily, interested in protecting Flanders' independence' (p. 258), or again, that 'de Man's concern with national peculiarity represented for him at that time the major critical tool for resisting the occupation forces and Nazi ideology' (p. 265). Also there is a problem – a logical tension – about claiming on the one hand that the early texts are more subtle, resistant, many-levelled (and so forth) than hostile critics have supposed while asserting on the other that those critics merely demonstrate their own obtuseness and malice by seeking out evidence of a continuity between the wartime journalism and de Man's later work. Still, as I say, this chapter makes a strong case on textual, historical, political, and even ethical grounds for rejecting much of the ill-informed commentary and ill-disguised academic rancour that has masqueraded as moral outrage on the part of de Man's detractors.

At any rate Gasché is quite justified in arguing that the de Man 'affair' has very often served as a pretext for avoiding any genuine engagement with those questions that are raised with such singular insistence and force in his later texts. Chief among them is the claim for reading – 'mere reading', as de Man provocatively puts it – as a powerful resource for the unmasking of 'aesthetic ideology', that is to say, for revealing the kinds of naive, phenomenalist, or naturalised 'commonsense' assumption that have so far exerted such a strong hold upon our thinking about issues in politics, ethics, philosophy, and literary theory.[5] There is no room here for an adequate account of de Man's radically heterodox approach to these issues, nor yet for a summary of Gasché's often just as difficult and at times even more tortuous exposition. Sufficient to say that de Man propounds a 'materialist' (as opposed to a phenomenalist) theory of the text that insists on the sheer *literality* of reading – quite aside from thematic concerns – and which moreover rejects any kind of expressive, intentionalist, anthropomorphic, referential, metaphorical, symbolic, or other such interpretive strategy for ensuring that texts turn out to have a meaning in accordance with received values of truth, coherence and intelligibility. This 'materialism' (which is also a radical formalism) involves the idea of a textual substrate made up of the mute, asemic elements – the very letters of the text – upon which meaning is momentarily imposed through a series of arbitrary 'positings' (*Setzungen*) that cannot be reduced to any order of intentional coherence or thematic continuity except by a kind of unwitting self-delusion on the reader's part, a resort to some form of naive 'aesthetic ideology'.

Hence de Man's contention (in his programmatic essay 'The Return to Philology') that the phenomenalist error – that of presupposing some 'natural' link between language, perception, and the realm of extralinguistic reality – is one which has characterised almost every school of philosophic and literary-critical thought, especially in the wake of Romanticism.[6] Hence also his claim that a 'resistant' reading must steadfastly abjure the various consoling illusions which have served to dissimulate the gap that opens up between language and world, thought and cognition, or the 'material' elements of textual inscription and the 'phenomenalist' appeal to modalities of sensory-perceptual experience. To go along with such illusions – so de Man argues – is not only to reveal a critically-disabling blindness to the workings of figural language but also, more crucially, to risk falling into a form of aesthetic ideology with potentially far-reaching ethical and political consequences. For we shall then be more easily persuaded by those forms of seductive organicist thinking which equate the naturalness – the pre-ordained growth and development – of some particular language or culture with the power of expression vested in privileged tropes such as metaphor and symbol, figures which claim to transcend or to reconcile the various (merely prosaic) antinomies of subject and object, mind and world, or language and phenomenal experience. Undoubtedly this is where de Man's later writings can be seen to constitute – in Geoffrey Hartman's phrase – a 'powerful though belated act of atonement' for the grievous errors of his wartime journalism.[7] For whatever one's view with respect to their moral, political, or strategic ambiguities those writings very often endorse just the kind of national-aestheticist thinking that de Man was later to repudiate by every means at his disposal.

All the same, as many readers have felt, de Man's way of setting about this task was highly equivocal – not to say evasive – in so far as it seemed to undermine the very basis of ethical judgement, or the grounds for holding persons presently accountable for their own past actions and utterances. Such would appear to be the upshot of his theory (derived in equal measure from Fichte, Nietzsche, and a highly tendentious reading of Rousseau) where the self becomes a kind of radical fiction brought into being by momentary acts of 'positing' which leave no room for any viable conception of substantive or enduring personhood.[8] 'However one interprets positing in Fichte', Gasché writes,

> its *Setzen* is not simply human. Nor is it to be mistaken for human law, for *Gesetz*. It is important to be aware of this, particularly because both Fichte's philosophy of positing and Austin's Speech Act Theory (which because of its notion of act is not to be mistaken simply for the act of speaking human beings) have been "humanized" in order to become applicable to a certain analysis of literature. (p. 41)

No doubt this is faithful to de Man and also to de Man's reading of Fichte, refracted as it is through a radically formalist (and in his sense 'materialist') theory of language that would treat the idea of continuing selfhood – or of present answerability for past speech-acts – as the merest of consolatory 'humanist' illusions, shown up as such through a reading attentive to the 'autonomous', self-positing power of linguistic figuration. All the same it is (to say the least) a highly questionable thesis and one that Gasché is over-ready to accept without sufficiently considering either its dire ethical implications or the range of objections that could well be put from alternative philosophic standpoints. On his account '[t]he analogy between Fichte's principle of the unconditioned identity of the self and the Act of Speech Act Theory cannot be overlooked', since '[i]n both cases it is by means of the purity of an "act upon an act itself, which specific act is preceded by no other whatever", that a subject becomes objective or that a speech act turns into an intentional act'.[9] But this is simply to ignore the whole range of contextual, institutional, social, cultural, interpersonal and suchlike factors which (according to Austin) must always be involved in any genuine speech-act transaction. Of course it may be said – with Derridean warrant – that there remain all sorts of unresolved problem with Austin's appeal to 'context' as a means of distinguishing 'normal' from 'deviant' instances of speech-act utterance.[10] Nevertheless even Derrida stops well short of suggesting – like de Man – that such appeals should be dismissed out of hand, or that performatives must somehow be conceived as issued by a self-positing Fichtean Ego that leaves them suspended in a state of radical disjunction 'preceded by no other [act] whatever'.

Thus it is hard to avoid the suspicion that one main purpose of de Man's late writings was to 'disarticulate' every notion of ethical responsibility and thereby disown any lingering guilt for his *vita ante acta* as represented by that yet-to-be-discovered cache of articles in the archives of *Le Soir*. Moreover, those writings are subject to the charge that they merely replace one kind of 'totalitarian' approach with another, more subtle but no less coercive in its claims to dictate what should properly count as a rigorous (undeluded) reading of texts. Gasché is well aware of this likely objection and indeed cites various passages from de Man – especially 'The Resistance to Theory' – where he preempts the charge by frankly owning up to it in his typical 'late' style of absolute, apodictic authority mixed with a deceptive tone of self-deprecating irony. Thus, for instance:

> technically correct rhetorical readings may be boring, monotonous, predictable and unpleasant, but they are irrefutable. They are also total-izing (and potentially totalitarian) for since the structures and functions they expose do not lead to the knowledge of an entity (such as language) but are an unreliable process of knowledge production that prevents all entities, including linguistic entities, from coming into discourse as such, they are indeed universals, consistently defective models of language's impossibility to be [sic] a model language.[11]

As I have said, Gasché is not one to underestimate the sheer affront that such a passage must offer to all the normative standards – of logic, coherence, conceptual precision, definitional clarity, etc. – that are commonly taken to decide what shall count as a valid (or meaningful) statement. Nor is he prone, like so many of de Man's literary-critical followers, to treat any objection along these lines as a sure sign that the objector has failed to fathom the incomparable depth and rigour of his thought. Indeed Gasché is at pains to emphasise the extreme singularity of de Man's project, that is to say, its utter and complete 'indifference' to the concepts, categories, and protocols of disciplined philosophic thought. Thus he is able to demon-strate, like others before him, that de Man more than once bases a whole elaborate structure of argument on a plain *misreading* of certain passages – for instance, in Kant or Hegel – which he annexes to his own heterodox purpose either through inaccurate translation of crucial phrases or by sup-plying a gloss wildly at odds with their manifest purport.[12] (I forget who first made the joke about 'DeMannuel Kant' but it does come persistently to mind when reading these essays.) Yet Gasché is still convinced – despite all this evidence of wilful misprision – that de Man's late work has a cogency and rigour that justify (indeed compel) the kind of closely attentive reading which his book sets out to provide.

III

Just why this should be is the chief question for any reviewer (myself included) who shares Gasché's fascination with that work but has come to suspect – after much hard reading – that the emperor's clothes, if not entirely absent, are distinctly threadbare in places. After all, what kind of 'rhetorical reading' is it that, in Gasché's words, 'focuses on the non-phenomenal and autonomous potential of language, rather than producing noumena, [and which] exhibits a fragmentary chaos of meaningless linguistic matter, repetitive mechanical rules, and absolutely opaque linguistic events'? (p. 76). Not, to be sure, the kind that could have any place in that traditional conception of rhetoric (or of language, literature, philosophy, or the human and social sciences) which stands in the service of humanist values, and which de Man therefore takes as the chief target of a properly 'rhetorical' reading. Gasché makes the point with particular force in a chapter ('Apathetic Formalism') where he contrasts de Man's peculiarly bleak or inhuman theory of language with the assumptions embodied in a canonical work such as Ernst Robert Curtius's *European Literature and the Latin Middle Ages*.[13] What 'rhetoric' stands for here is the continuity of tradition and the power of language to communicate meaning across distances of time and culture through a shared sense of ethical and intellectual values that somehow tran-scends all the obstacles placed in its way. To de Man's way of thinking, on the contrary, this is the merest of naive humanist illusions, a belief which must be rejected if we are ever to break the hold of that pervasive 'aesthetic ideology' which denies the stark truth of our linguistic predica-ment as revealed through a properly demystified reading in the prescribed (deconstructive) rhetorical mode.

    In the end – and despite all his express misgivings – Gasché comes out in defence of de Man as a thinker whose absolute 'singularity' places him beyond reach of criticism on any of the terms laid down by received forms of philosophical, ethical, political, or literary-critical judgement. Not that he advances this claim lightly or without a due sense of its outrageous character as measured against any reasonable standards of intellectual probity and truth. After all, '[i]f the material linguistic event has as such no relation whatsoever to a meaning intention, how then can it be said to make such intention possible or to subvert it?' (p. 84). And again: what are we to make of a practice of reading which raises 'indifference' to a high point of principle, or which refuses point-blank to meet the most basic requirements of interpretive fidelity, textual warrant, good-faith communicative purpose, etc.? Gasché puts the case with typical directness though also – just as typically – with a strong suggestion that de Man is so utterly unique a thinker as to place his work in a realm quite beyond those otherwise imperative requirements. 'His is a world', Gasché writes, 'of unrelated singulars, each so idiosyncratic that in it everything universal becomes extinguished; it is a world of heterogeneous fragments forming a whole only insofar as, by their mutual indifference and lack of generative power, they are all the same, endlessly repeating the punctuality of their lone meaninglessness' (p. 82). To which one may well be tempted to respond that this is on the face of it sufficient reason to view de Man's entire project as a massive aberration of critical intelligence, a project driven by his maybe understandable need to find ever more complicated ways of 'dissociating the cognition from the act' (de Man's phrase), or denying present responsibility for past deeds and utterances.

Gasché draws the line at such psychobiographical speculations, regarding them as merely a pretext for evading any real and sustained critical engagement with de Man's texts. No doubt this was the strategy adopted by many hostile commentators – David Lehmann and Jon Wiener among them – who seized on a few such passages taken out of context and used them as 'evidence' in support of their case that de Man's work (and 'deconstruction' in general) amounted to an all-purpose ploy for excusing any amount of collaborationist guilt.[14] Still the absurdity of arguments like this should not be allowed to rule out other, more considered attempts to understand de Man's later texts as at least in part designed to avoid any direct acknowledgment of the guilt-feelings engendered by the memory of his wartime journalism. It seems to me very hard to resist this conclusion when one reads (say) de Man on Nietzsche and the virtues of an active power of forgetting, a transformative or strong-revisionist outlook that would lift the dead hand of a merely 'antiquarian' (truth-fixated) historical approach and leave us free to explore the full range of possibilities for self-redescription.[15] And again, how else should we interpret those passages from his essay on Rousseau's *Confessions* where de Man treats of the confessional text as a 'machine' for generating guilt, a narrative mode wherein past (maybe fictive or imaginary) misdemeanours can be multiplied at will, and thereby offer a pretext for claiming all the more credit for frank and fearless self-exposure? Thus 'what Rousseau really wants' – in recounting the episode of the servant-girl Marion whom he falsely accused of having stolen a ribbon – 'is neither the ribbon nor Marion, but the public scene of exposure which he actually gets. ... This desire is truly shameful, for it suggests that Marion was destroyed, not for the sake of [Rousseau's] saving face ... but merely in order to provide him with a stage on which to parade his disgrace, or, what amounts to the same thing, to furnish him with a good ending for Book II of his *Confessions*'.[16] In which case, de Man concludes, such 'honest' self-reckoning will always be subtended by a covert (self-justificatory) motive, one which 'will indeed exculpate the confessor, making the confession (and the confessional text) redundant as it originates'.[17] No doubt – as Gasché would argue – this reading must be taken on its textual merits and not referred back to de Man's life-history in any vulgar-reductionist fashion. All the same, as so often in his later work, there is a need to explain why he should make such a capital point of collapsing the difference between fact and fiction, and moreover present it as somehow preferable – more honest, less self-indulgent – to refrain from 'confessing' to past faults lest the speech-act in question turn out to be a form of roundabout self-exoneration.

It seems to me that Gasché goes too far in making allowance for the utter 'singularity' of de Man's thought and the consequent need – as he sees it – to suspend the normative criteria that apply in the reading of *all* texts other than those of Paul de Man. This claim is pushed hardest in a chapter on Derrida's essay 'Plato's Pharmacy' where Gasché points out – among other things – the persistence of certain quite traditional assumptions and values in Derrida's reading, among them the commitment to intelligibility and the principle that an adequate interpretation must in some sense do justice to the subtleties and complexities of the text in hand.[18] The passage is worth quoting at length since it shows just how much he is willing to grant by way of special licence to de Man's very different 'deconstructionist' approach.

> The Derridean reading ... does not presume that the rhetoricity of Plato's text fatally flaws any attempt to interpret and come to understand it. On the contrary, the way Derrida understands text, that is, as a structure of referral, invites productive readings, readings that not only weave new interpretative threads into it but compose so many rewritings of it as well. Like Derrida, de Man also assumes the referentiality of language, but this referentiality is strictly intralinguistic, and ... always saturated by an exact opposite such that only negative knowledge is possible. ... From the perspective of de Manean mere reading, Derrida's philosophical claim – that is, that an essential, however subtle, difference obtains between *logos* and *mythos*, concept and metaphor, philosophy and sophistics, even though this difference rests on a constituting commerce between the oppositions – is an aberration. In mere reading, relation to an opposite amounts to undermining all claims to distinctness. ... [This] assumption ... is, for de Man, a last hideout of the philosophical illusion of a reconciliation of language and the phenomenal world. (pp. 176–7)

Still there is the question – one that Gasché never quite brings himself to answer – as to whether de Man would be justified in laying this charge against Derrida's reading of Plato. For it is far from clear that a de Manean 'mere reading' could come anywhere close to the level of intelligence, analytic acuity, conceptual rigour, and long-range textual-interpretive grasp that distinguishes Derrida's Plato commentary.

As I have said, there are some (albeit muted) indications that Gasché is uneasily aware of all this and that he knows full well the strength of those counter-arguments that would see nothing more to de Man's late work than a single-minded will to 'disarticulate' every last notion of truth, meaning, and ethical responsibility. What allows him to keep these doubts at bay is the fact that so much of his book is couched in a style of oblique or free-indirect paraphrase which remains indeterminate as between neutrally reporting what de Man has to say and signalling endorsement or at least qualified approval on his own part. Thus, for instance, '[e]verything besides language is of the order of phantasm, and it [language], therefore, must enjoy the unconditional interest of the reader. Its injunction is to be repeated, to be infinitely reenacted in the randomness, uniqueness, and incomprehensibility of its occurrence' (p. 233). Well yes, one wants to say: so it goes in any number of passages from late de Man, and this can scarcely be faulted as an accurate account of what 'occurs' – or what is supposed to occur – when we follow the letter of de Man's prescription for a properly 'materialist' reading. However Gasché never fully acknowledges the chief objection to this whole strange project: namely, that it cannot be carried through without ceasing to 'read' in any genuine sense and adopting an attitude of stupefied indifference to everything except the mute, asemic, sheerly 'material' letters on the page. 'In short', Gasché writes,

> the literary and the philosophical discourse are, for de Man, meaningful enterprises involved in forgetting or recuperating the non-phenomenal properties of the material and formal act of figuration, properties that come into view, as he insists, through figuration itself, precisely to the extent in which figuration is itself a repetition of the originary violence of positing. (p. 85)

But then one has to ask how those figural 'properties' could possibly 'come into view', given de Man's absolute insistence on the 'nonphenomenal' character of language (i.e., its irreducibility to the order of sensuous or perceptual-cognitive experience), along with his idea that figuration some-how *precedes and disrupts* any 'meaningful' construal that we – or the deluded philosophers and critics – might wish to place upon it. Quite frankly I can make no sense of this claim and think that Gasché would himself be hard put to make sense of it if he exited briefly from the paraphrastic mode and took up a somewhat more critical stance toward de Man's mesmerising rhetoric.

IV

There is (or used to be) a joke going the rounds of literary academe that the world was full of unwritten books and untenured critical theorists due to the massively inhibiting effect of de Man's teaching and writing. Gasché is untouched by this particular malaise but does show the symptoms of a variant condition, one that comes out in his curious unwillingness to press the kinds of question that would seriously challenge de Man's project with regard not only to its flagrant misreading of source-texts and its dubious philosophical credentials but also its motivating interests and purposes. Toward the end of his book Gasché proposes an unlikely comparison between that project and the logical positivists' attack on what they considered mere 'pseudo-problems' in philosophy. Such were the problems that typically arose when thinkers relinquished the firm ground of empirical observation and logical reasoning and yielded to various forms of delusive 'metaphysical' abstraction.[19] As Gasché sees it, 'de Man's critical debunking of all attempts to unify, or gather, though considerably more intransigent, is not unrelated to the Vienna School's critique of metaphysics, in that it proposes a categorical abandonment of all traditional philosophical issues' (p. 232). Well, to be sure, everything is related to everything else if one frames the terms of comparison broadly or vaguely enough. Still there is a vast difference – except (of course) from de Man's undifferentiating viewpoint – between the logical positivists' idea of philosophy as a science-led quest for rigour and precision in the asssessment of various theories, methods, truth-claims, observation-statements, etc., and an approach like de Man's that would utterly repudiate all such pointless philosophical strivings.

Gasché pretty much acknowledges this when he proceeds to develop the comparison. Thus:

> Whereas the logical positivists relinquished many traditional philosophical problems as meaningless because no empirical (or rather material) truth criteria could be provided to verify them, de Man abandons them in their entirety because the criteria for there to be truth have been expanded to such a degree as to definitely foil all possibility of judgment. The criterion being the total transparency and absolute coinciding of the way meaning is conferred and meaning itself, all one is left with is hopeless juxtaposition, disjunction, contradiction, and so forth. (pp. 232–3)

Now it may be said that logical positivism itself ran afoul of various contradictions or internal anomalies, among them – most famously – the fact that the verification-principle could not be stated in terms which satisfied its own stringent condition, i.e., that in order to count as 'meaningful' a statement must be *either* empirically verifiable *or* self-evidently valid in virtue of its logical form.[20] However, these objections clearly arose from a mode of critical analysis that continued to respect all the basic criteria – of logic, consistency, definitional rigour, self-reflexive application, etc. – which have long been taken to define what counts as an adequate philosophical argument. In other words they are as remote as can be from the kind of relentlessly sceptical approach – or the attitude of downright cavalier indifference to all such operative concepts and distinctions – which Gasché takes as the hallmark of de Man's late writing.

I must confess to having no idea what he means by his claim that, with de Man, 'the criteria for there to be truth' have somehow 'been expanded to such a degree' that there remains no 'possibility of judgment' (as between meaningful and meaningless statements) in the old, presumptively deluded logical-positivist manner. Some clue is perhaps offered by the next sentence where Gasché holds out the impossible ideal of a 'total transparency and absolute coinciding of the way meaning is conferred and meaning itself', failing which – so the passage implies – we are compelled to follow de Man into the morass of 'hopeless juxtaposition, disjunction, contradiction, and so forth'. But there is no reason to grasp either horn of this false and absurdly overstated de Manean dilemma. That it has seemed persuasive to some literary theorists – even a few with well-developed philosophical interests – may to some extent be explained by the problems with logical positivism and also (as Quine pointed out in a well-known essay) with its logical-empiricist successor movement.[21] However those problems are as nothing compared to the confusions that result – or that would result if the project could be carried through – from de Man's attitude of resolute 'indifference' toward all such strictly indispensable concepts, categories, and distinctions. To call them 'indispensable' is of course to deny what Gasché finds so compelling about de Man's arguments despite and against his own admission of their weakness on just about every count when assessed by normative (philosophical) standards of probity and truth. Still there is something odd – even perverse – about his constant willingness to give those arguments the benefit of the sceptical doubt when that doubt is pressed so far beyond the limits of rational intelligibility.

It is perhaps worth recalling, in this context, that one main target of the logical positivists' critique was that strain of Heideggerian depth-ontological thinking which likewise claimed to penetrate beyond the entirety of 'Western metaphysics' to a realm of authentic truth-as-unconcealment (*aletheia*) which had been covered over throughout the history of Western post-Platonic thought.[22] Gasché takes Heidegger as his prime authority for asserting that 'singular' thinkers – such as de Man – cannot be held accountable to received (conventionally sanctioned) standards of interpretive warrant or fidelity to the text in hand. Here again the relevant passage needs quoting at length in order to bring out the contortions imposed upon Gasché's attempt to think the unthinkable in response to de Man's summons. In so far as such a thought informs de Man's writing, he suggests,

> it is one that is so singular as to destroy its oneness and, with it, the
> unifying power that thought must be able to exercise to be the one

thought in the first place. It is therefore a thought so singular that it risks incomprehensibility. Yet in that very risk it appeals to thinking, which must face the challenge of the uniqueness of such an idea. Uniqueness on the level of thought, however, is not only exceptional, as is often believed in total disregard of the essence of thinking. Uniqueness, ultimately, is what thought *itself* makes impossible. Although absence of uniqueness does in no way preclude the independence or autonomy of a thinkng enterprise, thinking begins with the fallout of all uniqueness. Yet to have tried to think the impossible singularity, uniqueness of thinking in its universality, is what, forever, will make de Man's 'impossible' thinking so *incontournable* for anyone who claims to be in the business of thinking. (p. 113)

Confronted with a passage like this one is tempted to cite some of Carnap's withering comments on the kinds of obscurantist bewitchment by language to be found in Heidegger's work, that is to say, his idea of certain long-forgotten primordial truths that can be brought to light only by a thinking-back into the prehistory of (so-called) 'Western metaphysics'.[23] Ironically enough, one of de Man's early essays ('Heidegger's Exegeses of Hölderlin') was mainly devoted to pointing out the errors and confusions that could result from this uncritical acceptance of etymology as a source of uniquely 'authentic' interpretive insight.[24] Gasché is too intelligent and perceptive a reader to fall for any wholesale version of that fallacy. Besides, his own argument is for the most part conducted in a manner of careful and consequential reasoning which (thankfully) declines any such resort to *Volkisch* ideas of the wisdom enshrined in such primordial words. However, it is clear from the above passage that Gasché's claims for the utter 'singularity' of de Man's thought – and hence for treating it as unbeholden to commonplace standards of logic, rationality, and truth – have a great deal do with Heidegger's notion of an authentic thinking which begins at the point where those standards no longer apply.

V

Having myself published a book about de Man some 12 years I should perhaps say something about my own, now very different view of his work.[25] Like Gasché I found it an enthralling, perplexing, in many way deeply disturbing experience which left me convinced that de Man must be wrong in some crucial and obscurely motivated way, yet also that his readings had an uncanny power to override many of the obvious objections that rose up against them on almost every page. In part that uncanniness came from his knack of preempting such criticism by applying it to others and then somehow contriving to present it as a chief virtue in their thought. Thus for instance, in the essay on Heidegger mentioned above, de Man makes a cardinal point of distinguishing between 'errors' and 'mistakes' in textual commentary, the latter due to mere carelessness, oversight, failure to notice salient details, etc., while the former result from the kind of strong-revisionist reading (like Heidegger's exegeses of Hölderlin) which fall into error by sheer necessity or force of interpretive will. So when Heidegger ignores some crucial exegetical point – as by silently eliding a negative or transforming a subjunctive-conditional construction into a straightforward assertoric statement – it is always (so de Man would have us believe) an 'error' whose significance far transcends commonplace standards of scholarly-critical accountability. And of course there is a strong implication here that his own thought is of a stature and uniqueness that justifies similar exceptionalist treatment.

How this might square with de Man's later insistence on the stubborn *literality* of reading – on the need to respect the letter of the text even (or especially) where such a reading turns out to disrupt every notion of interpretive consistency and truth – is a question that finds no answer in his work. As I have said, Gasché is not always inclined to adopt this all-licensing approach on de Man's behalf. However there are many passages in his book – some of which I have cited above – where he does seem committed to the special-case view that de Man, like Heidegger, is a thinker of such originality as to defy comprehension and disqualify criticism on any but his own, intransigently 'singular' terms. Thus: 'they [de Man's readings] are "different", idiosyncratic to a point where, by making no point, they will have made their point – so singular as to make no difference but, perhaps, in that total apathy, a formidable challenge to philosophical difference' (p. 90). It seems to me now – coming back to de Man after a period mainly devoted to reading in the 'other' (analytic) tradition – that a thinker whose influence can work such contagious effects on a commentator of Gasché's undoubted intelligence is best regarded as a brilliant, subtle, but perverse exponent of what Carnap called 'pseudo-problems in philosophy'.[26] After all that tradition has come a long way since the heyday of logical positivism, not least in the matter of providing alternatives to the kind of sharply disjunctive thinking that characterized both the positivist programme and de Man's more extreme (and more rhetorically adroit) variations on the sceptical theme.

Indeed Gasché might not have been driven to such desperately wire-drawn paradoxical conclusions had he taken some account of those developments in recent philosophy of language that are likewise critical of empiricist (or phenomenalist) theories of meaning and reference, but which don't jump straight to the opposite fallacy of counting reference a purely textual or 'intralinguistic' function.[27] To be sure, as de Man says, 'it is not *a priori* certain that language functions according to principles which are those, or which are like those, of the phenomenal world'.[28] But there can be few philosophers nowadays who would wish to defend such a cratylist thesis, despite de Man's artfully rigged suggestion that *any* argument in support of the claim that language refers to a world 'outside' itself must be in thrall to some version of cratylism or – what amounts to the same thing – some form of delusive 'aesthetic ideology'. So it is that Gasché feels able to assert, following de Man, that 'reference is a function of language itself and remains entirely within its bounds'; moreover that, 'since language interconnects only elements within itself, it is shielded from being linked to extralinguistic referents, disconnected from the cognitive process and the value considerations characteristic of the phenomenal world' (p. 132). But this structuralist-derived theory of reference can be made to look plausible only through another of de Man's forced or artificial dilemmas, that is to say, by presenting it as the only alternative to a naive 'phenomenalist' theory that equates reference with some kind of direct, unmediated access to objects and events in the real-world domain. Hence his curious idea that anyone who thinks of reference in 'extralinguistic' terms, i.e., as not (or not exclusively) a function of language's 'autonomous' signifying power, must have fallen prey to the cratylist delusion which upholds the existence of a *natural* link between signifer and signified, or sign and referent.[29]

Thus, according to de Man, 'the convergence of sound and meaning ... [is] a mere *effect* which language can perfectly well achieve, but which bears no relationship, by analogy or by ontologically grounded imitation, to anything beyond that particular effect'.[30] If this were all that his argument amounted to then one could simply agree and moreover remark that it is a view which has been shared by the vast majority of philosophers and linguists from Plato down. That is, they have accepted the 'arbitrary' (non-natural and non-mimetic) relationship between word and object, except in those markedly deviant cases – such as onomatopoeia – which are taken to prove the general rule. (Those few who have disagreed – in the line of descent from Cratylus himself to Horne Tooke – have mostly had a poor press or been regarded as holding some highly idiosyncratic views.) But this is not to say that the relationship is 'arbitrary' in the sense of that term espoused by many post-structuralists and pushed beyond the limit of intelligibility in de Man's late writing. For once a word has acquired meaning (and reference) as a matter of shared linguistic convention then clearly it is the case – as Saussure, among others, was quick to acknowledge – that its usage cannot be simply a matter of 'arbitrary' imposition.[31] More than that: there are certain additional constraints having to to do with grammar, logic, and propositional content which narrow down the range of possible interpretations in any given case and which thus enable communicative grasp across across otherwise large distances of linguistic and cultural context. Here again, Gasché might have been less impressed by the ineluctable 'rigour' of de Man's arguments had he taken some account of the treatment of these issues by Donald Davidson and other philosophers in the post-Quinean tradition.[32] For one major theme in their work is this question of just where the line is to be drawn – and on just what principled grounds – between the 'arbitrary', the conventional, and the strictly non-conventional (since trans-culturally valid) aspects of linguistic-communicative grasp.[33]

De Man's main purpose in his later writing is to scramble these distinctions to the point where communication breaks down altogether and language becomes an impenetrable chaos of 'arbitrary' sounds or inscriptions. I have cited several passages from Gasché's book to just this effect but will offer one further example of the kind lest the reader doubt – as well she might – whether anyone could possibly endorse such a view.

> Considering the sheer arbitrariness and intrinsic senselessness of the material and signifying agencies of language, the randomness of their individual occurrences, the relative independence of their play, and the opacity of their literal materiality, all experienceable meaning appears *superimposed* on them. .... As these literal instances become thematized in the text's inscribed reference to its own figuration, they tend to exhibit a sphere of irreducible heterogeneity characterized by the absolute impenetrability and material singularity of the linguistic sounds or letters that, therefore, do not lend themselves to any meaningful interaction. These instances form a chaotic sphere of radically fragmented material agencies between which no text can ever be woven. (p. 71)

In which case – it seems fair to ask – how is it that de Man's texts ever got written or, once written, subject to commentary in Gasché's (sometimes) lucid exegetical mode? Then again, how is that we are *given to read* Gasché's book in the expectation – not always disappointed – that it will make sense of certain passages of de Man in a way that those passages (sometimes, not always) fail to make sense in and of themselves? 'Giving to Read' is Gasché's title for his chapter contrasting Derrida with de Man, and I recall it here in order to emphasise how utterly different is Derrida's sense of what constitutes an adequately complex, subtle, and responsive textual reading. For de Man it is a matter of taking away – showing up as naive or deluded – every last source of readerly assurance that we might have some chance of getting things right or at least of reading in a way that doesn't 'arbitrarily' impose its own meanings on an otherwise recalcitrant ('opaque', 'material', or 'heterogeneous') textual substrate. Yet neither he nor Gasché could advance this case with any hope of being read or understood were it not for the falsity of de Man's arguments and the self-exempting clause that implicitly attends their every attempt at consistent formulation.

In short, there is a massive performative contradiction involved in the sorts of claim put forward in the paragraph cited above. Gasché is misled – or so it seems to me – by his over-willingness to grant de Man's writings a genuine *philosophical* import despite all the evidence (which Gasché lays out in some detail) that they belong to some different, wholly 'singular' mode of oblique confessional discourse or perhaps to some hybrid, quasi-philosophical, displaced narrative *genre* that has more in common with the texts of writers like Beckett, Blanchot, or E.M. Cioran. Once in a while Gasché admits to certain misgivings in this regard, or the suspicion that maybe de Man is just a bad philosopher by any (not just conventional) criteria of reason, consistency, and truth. Thus:

> [i]s one not, in light of the results produced by this truly systematic levelling of difference and positive analogization – a levelling that is clearly deliberate, and not attributable to mere oversight or philosophical naiveté in general – immediately reminded of Hegel's famous dictum concerning those philosophers for whom thought is a night in which all cows are black? (p. 64–5)

This strikes me as a fair assessment of de Man's 'philosophical' claims, despite Gasché's strenuous efforts to lessen the gravity of the charge by treating his work as a special case whose 'singularity' places it far beyond reach of any such conventional judgement. By asking us to think of that levelling as 'deliberate' – and not just the upshot of 'oversight' or 'naiveté' – Gasché is clearly banking on de Man's own distinction (propounded in the essay on Heidegger) between mere 'mistake' and significant or motivated 'error'. But then we have to ask what could possibly *justify* so perverse and single-minded an effort to plunge philosophy back into the realm of chaos and old night. Gasché has written the best, most intelligent book we are likely to get on de Man from a critical standpoint closely aligned with its subject's ruling preoccupations. What is now needed is a more detached, resistant, or sceptical reading which holds out against the seductive power of de Man's nihilist rhetoric.

CHAPTER 8

Conflict, Compromise or Complementarity: ideas of science in modern literary theory

I

In this chapter I shall discuss some salient aspects of twentieth-century literary criticism in relation to science and philosophy of science. Up to now I have suggested a number of ways in which current debates about disciplinarity – about the relationship between different orders of knowledge and judgement – have challenged the idea of scientific reason as possessing any kind of superior status or privileged epistemic warrant. 'Postmodernism' may be taken as a blanket term for this outlook of generalised sceptical disdain for any discourse that falsely sets itself up – so the argument goes – as a paradigm of truth, method, or rational enquiry to which all others should aspire.[1] A similar deflationary drive is at work in the 'strong' sociology of knowledge (especially when applied to the physical sciences) and in various kindred movements of thought which seek to establish the context-dependent, culture-relative, historically emergent, discursively constructed, or socially mediated character of all such claims.[2] What these movements have in common is a will to challenge that ranking-order among the disciplines – as with the 'unity of science' programme advanced by the Logical Positivists – which placed them on a scale from physics (at the top), through chemistry and biology, to history, anthropology, sociology, psychology, and thence on down to such merely subjective or 'emotive' discourses as ethics, aesthetics, and literary criticism.[3] This conception has come under attack for various reasons, among them the emergence of research areas (like molecular biology) that cut across established disciplinary bounds and the extent to which developments in quantum theory have been thought to discredit the idea of science as aimed toward providing more detailed and accurate knowledge of an objective, observer-independent microphysical reality. But there is also a clearly-marked desire among cultural and literary theorists to exploit these supposed signs of 'crisis' in the discourse of the natural sciences and to stake their own claim as expert readers of the paradigm-change (or the large-scale discursive mutation) that is currently under way.

Hence, for instance, a book like John Dupré's *The Disorder of Things* whose title very pointedly evokes Foucault on the shifting configurations of knowledge or discourse from one period to the next, and whose nominalist theme is the sheer impossibility of fixing natural-kind classifications in biology and the life-sciences.[4] Hence also the notion of 'postmodern' science as no longer concerned with such old-fashioned values as truth, consistency, evidential warrant, explanatory power, and so forth, but rather – so it is said – with the kinds of 'paralogistic' reasoning that have emerged in the wake of quantum mechanics, chaos theory, and other such classically unthinkable *topoi*.[5] These ideas have lately gained wide currency, not least among postmodern culture-critics and those who have pursued the linguistic 'turn' to the point of claiming that reality is indeed nothing more than a product of our various language-games, discourses, paradigms, conceptual schemes, etc.[6] In earlier chapters I traced this development back to its starting-point in Kant's 'doctrine of the faculties', that is to say, in the various potential conflicts and tensions that existed within that doctrine and which later gave rise to just the sorts of boundary-dispute that are nowadays seized upon by postmodern thinkers as a lever for dismantling ('deconstructing') the entire edifice of modern philosophico-scientific thought. I also suggested that such arguments were both philosophically confused and very far from progressive – if perhaps 'radical' in some vague all-purpose sense of that term – with regard to their ethical and socio-political implications. What I want to do now is look more closely at some previous episodes in the complex history of relationships between literary criticism and science (or received ideas of science) during the period since 1900. Of course it is impossible to cover such a large topic without some kind of classificatory system, or at any rate a broad narrative structure on which to hang the relevant contrasts and comparisons. I shall therefore begin by distinguishing four main schools of thought whose differences can be mapped in broadly generic terms and also on a roughly chronological scale extending from the early years of the century to its final decades. Along the way I shall somewhat complicate the picture – or qualify this overly schematic approach – through a more detailed discussion of individual thinkers, some of whom stand decidedly apart from any general movement or trend.

II

First there is the markedly defensive attitude, typified in the early work of I.A. Richards, which sought to maintain some viable conception of poetic meaning or truth despite the perceived threat to such values from a narrowly positivist (science-based) epistemology.[7] On this view it appeared that the physical sciences were not only acquiring greater prestige than the humanistic disciplines but also challenging the very idea of literature as a source of imaginative insights unavailable elsewhere. Second, there is the more confident belief – descending from nineteenth-century hermeneutic theorists such as Schleiermacher and Dilthey – that literary criticism and the *Geisteswissenschaften* have their own distinctive mode of understanding, one that is in no way threatened by the methods and procedures of the natural sciences.[8] Third, there is the kind of systematic approach (first adopted by Aristotle and taken up by various latterday formalist and structuralist schools) which seeks to place criticism on a more scientific, that is to say, a more disciplined or methodical footing, and thereby avoid the disreputable vagaries of 'mere' interpretation or impressionistic reader-response. The fourth category is one that emphatically repudiates any such appeal to the *Naturwissenschaften* as a model or paradigm for criticism and the humanistic disciplines. This is the idea – most vigorously canvassed by postmodernist thinkers such as Lyotard and neo-pragmatists like Richard Rorty – that the physical sciences should themselves be regarded as interpretive constructs and hence as open to the full range of textual, hermeneutic, or rhetorical approaches.[9] Thus one way of writing this narrative would be to plot it in terms of a growing self-assurance, among literary theorists, that theirs is a practice which yields nothing to scientists (let alone philosophers or historians of science) in point of methodological rigour, objectivity, or truth. Rather, such values must be seen as belonging to an old, presumptively discredited paradigm whose eclipse marks the passage to a 'postmodern' epoch where the natural sciences no longer enjoy any kind of epistemic or cognitive privilege.

This is all about as remote as can be from the situation of literary studies as perceived by certain influential thinkers in the early years of this century. A predominant theme at the time was the idea of scientific knowledge as a threat to the kinds of imaginative insight provided by works of literature, an idea first expressed by Matthew Arnold and taken up by I.A. Richards in his writings of the 1920s.[10] For Arnold and his contemporaries – Tennyson most famously among them – this evoked a strong sense of existential anguish, or sometimes of forlorn resignation in the face of a materialist worldview that found no room for our all-too-human hopes, wishes, and beliefs. It had to do mainly with the encroachment of Darwinian and other naturalistic creeds upon the value-sphere of religious and moral belief, a realm that might yet survive this scientific onslaught – so Arnold maintained – if poetry lived up to its 'high destiny' and assumed the role which religion had performed until the advent of the Higher Criticism.[11] In Richards the pathos is considerably toned down while the general diagnosis remains much the same. Perhaps poetry can save us, as Arnold thought, but only on condition that it somehow make terms with the onward march of a scientific culture that had come to dictate what should count as 'knowledge' in the proper (i.e., scientifically certified) sense. At this time Richards was himself much influenced by the doctrines of

Logical Positivism, in particular the Verification Principle according to which any statement must be counted strictly meaningless – or emptily 'metaphysical' – unless it can be *either* verified as a matter of straightforward empirical warrant like the observation-sentences of physical science, *or* held self-evidently valid in virtue of its constituent meanings and logical form.[12] Since the 'statements' of poetry satisfied neither criterion – since their truth-conditions (if any) were not subject to assessment on factual-empirical or logical grounds – therefore those statements could only be construed as a species of 'emotive' utterance, one that laid no claim to veridical import but which served to evoke certain valuable kinds of affective or attitudinal response in the reader.

So it was that Richards in effect carried through on T.S. Eliot's well-known pronouncement that the great task of modern literature and criticism was to effect 'a complete severance between poetry and belief', thus leaving poetry free to explore ranges of human experience and cultural memory untouched by the encroachments of modern secular rationalism.[13] Other critics – F.R. Leavis most prominent among them – raised this doctrine to a high point of anti-scientistic principle which ascribed all the ills of our present-day 'technologico-Benthamite' civilisation to the advent of a narrowly means-end rationality that found no room for the redeeming values of creative and imaginative insight. Leavis's notorious 'debate' with C.P. Snow – not so much a debate as a mutual exchange of uncomprehending hostilities – may be seen as having marked a low-point in this history of strained relations between self-appointed advocates of the 'two cultures'.[14] However the case was somewhat different with Richards since his own approach to literary criticism bore the imprint of various scientifically-oriented currents of thought, in particular behavioral psychology and Bronislaw Malinowski's functionalist anthropology.[15] These allegiances – along with his uneasy endorsement of the Verificationist Principle – left Richards awkwardly placed when attempting (like Arnold before him) to justify poetry's claim upon the interests of a modern, scientifically informed readership. What made this problem yet more acute was Richards's central role in the establishment of so-called 'Cambridge English', a project whose chief aim was to vindicate the study of vernacular literature (against some fairly stiff local opposition) as a genuine academic discipline with its own criteria of method and evaluative judgement. By that standard there was something decidedly suspect – not to say shuffling and evasive – about his idea of poetry as proffering 'pseudo-statements' which were simply not candidates for rational assessment in terms of truth or falsehood, but valuable only in so far as they evoked certain rich and complex attitudinal states in the reader's mind.

One way out of this dilemma was that taken by the so-called 'New Criticism', a mainly US movement of thought which flourished from the mid-1940s until the late 1960s, and which exerted a widespread influence on the teaching of literature in schools and universities.[16] The New Critics shared Richards's concern with the threat to humane values – as they saw it – of a technocratic culture given over to rampant scientism and the utilitarian calculus of interests based on a merely instrumental conception of means-end rationality. This attitude was further reinforced by their collective self-image as a Southern Agrarian movement strongly opposed not only to the dominant ethos of the industrialised US North but also to the various secular forces that had brought about the increasing fragmentation of tradition-based communal values. Their response was a curious mixture of the classicising (anti-romantic and anti-humanist) bias inherited from T.S. Eliot, the romantic idea of 'aesthetic education' with its origins in poet-philosophers like Schiller and Coleridge, and a markedly methodical or systematising bent which stood in sharp contrast to their programmatic statements concerning the limits and the perils of applied technique. In brief, their approach to poetry involved the close-reading of individual texts with a strictly-enforced veto on 'extraneous' (e.g., biographical, historical, or socio-documentary) sources, and with maximum attention to 'intrinsic' details of structure, texture, and form. Only thus, they argued, could poetry be saved from the wrong sorts of critical interest that would reduce it to the level of plain-prose paraphrase or mere propositional content.

Hence the New Critics' constant recourse to a range of favoured rhetorical tropes – 'irony' and 'paradox' among them – that were held to characterise the best poetry in virtue of providing a highly-wrought verbal structure which allowed for the greatest variety of meanings yet could also be thought of as somehow objectively 'there' in the words on the page. Such was their answer to Richards's problem: a method that endorsed his high valuation of complex attitudinal states while claiming to locate them in the poem itself, rather than appealing to some vague idea of affective or 'emotive' reader-response. This was also their answer to the 'science and poetry' question in so far as poetry could now be viewed as possessing its own kind of 'logic', one that dealt chiefly in irony and paradox, and which thereby gave access to imaginative truths beyond the furthest reach of scientific reason. Still there was a certain defensiveness about the New Critics' attitude to science, resulting as it did – no less than with Richards – from a sense that such truths could only be preserved by imposing a whole elaborate system of doctrinal checks and sanctions. Hence W.K. Wimsatt's idea of the poem as 'verbal icon', that is to say, as a strictly inviolable structure of inwrought meanings and attitudes whose autonomy required absolute respect on the critic's part and could only be compromised by those various critical 'heresies' which sought to make terms with the rational prose intellect.[17]

If Richards's dilemma now looks strangely unreal then this is in part because philosophy of science has long since abandoned the verificationist doctrine, at least in its strict or canonical form, as outlined above.[18] One reason was the fact that it could not be stated or paraphrased so as to satisfy its own stipulative conditions. That is to say, the Verification Principle was neither empirically verifiable nor yet self-evidently valid in virtue of its logical structure and the meaning assigned to its constituent terms. The most telling attack on this whole programme in epistemology and philosophy of science was W.V. Quine's celebrated essay 'Two Dogmas of Empiricism'.[19] The 'two dogmas' in question were, first, the idea that meaningful statements could be exhaustively categorised according to the standard distinction between empirical 'matters of fact' and logical (or analytic) 'truths of reason', and second, the idea that empirical truth-claims could be checked one-by-one against various items of discrete observational evidence. On the contrary, Quine maintains: observation-statements are ineluctably 'theory-laden' in so far as they involve all manner of implicit ontological commitments, metaphysical assumptions, auxiliary hypotheses, etc. And theories are likewise 'underdetermined' by the evidence in so far as the empirical data in any given case are always capable of various construals depending on one's choice between alternative ways of fitting them into some overall descriptive or explanatory scheme. Thus, according to Quine, we should think of knowledge as a 'man-made fabric' that extends all the way from those logical axioms (or so-called 'truths of reason') that occupy a space near the centre to those observation-statements (or empirical 'matters of fact') which we currently accept as well borne out by the best scientific evidence but none the less hold to be revisable in light of future conflicting or recalcitrant data.

Quine's point is that *every* statement – analytic or synthetic – is in principle subject to reinterpretation by tweaking this or that thread of the fabric in order to conserve some especially cherished item, whether at the logical 'centre' or closer to the observational 'periphery'. What typically governs our choice in such matters is a conservative desire to save as much as possible of the existing stock of belief while at the same time seeking to minimize conflicts by making whatever pragmatic adjustments are required in order to maintain overall coherence. Thus it may be that sometimes – in periods of radical theory-change – we are driven to revise the very ground-rules of logic, as for instance should the evidence of quantum-physical phenomena like wave/particle dualism turn out to require the supension of logical laws such as bivalence or distributive truth/falsehood. Or again, it may be that we want to hang onto some particularly cherished core-principle and therefore elect to reinterpret the empirical evidence, as for instance by adducing perceptual distortion or (again as in quantum mechanics) the effect of observation on that which we observe. Thus no statement is in principle immune from revision since adjustments can be made at any point in the existing fabric of beliefs under pressure from anomalies elsewhere. Moreover it follows that every such statement must be thought of as confronting the entire 'tribunal of experience' and hence as neither confirmed nor falsified by any one piece of empirical data or the result of any one crucial experiment. Rather there is always an appeal open to the various auxiliary hypotheses that enter tacitly into the framing of even the most basic observation-statement, and may therefore be held responsible for any conflicts that arise between some particular item of recalcitrant evidence and the best state of present-day scientific knowledge. All of which amounts – on Quine's submission – to a knockdown case against the two last 'dogmas' of Logical Empiricism and an argument for the kind of holistic approach that would draw no firm or categorical line between truth-claims in the physical sciences and the rest of our standing ontological commitments as witnessed by the various items that figure in our everyday habits of talk.

III

I have discussed Quine's essay at length since it has had a great impact on philosophy of science during the past three decades and has also contributed to a wider sense that the 'old' disciplinary boundaries – including that between science and literature – are currently in process of radical trans-formation. Thus it is often argued that scientific knowledge cannot be divorced from those various background contexts (of language, culture, ideology, inherited belief-systems and so forth) which require the same kinds of interpretative treatment – or depth-hermeneutic understanding – as are standardly brought to bear by literary critics or other people in the human and social sciences.[20] For the Logical Positivists such thinking bore witness to a straightforward confusion of realms, namely that between the 'context of discovery' (where all sorts of historical, cultural, or psychobiographical factors might play a role) and the properly scientific 'context of justification' (where truth-claims and theories were tested on their merits and subject to the most rigorous standards of observational, predictive, or causal-explan-atory warrant).[21] However this distinction is thrown into doubt if one accepts Quine's arguments for meaning-holism, the 'theory-laden' character of observation-statements, and the 'underdermination' of theories by evidence. For it will then seem just another dogma of old-style Logical Empiricism that strives to hold the line between genuine, first-order scientific enquiry and whatever belongs to the lesser domains of history or sociology of science. And this despite Quine's many well-known statements to the effect that science – physics especially – is our most reliable method of belief-formation and should therefore take precedence, if only on 'pragmatic' grounds, over any hypotheses put forward by those other disciplines.

My point is to suggest how far the terms of debate have changed since Richards confronted his Arnoldian dilemma about poetry, science, and belief. For the idea has taken hold across a range of disciplines – sociology, psychology, historiography, literary criticism, even philosophy of science – that interpretation in some sense goes 'all the way down', in which case supposedly there is nothing (no standard of rigorous procedure or valid reasoning on the evidence) which can serve to distinguish the 'hard', i.e. physical or natural sciences from the 'soft', i.e. arts-and-humanities disciplines. This idea has various sources, among them Thomas Kuhn's distinctly Quinean argument – in his influential book *The Structure of Scientific Revolutions* – that scientists on each side of some major paradigm-change may be said to inhabit 'different worlds' since there exists no common framework (or shared ontological scheme) to which they might refer in order to establish genuine grounds for comparison.[22] Thus where Aristotle saw matter seeking out out its rightful place in the order of sublunary nature, Galileo saw a case of gravitationally-induced pendular motion. And likewise, where Priestley found strong experimental warrant for an intangible substance ('phlogiston') given out in the process of combustion, Lavoisier witnessed all the evident signs that combustion involved the uptake of oxygen.

There is some room for doubt as to just how strongly or literally Kuhn intended his claim about changes of paradigm being equivalent to changes of 'world'.[23] At times he appears to moderate the claim or suggest that we construe it in epistemological rather than ontological terms. Such would at any rate seem to be the implication when he uses the more cautious metaphor of scientists before and after a revolution viewing the world through differently tinted spectacles. All the same it is clear that Kuhn is prepared to go a long way with the Quinean holistic or framework-relativist argument which takes it that everything is in principle subject to revision, from perceptions (as recorded in observation-statements) to logical 'laws of thought'. Indeed the only items that remain invariant between observers with different theories are the bare, uninterpreted sensory 'stimuli' which Kuhn (like Quine) thinks sufficient to provide the basis of a thoroughly physicalist or naturalised epistemology. But in that case – as full-fledged cultural relativists are quick to point out – one might as well admit that for all practical purposes the observers do indeed inhabit 'different worlds' since their perceptions diverge at the most basic level where sense-data acquire significant content. And from here it is no great distance to Kuhn's case for the 'incommensurability' of different scientific paradigms, or the lack of any common (scheme-independent) criteria that might enable meaningful comparisons to be drawn with respect to such values as truth, objectivity, theoretical grasp, or rational inference to the best explanation. For these comparisons would always be made from within some particular paradigm or framework, and would therefore – by the incommensurability-thesis – fail to understand whatever lay beyond its internal (paradigm-specific) criteria of truth and method. Thus any talk of scientific 'progress' must henceforth be viewed as merely the kind of wishful illusion that comes of projecting our own favoured theories, ontologies, truth-claims, etc., onto past ways of thinking which are then judged wanting by our own presumptively more adequate standards.

I have written elsewhere about the problems – as I see them – with this relativist approach to the history and philosophy of science.[24] What I wish to do here, more neutrally, is emphasise the various points of convergence between recent developments in literary theory and the kinds of thinking that have gained ground among philosophers (and especially sociologists) of science in the wake of Logical Positivism. One result has been the shift toward a broadly hermeneutic conception of scientific enquiry which stresses the element of tacit knowledge – the background assumptions, cultural values, or shared habits of belief – that enter into each and every act of judgement, whether in the human or the natural sciences. This approach has a number of sources, among them (as I have said) the mainly German tradition of philosophical hermeneutics descending from Schleiermacher and Dilthey to Heidegger and Gadamer, and also the late writings of Wittgenstein, where science is viewed as just one of many 'language-games' or cultural 'forms of life', with no privileged claim to reason or truth except within certain specialised communities where its own criteria apply.[25] At the furthest extreme – as in the writings of a 'strong' textualist like Richard Rorty – it takes the form of downright denial that there is anything to distinguish the natural from the human sciences in point of methodological rigour or explanatory power.[26] It is not hard to see why such ideas should appeal to literary critics and cultural theorists with an interest in challenging the high prestige – not to mention the greater share of material resources – typically enjoyed by their scientist colleagues.

Indeed one could view the history of recent (post-1960) literary theory as a series of periodic pendulum swings between the twin poles of emulating science in a different field of endeavour and repudiating science as a 'discourse' backed up by all kinds of academic and state-sponsored institutional control. Two movements in particular typify this pattern, the first (structuralism) aspiring to the status of a 'science' of the literary text, the second (post-structuralism) firmly rejecting any such idea that literature can or should be theorised in accordance with the dictates of applied system and method. These movements have received a vast amount of commentary over the past two decades so I shall treat them here only in relation to the 'science and literature' theme.[27] Sufficient to say that the structuralist paradigm was one that took Saussure's theoretical 'revolution' in linguistics as a model for the analysis of various signifying systems, from styles of dress or culinary codes to myths, narratives, poetic structures, and – beyond that – the whole range of generic constraints that supposedly governed the production and reception of literary, historical, scientific, and other types of text.[28] In this sense it was firmly aligned with the ideals of systematicity and scientific rigour which had characterised previous schools of thought such as the Russian and Czech Formalist movements of the 1920s and 1930s. In another sense, however, it defined 'science' – or what should count as a truly 'scientific' approach – in terms that gave priority to language, discourse, or representation as the limit-point of all understanding and the main focus of enquiry for every branch of knowledge, the physical sciences included.

Hence Paul Ricoeur's well-known description of structuralism as 'Kantianism without the transcendental subject'.[29] That is say, it was a theory which maintained – like Kant – that we could have no access to reality except through the various concepts and schemas that we ourselves imposed upon it, but which denied Kant's claim that these were vested in the *a priori* forms and modalities of human understanding, and could thus provide intersubjectively valid knowledge. From a structuralist viewpoint, those forms were as many and diverse as the signifying systems – the cultural codes and conventions – that existed in various language-communities. Thus structuralism claimed scientific warrant but only in virtue of its further claim to be the master-discipline of knowledge, one that subsumed all merely regional sciences (from mathematics to anthropology, from history to psychoanalysis, from philosophy of science to narrative poetics) under the sovereign gaze of a method whose theoretical source was Saussure's project of a unified general semiology, a study of signs and their various modes of discursive articulation. For if language was indeed the key to all understanding then structural linguistics was the pilot science that alone provided an adequate grasp of the various discourses (narratives, paradigms, modes of representation, etc.) which comprised the entirety of knowledge at any given time.

In short, structuralism already went some way toward challenging the received idea that the disciplines could be ranked in descending order with the natural sciences in pride of place (physics, chemistry, and biology), and the humanities subjects (history, economics, anthropology, sociology, psychology, down to aesthetics and literary criticism) as subject-areas that were not to be thought of as 'sciences' in the strict sense of that term. Of course there were boundary-disputes in plenty, with claims for genuine scientific status advanced on behalf of disciplines like economics and sociology where there seemed at least a plausible case to be made that these were amenable to rigorous (e.g., statistical or causal-explanatory) treatment, rather than subject to the vagaries of mere 'interpretation'. Still it seemed clear that literary criticism was at best an interpretative discipline and hence beyond the pale of 'scientific' method in any but an honorific sense of that term. Such was at any rate the viewpoint adopted by advocates of the 'unity of science' programme which enjoyed wide support among logical positivists and their logical-empiricist descendents. As we have seen, it quickly came under attack by philosophers of science such as Quine and

Kuhn who rejected its most basic tenets and in stead proposed a holistic (or contextualist) theory of knowledge with strong relativist implications. So it is not surprising that the structuralist 'revolution' in various, mainly French-influenced fields of thought should have attained its maximum impact at about the same time – the late 1960s – when Anglophone philosophy of science was likewise starting to question those hitherto sacrosanct ideas of method, objectivity, and truth.

IV

Post-structuralism is commonly viewed as marking a further, yet more decisive break with such old-style 'scientistic' aims and ambitions. Thus for instance one finds Roland Barthes, in his book *S/Z* (1970), denouncing the methodological ideal that had guided much of his own previous work, namely the quest for a narrative poetics – or a generalised theory of 'the text' – which would place criticism on a properly rigorous footing.[30] Rather, as he now thinks, we should acknowledge the uniqueness and the infinite complexity of every text we encounter, and read henceforth with a finely tuned sense of the various codes, intertextual allusions, narrative cross-cuts, moments of representational crisis, ideological blind-spots, etc., which elude any treatment of the sort prescribed by classic structuralist theory. To this extent it is true to say that the prefix 'post-' in the term 'post-structuralism' denotes a sharp turn against the claims of system and method, one that entails a high degree of scepticism with regard to any claim that literary theorists might take a lesson from the physical sciences, above all from that positivist tradition of thought in French literary scholarship which Barthes regards as just another form of collusive 'commonsense' ideology.[31] This in turn goes along with a deep hostility – on the part of many post-structuralists and their current postmodernist *confrères* – toward the idea of science as a constructive, truth-seeking endeavour characterized by certain distinctive values such as truth, rationality, hypothesis-testing, and inference to the best (most adequate) explanation.

Thus for some – Jean-François Lyotard most prominent among them – we have now entered an epoch of 'postmodern' science where the most significant advances have to do with incompleteness, undecidability, indeterminacy, complementarity, the 'limits of precise measurement', fracta, paradox, catastrophe, wave/particle dualism, quantum superposition, and so forth, none of them capable of theorization in classical ('modernist') scientific terms.[32] In so far as truth still has some role to play it is 'truth' as a matter of sheerly *performative* effects – the ability to persuade, to influence people, to get a hearing for one's ideas or raise the necessary research funds – rather than 'truth' as a strictly *constative* ideal, a matter of theories or explanatory hypotheses that hold good quite apart from such extraneous socio-cultural factors. What this amounts to, in effect, is a total repudiation of the 'two-contexts' theory advanced by the logical empiricists, namely the distinction between 'context of discovery' and 'context of justification', the one having to do with motivating interests, pressures and incentives that play some role in the genesis of scientific theories, the other with standards of rational accountability that involve quite different (more precise or conceptually rigorous) criteria.[33] 'Postmodern' science therefore works out as something very like Paul Feyerabend's notion of 'epistemological anarchism', that is to say, an attitude of 'anything goes!', adopted in the hope that this will allow a thousand speculative flowers to bloom by lifting the kinds of orthodox methodological constraint that deter scientists from following out their own pet theories and conjectures.[34] It can thus be seen as a reversal of Kuhn's (to this extent) conservative idea that 'normal' science is by very definition the sort that goes on most of the time, while 'revolutionary' science is what goes on during just those infrequent and exceptional periods of crisis when even the most basic scientific beliefs are open to radical challenge.

Postmodernism views that state of crisis as affecting every branch of knowledge and indeed every area of present-day life, from the physical sciences to ethics, politics, and modes of historical representation.[35] In each case – so it is argued – we have lost the old sense of 'meta-narrative' security that came of telling a Whiggish story about truth, reason, progress, critique, and the convergence on a rational (enlightened) consensus that would finally remove all obstacles to agreement among like-minded enquirers. What we are left with is a medley of competing beliefs – 'first-order natural pragmatic narratives', as Lyotard calls them – none of which can rightfully claim such status, but all of which exist in an ongoing 'cultural conversation' (Rorty's term) that can best be promoted by learning to respect these strictly irreducible differences of view. Here again there are obvious points of resemblance to Kuhn's paradigm-relativist philosophy of science, as well as to Feyerabend's yet more extreme variations on the theme of paradigm-incommensurability.

To some extent these notions find a parallel in the broadly post-structuralist 'theory' of truth as a linguistic (or discursive) construct whose ultimate sources may be as much metaphorical as conceptual, or as much dependent on certain privileged narrative constructions as on processes of disciplined observation, inductive inference, hypothetico-deductive reasoning, etc. However there is a strong countervailing tendency that has left its mark on a good deal of recent Francophile literary theory, despite the appeal of such heady (ultimately Nietzsche-derived) sceptical arguments. This has its roots in Gaston Bachelard's critical-rationalist approach to the history and philosophy of science, an approach that exerted considerable influence on the early generation of structuralist thinkers, since it offered a range of highly developed concepts and categories for describing how progress came about in the physical and the human sciences.[36] Most crucial here was Bachelard's theory of the 'epistemological break' which marked the decisive stage of advance from a pre- or protoscientific way of thinking – one typified by residual elements of myth, metaphor, anthropomorphism, imagistic 'reverie', and so forth – to a mature science with adequate powers of descriptive, conceptual, and explanatory grasp. This theory itself marked a definite break with the Cartesian rationalist tradition wherein knowledge was conceived as a matter of the mind's having access to 'clear and distinct ideas', ideas whose apodictic truth would then provide an anchor-point proof against the demons of sceptical doubt. However – so Bachelard argued – that conception was no longer viable in the wake of various scientific advances (such as non-Euclidean geometry, relativity-theory, and quantum mechanics) which were simply incompatible with any such approach. Rather, those advances could only have occurred through a decisive break with the idea of knowledge as grounded in concepts or representations that were somehow self-evident to reason. After all, it was just that kind of *a priori* thinking which had led Kant – despite his criticism of Descartes' 'rational psychology' – to erect an entire theory of knowledge on the supposedly absolute truths of Euclidean geometry and Newtonian physics.[37] What had since become clear was the need for philosophy of science to free itself from any such lingering Cartesian influence and attend more closely to particular episodes in the history of scientific theory-construction and paradigm-change.

However Bachelard maintains – unlike Kuhn – that there are certain trans-paradigm standards of method, validity, and truth which the historian has to apply when reconstructing those episodes and which make it possible to compare different theories (or different stages of conceptual advance within a given theory) according to properly scientific criteria. Thus, for instance, a theory may have its origins in the kind of poetic 'reverie' that throws up some suggestive image or metaphor – such as the ancient atomists' conception of matter – which is then developed and refined to the point where it becomes an item of mature scientific knowledge capable of rigorous statement or precise formulation. This process of 'rectification and critique' is the means by which science itself makes progress and also the means by which historian-philosophers of science can distinguish progressive from retrograde, stagnant, or ultimately dead-end episodes in its history to date. It is here that Bachelard's critical-rationalist approach differs most sharply from Kuhn's idea that scientific 'revolutions' involve such a wholesale change in the meaning of observational and theoretical terms that no comparison is possible across or between successive paradigms. On the contrary, he argues: we can and must make such comparisons if philosophy is to offer any adequate account of scientific knowledge and progress.

V

As I have said, French structuralism derived some important lessons from Bachelard's epistemology, among them its basic working principle that the human sciences could achieve methodological rigour only by adopting a synchronic approach that allowed them adequately to theorise their own conceptual premises and presuppositions. In this respect it lent powerful support to Saussure's programme for structural linguistics and, beyond that, for a generalised semiology encompassing all the manifold forms of human social exchange. However Bachelard's philosophy was subject to various revisionist readings in the course of its migration from philosophy and history of science to critical, cultural, and literary theory. For Louis Althusser, seeking to justify the claims of Marxist 'theoretical practice', it offered the idea of a decisive epistemological break between the realm of ideological (imaginary) misrecognition and the standpoint of a genuine Marxist 'science' that would enable the theorist to achieve at least a momentary view from outside that realm.[38] Thus Althussser's project of structural Marxism preserved this main feature of Bachelard's critical epistemology even though it involved some considerable stretching of terms – 'science' among them – and also gave rise to many other problems for his disciples and exegetes.[39] In Foucault's early work, conversely, the notion of 'epistemological break' took on such a wide and loose application that it became pretty much synnoymous with Kuhn's idea of paradigm-change. That is to say, it is envisaged as a large-scale shift of interpretative framework occurring at certain vaguely-defined historical junctures for no specifiable reason and amounting to a kind of random drift which somehow affects all the discourses of knowledge from one *episteme* (or order of knowledge and representation) to the next. Foucault's interest is directed chiefly toward those middle-range disciplines on the standard 'hard-to-soft' scale – biology (or the life-sciences), economics (or the earlier 'analysis of wealth'), sociology, psychology, philology, historiography – which have undergone various marked transformations in their scope of 'legitimate' enquiry, and whose scientific status has therefore very often been a matter of intense methodological dispute.

It is not hard to see why Foucault should have taken these subject-areas (rather than, say, the history of atomic physics from its ancient Greek speculative origins to Dalton, Mendeleev, Rutherford, Einstein, Bohr et al.) as his basis for arguing the relativist case that notions such as truth, reason, or progress are always internal to some given 'discourse' or framework of representation. The advantage they offer – from Foucault's point of view – is that they make it more plausible to suggest by analogy that *all* the sciences ('hard' and 'soft') are subject to the same sorts of boundary-dispute and can thus be brought within the overarching compass of a theory of shifting discursive formations which treats them as indifferently ranked with respect to objectivity or truth. The chief problem here, as with Kuhn and Feyerabend, is that of explaining *in rational terms* why such changes in scientific thinking should ever occur, given the holistic (or framework-relativist) character of all these theories and their failure to provide any adequate account of just what grounds scientists might have for abandoning one and adopting another 'discourse', 'paradigm', 'narrative', etc.

Literary theorists – at any rate those of a broadly postmodernist persuasion – have tended to ignore this problem in their keenness to exploit the resultant opportunities for levelling the science/literature distinction, or for treating 'science' as a strictly non-privileged field of textual representations open to their own well-practised techniques of rhetorical analysis. Elsewhere there has been much talk of fashionable topics in present-day 'popular' science – chaos theory especially – as somehow supporting (or supported by) the most advanced forms of literary-speculative thought.[41] Such arguments tend to work best when they focus on well-chosen passages of specific literary texts and not when advanced as sweeping claims about the passage to a new 'postmodern' epoch in science, or the eclipse of values such as reason and truth through the advent of a paradigm whose signs are those of paralogism, undecidability, etc. Thus, for instance, N. Katherine Hayles has produced some informative and well-documented work comparing the emergence of field-theoretical concepts – from Faraday and Maxwell down – with related or broadly analogous developments in nineteenth- and twentieth-century poetry and fiction.[42] Such studies gain in depth and precision what they sacrifice in the rhetoric of epochal change or world-transformative paradigm shifts.

This is also the case with various attempts to establish a link between literary theory and developments in mathematics or theoretical physics. Such comparisons often make considerable play with Gödel's incompleteness-theorem (to the effect that any arithmetical system beyond a certain order of complexity will contain at least one axiom the truth of which is not provable within that system), and the uncertainty-relations which – according to the orthodox theory – specify the limits of attainable knowledge with regard to quantum phenomena.[43] At times such analogies are pushed pretty hard, as for example by Arkady Plotnitsky, who argues at length for a reading of Derrida's work in conjunction with that of the quantum physicist-philosopher Niels Bohr.[44] In this instance it is Bohr's formulations – including his celebrated complementarity-principle – which leave one doubting their philosophic rigour while Derrida emerges (contrary to widespread report) as a thinker of the utmost conceptual precision and sustained analytic power. Here again it is through the detail of Derrida's texts that the case is most convincingly made and not through the kinds of blanket claim that would have the entirety of 'Western metaphysics' somehow undermined by a generalised appeal to such deconstructive key-terms as 'writing', 'difference', and 'supplementarity'.[45]

This distinction can also be drawn with respect to the various quantum-physical analogies proposed by literary theorists, beginning with some quirkish but brilliant pages in William Empson's *Seven Types of Ambiguity* (1930), taken up by I.A. Richards in his speculative middle-period writings, and continued – as I have said – by postmodernist thinkers such as Lyotard.[46] Most often their interest is focused on the well-known problems that arise in assigning any consistent or intelligible realist interpretation to quantum-physical phenomena. These problems include wave/particle dualism, the inherent uncertainty attaching to measurements of particle location or momentum, the (supposedly) observer-induced 'collapse of the wave-packet', and the evidence of remote simultaneous interaction between widely separated particles.[47] Hence the range of often far-fetched speculative 'solutions' that theorists have typically produced in response to what they see as the insuperable problems now confronting any realist or 'classical' scientific worldview.[48] Then again there is the notion that since quantum mechanics is deeply mysterious therefore it must be somehow connected with other such likewise mysterious matters as the nature of consciousness or the possibility of human freewill as against the claims of old-style scientific determinism.[49]

Empson's reflections were a good deal more circumspect and better-informed than much of this subsequent discussion, not least as a result of his having read mathematics and taken a keen interest in the new physics during his first two years of undergraduate study at Cambridge. What chiefly engaged his interest in *Seven Types* was the relevance of Heisenberg's Uncertainty Principle to issues of meaning, objectivity and truth in the interpretation of literary texts. That is to say, just as quantum physics entailed certain ultimate limits to our powers of objective measurement and observation when applied to events in the subatomic domain, so likewise it was strictly impossible to conceive of poetic meaning as somehow objectively 'there' in the words on the page, quite apart from our response to them as more or less sensitive, intelligent, or well-trained readers. On the other hand Empson was far from drawing the subjectivist conclusion that the poem should therefore be assumed to 'mean' whatever the reader might suppose it to mean according to his or her private associations, preferences, habits of response, etc. After all, quantum physics assigned a precise value to the degree of uncertainty that applied in any given case, or the likelihood of obtaining this or that measurement under certain specified experimental conditions. This value was a product of the wavefunction – itself calculated according to Schrödinger's Equation – which determined the *objective* probability of recording such measurements at a given locus or a given point in the field of propagating wavelike events.[50] No doubt there were problems in conceiving the nature of any putative quantum-physical 'reality' which could somehow manifest itself in different ways (i.e., in wave- or particle-form) according to the kind of experiment conducted or the momentary setting of the measurement apparatus. Still these problems had to do with the limits of human (technologically-assisted) observation – or maybe with the limits of our present-best theories and conceptual powers – rather than pertaining to some ultimate mystery in the nature of quantum-physical reality.

In literary criticism likewise (so Empson thought) there was no valid argument from the manifest shortcomings of a naive objectivist approach to the denial of any constraints upon interpretative freedom exerted by the words on the page. Rather, what critics might usefully learn from these new developments in physical science was the impossibility of conceiving knowledge as the Logical Positivists conceived it, i.e., a process by which 'the mind, otherwise passive, collects propositions about the outside world'.[51] If this was the dominant approach in philosophy of science at the time – not to mention its influence (as we have seen already) on scientifically-aware critics such as I.A. Richards – nevertheless it was one that came sharply into conflict with the latest quantum-physical findings. In the case of poetry, Empson remarks, 'the act of knowing is itself an act of sympathizing; unless you are enjoying the poetry you cannot create it, as poetry, in your mind'. Thus the attempt to apply positivist principles in the field of literary criticism might at least have some use in bringing out the inherent limitations of any such approach or 'reduc[ing] that idea of truth (much more intimately than elsewhere) to a self-contradiction'.[52] Such was at any rate Empson's understanding of the 'science and literature' debate at a time when the so-called 'two cultures' were already maintaining in a kind of uneasy truce which would soon break down and give rise to the overt hostilities enacted in Leavis's notorious 'debate' with C.P. Snow.

Richards was Empson's supervisor at Cambridge and it seems fairly clear that when Empson alludes to the problems with Logical Positivism he is talking at least in part about the problems with Richards's attempt to make terms with science by adopting an emotivist (i.e., noncognitivist or non-truth-functional) theory of poetic meaning. In fact Richards himself shortly afterwards abandoned that position and turned to Niels Bohr's quantum-derived notion of 'complementarity' as an alternative means of confronting the issue.[53] For Bohr, the only answer to problems such as wave/particle dualism or the impossibility of obtaining precise simultaneous measurements of particle position and momentum was to accept the need for 'complementary' descriptions, that is to say, descriptions which in some sense applied to the 'same' physical phenomenon, but which construed it in accordance with two (non-conflicting since strictly incommensurable) theories, frameworks, ontological schemes, etc.[54] Richards, like Bohr, thought of this approach as a major advance not only in philosophy of science but also in other areas of human concern – ethics, aesthetics, and politics among them – where disagreement typically led on to a stalemate situation where the opposing parties could envisage no way beyond some deep-laid clash of ultimate values or priorities. However this escape-route might seem a mere evasion of the issue, whether as regards the conceptual dilemmas of orthodox (Bohr-derived) quantum theory or the genuine problems that often arise when we try to reconcile differences of ethical view or antinomies such as that between freewill and determinism. At any rate Empson saw little virtue in those later attempts by literary theorists – the New Critics among them – to avoid confronting such issues by treating poetry as a privileged realm where contradiction could have no place since poetic truth was 'paradoxical' in its very nature, and must therefore be thought to transcend all the vexing antinomies of plain-prose reason.[55] On the contrary, he argued: if poetry failed to make sense by rationally accountable standards then this should at least give pause to any 'deep' interpretation (or any saving recourse to the complementarity-doctrine) whose effect was simply to push these problems conveniently out of sight.

VI

Postmodernists have gone much further than Empson, or indeed Richards, in their claim to draw radical implications from the quantum revolution in physics. Hence the idea that present-day science has abandoned any notion of an objective or mind-independent 'reality' and come around to an outlook of full-fledged postmodernist scepticism with regard to such naive beliefs. This thesis can be made to look all the more plausible by citing authorities like Bohr whose statements often invite such a reading on account of their highly paradoxical quality and fondness for all sorts of far-reaching metaphysical claims.[56] Indeed a good many fashionable forms of anti-realist and cultural-relativist doctrine take it for granted that their position finds support from the most advanced quarters of current theoretical physics. Typical of these is Lyotard's sweeping conclusion that 'postmodern' science has nothing to do with truth – even truth 'at the end of enquiry' – but everything to do with uncertainty, undecidability, chaos, paralogistic reasoning and the observer-dependent nature of physical 'reality'.[57]

This whole situation is deeply ironic, given the problems that arise with quantum theory and the extent of disagreement (among physicists and philosophers alike) with regard to its implications for our basic concepts of the physical world. Nevertheless it often figures as a background source of 'scientific' assurance for those on the more extreme postmodernist wing who are happy to count reality a world well lost for the sake of pursuing their own favoured kinds of hyperreal fantasy projection. The results are evident not only in literary studies – a fairly safe zone for such ideas – but also in other disciplines which have likewise taken the postmodern-textualist turn, among them history, sociology, political theory and even philosophy of science.[58] One is put in mind of a remark by the philosopher Wesley Salmon – himself a convinced and resourceful proponent of causal realism – to the effect that 'anyone who isn't worried about quantum mechanics must have rocks in their head'.[59]

One source of its widespread appeal, I suggest, is the taken-for-granted background belief that quantum physics has undermined the case for any kind of scientific realism, whether in the subatomic or the macrophysical domain. And this despite the well-known paradox of Schrödinger's Cat, which amounts to a *reductio ad absurdum* of orthodox QM theory when extended to the realm of observable objects and events.[60] In this somewhat repellent thought-experiment, the cat was imagined as shut in a box along-side a lump of fissile material with a 50 per cent probability of decaying and thus emitting a particle within a certain period of time. Should emission occur then the particle would trigger an electro-mechanical device which in turn shattered a fragile container of some volatile poisonous liquid. But, according to orthodox QM, there is simply no possibility of knowing how things have turned out unless and until the quantum probability is 'reduced' by some conscious act of observation/measurement. So we are supposed to think of the unfortunate cat as somehow existing in a 'superposed' (dead-and-alive or neither-dead-nor-alive) state which continues until the box is opened up for inspection and the wave-packet is thereby 'collapsed' into one or another determinate (measurable) value. Schrödinger clearly intended this as a lesson in the limits of orthodox QM theory and as a pointer to the need for some alternative account that would resolve the paradox without any such massive affront to our straightforward commonsense-realist convictions when applied to objects, processes, and events in the macrophysical domain. However it has enjoyed a whole rich afterlife of popularising accounts which ignore that original intention and treat it as a 'strange-but-true' indication of the mysteries of the quantum world.

It is not surprising that literary theorists should have looked to quantum theory in search of 'scientific' endorsement for some of their more extreme anti-realist or cultural-linguistic-relativist claims. Still it is far from clear that such support is to be had except by ignoring the problems that continue to arise whenever physicists abandon their orthodox pragmatic-instrumentalist stance ('don't worry about the interpretation just so long as the measurements and predictions come out right!') and ask what possible sense can be made of the reality behind quantum-physical appearances. Post-structuralists and postmodernists – like orthodox QM theorists – may elect not to worry about such things and count those anxieties merely a symptom of the hankering for long-lost ontological and epistemic certitudes. All the same there is some cause for concern when this outlook goes along with an eagerness to collapse a whole range of related distinctions, as for instance between historical and fictive modes of narrative discourse, or ethical judgements informed by a knowledge of real-world situated human concerns, and ethical decisions – Lyotard again – thought of as issuing from a giddy moment of groundless or unmotivated choice between rival ('incommensurable') interests and value-commitments.

No doubt such thinking has other sources, among them the Saussure-derived concept of 'difference' extended to areas far outside the structural-linguistic domain, and also the notion of absolute 'alterity' or radical 'otherness' which is often taken – e.g., by followers of the philosopher Emmanuel Levinas – as opening the way to an ethical dimension beyond the metaphysical 'closure' of Western post-Hellenic thought.[61] Nevertheless these ideas have gained a large measure of added plausibility from the 'crisis' of knowledge and representation that is widely assumed to have overtaken the physical sciences with the advent of quantum mechanics and its challenge to earlier (realist and causal-explanatory) norms of understanding. What is remarkable about this situation is the fact that it has lasted so long, indeed from the year 1900 (when Max Planck introduced the quantum hypothesis as a means of accounting for certain anomalous features of black-body radiation) right down to the present day.

VII

I have focused here on some of the more striking ways in which literary critics and theorists have responded to this radical questioning of our basic concepts of knowledge and physical reality. How they might yet respond to some future shift of thought – perhaps toward a Bohm-type (albeit nonlocal) realist theory or an objective (non-observer-relative) account of the kind that Einstein so fervently hoped to achieve – is very much an open question.[62] What can be said with more confidence is that realism in both fields still has some highly resourceful defenders and that the burden of proof should not be assumed – as so often it is – to rest entirely on their side of the argument.[63] No doubt there is a sense (a traditional sense) in which literary theory has concerned itself chiefly with whatever *distinguishes* literary language – fictive, poetic, metaphorical, etc. – from those other sorts of language that are properly assessed in terms of their truth-conditions or veridical import. To this extent defences of literary 'realism' have more to do with certain narrative-textual effects – what post-structuralists would call the illusion of *vraisemblance* – than with first-order issues in epistemology, ontology or philosophy of science. However, as I have said, the upshot of much current theorizing is precisely to annul this distinction by treating all discourses (those of history and the natural sciences included) as possessing equal claim to a notional 'truth' which itself becomes nothing more then a product of fictive, rhetorical or narrative contrivance.

There are several problems with this line of argument. One is the way that it relativises truth to the point where rational debate is pretty much ruled out since there is no appeal to standards of evidence, factual warrant, logical consistency, etc., except as construed by the interpretive lights of some particular language-game or 'discourse'. Hence – at its most extreme – the postmodernist idea that historical 'facts' or scientific truth-claims have no kind of epistemic privilege but should rather be treated as textual constructions and valued according to their strong-revisionist or world-transformative capacity. Such is at any rate Rorty's proposal, one that effectively inverts Kuhn's distinction between 'normal' and 'revolutionary' science by giving it a Nietzschean/post-structuralist spin and envisaging a state of permanent revolution where truth-values are no sooner affirmed than subject to radical challenge.[64] In which case – so the argument goes – we had better look to the poets, novelists, and culture-critics rather than the scientists and philosophers if we want to push the process along and avoid getting stuck with normal (= boring and old-fashioned) habits of talk. But if this gives literature a welcome boost in its ancient quarrel with science, history, and philosophy it also has the surely less welcome effect of reducing literature to just another discourse among others, devoid of those distinctive features – imaginative truth, metaphorical depth, complexity of moral insight – that philosophers from Aristotle down have regarded as its chief claim to serious attention. For there is no making sense of such claims unless they are taken as describing what is special about literature, that is to say, what sets it apart from other modes of discourse (such as history and science) where different standards and criteria apply.

'Postmodernism' is one name for this blurring of distinctions between fictive or poetic discourse on the one hand and factual, veridical, or assertoric discourse on the other. As I have said, it marks an extreme point in the reaction against Logical Positivism and also against the idea – so plangently expressed in Richards's early writings – that science must be seen as setting the terms for any adequate present-day defence of literature. What complicates the picture yet further is the extent to which developments in recent physics (quantum theory especially) have appeared to bear out some of the claims advanced by postmodernist thinkers. All the same it would be premature to accept those claims at face value given the highly problematical and speculative character of much that now passes for 'scientific' wisdom among cultural theorists. At very least there is a case for suspending judgement – or not pushing these analogies too hard – until such time as scientists (or maybe philosophers of science) achieve a better grasp of their implications for our knowledge of the physical world. In Chapter Nine I shall examine some of the confusions that typically result when such caution is thrown to the winds and theorists indulge in discipline-hopping without due regard for the requisite standards of knowledge, competence, and relevance that properly apply in differing (e.g., scientific and literary-cultural) contexts of debate.

CHAPTER 9

Sexed Equations and Vexed Physicists: the 'two cultures' revisited

I

Intellectual Impostures – coauthored by an American physicist and a Belgian colleague – grew out of a now-famous hoax which the former pulled off a couple of years ago to the jubilant acclaim of some of his scientific colleagues and the angry discomfiture of many on the 'cultural left'.[1] For those who somehow didn't latch on when the piece first appeared I should perhaps explain briefly what the fuss was all about. It involved the composition of a spoof article ('Transgressing the Boundaries: toward a transformative hermeneutics of quantum gravity') which Alan Sokal submitted to the US journal *Social Text* and which the editors accepted for publication after apparently putting it through the standard review procedures.[2] Very shortly thereafter Sokal went public with a piece ('A Physicist Experiments with Cultural Studies') where he described his own article as a farrago of nonsense cobbled together from various fashionable sources but taking care not to misquote or misrepresent those sources.[3] His wager was that the editors would let it through first because here was a real live physicist who actually agreed with their half-baked doctrines and second because the nonsense contained in the article was just the sort of stuff – much of it verbatim transcription – that normally appeared in their pages. It is reprinted in full as an appendix to the book so that readers can form their own judgement – though not without some previous heavy nudging from Sokal and Jean Bricmont – as to just how badly the editors fared and just how intellectually bankrupt is the state of present-day cultural studies.

My own view is that it is a highly plausible, indeed very expertly calculated spoof which contains just enough 'genuine' science (including some confused or incautious statements by respected quantum physicists) to get the editors at least partly off the hook. On the other hand it does expose a great deal of pretentious, self-promoting and scientifically ill-informed work that too easily passes muster among the target readership of books and journals in the cultural-studies field. At any rate some stronger defence is called for than that quickly mounted by Stanley Fish – nimblest of lit-crit polemicists and director of Duke University Press, the publisher of *Social Text* – who tried to turn the tables on Sokal by claiming that his hoax had undermined those basic standards (of integrity, good faith, and mutual trust) that were essential to the well-regulated conduct of academic life.[4] The editors came back with some spirited ripostes but were visibly bruised by the whole affair and – to their credit – keen to prevent it from reflecting too badly on their colleagues and other contributors.

The repercussions are still rumbling on in various quarters of scientific and literary-cultural academe. They have also provoked a stream of commentary in the up-market dailies and weeklies where the 'Sokal Affair' has become a main focus for debate about the current 'Science Wars', themselves basically just another outbreak of the old 'Two Cultures' controversy initiated by C.P. Snow in the early 1960s.[5] Sokal professes himself surprised and somewhat embarrassed by the storm that has blown up around his spoof article, not least because it has often been taken – especially by right-wing commentators – as a blanket attack on feminists, multiculturalists, proponents of affirmative action, responsible critics of certain developments in applied scientific research, and just about anyone of left-leaning or progressive political views. In fact he and Bricmont are anxious to establish their own broadly left credentials (Sokal having taught physics in Nicaragua during the period of Sandanista government) and the fact that they are in no way sympathetic to the kinds of anti-liberal or left-bashing tendency exhibited by some of their less welcome allies. All the same they might have guessed that this would be the case given the sharply polarised climate of debate and the way that public promoters of science are currently lining up to denounce its enemies, real or imagined. Sokal's article entered the fray against a background of large-scale cuts in research spending and fierce competition for state support both between different branches of science and – more to the point – between the physical sciences on the one hand and the arts, humanities, and social-science disciplines on the other. So there is something just a tad disingenuous about Sokal and Bricmont's claim to have been quite amazed to find themselves suddenly thrust into the thick of all these high-profile media polemics.

The offenders fall into two main groups. On the one hand are those who invoke theories or concepts from various branches of mathematics or the physical sciences in order to gain credibility for vaguely analogous ideas of their own. On the other are those who attack the basic values of scientific enquiry – rationality, truth, method, inductive warrant, hypothesis-testing, empirical observation, experimental controls, replication of results, conceptual refinement, cooperative problem-solving endeavour and so forth – as just a set of outworn 'enlightenment' (= authoritarian) beliefs that are standardly deployed in order to suppress dissident or marginalized views. The first group tend to be treated by Sokal and Bricmont with a certain pitying fondness as well-meaning dabblers in disciplines beyond their technical grasp who should at least be awarded a few marks for trying. However this patience quite often runs out, as for instance when they discuss Jacques Lacan's (to say the least) impressionistic use of ideas from topology and mathematical logic as a key to the ultimate truths of Freudian psychoanalysis, or Julia Kristeva's early attempt to elaborate the notion of poetic language as 'a formal system whose theorization can be based on mathematical set theory'.[6]

They also devote some less than kind commentary to the idea, proposed by Luce Irigaray, that the 'underdevelopment' of fluid mechanics as compared with solid mechanics can best be explained (and put to radical use) through a feminist critique along fairly predictable lines.[7] It has to be said that these theorists are often caught out – Lacan to most damaging effect – in abusive extrapolations from various fields which would scarcely serve the intended purpose even if they made adequate sense in scientific terms. After all, as Sokal/Bricmont remark, 'solid mechanics is far from being complete; it has many unsolved problems, such as the quantitative description of fractures'. Conversely, 'fluids in equilibrium or laminar flow are relatively well understood [since] we know the equations . . . that govern the behavior of fluids in a vast number of situations' (p. 104). Where the real problems come in is with turbulent flow-patterns which involve nonlinear partial differential equations whose solution can be extremely difficult.

However this is not the main point of their critique. What they object to, I think justifiably, is the idea that *feminists* of all people should find comfort or political motivation in this kind of wire-drawn analogy. For there would seem to be nothing very radical or counter-hegemonic about a theory which – granting its validity for the sake of argument – equates the less 'developed' branches of science with (supposedly) feminine qualities and which thereby effectively confines women scientists to the sphere of intuitive or experiential knowledge. Now some of this is certainly knockabout stuff and lays the authors open to an obvious rejoinder. For of course it may be said that the whole point of such arguments is to reveal the deep-laid sexist bias that sets the very terms for what shall *count* as a 'developed' branch of science (rigorous, precise, quantifiable, predictively accurate, etc.), and sets them moreover in just such a way as to exclude or marginalize other ways of knowing. Sokal and Bricmont acknowledge this possibility in passing but prefer – understandably – to focus on the more extreme statements and dubious versions of the case for gender difference as a crucial factor in science. Thus they cite an 'American feminist pedagogue of mathematics' whose professed aim of encouraging young women to enter scientific careers they briefly applaud but whose argument in terms of the 'experiential cyclical time of the menstrual body' they proceed to take apart with considerable relish. 'Is it obvious', she asks, 'to the female mind-body that intervals have end-points, that parabolas neatly divide the plane, and, indeed, that the linear mathematics of schooling describes the world of experience in intuitively obvious ways?'[8] To which Sokal and Bricmont respond that it is an odd sort of feminist theory that would have us believe young women to experience problems with the elementary truths of geometry on account of their menstrual cycle. In fact it strikes them as 'uncannily reminiscent of the Victorian gentlemen who held that women, with their delicate reproductive organs, are unsuited to rational thought and to science' (pp. 111–12).

Still this is fairly mild stuff compared with their treatment of the second-wave theorists whose influence is currently much greater. For these thinkers there is no question of acquiring a certain added prestige by emulating science in a different field of study or borrowing from it (however confusedly) so as to give their own endeavours a certain veneer of pseudo-scientific rigour. Rather they seek to postmodernize science by treating it as a 'discourse', a textual or narrative construct with no special claim to rationality or truth except in so far as these are defined according to prevalent socio-cultural norms. Thus 'science studies' becomes – in effect – just another sub-branch of their own academic specialism. For Sokal and Bricmont this is symptomatic of a widespread intellectual malaise that also goes under the various names of 'post-structuralism', 'literary theory', 'cultural criticism', 'deconstruction', or – on somewhat different but related grounds – the 'strong programme' in sociology of knowledge.

What these all have in common, they argue, is a failure to grasp the basic principles of science along with a habit of throwing out casual references to it as if to support their wilder assertions through a show of up-to-the-minute scientific expertise. Previously – as in the heyday of French structuralism – this took the form of a misplaced desire to imitate the 'discourse' of mathematics or physics by devizing all manner of far-fetched analogies, pseudo-formalisms, or vaguely metaphorical borrowings. Later on, it entered a more militant phase where science was equated with the grim paternal law of reason, progress and truth. Theorists then took a lead from Foucault in denouncing the complicity between these typecast 'enlightenment' values and the repressive apparatus of power/knowledge along with its 'phallogo-centric' promotion of sexist and authoritarian attitudes.[9] However this line of attack soon gave way to the notion – advanced by thinkers like Jean-François Lyotard – that science has itself now moved on into a postmodern phase that involves renouncing all the old illusory certitudes. Thus, according to Lyotard, knowledge must be henceforth a matter of undecid-ability, conflicting hypotheses, rival ('incommensurable') paradigms, chaotic phenomena, paralogistic reasoning, the 'limits of precise measurement', and speculative thought that exceeds the furthest bounds of classical (determinate or bivalent) truth and falsehood.[10]

II

Sokal and Bricmont have quite a field-day pointing out the various errors and confusions that make up this wildly composite image of 'postmodern' science. These include a whole range of mistaken ideas about Gödel's undecidability-theorem, about chaos theory (a rich source of quotes which the authors exploit to maximum effect), about quantum 'uncertainty' and its supposed implications for events in the macrophysical domain – not to mention its bearing on social and political issues – and of course about Einstein's Special and General Theories of Relativity which are often mixed up and put to all kinds of illicit or extravagant uses. On the whole it seems to me that Sokal and Bricmont distribute the blame quite fairly and reserve their passages of fiercest scorn for the worst examples of fashionable nonsense passed off as authoritative wisdom. Thus they show more charity in cases where the writer has made an honest attempt to comprehend difficult ideas which even physicists – or specialist workers in the field – have problems in explaining clearly. Sometimes they are perhaps over-charitable, as when they express puzzlement – nothing stronger – that a 'renowned thinker' such as Vaclav Havel should have taken the fall of Communism in Eastern Europe as 'a sign that modern thought – based on the premise that the world is objectively knowable – has come to a final crisis'.[11] For it is just this kind of confusion that elsewhere attracts some of their harshest comment, not only on scientific grounds (since 'objectivity' becomes a mere plaything of dominant social forces) but also because it threatens to undermine all the values that a dissident intellectual such as Havel presumably holds dear. That is to say, if the postmodernists are right – whatever that could mean – and if truth is nothing more than an ideological (for which also read: textual, rhetorical, or narrative) construct then what could be the point of expressing dissident views or challenging the untruths forcibly imposed by totalitarian regimes?

Historical truth is one of the first things to go, as the authors bring out by enlisting Eric Hobsbawm as an unrepentant 'old left' historian who has waged his own battle against this current postmodernist assault on the values of truth, objectivity, and critical reason. In their words Hobsbawm has shown very effectively 'how rigorous historical work can refute some of the fictions propounded by reactionary nationalists in India, Israel, the Balkans and elsewhere' (p. 195). So it is not hard to see why Sokal is annoyed that the fall-out from his *Social Text* article has included charges that he is just another front-man for the widespread neoconservative reaction against feminism, multiculturalism, socialism, liberalism, interdisciplinarity, and the very idea that some kinds of applied scientific research might be subject to criticism on ethical or sociopolitical grounds. His point, quite simply, is that opponents on the 'cultural left' are deceiving themselves if they think that a wholesale sceptical rejection of truth, objectivity, and method can substitute for the hard work of understanding what science has produced so far in the way of reasonably secure knowledge and what it might yet achieve if informed by a realistic sense of its potential for good or ill. Thus 'scientists are the *first* to advise scepticism in the face of other people's (and one's own) truth claims'. On the other hand 'a sophomoric scepticism, a bland (or blind) agnosticism, won't get you anywhere [since] cultural critics, like historians or scientists, need an *informed* scepticism, one that can evaluate evidence and logic, and come to reasoned (albeit tentative) judgements based on that evidence and logic' (p. 254).

This strikes me as a strong argument not only against the wilder fringes of postmodern cultural theory but also against the more 'respectable' kinds of thinking – influenced by philosophers of science such as Kuhn and Quine – that likewise tend toward a relativist position when it comes to defining what counts as truth within this or that paradigm, conceptual scheme, or ontological framework.[12] Sokal and Bricmont have some good arguments here but concentrate their fire on the French connection and are hence rather apt to let things go with a mild rebuke when it comes to criticizing Anglo-American thinkers. One point they make very forcefully with regard to Kuhn is the strange inversion of priorities whereby truth-claims in the physical sciences are in principle subject to sceptical doubt while truth-claims in history, sociology or cultural theory are somehow magically exempt from any such doubt and indeed provide the very grounds for attacking notions of scientific objectivity and truth. After all, 'why speak in a realist mode about historical categories, such as paradigms, if it is an illusion to speak in a realist mode about scientific concepts (which are in fact much more precisely defined) such as electrons or DNA?' (p. 72). It is a good question and one that receives no adequate answer in the great mass of literature lately devoted to 'science studies' and the strong programme in sociology of knowledge.

This latter is a chief target of the book for fairly obvious reasons. According to the strong programme – as described by its chief proponents Barry Barnes and David Bloor – historians and sociologists of science should not be at all concerned with issues regarding the validity or truth of those theories, hypotheses, causal explanations, etc., which they pass in review.[13] Rather they should treat *all* such theories as themselves requiring some causal explanation on socio-historical grounds and hence as strictly on a par with respect to their possible truth-content. There are some fairly cautious statements of this parity-principle (which Sokal and Bricmont dutifully cite) and others less cautious or more fully given over to the cultural-relativist doctrine (which they cite at greater length and with more relish). An example of the latter is the claim by Barnes and Bloor that 'for the relativist there is no sense attached to the idea that some standards or

beliefs are really rational as distinct from merely locally accepted as such'
(cited p. 82). An example of the former (same source) is that 'all these
questions can, and should, be answered without regard to the status of the
belief as it is judged and evaluated by the sociologist's own standards' (ibid).

There is something to be said for this in so far as it allows the sociologist
of knowledge to maintain a critical distance from currently prevailing ideas
of scientific knowledge and truth. After all it is a basic premise of realism
that truth is 'verification-transcendent', that is to say, a matter of what is
actually the case respecting a realm of objective (mind-independent) reality
and not a matter of the way it is represented according to our current best
beliefs or evidence.[14] However this is just what the strong sociologists
deny – in their less cautious moments – by insisting that objectivity and
truth are *nothing but* social or cultural constructs, and hence that all scientific
theories should be treated on a strict principle of parity. From their point of
view there is no difference, sociologically speaking, in point of truth between
astronomy and astrology, or raindance rituals and the methods of present-
day meteorological prediction, or Darwinism and 'creation science', or
Priestley's phlogiston-based theory of combustion and Lavoisier's account of
the same process in terms of oxygen uptake.[15] No difference, that is, except
in so far as some of these theories happens to have gained scientific credence
in our particular cultural locale, while others have never enjoyed such status
or – as in Priestley's case – have since been consigned to the history of past
(presumptively false or discredited) beliefs. Thus, according to Barnes and
Bloor, 'instead of defining it as true belief – or perhaps justified true
belief – knowledge for the sociologist is whatever people take to be
knowledge' (cited p. 81n). And this despite the fact that sociologists – like
scientists, historians or philosophers – cannot do without some working
distinction between veridical belief and beliefs which, no matter how firmly
held, must yet be considered false or at least insufficiently supported by the
best available evidence. However this problem can be got around, they
argue, 'by reserving the word "knowledge" for what is collectively endorsed,
leaving the individual and idiosyncratic to count as mere belief' (ibid).[16]

Sokal and Bricmont have no trouble in showing that this is a pseudo-
solution which in fact leaves the problem firmly in place since it still defines
'knowledge' solely in terms of communal beliefs which might be flat wrong
even if shared by all members of some given cultural community.
Wittgenstein is the chief source of such ideas – imported into the social
sciences by thinkers like Peter Winch – though the authors fail to make this
connection and thereby ignore the extent of cultural-relativist thinking among
philosophers largely untouched by modish (i.e., French-derived) currents of
thought.[17] Yet the Wittgensteinian doctrine has probably done more harm
through its placid endorsement of the way people talk and think within this or
that language-game or cultural life-form, and hence its refusal to acknowledge

that some such language-games might just be wrong – scientifically misinformed – or objectionable on other (e.g., moral or political) grounds.

In its orthodox form this doctrine has acquired a remarkable, almost talismanic power to stifle thought and produce the kind of reflex conformist response that declares – in effect – 'this is our (or their) language-game so critics had better keep off'. Its impact has been greatest in the social sciences and cultural theory where one regularly comes across the argument that in order to criticize a belief, ideology, institution, or social practice one must first have *understood* it in the same way as those for whom it constitutes a way of life. So one could only have missed the point – or adopted an uncomprehending 'externalist' view – if one presumed to take issue with some item of faith (say in witchcraft, or Azande magic, or the Christian doctrine of Atonement) which happened not to fit with one's own ideas of rational belief.[18] After all, did not Wittgenstein draw this salutary lesson from his own early attempt, in the *Tractatus Logico-Philosophicus*, to devize a truth-functional language that would include just those statements which made sense according to the strictest requirements of logic or empirical science?[19] Was it not the main point of his subsequent 'therapeutic' writings to wean us away from this narrow conception of language, logic, and truth by reminding us just how many and varied are the language-games or cultural forms of life whereby human beings make sense of the world and their place in it?[20]

Such has at least been the usual understanding of the mid-life 'turn' in Wittgenstein's thought. It was the turn clean away from an atomistic theory of language consonant with the doctrines of logical positivism to a wiser, more tolerant and pluralist acceptance that no single language-game – least of all that one – could ever lay claim to an adjudicative standpoint above all those other culturally sanctioned and hence (by their own 'internal' criteria) perfectly legitimate modes of thought. Commentators have of course differed on the question of just how far the *Tractatus* should be seen as already, in its last few paragraphs, marking a break with the precepts of Russell-style logical atomism. For those paragraphs famously contain some passages which suggest that Wittgenstein's main purpose in adopting this approach was to point beyond it to regions of enquiry – ethics, aesthetics, religious belief – any statement of which was bound to be meaningless (or emptily 'metaphysical') by verificationist criteria, but which none the less concerned matters of the deepest moral and spiritual import. Hence his various cryptic suggestions: that the *Tractatus* should best be treated like a ladder, kicked away as no longer of use when one has reached the topmost rungs; that certain truths may be *shown* but not *stated* through language since they belong to a realm beyond the strict confines of logical sense or propositional form; and hence that 'the limits of my language are the limits of my world' in so far as language can state everything that is the case concerning the world as I know it and yet leave room for whatever exceeds or transcends the bounds of verifiable knowledge. So the best way forward – or at least that taken by the majority of Wittgenstein's exegetes – is to give up the whole idea that there exists any means of assessing or contrasting language-games in point of truth, logical consistency, descriptive precision or causal-explanatory power. Rather, those values should be viewed as 'internal' to this or that particular language, and therefore as exerting no legitimate claim to criticize expressions of belief which fail to accord with their own criteria. So it was – in short – that those obscurely-phrased passages in Wittgenstein's early text were read as a kind of coded rehearsal for the doctrine of language-games, life-forms, and meaning-as-use that emerged more plainly in his later writings.

One can therefore see why Russell started out by admiring the *Tractatus* as a full-scale exercise of rigorous analysis in the verificationist mode, but then came around – at the time of Wittgenstein's later, more overt apostasy – to a view of it as opening the way to all manner of irrationalist or quasi-mystical beliefs. For if indeed it is the case that 'the limits of my language are the limits of my world' then this can take philosophy in one or other of two very different directions. *Either* it can mean, on the verificationist reading, that 'the world' is a vast collection of factual states of affairs to which there correspond all those true (empirically warranted) statements and the various entailment-relations between them that make up an accurate picture of that world in its every last detail. (Such was Russell's original understanding and the version that gained Wittgenstein his brief high standing with the Vienna-Circle Logical Positivists.) *Or* it can mean that 'the world' *as it exists for me* is always the world as viewed from within some given range of language-games, cultural life-forms, or shared beliefs that constitute the very horizon of meaningful experience for myself and other members of my own interpretive community. Whence the idea – so repugnant to Russell and so cherished by many Wittgensteinians – that we can never be justified in criticizing beliefs of any kind (philosophical, scientific, historical, political, moral, or religious) with which we are so far out of sympathy that we cannot judge them by the same criteria as are daily, routinely, un-self-consciously applied by those for whom they constitute a genuine faith or mode of social existence. Indeed a case could be made that the Wittgenstein-cult has often gone along with a marked devaluation of Russell's work partly on account of the latter's refusal – in his 'technical' and 'popular' writings alike – to endorse this idea of truth and moral values as internal (i.e., relative) to some given cultural tradition. At any rate one lesson frequently drawn from Wittgenstein's later philosophy is that dissident views such as Russell's are hopelessly off-the-point since they just don't engage with what it means to be a Christian believer or to live in accordance with the communal mores of one's own time and place.

Thus Russell is very often made out to be some kind of village atheist attacking a religious form of life which he fails to understand through applying the wrong kinds of criteria. And he is likewise mistaken – so the Wittgensteinians argue – when he seeks to rectify some of the errors and confusions supposedly embodied in our everyday habits of linguistic usage. In Russell, as in Frege, this takes the form of a logico-semantic analysis intended to reveal those underlying structures of sense and reference that are often disguised by the surface form of natural-language grammar.[21] However such efforts can only be misguided if, as Wittgenstein maintained, everything is perfectly in order with language as we use it and philosophy can therefore do no more than draw attention to the various features of language in its various contexts of utterance. Least of all should it presume to correct or to criticise what makes good sense by the interpretative lights of this or that language-game, communal life-form, or shared tradition of belief. For this is to fall into the same error as those old-style rationalist thinkers – the anthropologist Frazer among them – whom Wittgenstein chides for their arrogant claim to have understood the workings of 'primitive' thought from a later, more adequate scientific or causal-explanatory standpoint.[22]

On this latter view there is no necessary relation between understanding and belief, that is to say, no requirement that in order to interpret or explain some customary life-form we should first have adjusted our criteria so as to think ourselves into the position of a true believer. Rather we are entitled to explain such beliefs – where they seem to us false or misguided – in terms of their causal aetiology, motivating interests, reliance on limited information, on fallible (error-prone) sources of perceptual evidence, etc. Moreover, in so doing, we may sometimes set aside or decline to accept any reasons or justifications that might be offered by participants in the cultural life-form concerned. Thus, for instance, we might have reason to suppose that they were suffering some form of perceptual distortion or subscribed to an animistic worldview or other such system of belief that explained why their ideas diverged so sharply from our own canons of rational warrant. But in that case, Wittgenstein argues, we shall cut ourselves off from any hope of understanding what is meant by the various customs, practices, rituals or expressions of belief which may seem aberrant (or downright irrational) from our point of view, but are none the less perfectly 'in order' for denizens of that particular lifeworld.

It seems to me that this cultural-relativist appropriation of late Wittgenstein amounts to a failure of intellectual nerve, a refusal to accept that we might on occasion have reasons – adequate justificatory grounds – for counting certain beliefs erroneous or certain practices morally repugnant by any defensible standard. Indeed, the chief effect of Wittgenstein's thinking on various academic disciplines – philosophy of science among them – has been to disarm rational debate by constantly adverting to the 'internal' (culture-relative) character of all such judgements, and hence the arrogance of any claim to criticize beliefs and practices belonging to cultures other than our own. One problem with Sokal and Bricmont's approach is that they concentrate their energies too narrowly on the French connection – along with the more extreme statements of strong-sociological doctrine – and thus play down the extent of these influences nearer home. They do have some well-chosen passages from Russell which put the case for objectivity and truth not only as values integral to the pursuit of scientific knowledge but also as a check upon the countervailing drive toward human self-aggrandisement at the expense of precisely those values. When such checks are removed, Russell writes, 'a further step is taken on the road towards a certain kind of madness – the intoxication with power which invaded philosophy with Fichte, and to which modern men, whether philosophers or not, are prone'.[23]

This may all seem pretty remote from Wittgenstein and the kinds of cultural-relativist thinking that currently dominate large sectors of the social and human sciences. But the connection will not seem so far-fetched if one considers the well-documented fact of his wide early reading in nineteenth-century German idealist philosophy and also the decidedly Fichtean cast of his statement that 'the limits of my language are the limits of my world'. It is this conviction that carries across into Wittgenstein's later philosophy and which links the solipsistic reflections to be found toward the end of the *Tractatus* with the idea of truth as internal to various language-games or cultural life-forms. That is to say, there is not after all such a sharp break between 'early' and 'late' Wittgenstein when considered in relation to Russell's point about the need that we acknowledge some objective (mind- and language-independent) check upon our tendency to fashion the world in accordance with our predisposed habits of belief. The authors pick up – predictably enough – on the passage from his intellectual autobiography where Russell recalls his own conversion from Hegelian idealism as having been brought about chiefly by his reading of the 'muddle-headed nonsense' to be found in the pages of Hegel's *Science of Logic* devoted to the differential and integral calculus (p. 28). All the same their argument might have been strengthened by a deeper sense of the conflicting strains within Anglophone philosophy during the past century as well as between the (so-called) 'analytic' and post-Kantian 'continental' lines of descent.

Where Sokal and Bricmont do follow Russell is in stressing the socio-political implications of a relativist outlook pushed to the point of declaring all beliefs equally valid by their own interpretative lights. This issue goes to the heart of their argument since it here that theorists on the 'cultural left' have attempted to claim the moral high ground as against old-style 'enlightenment' thinkers who are purportedly embarked upon a rearguard defence of the elitist, ethnocentric, and patriarchal values enshrined in the discourse of Western rationality and truth. In a brief section on 'Relativism in the Third World' they cite the example of an Indian politician who had run into trouble and was advised, according to Vedic belief, that he should enter his office through an east-facing gate and thereby solve all his problems. However this area contained a large slum through which his car was unable to pass so he ordered the slum to be demolished. Their source here is Meera Nanda, a biochemist with close ties to the Indian 'Science for the People' movement, and currently (we are told) conducting a study of the US sociology of science movement. It is worth quoting his comments at length since they sum up both his and the authors' case against what they see as the illogicality and the weird inversion of social and moral priorities involved in such cultural-relativist thinking.

> If the Indian left were as active in the people's science movement as it used to be, it would have led an agitation not only against the demolition of people's homes, but also against the superstition that was used to justify it .... A left movement that was not so busy establishing 'respect' for non-Western knowledge would never have allowed the power-wielders to hide behind indigenous 'experts'.[24]

Nanda goes on to recount how he presented this case to some US 'social constructionist' colleagues and how they came back – predictably enough – with the argument from parity of cultural esteem to parity of truth-claims, belief-systems, or causal-explanatory hypotheses. In his view (endorsed by Sokal and Bricmont) it is an indefensible argument, philosophically confused and ethically bankrupt as well as a patronising First-World insult to just those people whose values and interests it claims to respect. In short it falls into the same way of thinking that equates the advancement of women in science with the advent of a different feminist science best suited to their special powers of intuitive insight.

III

So there is a lot that needed saying and much that is well said in this follow-up to Sokal's hoax article. On the other hand the book does have its weaknesses, some of which have left the way open for critics to dismiss it as just another ill-tempered salvo in the current bout of 'science wars' polemics. One is the lack of any adequate acknowledgement that there exists a good deal of recent work in the history and sociology of science written by people on the 'cultural left' who do have a detailed and sophisticated grasp of the relevant scientific issues.[25] Thus the authors often make things a bit too easy for themselves by plucking out some especially absurd statement – such as Irigaray's idea that $E = Mc^2$ is a 'sexed equation' not so much because it went into the making of nuclear weapons but rather because it 'privileges what goes the fastest' – and letting it stand as a typical instance of what goes wrong when feminists and others wander onto specialist scientific ground (p. 100). In fact their whole treatment of the gender-bias issue lies open to the charge of gender-bias in so far as it omits any mention of a writer like Evelyn Fox Keller, one who undoubtedly knows enough science to avoid the sorts of error that Sokal and Bricmont are intent upon exposing.[26]

This goes along with their frequent tendency to pick the wrong targets for heaviest attack and then quote selectively or out of context so as to leave a distorted impression of what these authors have to say. The worst case here is their treatment of Bruno Latour, a French sociologist/anthropologist of scientific knowledge to whom they devote a whole chapter focusing on one (not very typical) essay which happens to fall within their own field of interest. Now Latour has certainly let drop some provocative remarks in the cultural-relativist vein, the sorts of remark that are pretty much *de rigueur* for sociologists in the French academic context where disciplinary rivalry is especially intense, no doubt for reasons that they (the sociologists) can go some way toward explaining. This particular piece is a semiotic reading of Einstein's introductory text *Relativity: the Special and General Theory* which applies ideas from structuralist poetics and narrrative analysis – principally that of the narrative frame – by way of drawing out some hitherto unnoticed implications of Einstein's well-known thought-experiments concerning relative velocities as between two spatio-temporal frames of reference.

Latour's point, briefly stated, is that the theory makes implicit appeal to a third such frame – one that 'collects information sent by [observers occupying] the two others' – while avowedly deploying only two frames and using the Lorentz transformation to establish coordinate relations between them. As he puts it:

> how can one decide whether an observation made in a train about the behaviour of a falling stone can be made to coincide with the observation made of the same falling stone from the embankment? If there are only one, or even *two*, frames of reference no solution can be found. ... Einstein's solution is to consider *three* actors: one in the train, one on the embankment and a third one, the author (enunciator) or one of its representants, who tries to superimpose the coded observations sent back by the two others.[27]

Sokal and Bricmont see nothing here but a series of 'elementary' blunders and terminological slippages, as between different senses of the term 'frame' (Lorentz-invariant and narratological), different understandings of what constitutes a 'privileged' or 'reference-frame', and – above all – differences concerning the role of the 'narrator' in scientific texts on the one hand and fictive or literary texts on the other. Also they object to Latour's further claim that this role is occupied by an 'enunciator' – Einstein *ipse* or his self-authorized narrative voice – with reference to whose 'privileged' status the theory assigns all other (observer-relative) frames, velocities, or space-time coordinates. It is in this sense that Latour describes his essay as a 'contribution to the sociology of delegation'. That is, he is interested in the kinds of jointly epistemic, disciplinary, and cultural 'gain' that effectively accrue from a scientific theory which works by establishing a hierarchy of viewpoints each of which possesses its own 'relative' truth, yet only one of which (the author's) can legitimately claim to encompass them all in a unified general theory. Thus 'it is the enunciator who has the privilege of accumulating all the descriptions of all the scenes he has delegated observers to'. Moreover, 'it is only when the enunciator's *gain* is taken into account that the difference between relativism and relativity reveals its deeper meaning'.[28] From this standpoint it possible to see how relativity-theory is constructed in the image of certain social relations that leave their definite though covert imprint on its modes of textual and narrative representation.

Now on the face of it there is much in this analysis which more than justifies the rough treatment it receives at the hands of Sokal and Bricmont. In particular they are right in pointing out that, according to Einstein, there is *no* ultimately privileged frame of reference since the Lorentz equations provide a means of translating the space-time coordinates of any event from one to another reference-frame without the need for such an overall commanding or unitary perspective. They also have good grounds for maintaining that it is simply a mistake – one characteristic of this strong-textualist approach – to suppose that the truth of scientific theories is in any way dependent on the author-function, or the narrative-rhetorical means by which some individual writer (such as Einstein) chose to put his arguments across. This applies especially in the case of a popularizing account whose pedagogical aims may very well require the use of metaphors, analogies, or other such illustrative devices by which to make the argument more vivid and avoid excessive technicality. In short, 'no reference frame plays any privileged role here; nor does the author (Einstein) exist at all – much less constitute a 'reference frame' – *within* the physical situation he is describing' (p. 119).

Thus Latour is definitely at fault if his claim in this analysis is (1) to interpret Einstein's theory *on its own scientific terms*, and (2) to 'relativize' relativity by showing how those terms are in fact socially or culturally constructed, and hence fair game for debunking treatment in the favoured style. In that case Sokal and Bricmont would be fully warranted in charging that Latour's 'sociological bias' had betrayed him into yet another 'elementary' error, namely his failure to understand that – according to Special Relativity – 'no inertial reference frame is privileged over any other' (p. 119). However this is to mistake his whole purpose and lump him together with those who think that '$E = Mc^2$' can itself be treated as a 'gendered equation' or as some kind of cultural construct. Rather he is arguing the very different case – one which the authors consider too 'modest' to be really what he has in mind – that scientific theories may indeed be *motivated* by all sorts of social, political, or ideological interest, but that this has no ultimate or necessary bearing on their truth-content. That is to say, Latour is far from collapsing the distinction between (social) 'context of discovery' and (scientific) 'context of justification', even though – naturally enough – the former is his main focus of interest. At any rate his work stands decidedly apart from the kinds of wholesale cultural-relativist thinking which treat that distinction as just another relic of old-style 'enlightenment' discourse. Rather he accepts – as a matter of working principle – that there *are and must be* standards of enquiry (of empirical warrant and careful reasoning on the evidence) against which to measure his own, albeit more detached observations of everyday scientific work. What has misled Sokal and Bricmont is the fact that Latour sets these standards very high, indeed so high that very little of science as actually practised comes anywhere near meeting them. Still if they had examined some of his other writing they would have found in Latour a devoted, meticulous student of the physical sciences whose attention to the conduct of everyday fieldwork and 'laboratory life' places him in a world quite apart from the purveyors of modish sceptical doctrine.[29]

There is an irony here which is worth dwelling on briefly since it goes to the heart of this particular misunderstanding and also points up another main problem with the Sokal/Bricmont approach. Thus, for instance, the authors characterise Latour as 'rejecting contemptuously' any comments or criticisms that scientists might offer concerning his work. Actually the passage in question reads as follows: 'the opinions of scientists about science studies are not of much importance. Scientists are the informants for our investigations of science, not our judges. The vision we develop of science does not have to resemble what scientists think about science' (cited p. 121). Now of course this conveys more than a touch of professional *amour propre*, along with a certain defensive edge which no doubt results from previous encounters of the type here staged by Sokal and Bricmont. Still there is another way of reading the passage that is more in touch with the general character and ethos of Latour's work. After all, it is just their own point with respect to Einstein and Special Relativity that the truth of such theories has nothing to do with the 'authority' vested in certain individuals, or – as Latour phrases it – 'what scientists think about science'. Rather this issue can only be decided through a process of continuing research, observation, experiment, theoretical refinement, conceptual criticism, alternative hypothesis-construction, and so forth. Indeed this is their main charge against the more reductive forms of strong-sociological approach: that by equating 'science' with the privileged viewpoint of certain individual scientists they are able to treat it as a reflex product of their hegemonic status, class-interests, or gender-bias. Undoubtedly Latour is cocking a snook when he denies that 'the opinions of scientists' are of much importance to people working in the field of science studies. In fact it is a claim decisively refuted by his own constant practice elsewhere of asking researchers all sorts of questions about their methods, criteria, investigative practices, theoretical commitments, or motivating interests. Moreover he notes their responses with assiduous care even if – very often – in order to remark the striking divergence between what actually goes on in day-to-day 'laboratory life' and what typically gets written up in the scientific journals from the sanitized viewpoint of selective hindsight. But this is just to say (as in the passage that provoked Sokal and Bricmont) that 'the vision of science we [i.e., sociologists] develop does not have to resemble what scientists think about science' (cited p. 121).

Clearly it would be a foolhardy sociologist who took this advice so much to heart as to abjure all reliance on expert or 'inside' testimony. However, just as clearly, there is strong warrant for Latour's claim that sociology of science has its own distinctive methods and criteria for assessing the kinds of evidence thereby obtained. For it is a main point of Sokal and Bricmont's argument that the social and human sciences need to preserve those distinctive standards of enquiry and can best do so if they manage to avoid two opposite temptations. One is the fallacy of misplaced 'scientific' rigour, that is, the typically structuralist tendency to emulate the physical sciences in fields where different criteria apply and where this habit gives rise to various kinds of false analogy or wire-drawn metaphor. In this context Sokal and Bricmont might have noted the distinctively French tradition in philosophy of science – descending from Bachelard and Canguilhem to Derrida's essay 'White Mythology' – which provides by far the most subtle and rigorous account of the way that scientific concepts develop out of the matrix of intuitive or metaphoric thought through stages of progressive elaboration and critique.[30] Such thinking retains its critical edge in the theory of 'epistemological breaks' taken up by the Marxist theoreticians Louis Althusser and Pierre Macherey, as likewise in Derrida's deconstructive reading of various (mainly philosophical) texts.[31] However these developments receive no mention from Sokal and Bricmont, partly – I suspect – because they don't fit in with the authors' polemical purpose or their typecast image of 'French intellectuals' as enemies of reason and truth. They are much keener to denounce the other tendency – nowadays more widespread – which treats every form of 'knowledge' as a cultural construct, a figment of narrative discourse, or a product of the epistemic will-to-power codified in various disciplinary regimes. For when carried to the limit (as by postmodernists or sundry followers of Nietzsche and Foucault) this results in an outlook of wholesale cultural relativism which effectively deprives the social and human sciences of any power to challenge received beliefs or to question the ideological self-images of the age.

Sokal and Bricmont make the point by distinguishing between two very different sorts of scepticism. The first is the sort that scientists and others (cultural theorists among them) very properly apply when they refuse to take any item of belief on trust and adopt the attitude that everything should in principle be open to criticism, their own beliefs included. On the other hand 'a sophomoric scepticism won't get you anywhere [since] cultural critics, like historians or scientists, need an *informed* scepticism, one that can evaluate evidence and logic, and come to reasoned (albeit tentative) judgments *based on that evidence and logic*' (p. 255). This states a simple though important truth which enables them to cut a swathe through large areas of the current discourse on knowledge and its socially 'constructed' character. Still it goes along with a certain deafness to other kinds of scepticism – irony especially – which writers like Latour use to powerful effect but which registers not at all in Sokal and Bricmont's very literal-minded reading of their texts. Thus they simply fail to grasp some of Latour's more pointedly ironic remarks about the relation between science and sociology of science, or his image of scientists as native 'informants' whose ideas about their own cultural practices the anthropologist should take with a sceptical pinch of salt.

IV

This also helps to explain why the Sokal hoax misfired to the extent of creating a host of enemies where he had hoped to find at least some allies and supporters on the cultural left. For the *Social Text* article is a classic case of what literary critics term 'unstable irony', that is, the kind of irony which lacks control of its own argumentative purposes and which thus lies open to all sorts of misconstrual or unforeseen reader-response.[32] The first paragraph gets off to a strong (pointedly ironic) start by remarking on the extraordinary circumstance that there are still some scientists, physicists in particular, who reject the idea that social and cultural theory 'can have anything to contribute, except perhaps peripherally, to their research' (p. 197). Stranger still, they persist in ignoring the claim 'that the very foundations of their worldview must be revised or rebuilt in the light of such criticism' (ibid). Instead they adhere to a range of hopelessly outworn 'enlightenment' beliefs, among them:

> that there exists an external world, whose properties are independent of any individual human being and indeed of humanity as a whole; that these properties are encoded in 'eternal' physical laws; and that human

beings can obtain reliable, albeit imperfect and tentative, knowledge of these laws by hewing to the 'objective' procedures and epistemological strictures prescribed by the (so-called) scientific method. (p. 199)

Up to this point the irony seems pretty stable, or at any rate sufficiently controlled to ensure that its purport won't be lost on those with ears to hear. Thus the passage asserts a number of propositions which are clearly endorsed by Sokal *ipse* and which – it is assumed – will likewise be endorsed by any reader with a basic (commonsense) grasp of the relevant issues. In other words there is a level of communication between 'implied author' and 'implied reader' such that the passage reliably conveys its parodic intent to any but those whose thinking has been warped by regular exposure to the kinds of article that appear in journals like *Social Text*. But of course it does so through the implied persona of a typecast cultural theorist who considers those 'truths' to be nothing but a set of ideological constructs or hegemonic values imposed by the discourse of 'enlightened' modernity and scientific method. At any rate the irony is heavy enough – or the signs (one would think) so clearly legible – that it is hard to understand why some warning lights didn't start to flash in the editorial office. The give-away is not so much the talk about 'objective' procedures and 'eternal' physical laws, since presumably there are few contributors to *Social Text* who would commit such phrases to paper without the obligatory scare-quotes, and few readers who would not suspect irony were the phrases used (apparently) in good earnest. Rather the joke is to reverse roles and put the knowing reader who has long seen through such talk into the position of one who is unknowingly the dupe of his or her own fixed habits of response. What gives the game away is that bit about obtaining 'reliable, albeit imperfect and tentative, knowledge'. For it would take a very fargone epistemological sceptic, even by *Social Text* standards, to assume that a fallibilist statement such as this could also be relied on to strike his readers as a throwback to bad old 'enlightenment' ways of thought.

However this first paragraph is untypical in keeping a fairly tight rein on its ironic intentions and thereby sorting the sheep from the goats among its target readership. Elsewhere one can understand more easily why the editors failed to spot the hoax since it is not at all clear just where the irony is aimed or where exactly the line is supposed to be drawn between reasonable (scientifically informed) opinion and the confusions endemic to cultural theory. In part this has to do with Sokal's unfortunate habit of lumping together a whole wide range of theoretical positions on the (so-called) 'cultural left' which in fact bear little resemblance to each other apart from their raising more-or-less pertinent questions with regard to the status of truth-claims or theoretical arguments in the physical, social, and human sciences. Thus the parody makes no distinction – and suggests that there is no important distinction to be made – between the wildest excesses of postmodernist scepticism, the kindred (though differently angled) approach of 'strong' sociologists of knowledge, the more moderate version of that approach to be found in writers like Latour, and the work of a philosopher such as Derrida whose intellectual depth and degree of analytical acumen far surpass anything advanced in his name by trend-spotting cultural theorists. Had they read some of Derrida's texts at first hand – especially those collected in *Margins of Philosophy* – then Sokal and Bricmont would have found him 'deconstructing' a good many of the modish cultural-relativist or social-constructivist fallacies which they are out to attack.[33] Indeed one of the more striking differences between Sokal's original essay and the subsequent book is that the authors wisely make a point of exempting Derrida from the general curse since his work (as opposed to its wider influence) cannot be counted just another product of current 'left-cultural' fashion. Still – as I have said – their argument is sometimes weakened by a failure to distinguish the kinds of critical thinking that genuinely deserve that title from the sorts of all-purpose routine scepticism which render such thinking altogether impossible.

There is another problem with Sokal's article that gets in the way of its parodic intent and which no doubt helped to bamboozle the *Social Text* editors. This is the trick by which it interweaves citations from cultural theorists (some but not all of them confused and pretentious) with passages from the writing of various scientists which are often themselves scarcely models of precision or lucid conceptual grasp. Thus he draws quite extensively on Heisenberg, Bohr, and other theorists of quantum mechanics with the aim – so it seems – of exposing the way their statements are often taken out of context and paraded as examples of 'postmodern' science by ill-informed or opportunist commentators. However this device misfires for various reasons, among them the fact that ever since its inception at the turn of the century quantum mechanics has been rife with paradoxes, conceptual dilemmas and deep-laid interpretative problems which are not yet resolved despite the best efforts of physicists and philosophers of science.[34] Sokal's point in quoting these passages – especially the excerpts from Bohr – is that they have since given rise to a whole genre of derivative pronouncements by cultural theorists who exploit the *topoi* of quantum uncertainty, wave/particle dualism, the limits of precise measurement, or (according to one interpretation) the observer-induced collapse of the wave-packet.[35] However this leaves him rather awkwardly placed when it comes to distinguishing the false extrapolations (i.e., the sorts of vulgarized notion put about about by theorists on the 'cultural left') from the pronouncements of qualified physicists like Heisenberg and Bohr who presumably knew what they were talking about. For the truth is that some of those pronouncements – precisely the ones with maximum 'postmodern' appeal – are subject to just the sorts of deep-laid philosophical confusion that Sokal and Bricmont find so offensive when retailed by cultural theorists.

The greatest irony about all this is that quantum physics is probably the one field where sociology of knowledge has come up with strong arguments *in support* of scientific realism rather than maintaining that any such talk of 'reality' or 'truth' is a product of the naive objectivist belief in a world outside or beyond our current range of discourses, language-games, textual constructions, or whatever. Sokal's article has a brief reference (duly footnoted) to 'Aronowitz's analysis of the cultural fabric that produced quantum mechanics' (p. 200). Stanley Aronowitz is a cultural theorist and one of the hapless editors who fell for Sokal's hoax so the reference has a certain added piquancy in this context. All the same it is worth noting that other cultural theorists have offered some powerful arguments for viewing the hegemony of orthodox QM theory, along with its various (so far) intractable puzzles and paradoxes, as a result of certain socio-historical factors which help to explain its conditions of emergence and continued widespread appeal despite the existence of alternative theories which provide a realist interpretation with nothing like this burden of unresolved problems and paradoxes.[36]

The chief such contender is David Bohm's 'hidden-variables' theory which resolves the wave/particle dualism by adopting the idea – first proposed by de Broglie – that particles are guided by a 'pilot-wave' which allows them to possess determinate values of location and momentum between measurements.[37] Measurement-values are probabilistic since the wave function is itself a quantum function (derived from various well-established formalisms) which distributes the probability of obtaining certain results under certain experimental conditions. Nevertheless Bohm's theory is realist in the sense that it places such uncertainties squarely on the side of the observer (i.e., puts them down to the limits of our knowledge or powers of precise measurement) rather than invoking some ultimate mystery in the quantum-physical nature of things. Thus it offers an intuitively far more acceptable alternative to the notion that quantum 'reality' is somehow *created* by our performing this or that type of experiment and thus bringing about a localized 'collapse' of the wavepacket into wave or particle form. On Bohm's account the particle does have determinate values of position and momentum between measurements, values that are assigned by the wavefunction (i.e., by applying Schrödinger's equation exactly as in orthodox QM), but which are taken to exist objectively and not as an effect of observer 'interference' or some strange mechanism whereby the very choice of value to be measured decides the observational outcome from case to case. For the great problem with this orthodox theory is the famous paradox of Schrödinger's cat, that is to say, the problem of deciding just how to draw a line between the subatomic realm of quantum phenomena where everything is uncertain or probabilistic and the realm of macrophysical reality where we know that the cat must be *either* alive *or* dead – rather than existing in some limbo of 'superposed' dead-and-alive states – before the box is opened up for inspection.[38]

Schrödinger's purpose in devizing this gruesome thought-experiment was to offer a *reductio ad absurdum* of the orthodox theory, thus proving that theory to be incomplete in some crucial respect and to require an alternative construal in line with our knowledge of the way things stand with respect to objects and events in the macrophysical domain. That it has often been taken as urging just the opposite case – the need to abandon our entire commonsense or scientific-realist ontology in response to this and other such quantum paradoxes – is one of those ironies that Sokal should appreciate since it has a lot to do with the widespread appeal of quantum mechanics among postmodernists, post-structuralists and cultural theorists of a like sceptical persuasion. However it is also a problem for Sokal since so much of the current debate among physicists regarding various rival (e.g., 'many-minds' and 'many-worlds') interpretations of QM phenomena takes place at a rarefied speculative level that is just as remote from any realist worldview and which leaves no room for pointed comparisons with the kinds of misunderstanding put about by people on the 'cultural left'.[39]

Indeed, as I suggested above, this is one area where cultural historians of science and even sociologists of knowledge may have something of value to contribute to the realist side of the argument. Thus a recent book by James T. Cushing puts the case that orthodox QM achieved hegemonic status and prevailed against Bohm's realist interpretation not so much on its superior scientific merits – since the two theories are observationally and predictively equivalent – but rather for reasons connected with the socio-cultural climate of belief in Europe (and Germany especially) during the inter-war period.[40] In brief, it responded to the widespread mood of reactive *Kulturpessimismus*, the turn toward irrationalist or subjectivist doctrines, and – above all – the prevalent mistrust of science and technology as forces bound up with the destructive drive for domination over nature and humankind alike which had brought catastrophe upon the world. There is no room here for a detailed account of Cushing's exceptionally well-researched and stimulating book. Sufficient to say that he brings out the depth of attachment to ideas such as these in the theoretical writings of Bohr, Heisenberg and other leading advocates of the orthodox view, along with their equally deep resistance to any interpretation of quantum mechanics – Bohm's 'hidden-variables' theory in particular – that would claim to resolve the QM paradoxes within a basically realist framework involving least conflict with the laws of classical, pre-quantum physics.

This is not to say that Bohm's interpretation is 'classical' (or indeed 'realist') in the sense of conserving all the precepts of physical science up to and including Special Relativity. In fact it has to admit at least one major anomaly – that of remote simultaneous interaction or 'entanglement' between widely separated particles – which contravenes Einstein's cardinal requirement that nothing can travel faster than the speed of light since this is the absolute reference-point for all assignments of space-time position and velocity. Ironically enough it was a thought-experiment conducted by Einstein and two of his colleagues – the famous EPR experiment – which set out to prove the incompleteness of orthodox QM on precisely these grounds, but which ended up by convincing most physicists that this problem was strictly inescapable (i.e., that there *must* be such superluminal effects) since the quantum predictions were so well borne out by observation and theory alike.[41] Later on the issue was posed more sharply by J.S. Bell's rigorous demonstration that no hidden-variables theory such as Einstein's or Bohm's could square with the QM predictions unless it allowed for the existence of superluminal (faster-than-light) 'communication' between particles that had once interacted and then moved apart to any distance of space-like separation.[42] And Bell's results were in turn confirmed by a series of highly ingenious laboratory experiments which offered proof that such effects did indeed occur and could not explained on any other theory than that which Einstein had hoped to rule out as involving what he called 'spooky action-at-a-distance'.

However Bohm was less worried since, in his view, such phenomena presented no challenge to a realist ontology – or created no paradoxes about time-travel, retroactive causation, and the like – just so long as they didn't allow *messages* to be broadcast from one observer to another at superluminal velocities. This principle (the 'no-first-signal' requirement) could not be infringed by the existence of remote correlation effects since there was simply no way that the two observers could decode the results of any measurements carried out except by prior agreement (which would undermine the whole point of the exercise) or else by having some other, even faster means of transmitting the requisite codes (which of course was impossible).[43] So the EPR 'paradox' and the Bell results could quite readily be taken on board – Bohm argued – without prejudice to the hidden-variables theory or its basic ontological-realist credentials. Moreover, it was the one interpretation of quantum mechanics that managed to conserve the theory's strong observational and statistical-predictive warrant while none the less avoiding its drastic break with so many hitherto well-entrenched laws of physics, including some of the most fundamental premises of causal-explanatory thought.

Sokal's bibliography appended to the spoof article contains just one reference to Bohm, an entry for his book *Wholeness and the Implicate Order* which presumably was thought to merit inclusion since it represents an aspect of his thinking quite remote from the quantum realism issue.[44] In fact it has acquired something of cult-following among 'New Age' adepts and those who look to the more speculative reaches of quantum theory for intimations of a paranormal world elsewhere or a deeper reality beyond the grasp of our quotidian sensory-cognitive powers. Perhaps it is understandable that his other (one is tempted to say) more serious and scientifically important work rates no mention either in the article or in Sokal and Bricmont's book. So far as the article is concerned any coverage of Bohm's hidden-variables theory would presumably have complicated matters by requiring that the idiot persona denounce it as just another hopeless last-ditch attempt to prop up 'realist', 'objectivist' or 'enlightenment' modes of thought. But this might well have raised editorial eyebrows when compared with the passage which links Einstein's 'spooky action-at-distance', Bell's theorem concerning remote particle correlation, and the possibility of 'an alternative worldview in which the universe is characterized by interconnectness and (w)holism: what physicist David Bohm has called "implicate order"' (pp. 205–6). Here again the irony is highly unstable – and the *Social Text* editors deserve at least a bit of sympathy – since it is far from clear whether the ridicule is directed toward Bohm's more credulous or scientifically ill-informed readers, toward Bohm himself for indulging a sideline in such speculative fancies, or toward the whole idea of remote superluminal interaction as required by Bell's extrapolation from the EPR thought-experiment. Nor is the innocent reader much helped by the next sentence which judiciously remarks: 'New Age interpretations of these insights from quantum physics have often gone overboard in unwarranted speculation, but the general soundness of the argument is undeniable' (p. 206). For one need only glance at a typical number of up-market popularizing journals like *New Scientist* or *Scientific American* to see how narrow is the line that separates 'advanced' theoretical physics from the crankier varieties of New Age thinking or sheer science-fiction fantasy.

The trouble is that a great deal of quantum-theoretical debate – including some by eminent physicists – has likewise 'gone overboard' in various speculative directions, beginning with Bohr's obscurely metaphysical thoughts on the topic and continuing with the kinds of argument nowadays advanced by adherents of the 'many-minds' and 'many-worlds' interpretations. In the latter case especially – witness the recent and much-publicised book by David Deutsch – what results is a quantum-based update on themes from the heyday of pre-Kantian rationalist metaphysics, or a literalization of modal-logical ('possible worlds') arguments which again go back to Leibniz and have lately been revived by philosophers such as David Lewis.[45] My point in all this is that Sokal's parody very often misses the mark because one just can't be sure – with so many shifting and often barely distinguishable targets – which are (supposed to be) the purveyors of mere fashionable nonsense and which the reputable scientific sources.

Once in a while he and Bricmont let on that they incline toward a realist interpretation of quantum mechanics and that they don't go along with the various orthodox-QM pronouncements of Bohr, Heisenberg and others cited at length in the hoax essay. Certainly these have provided inspiration for some of the more blanket anti-realist doctrines or extreme varieties of postmodern-sceptical thinking which they identify with the present-day cultural left. But of course it would be hard for Sokal and Bricmont to come straight out and declare in favour of a Bohm-type realist QM theory without implicitly conceding that much of what has counted as the most advanced work in theoretical physics over the past near-century has in fact been committed to a range of highly dubious premises which are not, after all, so very different from those of the bother-headed theorists whom the authors here take to task. Also, as I have said, it is an awkward fact from their point of view that some of the most telling arguments against orthodox QM and in support of Bohm's realist alternative are those provided by historians, sociologists, and contextually-minded philosophers of science.

Of course there is a crucial distinction to be drawn – as Cushing is careful to insist – between different ways of interpreting the case that science may be influenced by social factors outside or beyond its specialized sphere of concern. On the one hand there is work in this field (such as his own) that respects the relative autonomy of scientific research and resists any move to simply conflate the socio-historico-cultural 'context of discovery' and the scientific 'context of justification' where the relevant standards of appraisal are those internal to the discipline concerned. On the other there is the 'strong' culturalist approach according to which sociological explanations go all the way down and leave no room for the critical assessment of scientific truth-claims, methods, or theories except on externalist (i.e., extra-scientific) grounds. Cushing very firmly rejects this latter line of argument and enters some explicit caveats with regard to other work on the cultural background and historical context of orthodox QM – e.g., the writings of Paul Forman – which strikes him as pressing the case too far in a social-constructivist direction.[46] Nevertheless he is clearly sympathetic to at least one aspect of Forman's studies, that is to say, the idea that the sociology of knowledge need not always come out (though very often it does) in alliance with an anti-realist position on epistemological issues and a sceptical or cultural-relativist stance as concerns the criteria of scientific method and truth. For it is just Forman's point – taken up by Cushing albeit in a more philosophically nuanced and less 'sociological' key – that attention to the cultural conditions of emergence for orthodox QM theory can go some way toward explaining the hegemony of anti-realist doctrines not only in debates about quantum mechanics but also across a wide range of disciplines (from philosophy of science to cultural theory) where those debates have left their mark. In other words there is no necessary conflict – such as Sokal and Bricmont tend to assume in their treatment of a thinker like Latour – between the aims and values of physical science and those of a qualified (scientifically informed) sociology of knowledge that is not merely out to promote its own interests.

V

Unfortunately their book has already become a rallying-point for some of the more strident media polemicists and warriors for the 'public understanding of science' who will brook no suggestion that philosophers and historians (let alone cultural theorists) might have something relevant to say on these topics. In the face of such attitudes it is worth recalling what Heisenberg remarked about Bohr – that he pursued a 'darkly metaphysical' habit of mind under the guise of theoretical physics[47] – and also the degree of speculative licence (often with dubious philosophic warrant) involved in some of the arguments advanced by present-day quantum physicists. Indeed one of the crowning ironies of Sokal's hoax essay is that it quotes a passage from Gilles Deleuze which comes out strongly *against* the kinds of subjectivist or cultural-relativist confusion which have characterized much of this debate.[48]

To some extent, as I have said, the book makes up for these unwitting ironies in the article by defining its targets more exactly and not adopting such a wide-angle or scatter-shot approach. Still there is a problem with the authors' tendency to shift around between various loosely-defined ideas of 'relativism' according to the particular theorist in view or the local context of debate. Thus they don't distinguish clearly enough between: (1) the sociologist's reasonable claim that cultural factors may often play a role in the scientific context of discovery; (2) the viewpoint of certain 'social epistemologists' according to whom this relativity extends to various culture-specific differences of interpretive framework or conceptual scheme[49]; and (3) the full-blown *ontological*-relativist argument which holds that 'reality' itself is either socially constructed or a product of the differing construals placed upon it by various observers. Even then there are further distinctions to be drawn, as for instance (within the last category) between those theorists who push all the way with this extreme version of the doctrine and those others – the majority – who tend to fall back on (2) at strategic moments or perhaps when suddenly struck by the extremity of their own position.

However the groupings don't fall out along anything like the lines suggested by Sokal and Bricmont, i.e., with French (or French-influenced) cultural theorists always adopting positions at the far-out relativist end of the scale while it is left to the scientists and (mainly Anglophone) defenders of commonsense realism to hold out against these wild sceptical excesses. Thus one often finds Bohr shifting back and forth – sometimes within a couple of sentences – from a standpoint of 'strong' (category 3) ontological anti-realism to a more moderate (category 2) position where phenomena such as wave/particle dualism are ascribed to the impossibility of achieving precise simultaneous measurements and/or the limits of human understanding, constrained as it is to work with certain 'classical' concepts and logico-semantic resources. Thus '[a]n independent reality in the ordinary physical sense can ... neither be ascribed to the phenomena nor to the agencies of observation' (cited p. 202). Here the ambiguity hinges on the word 'phenomena', properly meaning 'that which appears or manifests itself to human observers' but in Bohr's usage tending to oscillate between this (broadly Kantian) sense of the term and a different, vaguely objectivist sense where it signifies a realm of quantum reality beyond the best powers of human conceptualization. Hence some of the problems that arise in interpreting Bohr's philosophy of quantum mechanics and the various alternative proposals which attempt to resolve those problems within the framework of orthodox (Bohr-derived) QM theory.

There is a similar kind of equivocation in Thomas Kuhn's talk of how the 'world changes' for scientists living before and after some decisive paradigm-shift.[50] Thus he sometimes appears to be arguing the case for a 'strong' (ontological) relativist approach while at other times phrasing his claims more cautiously so as to leave room for a Category 1 or 2 interpretation. With Quine also – in those passages of his work that clearly influenced Kuhn – it is often hard to decide which construal best makes sense of his various statements on the topic of ontological relativity.[51] Meanwhile there are Anglophone philosophers (such as Nelson Goodman) who push so far toward a strong-constructivist or framework-relativist position that their dicta would scarcely be out of place in a postmodern manifesto.[52] And there are others again – Hilary Putnam most prominent among them – who have made the long trek from a full-fledged realist standpoint to a doctrine of 'internal realism' (Putnam's phrase) which amounts to little more than a relativism that dare not speak its name.[53] What is more, these thinkers can often be found alluding to quantum mechanics – on the orthodox interpretation – as a prime instance of the problems faced by any realist ontology or epistemology that seeks to hold the line against this widespread retreat from the values of truth and objectivity. At any rate it is a highly simplified picture which would count 'French intellectuals' chiefly responsible for undermining those values or creating the conditions where science can itself be called to witness in support of relativist or anti-realist arguments.

It seems to me that this blurring of ironic focus is one sure sign that Sokal and Bricmont have picked some wrong targets and rested their case on some dubious sources of scientific warrant. According to Stanley Fish – publisher of *Social Text* and himself a nifty ironist – we are deluded if we think that irony can ever be 'stable' or that there should be some clear-cut difference between the sorts of irony that deftly separate knowing from idiot readers and the sorts that open up endless possibilities of cross-purpose (non)communication.[54] For Fish this is just another version of the old objectivist fallacy which takes meanings to be somehow 'there' in the text, rather than viewing them as transient stages in the open-ended process of cultural negotiation whereby texts are constantly refashioned according to the prevalent norms and values of this or that 'interpretive community'. This is the case – he argues – not only with novels and poems but across the whole range of academic disciplines from history, sociology, anthropology, linguistics and the other human sciences to biology, chemistry, and physics. Interpretation *always* goes 'all the way down', whatever its illusory claims to objectivity or truth, and the problems with irony are a good way of showing how groundless is the hope that we could ever achieve any basis for rational agreement save that which comes of our belonging to one or another such community. It is this kind of corrosive all-purpose scepticism that has found its way from literary theory into the wider 'postmodernist' cultural sphere and thence into some versions of the strong-sociological programme.

Nevertheless it is worth pointing out that these ideas have gained ground for a variety of reasons, among them the fact that quantum mechanics (on the orthodox interpretation) appears to give 'scientific' warrant for some of the wilder anti-realist claims that are nowadays routinely advanced by postmodern culture critics. Also – as I have said – there are other influences at work, among them that of Wittgensteinian social philosophy, which here receive nothing like their due share of critical attention. Sokal and Bricmont do a fair job of exposing the worst excesses but too often give way to a polemical narrowing of sights that ironically rebounds against their own argument. In this book I have criticised some of the same tendencies and – more constructively – put the case for a reaffirmation of those values and principles that constitute the 'unfinished project' of modernity. One way to characterise the counter-movement which rejects such values *tout court* is in terms of a distinctively postmodern irony devoid of affirmative or critical content and veering from scepticism to downright cynicism in its desire to come out on the far side of that delusive 'enlightenment' ethos. At any rate I would hope to have suggested some promising directions for a large-scale reassessment of our (so-called) postmodern condition and a vigorous deployment of the various resources that can yet be mustered against it.

Notes

Chapter 1 Deconstruction *versus* Postmodernism: epistemology, ethics, aesthetics

1 A.O. Lovejoy, 'On the Discrimination of Romanticisms', in *Essays in the History of Ideas* (Baltimore: Johns Hopkins University Press, 1948).

2 See especially David Lodge, *The Modes of Modern Writing: metaphor, metonymy and the typology of modern literature* (London: Longman, 1977); also Malcolm Bradbury and James McFarlane (eds), *Modernism* (Harmondsworth: Penguin, 1976) and Peter Nicholls, *Modernism: a literary guide* (London: Macmillan, 1995).

3 See for instance Donald Mitchell, *The Language of Modern Music* (London: Faber, 1963).

4 René Descartes, *Meditations on First Philosophy*, trans. J. Cottingham (Cambridge: Cambridge University Press, 1986).

5 Immanuel Kant, *Critique of Pure Reason*, trans. Norman Kemp Smith (London: Macmillan, 1964); *Critique of Practical Reason*, trans. Lewis White Beck (Indianapolis: Bobbs-Merrill, 1975); *Critique of Judgement*, trans. J.C. Meredith (Oxford: Clarendon Press, 1978).

6 See for instance Jürgen Habermas, *Knowledge and Human Interests*, trans. J. Shapiro (London: Heinemann, 1972).

7 Habermas, *Theory of Communicative Action*, 2 vols, trans. T. McCarthy (Boston: Beacon Press, 1984 and 1987).

8 For a useful comparative survey, see Timothy J. Reiss, *The Discourse of Modernism* (Ithaca, NY: Cornell University Press, 1982).

9 See especially Fredric Jameson, *Postmodernism, or, the Cultural Logic of Late Capitalism* (London: Verso, 1991).

10 Jean-François Lyotard, *The Postmodern Condition: a report on knowledge*, trans. Geoff Bennington and Brian Massumi (Manchester: Manchester University Press, 1984).

11 G.W.F. Hegel, *The Phenomenology of Spirit*, trans. Parvis Emad and Kenneth Maly (Bloomington, Ind.: Indiana University Press, 1988).

12 Lyotard, *The Differend: phrases in dispute*, trans. Georges van den Abbeele (Manchester: Manchester University Press, 1988).

13 See entries under Notes 2 and 3, above; also Karl-Oto Apel, *Understanding and Explanation: a transcendental-pragmatic perspective*, trans. Georgia Warnke (Cambridge, Mass.: MIT Press, 1985).

14 Kant, *Critique of Pure Reason* (op. cit.).

15 Kant, *Critique of Practical Reason* (op. cit.).

16 See for instance Michael Sandel, *Liberalism and the Limits of Justice* (Cambridge: Cambridge University Press, 1982); Michael Walzer, *Spheres of Justice* (Oxford: Blackwell, 1983); Bernard Williams, *Ethics and the Limits of Philosophy* (London: Fontana, 1985).

17 Kant, *Critique of Judgement* (op. cit.).

18 Kant, *Critique of Pure Reason* (op. cit.), p. 112.

19 See for instance Frederick C. Beiser, *The Fate of Reason: German philosophy from Kant to Fichte* (Cambridge, Mass.: Harvard University Press, 1987).

20 See Emmanuel Chukwudi Eze (ed.), *Race and the Enlightenment: a reader* and *Postcolonial African Philosophy; a reader* (both Oxford: Blackwell, 1997).

21 Lyotard, *The Differend* (op. cit.).

22 Lyotard, *The Differend* (op. cit.).

23 See Hayden White, *Tropics of Discourse* (Baltimore: Johns Hopkins University Press, 1978) and *The Content of the Form* (Baltimore: Johns Hopkins University Press, 1988).

24 Roland Barthes, 'The Discourse of History' and 'The Reality Effect', in *The Rustle of Language*, trans. Richard Howard (Oxford: Blackwell, 1986), pp. 127–40 and 141–8.

25 See especially Michael Dummett, *Truth and Other Enigmas* (London: Duckworth, 1978); also Crispin Wright, *Realism, Meaning and Truth* (Oxford: Blackwell, 1987).

26 See Dummett, *Elements of Intuitionism* (London: Oxford University Press, 1977).

27 Ludwig Wittgenstein, *Philosophical Investigations*, trans. G.E.M. Anscombe (Oxford: Blackwell, 1958); Gottlob Frege, 'On Sense and Reference', in Peter Geach and Max Black (eds), *Translations from the Philosophical Writings of Gottlob Frege* (Oxford: Blackwell, 1952), pp. 56–78.

28 See especially Keith Jenkins, *Re-Thinking History* (London: Routledge, 1991) and *On 'What Is History'?: from Carr and Elton to Rorty and White* (London: Routledge, 1995).

29 See also various contributions to Keith Jenkins (ed.), *The Postmodern History Reader* (London: Routledge, 1997).

30 Simon Schama, *Dead Certainties (unwarranted speculations)* (Harmondsworth: Penguin/Granta, 1992).

31 Linda Hutcheon, *The Politics of Postmodernism* (London: Routledge, 1989).

32 For a representative sampling, see Jean Baudrillard, *Simulations*, trans. Paul Foss, Paul Patton, and Philip Beitchman (New York: Semiotext(e), 1983); also *Jean Baudrillard: selected writings*, ed. Mark Poster (Cambridge: Polity Press, 1989) and *Revenge of the Crystal: a Baudrillard reader* (London: Pluto Press, 1990).

33 Ferdinand de Saussure, *Course in General Linguistics*, trans. Wade Baskin (London: Fontana, 1974).

34 See especially Ruth A. Ronen, *Possible Worlds in Literary Theory* (Cambridge: Cambridge University Press, 1994); also Thomas Pavel, *Fictional Worlds* (Harvard, Mass.: Harvard University Press, 1986).

35 Terry Eagleton, *The Illusions of Postmodernism* (Oxford: Blackwell, 1996).

Chapter 2   Postmodern Ethics and the Trouble with Relativism

1 See for instance F.R. Ankersmit, *History and Tropology* (Berkeley and Los Angeles: University of California Press, 1994); Robert F. Berkhofer, *Beyond the Great Story: history as text and discourse* (Cambridge, Mass.: Harvard University Press, 1995); Elizabeth Deeds Ernarth, *Sequel to History: postmodernism and the crisis of time* (Princeton, NJ: Princeton University Press, 1992); Keith Jenkins, *Re-Thinking History* (London: Routledge, 1991) and *On 'What Is History?': From Carr and Elton to Rorty and White* (London: Routledge, 1995); Jenkins (ed.), *The Postmodern History Reader* (London: Routledge, 1997): H. Aram Veeser (ed.), *The New Historicism Reader* (London: Routledge, 1994).

2 See especially Michael Dummett, 'Bringing About the Past' and 'The Reality of the Past', in *Truth and Other Enigmas* (London: Duckworth, 1978), pp. 333–50 and 358–74.

3 Dummett, 'The Reality of the Past' (op. cit.), p. 363.

4 Gottlob Frege, 'On Sense and Reference', in Max Black and P.T. Geach (eds), *Translations from the Philosophical Writings of Gottlob Frege* (Oxford: Blackwell, 1952), pp. 56–78; Ludwig Wittgenstein, *Philosophical Investigations*, trans. G.E.M. Anscombe (Oxford: Blackwell, 1953).

5 Dummett, 'The Reality of the Past' (op. cit.), p. 374.

6 See for instance Christopher Hookway, *Scepticism* (London: Routledge, 1992); A.C. Grayling, *The Refutation of Scepticism* (London: Duckworth, 1985); Arne Naess, *Scepticism* (London: Routledge & Kegan Paul, 1970); Michael Williams, *Unnatural Doubts: epistemological realism and the basis of scepticism* (Princeton, NJ: Princeton University Press, 1996).

7 See Lyotard, *The Differend*, trans. Georges van den Abbeele (Manchester: Manchester University Press, 1988).

8 See for instance Robert L. Arrington (ed.), *Rationalism, Realism, and Relativism: perspectives in contemporary moral epistemology* (Ithaca, NY: Cornell University Press, 1989); David O. Brink, *Moral Realism and the Foundations of Ethics* (Cambridge: Cambridge University Press, 1989); Alan H. Goldman, *Moral Knowledge* (London: Routledge, 1988); Sabina Lovibond, *Realism and Imagination in Ethics* (Oxford: Blackwell, 1983).

9 Gilles Deleuze, *Kant's Critical Philosophy: the doctrine of the faculties*, trans. Hugh Tomlinson and Barbara Habberjam (London: Athlone Press, 1984).

10 Michel Foucault, *The Order of Things*, trans. A. Sheridan-Smith (London: Tavistock, 1970).

11 See especially Jean-François Lyotard, *Lessons on the Analytic of the Sublime*, trans. Elizabeth Rottenberg (Stanford, Ca: Stanford University Press, 1994).

12 Onora O'Neill, *Constructions of Reason: explorations of Kant's practical philosophy* (Cambridge: Cambridge University Press, 1989). See also Christopher Norris, 'Kant Disfigured: ethics, deconstruction, and the textual sublime', in *The Truth About Postmodernism* (Oxford: Blackwell, 1993), pp. 182–256.

13 See Emmanuel Levinas, *Totality and Infinity*, trans. A. Lingis (Pittsburgh, Pa.: Duquesne University Press, 1969) and *Otherwise Than Being, or Beyond Essence*, trans. Lingis (The Hague: Martinus Nijhoff, 1981).

14 Jacques Derrida, 'Violence and Metaphysics: an essay on Emmanuel Levinas', in *Writing and Difference*, trans. Alan Bass (London: Routlege & Kegan Paul, 1978), pp. 79–153.

15 See Edmund Husserl, *Formal and Transcendental Logic*, trans. Dorian Cairns (The Hague: Martinus Nijhoff, 1969); also *The Crisis of European Sciences and Transcendental Phenomenology*, trans. David Carr (Evanston: Northwestern University Press, 1970); *Logical Investigations*, two vols, trans. J.N. Finlay (New York: Humanities Press, 1970); *Experience and Judgement: investigations in a genealogy of logic*, ed. Ludwig Landgrebe, trans. J.S. Churchill and K. Ameriks (Evanston: Northwestern University Press, 1973); *Ideas: general introduction to pure phenomenology*, trans. W.R. Boyce Gibson (London: Collier Macmillan, 1975).

16 Husserl, *Cartesian Meditations: an introduction to phenomenology*, trans. Dorian Cairns (The Hague: Martinus Nijhoff, 1973).

17 Immanuel Kant, *Critique of Pure Reason*, trans. Norman Kemp Smith (London: Macmillan, 1964).

18 See especially Martin Heidegger, *Kant and the Problem of Metaphysics*, trans. James S. Churchill (Bloomington, Ind.: Indiana University Press, 1962); also Frederick C. Beiser, *The Fate of Reason: German philosophy from Kant to Fichte* (Cambridge, Mass.: Harvard University Press, 1987).

19 Robert Brandom, *Making It Explicit: reasoning, representing, and discursive commitment* (Cambridge, Mass.: Harvard University Press, 1994); John McDowell, *Mind and World* (Cambridge:, Mass.: Harvard University Press, 1994); also Thomas Nagel, *The Last Word* (Oxford: Oxford University Press, 1997).

20 Bernard Williams, *Ethics and the Limits of Philosophy* (Cambridge, Mass.: Harvard University Press, 1985).

21 Derrida, ' "Genesis and Structure" and Phenomenology', in *Writing and Difference* (op. cit.), pp. 154–68; also *Speech and Phenomena and Other Essays on Husserl's Theory of Signs*, trans. David B. Allison (Evanston, Ill.: Northwestern University Press, 1973); *La problème de la genèse dans la philosophie de Husserl* (Paris: Presses Universitaires de France, 1990).

22 See for instance Norris, *Truth and the Ethics of Criticism* (Manchester: Manchester University Press, 1994) and *Reclaiming Truth: contribution to a critique of cultural relativism* (London: Lawrence & Wishart, 1996).

23 Zygmunt Bauman, *Postmodern Ethics* (Oxford: Blackwell, 1993).

24 W.V. Quine, 'Two Dogmas of Empiricism', in *From a Logical Point of View*, 2nd edn (Cambridge, Mass.: Harvard University Press, 1961), pp. 20–46; also Quine, *Ontological Relativity and Other Essays* (New York: Columbia University Press, 1969).

25 See especially Rudolf Carnap, *The Logical Structure of the World and Pseudoproblems in Philosophy*, trans. R. George (Berkeley and Los Angeles: University of California Press, 1969); also A.J. Ayer, *The Foundations of Empirical Knowledge* (London: Macmillan, 1955); Ayer (ed.), *Logical Positivism* (New York: Free Press, 1959); Oswald Hanfling (ed.), *Essential Readings in Logical Positivism* (Oxford: Blackwell, 1981); Carl G. Hempel, *Fundamentals of Concept Formation in Empirical Science* (Chicago: University of Chicago Press, 1972); Hans Reichenbach, *Experience and Prediction* (Chicago: Univsersity of Chicago Press, 1938).

26 See Sandra G. Harding (ed.), *Can Theories Be Refuted? essays on the Duhem-Quine thesis* (Dordrecht and Boston: D. Reidel, 1976).

27 Quine, *Philosophy of Logic* (New York: Prentice-Hall, 1970). See also Susan Haack, *Deviant Logic: some philosophical issues* (Cambridge: Cambridge University Press, 1974).

28 Thomas S. Kuhn, *The Structure of Scientific Revolutions*, 2nd edn (Chicago: University of Chicago Press, 1970).

29 Hilary Putnam, *Pragmatism: an open question* (Oxford: Blackwell, 1995), p. 53n.

30 See for instance Hilary Putnam, *The Many Faces of Realism* (La Salle: Open Court, 1987) and *Realism With a Human Face* (Cambridge, Mass.: Harvard University Press, 1990).

31   Norris, *Resources of Realism: prospects for 'post-analytic' philosophy* (London: Macmillan, 1997); *New Idols of the Cave: on the limits of anti-realism* (Manchester: Manchester University Press, 1997); *Against Relativism: philosophy of science, deconstruction and critical theory* (Oxford: Blackwell, 1997).

32   See for instance Martin Gardner, 'Realism and Instrumentalism in Nineteenth-Century Atomism', *Philosophy of Science*, Vol. 46, No. 1 (1979), pp. 1–34; Mary Jo Nye, *Molecular Reality* (London: MacDonald, 1972); J. Perrin, *Atoms*, trans. D.L. Hammick (New York: Van Nostrand, 1923); Wesley C. Salmon, *Scientific Explanation and the Causal Structure of the World* (Princeton, NJ: Princeton University Press, 1984).

33   See Paul Feyerabend, *Against Method* (London: New Left Books, 1975) and *Science in a Free Society* (London: New Left Books, 1978).

34   See especially David Bloor, *Knowledge and Social Imagery* (London: Routledge and Kegan Paul, 1976) and *Wittgenstein: a social theory of knowledge* (New York: Columbia University Press, 1983); Barry Barnes, *T.S. Kuhn and Social Science* (Oxford: Blackwell, 1982) and *About Science* (Oxford: Blackwell, 1985); Bruno Latour and Steve Woolgar, *Laboratory Life: the social construction of scientific facts* (London: Sage, 1979); Steve Fuller, *Social Epistemology* (Bloomington, Ind.: Indiana University Press, 1988); Steve Woolgar, *Science: the very idea* (London: Tavistock, 1988); Woolgar (ed.), *Knowledge and Reflexivity: new frontiers in the sociology of knowledge* (London: Sage, 1988).

35   Quine, 'Two Dogmas of Empiricism' (op. cit.).

36   See Note 6, above.

37   For some strong arguments to just this effect, see Michael Devitt, *Realism and Truth*, 2nd edn (Oxford: Blackwell, 1986); also D.M. Armstrong, *Universals and Scientific Realism* (2 vols) (Cambridge: Cambridge University Press, 1978); J. Aronson, R. Harré and E. Way, *Realism Rescued: how scientific progress is possible* (London: Duckworth, 1994); Roy Bhaskar, *Scientific Realism and Human Emancipation* (London: Verso, 1986); Jarrett Leplin (ed.), *Scientific Realism* (Berkeley and Los Angeles: University of California Press, 1984); Karl Popper, *Realism and the Aim of Science* (London: Hutchinson, 1983); J.J.C. Smart, *Philosophy and Scientific Realism* (London: Routledge & Kegan Paul, 1963); Peter J. Smith, *Realism and the Progress of Science* (Cambridge: Cambridge University Press, 1981).

38   Hartry Field, 'Theory Change and the Indeterminacy of Reference', *Journal of Philosophy*, Vol. 70 (1973), pp. 462–81; 'Conventionalism and Instrumentalism in Semantics', *Nous*, Vol. 9 (1975), pp. 375–405; 'Quine and the Correspondence Theory', *Philosophical Review*, Vol. 83 (1974), pp. 200–28.

39   See Note 32, above.

40   See for instance the essays and interviews collected in Paul Rabinow (ed.), *The Foucault Reader* (Harmondsworth: Penguin, 1986).

41   Jürgen Habermas, *Knowledge and Human Interests*, trans. J. Shapiro (London: Heinemann, 1972).

42   See especially Richard Rorty, *Objectivity, Relativism, and Truth* (Cambridge: Cambridge University Press, 1991); also *Consequences of Pragmatism* (Brighton: Harvester, 1982); *Essays on Heidegger and Others* (Cambridge: Cambridge University Press, 1991); *Truth and Progress* (Cambridge: Cambridge University Press, 1998).

43   See especially Søren Kierkegaard, *Fear and Trembling* and *The Sickness Unto Death*, trans. W. Lowrie (Princeton, NJ: Princeton University Press, 1974).

44   See Note 34, above.

45   Ludwig Wittgenstein, *Philosophical Investigations*, trans. G.E.M. Anscombe (Oxford: Blackwell, 1953).

46   Richard Rorty, *Contingency, Irony, and Solidarity* (Cambridge: Cambridge University Press, 1989).

47   See especially Habermas, *Communication and the Evolution of Society*, trans. Thomas McCarthy (London: Heinemann, 1979); *Theory of Communicative Action*, 2 vols, trans. McCarthy (London: Heinemann, 1984 and 1987); *Justification and Application: remarks on discourse ethics*, trans. C.P. Cronin (Cambridge: Polity Press, 1993).

48   Peter Winch, *The Idea of a Social Science and its Relation to Philosophy* (London: Routledge & Kegan Paul, 1958).

49   Donald Davidson, 'On the Very Idea of a Conceptual Scheme', in *Inquiries into Truth and Interpretation* (London: Oxford University Press, 1984), pp. 183–98.

50   See also David Papineau, *Theory and Meaning* (London: Oxford University Press, 1979) and *Philosophical Naturalism* (Oxford: Blackwell, 1993).

51   See Jonathan Bennett, *Linguistic Behaviour* (Cambridge: Cambridge University Press, 1976).

52 See Notes 41 and 47, above; also Karl-Otto Apel, *Understanding and Explanation: a transcendental-pragmatic perspective*, trans. Georgia Warnke (Cambridge, Mass.: MIT Press, 1985) and *From a Transcendental-Semiotic Point of View*, ed. Marianna Papastephanou (Manchester: Manchester University Press, 1998); Albrecht Wellmer, *Critical Theory of Society*, trans. John Cumming (New York: Seabury Press, 1974) and *The Persistence of Modernity: aesthetics, ethics and postmodernism* (Cambridge: Polity Press, 1991).

53 Davidson, *Inquiries into Truth and Interpretation* (op. cit.); also Alfred Tarski, 'The Concept of Truth in Formalized Languages', in *Logic, Semantics and Metamathematics*, trans. J.H. Woodger (Oxford: Oxford University Press, 1956), pp. 152–278.

54 See especially Foucault, *Power/Knowledge: selected interviews and other writings* (Brighton: Harvester, 1980).

55 Habermas, *The Philosophical Discourse of Modernity: twelve lectures*, trans. Frederick Lawrence (Cambridge: Polity Press, 1987).

56 Norris, 'Kant Disfigured' (op. cit.).

57 Habermas, *The Philosophical Discourse of Modernity* (op. cit.).

58 Derrida, 'Afterword: toward an ethic of conversation', in *Limited Inc*, ed. Gerald Graff (Evanston, Ill.: Northwestern University Press, 1989), pp. 111–54.

59 See Note 61, below.

60 Derrida, *Writing and Difference* (op. cit.); *Of Grammatology*, trans. G.C. Spivak (Baltimore: Johns Hopkins University Press, 1975); *Dissemination*, trans. Barbara Johnson (London: Athlone Press, 1981); *Margins of Philosophy*, trans. Alan Bass (Chicago: University of Chicago Press, 1982).

61 On this issue of deconstruction *vis-à-vis* the discourse of Enlightenment critique, see especially Derrida, 'The Principle of Reason: the university in the eyes of its pupils', *Diacritics*, Vol. 19 (1983), pp. 3–20; 'Mochlos, or the Conflict of the Faculties', in Richard Rand (ed.), *Logomachia* (Lincoln and Nebraska: University of Nebraska Press, 1992), pp. 3–34; 'Of an Apocalyptic Tone Newly Adopted in Philosophy', in Harold Coward and Toby Foshay (eds), *Derrida and Negative Theology* (Albany, NY: State University of New York Press, 1992), pp. 24–71.

62 Derrida, 'Violence and Metaphysics' (op. cit.).

Chapter 3   Deconstruction and the 'Unfinished Project of Modernity'

1   Jürgen Habermas, *The Philosphical Discourse of Modernity: twelve lectures*, trans. Frederick Lawrence (Cambridge: Polity Press, 1987).

2   Richard Rorty, 'Philosophy as a Kind of Writing: an essay on Derrida', in *Consequences of Pragmatism* (Brighton: Harvester Press, 1982), pp. 89–109. See also Christopher Norris, 'Philosophy as *Not* Just a "Kind of Writing": Derrida and the Claim of Reason' and Rorty, 'Two Meanings of "Logocentrism": a reply to Norris', both in Reed Way Dasenbrock (ed.), *Re-Drawing the Lines: analytic philosophy, deconstruction, and literary theory* (Minneapolis: University of Minnesota Press, 1989), pp. 189–203 and 204–16.

3   Rorty, 'Philosophy as a Kind of Writing' (op. cit.). See also his essays 'Deconstruction and Circumvention', *Critical Inquiry*, Vol. XI (1984), pp. 1–23 and 'Is Derrida a Transcendental Philosopher?', in David Wood (ed.), *Derrida: a critical reader* (Oxford: Blackwell, 1992), pp. 235–46.

4   Rodolphe Gasché, *The Tain of the Mirror: Derrida and the philosophy of reflection* (Cambridge, Mass.: Harvard University Press, 1986).

5   See Habermas, 'On Levelling the Genre Distinction Between Philosophy and Literature', in *The Philosophical Discourse of Modernity* (op. cit.), pp. 185–210.

6   See Jacques Derrida, 'Signature Event Context' and John R. Searle, 'Reiterating the Differences', both in *Glyph*, Vol. 1 (Baltimore: Johns Hopkins University Press, 1977), pp. 172–97 and 198–208; also Derrida, 'Limited Inc a b c', in *Glyph*, Vol. 2 (Baltimore: Johns Hopkins University Press, 1977), pp. 162–254.

7   Michael Dummett, *The Origins of Analytic Philosophy* (London: Duckworth, 1993).

8   Jacques Derrida, 'Afterword: toward an ethic of conversation', in *Limited Inc a b c* (Evanston, Ill.: Northwestern University Press, 1989), pp. 111–60.

9   Habermas, *The Philosophical Discourse of Modernity* (op. cit.).

10 Rorty, *Consequences of Pragmatism* (op. cit.); also *Objectivity, Relativism, and Truth* and *Essays on Heidegger and Others* (both Cambridge: Cambridge University Press, 1991).

11 Searle, 'Reiterating the Differences' (op. cit.); also 'Literary Theory and its Discontents', *New Literary History*, Vol. XXV, No. 3 (1994), pp. 637–67 and 'The World Turned Upside Down', *New York Review of Books*, Vol. XXX, No. 16 (27 Oct. 1983), pp. 74–9.

12 See Norris, *Derrida* (London: Fontana, 1987); *Truth and the Ethics of Criticism* (Manchester: Manchester University Press, 1994); *Reclaiming Truth: contribution to a critique of cultural relativism* (London: Lawrence & Wishart, 1996); *Against Relativism: philosophy of science, deconstruction and critical theory* (Oxford: Blackwell, 1997).

13 See especially the texts brought together in Derrida, *Du droit à la philosophie* (Paris: Galilée, 1990); also *Institutions of Reason*, ed. Deborah Esch and Thomas Keenan (Minneapolis: University of Minneapolis Press, 1992); 'Economimesis', *Diacritics*, Vol. XI, No. 2 (Summer 1981), pp. 3–25; 'The Principle of Reason: the university in the eyes of its pupils', trans. Catherine Porter and Edward P. Morris, *Diacritics*, Vol. XIII. No. 3 (Fall 1983), pp. 3–20; 'Parergon', in *The Truth in Painting*, trans. Geoff Bennington and Ian McLeod (Chicago: University of Chicago Press, 1987), pp. 15–147; 'Mochlos – or the conflict of the faculties', in Richard Rand (ed.), *Logomachia* (Lincoln, Nebr.: University of Nebraska Press, 1992), pp. 1–34.

14 Derrida, 'Mochlos' (op. cit.).

15 Gilles Deleuze, *Kant's Critical Philosophy: the doctrine of the faculties*, trans. Hugh Tomlinson and Barbara Habberjam (London: Athlone Press, 1984).

16 Immanuel Kant, *The Conflict of the Faculties*, trans. Mary J. Gregor (New York: Abaris Books, 1979).

17 Derrida, 'Mochlos' (op. cit.), p. 24.

18 Ibid, pp. 25–6.

19 For some relevant historico-philosophical detail, see Frederick C. Beiser, *The Fate of Reason: German philosophy from Kant to Fichte* (Cambridge, Mass.: Harvard University Press, 1987).

20 Kant, *Religion Within the Limits of Reason Alone*, trans. Theodore M. Greene and Hoyt H. Hudson (Chicago: Open Court, 1934).

21 See Derrida, 'The Principle of Reason' (op. cit.) and 'No Apocalypse, Not Now: seven missiles, seven missives', *Diacritics*, Vol. XX (1984), pp. 20–31.

22 J.L. Austin, *How to Do Things With Words* (London: Oxford University Press, 1963).

23 See Note 6, above.

24 See for instance Stanley Cavell, *A Pitch of Philosophy: autobiographical exercises* (Cambridge, Mass.: Harvard University Press, 1994); Jonathan Culler, 'Convention and Meaning: Derrida and Austin', *New Literary History*, Vol. XIII (1981), 15–30; Shoshana Felman, *The Literary Speech-Act: Don Juan with J.L. Austin, or seduction in two languages*, trans. Catherine Porter (Ithaca, NY: Cornell University Press, 1983); Stanley Fish, 'With the Compliments of the Author: reflections on Austin and Derrida', *Critical Inquiry*, Vol. VIII (1982), pp. 693–72.

25 Derrida, 'Mochlos' (op. cit.), p. 18.

26 Ibid, pp. 19–20.

27 See especially Kant, 'What Is Enlightenment?' and other texts collected in Lewis W. Beck (ed.), *Kant: On History* (Indianapolis: Bobbs-Merrill, 1963); also Kant, *Political Writings*, ed. Hans Reiss (Cambridge: Cambridge University Press, 1976).

28 Kant, *Critique of Pure Reason*, trans. Norman Kemp Smith (London: Macmillan, 1964).

29 Kant, *Critique of Practical Reason*, trans. Lewis W. Beck (Indianapolis: Bobbs-Merrill, 1977).

30 Kant, *Critique of Judgement*, trans. J.C. Meredith (Oxford: Clarendon Press, 1978).

31 For a useful conspectus of these differing approaches, see Paul Guyer (ed.), *The Cambridge Companion to Kant* (Cambridge: Cambridge University Press, 1992).

32 Martin Heidegger, *Kant and the Problem of Metaphysics*, trans. James S. Churchill (Bloomington, Ind.: Indiana University Press, 1982); Jean-François Lyotard, *Lessons on the Analytic of the Sublime*, trans. Elizabeth Rottenberg (Stanford, Ca: Stanford University Press, 1994).

33 Pierre Bourdieu, *The Political Ontology of Martin Heidegger*, trans. Peter Collier (Oxford: Polity Press, 1991).

34 Derrida, 'Mochlos' (op. cit.), p. 23.

35 See Note 13, above.

36 Kant, 'Transcendental Dialectic', in *Critique of Pure Reason* (op. cit.), pp. 297–484.

37 Pierre Bourdieu, *Distinction: a social critique of the judgement of taste*, trans. R. Nice (Cambridge, Mass.: Harvard University Press, 1984).

38 See also Bourdieu, *Language and Symbolic Power*, ed. John B. Thompson, trans. Gino Raymond and Matthew Adamson (Cambridge: Polity Press, 1991).

39 Mark A. DeBellis, *Music and Conceptualization* (Cambridge: Cambridge University Press, 1995), p. 94.
40 See Note 37, above.
41 Theodor W. Adorno, *Prisms*, trans. Samuel and Shierry Weber (Cambridge, Mass.: MIT Press, 1981).
42 See especially Adorno, *Negative Dialectics*, trans. E.B. Ashton (London: Routledge & Kegan Paul, 1973).
43 Adorno, *Against Epistemology: a metacritique*, trans. Willis Domingo (Oxford: Blackwell, 1982).
44 For the most perceptive and interesting version of this argument – albeit hedged about with numerous qualifications – see Frederic Jameson, *Late Marxism: Adorno, or the persistence of the dialectic* (London: Verso, 1990).
45 See Habermas, *The Philosophical Discourse of Modernity* (op. cit.).
46 See entries under Note 13, above.
47 See Rorty, *Consequences of Pragmatism* (op. cit.); also *Contingency, Irony, and Solidarity* (Cambridge: Cambridge University Press, 1989).
48 Cited by Derrida, 'Mochlos' (op. cit.), p. 28.
49 Deleuze, *Kant's Critical Philosophy* (op. cit.).
50 Derrida, 'Mochlos' (op. cit.), p. 26.
51 See especially Lyotard, *The Postmodern Condition: a report on knowledge*, trans. Geoff Bennington and Brian Massumi (Manchester: Manchester University Press, 1984).
52 Derrida, 'Mochlos' (op. cit.), pp. 26–7.
53 Ibid, p. 12.
54 Ibid, p. 14.
55 Ibid, p. 16.
56 Ibid, p. 17.
57 Ibid, p. 5.
58 See especially Rorty, *Objectivity, Relativism, and Truth* (op. cit.).
59 Rorty, 'Philosophy as a Kind of Writing' (op. cit.).

Chapter 4 Deconstruction, Postmodernism and Philosophy of Science

1 On this topic see also Christopher Norris, *New Idols of the Cave: on the limits of anti-realism* (London: Macmillan, 1997) and *Against Relativism: philosophy of science, deconstruction and critical theory* (Oxford: Blackwell, 1997).
2 See for instance Jacques Derrida, *Of Grammatology*, trans. G.C. Spivak (Baltimore: Johns Hopkins University Press, 1975), p. 158.
3 See Derrida, *Of Grammatology* (op. cit.); also '*Speech and Phenomena*' *and other Essays on Husserl's Theory of Signs*, trans. David B. Allison (Evanston, Ill.: Northwestern University Press, 1973); *Margins of Philosophy*, trans. Alan Bass (Chicago: University of Chicago Press, 1982); *Dissemination*, trans. Barbara Johnson (London: Athlone Press, 1981).
4 Derrida, 'White Mythology: metaphor in the text of philosophy', in *Margins of Philosophy* (op. cit.), pp. 207–71; henceforth referred to as 'WM'.
5 Richard Rorty, 'Philosophy as a Kind of Writing: an essay on Derrida', in *Consequences of Pragmatism* (Brighton: Harvester, 1982), pp. 89–109. See also Norris, 'Philosophy as *Not* Just a "Kind of Writing": Derrida and the claim of reason' and Rorty, 'Two Meanings of "Logocentrism": a reply to Norris', both in R.W. Dasenbrock (ed.), *Redrawing the Lines: analytic philosophy, deconstruction, and literary theory* (Minneapolis: University of Minnesota Press, 1989), pp. 198–202 and 204–16.
6 Derrida, *The Post Card: from Socrates to Freud and beyond*, trans. Alan Bass (Chicago: University of Chicago Press, 1987).
7 See Norris, 'Of an Apoplectic Tone Recently Adopted in Philosophy', in *Reclaiming Truth: contribution to a critique of cultural relativism* (London: Lawrence & Wishart, 1996), pp. 222–53.
8 Rorty, *Philosophy and the Mirror of Nature* (Oxford: Basil Blackwell, 1979).
9 See entries under Note 3, above.
10 Friedrich Nietzsche, 'On Truth and Falsity in their Ultramoral Sense', in *The Complete Works of Friedrich Nietzsche*, ed. Oscar Levy, Vol. 2 (New York: Russell & Russell, 1964); Anatole France, *The Garden of Epicurus*, trans. Alfred Allinson (New York: Dodd, Mead, 1923).

11   France, 'The Garden of Epicurus' (op. cit.), p. 213.

12   Martin Heidegger, *Early Greek Thinking*, trans. David F. Krell and Frank Capuzzi (New York: Harper & Row, 1975); *Poetry, Language, Thought*, trans. Albert Hofstadter (New York: Harper & Row, 1971); *What Is Called Thinking?*, trans. Fred D. Wieck and J. Glenn Gray (New York: Harper & Row, 1968).

13   Aristotle, *Poetics*, trans. I. Baywater (London: Oxford University Press, 1924); *Metaphysics*, trans. Hugh Tredenick (Cambridge, Mass.: Harvard University Press, 1933): *Categories and On Interpretation*, trans. J.L. Ackrill (Oxford: Clarendon, 1963); also *The Complete Works of Aristotle*, 2 vols, ed. Jonathan Barnes (Princeton, NJ: Princeton University Press, 1984).

14   See for instance – from a range of philosophical viewpoints – Max Black, *Models and Metaphors* (Ithaca, NY: Cornell University Press, 1962); Donald Davidson, 'What Metaphors Mean', in *Inquiries into Truth and Interpretation* (London: Oxford University Press, 1984), pp. 245–64; William Empson, *The Structure of Complex Words* (London: Chatto & Windus, 1951); Eva Feder Kitay, *Metaphor: its cognitive force and linguistic structure* (Oxford: Clarendon Press, 1987); Sarah Kofman, *Nietzsche and Metaphor*, trans Duncan Large (Stanford, Ca.: Stanford University Press, 1993); W.H. Leatherdale, *The Role of Analogy, Model and Metaphor in Science* (Amsterdam: North-Holland, 1974); Andrew Ortony (ed.), *Metaphor and Thought* (Cambridge: Cambridge University Press, 1979); I.A. Richards, *The Philosophy of Rhetoric* (New York and London: Oxford University Press, 1936).

15   See especially the essays on Husserl, Levinas, Foucault and others collected in Derrida, *Writing and Difference*, trans. Alan Bass (London: Routledge & Kegan Paul, 1978).

16   On this aspect of Derrida's work see Rodolphe Gasché, *The Tain of the Mirror: Derrida and the philosophy of reflection* (Cambridge, Mass.: Harvard University Press, 1986).

17   See Gaston Bachelard, *La formation de l'esprit scientifique* (Paris: Corti, 1938); *Le Rationalisme appliqué* (Paris: Presses Universitaires de France, 1949); *L'Actualité de l'histoire des sciences* (Paris: Palais de la Découverte, 1951); *L'Activité rationaliste de la physique contemporaine* (Paris: Presses Universitaires de France, 1951); *Le Materialisme rationnel* (Paris: Universitaires de France, 1953); *The Philosophy of No: a philosophy of the new scientific mind* (New York: Orion Press, 1968); *The New Scientific Spirit* (Boston: Beacon Press, 1984).

18   Georges Canguilhem, *Etudes d'historire et de philosophie des sciences* (Paris: Vrin, 1969); *La connaissance de la vie*, 2nd edn (Paris: Vrin, 1969); *On the Normal and the Pathological* (Dordrecht: D. Reidel, 1978); *Ideology and Rationality in the History of the Life Sciences*, trans. Arthur Goldhammer (Cambridge, Mass.: MIT Press, 1988).

19   Canguilhem, *La connaissance de la vie* (op. cit.), p. 49 ff.

20   See Imre Lakatos and Alan Musgrave (eds), *Criticism and the Growth of Knowledge* (Cambridge: Cambridge University Press, 1970).

21   For the best-known statement of this strong-sociological 'principle of parity', see David Bloor, *Knowledge and Social Imagery* (London: Routledge & Kegan Paul, 1976); also Barry Barnes, *Scientific Knowledge and Sociological Theory* (London: Routledge & Kegan Paul, 1974); Steve Fuller, *Social Epistemology* (Bloomington, Ind.: Indiana University Press, 1988); Bruno Latour and Steve Woolgar, *Laboratory Life* (London: Sage, 1979); Andrew Pickering, *The Mangle of Practice* (Chicago: University of Chicago Press, 1995); Steven Shapin and Simon Schaffer, *Leviathan and the Airpump* (Princeton, NJ: Princeton University Press, 1985); Steven Shapin, 'History of Science and its Sociological Reconstructions', *History of Science*, Vol. 20 (1982), pp. 157–212; Steve Woolgar, *Science: the very idea* (London: Tavistock, 1988). For further critical discussion, see Martin Hollis and Steven Lukes (eds), *Rationality and Relativism* (Oxford: Blackwell, 1982); W.H. Newton-Smith, *The Rationality of Science* (London: Routledge, 1981); R. Nola (ed.), *Relativism and Realism in Science* (Dordrecht: Kluwer, 1988); Christopher Norris, *Against Relativism* (op. cit.).

22   Ludwig Wittgenstein, *Philosophical Investigations*, trans. G.E.M. Anscombe (Oxford: Blackwell, 1958); Thomas S. Kuhn, *The Structure of Scientific Revolutions*, 2nd edn (Chicago: University of Chicago Press, 1970); also entries under Note 21, above.

23   See for instance Michel Foucault, *The Archaeology of Knowledge*, trans. A. Sheridan-Smith (London: Tavistock, 1971) and *Language, Counter-Memory, Practice*, ed. D.F. Bouchard (Oxford: Blackwell, 1977); Jean-François Lyotard, *The Postmodern Condition: a report on knowledge*, trans. Geoff Bennington and Brian Massumi (Manchester: Manchester University Press, 1984); Stephen Mulhall, *On Being in the World: Wittgenstein and Heidegger on seeing aspects* (London: Routledge, 1990); Joseph Rouse, *Knowledge and Power: toward a political philosophy of science* (Ithaca, NY:

Cornell University Press, 1987); Richard Rorty, *Relativism, Objectivity, and Truth* (Cambridge: Cambridge University Press, 1991).

24 Jürgen Habermas, 'On Levelling the Genre Distinction Between Philosophy and Literature', in *The Philosophical Discourse of Modernity: twelve lectures*, trans. Frederick Lawrence (Cambridge: Polity Press, 1987), pp. 185–210.

25 See Norris, 'Deconstruction, Postmodernism and Philosophy: Habermas on Derrida', in *What's Wrong with Postmodernism: critical theory and the ends of philosophy* (Hemel Hempstead: Harvester-Wheatsheaf, 1990), pp. 49–76.

26 See for instance Jacques Derrida, 'Of an Apocalyptic Tone Recently Adopted in Philosophy', trans. John P. Leavey, in Harold Coward and Toby Froshay (eds), *Derrida and Negative Theology* (Albany, NY: State University of New York Press, 1992), pp. 25–71; also 'The Principle of Reason: the university in the eyes of its pupils', *Diacritics*, Vol. 8, No. 3 (Fall 1983), pp. 3–20 and various texts collected in *Du Droit à la philosophie* (Paris: Minuit, 1990).

27 See entries under Note 17, above; also Bachelard, *The Poetics of Space*, trans. Maria Jolas (Boston: Beacon Press, 1963); *The Poetics of Reverie*, trans. Daniel Russell (Boston: Beacon Press, 1971).

28 Louis Althusser, *For Marx*, trans. Ben Brewster (London: Allen Lane, 1969); Althusser and Etienne Balibar, *Reading Capital*, trans. Brewster (London: New Left Books, 1970).

29 See Ted Benton, *The Rise and Fall of Structural Marxism* (London: New Left Books, 1984); Gregory Elliott, *Althusser: the detour of theory* (London: Verso, 1987); Christopher Norris, 'Spinoza, Marx, Althusser: "structural Marxism" twenty years on', in *Reclaiming Truth* (op. cit.), pp. 127–53.

30 Michel Foucault, *The Order of Things: an archaeology of the human sciences*, trans. Alan Sheridan-Smith (London: Tavistock, 1970); *The Archaeology of Knowledge* (op. cit.).

31 Foucault, *The Order of Things* (op. cit.), p. 387.

32 Immanuel Kant, *Critique of Pure Reason*, trans. Norman Kemp Smith (London: Macmillan, 1964).

33 Edmund Husserl, *Cartesian Meditations: an introduction to phenomenology*, trans. Dorian Cairns (The Hague: Martinus Nijhoff, 1973); *Ideas: general introduction to pure phenomenology*, trans. W.R. Boyce Gibson (The Hague: Martinus Nijhoff, 1950).

34 René Descartes, *The Philosophical Works of Descartes*, 2 vols, trans. Elizabeth S. Haldane and G.R.T. Ross (Cambridge: Cambridge University Press, 1967).

35 For a good brief account of the Michelson-Morley findings, see Rom Harré, *Great Scientific Experiments* (London: Oxford University Press, 1983).

36 Niels Bohr, *Atomic Theory and the Description of Nature* (Cambridge: Cambridge University Press, 1934); *Atomic Physics and Human Knowledge* (New York: Wiley, 1958); also John Honner, *The Description of Nature: Niels Bohr and the philosophy of quantum mechanics* (Oxford: Clarendon Press, 1987).

37 See for instance David Bohm and Basil J. Hiley, *The Undivided Universe: an ontological interpretation of quantum theory* (London: Routledge, 1993); James T. Cushing, *Quantum Mechanics: historical contingency and the Copenhagen hegemony* (Chicago: University of Chicago Press, 1994); Arthur Fine, *The Shaky Game: Einstein, realism, and the quantum theory* (Chicago: University of Chicago Press, 1986); Peter Gibbins, *Particles and Paradoxes* (Cambridge: Cambridge University Press, 1987); Christopher Norris, *Quantum Theory and the Flight from Realism: philosophical responses to quantum mechanics* (London: Routledge, 2000); Michael Redhead, *Incompleteness, Nonlocality and Realism: a prolegomenon to quantum mechanics* (Oxford: Clarendon Press, 1987); Euan Squires, *The Mystery of the Quantum World* (Bristol and Philadelphia: Institute of Physics Publishing, 1986).

38 See Gordon G. Brittan, *Kant's Theory of Science* (Princeton, NJ: Princeton University Press, 1978) and Michael Friedman, *Kant and the Exact Sciences* (Hemel Hempstead: Harvester, 1992).

39 J. Alberto Coffa, *The Semantic Tradition from Kant to Carnap: to the Vienna Station* (Cambridge: Cambridge University Press, 1991).

40 Lyotard, *The Postmodern Condition* (op. cit.).

41 W.V. Quine, 'Two Dogmas of Empiricism', in *From a Logical Point of View*, 2nd edn (Cambridge, Mass.: Harvard University Press, 1961), pp. 20–46.

42 Aristotle, *Poetics* (op. cit.).

43 Richard Rorty, 'Texts and Lumps', in *Relativism, Objectivity, and Truth* (op. cit.), pp. 78–92.

44 See Kuhn's 'Postscript' to *The Structure of Scientific Revolutions* (2nd edn, op. cit.); also *The Essential Tension: selected studies in scientific tradition and change* (Chicago: University of Chicago Press, 1977).

45 See entries under Note 3, above.

46 Derrida, *Limited Inc a b c* (Evanston, Ill.: Northwestern University Press, 1989).

47 John R. Searle, 'Reiterating the Differences', *Glyph*, Vol. 1 (Baltimore: Johns Hopkins University Press, 1977), pp. 198–208.

48 Searle, *Speech Acts: an essay on the philosophy of language* (Cambridge: Cambridge University Press, 1969) and *Expression and Meaning: studies in the theory of speech acts* (Cambridge: Cambridge University Press, 1979).

49 Derrida, *Of Grammatology* (op. cit.), p. 158.

50 Searle, 'Reiterating the Differences' (op. cit.).

Chapter 5 'The Idea of the University': some interdisciplinary soundings

1   See for instance Timothy Clark and Nicholas Royle (eds), *The University in Ruins, Oxford Literary Review*, Special Number, Vol. XVII, Nos. 1 and 2 (1995); Sandy Cohen, *Academia and the Lustre of Capital* (Minneapolis: University of Minnesota Press, 1993); Richard Rand (ed.), *Logomachia: the conflict of the faculties* (Lincoln, Nebraska: University of Nebraska Press, 1992).

2   See Michel Foucault, *The Archaeology of Knowledge*, trans. Alan Sheridan-Smith (London: Tavistock, 1972) and *Language, Counter-Memory, Practice*, trans. D.F. Bouchard and Shierry Weber (Oxford: Blackwell, 1977); Jean-François Lyotard, *The Postmodern Condition: a report on knowledge*, trans. Geoff Bennington and Brian Massumi (Manchester: Manchester University Press, 1984) and *The Differend: phrases in dispute*, trans. Georges van den Abbeele (Manchester: Manchester University Press, 1988); Clifford Geertz, *The Interpretation of Cultures: selected essays* (New York: Basic Books, 1973); Thomas Kuhn, *The Structure of Scientific Revolutions*, 2nd edn (Chicago: University of Chicago Press, 1970); Paul Feyerabend, *Against Method* (London: New Left Books, 1975).

3   Donald Davidson, 'On the Very Idea of a Conceptual Scheme', in *Inquiries into Truth and Interpretation* (Oxford: Clarendon Press, 1984), pp. 183–98.

4   See for instance W.V. Quine, 'Two Dogmas of Empiricism', in *From a Logical Point of View* (Cambridge, Mass.: Harvard University Press, 1961), pp. 20–44; also Quine, *Ontological Relativity and Other Essays* (New York: Columbia University Press, 1969).

5   Ferdinand de Saussure, *Course in General Linguistics*, trans. Wade Baskin (London: Fontana, 1974).

6   Davidson, 'Communication and Convention', in *Inquiries into Truth and Interpretation* (op. cit.), pp. 265–80 (p. 279).

7   Davidson, 'Thought and Talk', in *Inquiries into Truth and Interpretation* (op. cit.), pp. 155–70 (p. 162).

8   See for instance Christopher Norris, 'Reading Donald Davidson: truth, meaning and right interpretation', in *Deconstruction and the Interests of Theory* (London: Pinter Publishers, 1988), pp. 59–83.

9   Davidson, 'A Coherence Theory of Truth and Knowledge', in Ernest Le Pore (ed.), *Truth and Interpretation: essays on the philosophy of Donald Davidson* (Oxford: Blackwell, 1986), pp. 307–19.

10 Davidson, 'The Structure and Content of Truth', *Journal of Philosophy*, Vol. 87 (1990), pp. 279–328.

11 Norris, 'Reading Donald Davidson' (op. cit.).

12 Davidson, 'Reality Without Reference', in *Inquiries into Truth and Interpretation* (op. cit.), pp. 215–25 (p. 225).

13 For a more developed and detailed version of this argument, see Robert Brandom, *Making It Explicit: reasoning, representing, and discursive commitment* (Cambridge, Mass.: Harvard University Press, 1994).

14 Davidson, 'On the Very Idea of a Conceptual Scheme' (op. cit.), p. 197.

15 Benjamin Lee Whorf, *Language, Thought and Reality: selected writings*, ed. J.B. Carroll (Cambridge, Mass.: MIT Press, 1956).

16 See entries under Note 2, above.

17 Quine, 'Two Dogmas of Empiricism' (op. cit.).

18 Davidson, 'On the Very Idea of a Conceptual Scheme' (op. cit.), p. 184.

19 Ibid, p. 195.

20 Ibid, p. 197.

21 For a more detailed critical account of these ideas, see Christopher Norris, *The Truth About Postmodernism* (Oxford: Blackwell, 1993), *Resources of Realism: prospects for 'post-analytic' philosophy* (London: Macmillan, 1997), and *Against Relativism: philosophy of science, deconstruction and critical theory* (Oxford: Blackwell, 1997).

22 See for instance Lyotard, *The Postmodern Condition* (op. cit.) and Michel Foucault, *Power/ Knowledge: selected interviews and other writings* (Brighton: Harvester, 1980).

23 For further discussion see Norris, *Truth and the Ethics of Criticism* (Manchester: Manchester University Press, 1994).

24 See especially Feyerabend, *Against Method* (op. cit.) and *Science in a Free Society* (London: New Left Books, 1978).

25 See for instance Richard Rorty, *Consequences of Pragmatism* (Brighton: Harvester, 1982) and *Objectivity, Relativism, and Truth* (Cambridge: Cambridge University Press, 1991).

26 Feyerabend, *Farewell to Reason* (London: Verso, 1987).

27 See for instance – from a range of associated viewpoints – Barry Barnes, *About Science* (Oxford: Blackwell, 1985); David Bloor, *Wittgenstein: a social theory of knowledge* (New York: Columbia University Press, 1983); Harry Collins and Trevor Pinch, *The Golem: what everyone should know about science* (Cambridge: Cambridge University Press, 1993); Derek L. Phillips, *Wittgenstein and Scientific Knowledge: a sociological perspective* (London: Macmillan, 1977); Andrew Pickering (ed.), *Science as Practice and Culture* (Chicago: University of Chicago Press, 1992); Joseph Rouse, *Knowledge and Power: toward a political philosophy of science* (Ithaca, NY: Cornell University Press, 1987); Steven Shapin, *A Social History of Truth: civility and science in seventeenth-century England* (Chicago: University of Chicago Press, 1994); Steven Shapin and Simon Schaffer, *Leviathan and the Air-Pump: Hobbes, Boyle, and the experimental life* (Princeton, NJ: Princeton University Press).

28 This distinction receives its classic statement in Hans Reichenbach, *Experience and Prediction* (Chicago: University of Chicago Press, 1938).

29 William Empson, review of E.A. Burtt, *The Metaphysical Foundations of Modern Science*, in Empson, *Argufying: essays on literature and culture*, ed. John Haffenden (London: Chatto & Windus, 1987), pp. 530–3.

30 Ibid, p. 532.

31 Ibid, p. 533.

32 Bruno Latour, *We Have Never Been Modern*, trans. Catherine Porter (Hemel Hempstead: Harvester-Wheatsheaf, 1993).

33 Ibid, p. 55.

34 Ibid, p. 54.

35 Ibid, p. 55.

36 Ibid, p. 55.

37 See for instance Bruno Latour, *Science in Action* (Milton Keynes: Open University Press, 1987); Bruno Latour and Steve Woolgar, *Laboratory Life: the social construction of scientific facts* (London: Sage, 1979).

38 Empson, review of Burtt (op. cit.), p. 532.

39 See especially Roy Bhaskar, *A Realist Theory of Science* (Leeds: Leeds Books, 1975); *Scientific Realism and Human Emancipation* (London: Verso, 1986); *Reclaiming Reality: a critical introduction to contemporary philosophy* (London: Verso, 1989).

40 Bhaskar, *Scientific Realism and Human Emancipation* (op. cit.), p. 283.

41 See T.W. Adorno and Max Horkheimer, *Dialectic of Enlightenment*, trans. John Cumming (New York: Seabury Press, 1972).

42 See especially Jürgen Habermas, *The Philosophical Discourse of Modernity*, trans. Frederick Lawrence (Cambridge, Mass.: MIT Press, 1987).

43 Bhaskar, *Scientific Realism and Human Emancipation* (op. cit.), p. 49.

44 Quine, 'Two Dogmas of Empiricism' (op. cit.).

45 See for instance Keith Jenkins, *Re-Thinking History* (London: Routledge, 1991); Hayden White, *Tropics of Discourse* (Baltimore: Johns Hopkins University Press, 1978).

46 For further discussion see Norris, *Against Relativism* (op. cit.) and *New Idols of the Cave: on the limits of anti-realism* (Manchester: Manchester University Press, 1997).

47 Foucault, *Power/Knowledge* (op. cit.).

Chapter 6   Ethics, Autonomy and Self-Invention: debating Foucault

1 Patrick Shaw, 'Whatever Happened to the French Foucault? Norris on Foucault', *Journal of the British Society for Phenomenology*, Vol. 30, No. 3 (1999), pp. 275–90. All further references given by page-number in the text.

2   See Christopher Norris, ' "What Is Enlightenment": Kant according to Foucault', in Gary Gutting (ed.), *The Cambridge Companion to Foucault* (Cambridge: Cambridge University Press, 1994), pp. 159–96; also Norris, *The Truth About Postmodernism* (Oxford: Blackwell, 1993) and *Truth and the Ethics of Criticism* (Manchester: Manchester University Press, 1994).

3   Gilles Deleuze, *Foucault*, trans. Seán Hand (Minneapolis: University of Minnesota Press, 1988); Richard Rorty, 'Moral Identity and Private Autonomy: the case of Foucault', in *Essays on Heidegger and Others* (Cambridge: Cambridge University Press, 1989), pp. 193–8.

4   See especially Michel Foucault, 'What Is Enlightenment?', in Paul Rabinow (ed.), *The Foucault Reader* (Harmondsworth: Penguin, 1986), pp. 32–50; also Foucault, 'Politics and Ethics' and interview with Rabinow, ibid, pp. 371–80 and 381–90.

5   See for instance Foucault, *Language, Counter-Memory, Practice*, trans. and ed. D.F. Bouchard and S. Weber (Oxford: Blackwell, 1977); *Power/Knowledge: selected interviews and other writings* (Brighton: Harvester, 1980); *Politics, Philosophy, Culture*, ed. L.D. Kritzman (London: Routledge, 1988).

6   Jürgen Habermas, *Communication and the Evolution of Society*, trans. Thomas McCarthy (London: Heinemann, 1979); *Theory of Communicative Action*, 2 vols., trans. Thomas McCarthy (London: Heinemann, 1984 and 1987); *Justification and Application: remarks on discourse ethics*, trans. C.P. Cronin (Cambridge: Polity Press, 1993); Karl-Otto Apel, *Understanding and Explanation: a transcendental-pragmatic perspective*, trans. Georgia Warnke (Cambridge, Mass.: MIT Press, 1985) and *From a Transcendental-Semiotic Point of View*, ed. Marianna Papastephanou (Manchester: Manchester University Press, 1998).

7   Foucault, *The Birth of the Clinic*, trans. Alan Sheridan (London: Tavistock, 1973); *Discipline and Punish: the birth of the prison*, trans. Sheridan (New York: Pantheon, 1977); *The History of Sexuality, Vol. One: an introduction*, trans. Robert Hurley (New York: Pantheon, 1978); *Madness and Civilization: a history of insanity in the age of reason*, trans. Richard Howard (London: Tavistock, 1971); *The Order of Things: an archaeology of the human sciences*, trans. Sheridan (New York: Pantheon, 1970).

8   Patrick Shaw, *Logic and its Limits*, 2nd edn, revised (Oxford: Oxford University Press, 1997).

9   Bertrand Russell is probably the earliest and best-known exponent of philosophic commentary in this 'rational-reconstructive' mode, while Jonathan Bennett has applied it to yet more vigorous effect in his studies of Spinoza, Kant, and others.

10 See Hans-Georg Gadamer, *Truth and Method*, trans. John Cumming and Garrett Barden (London: Sheed & Ward, 1979) and *Philosophical Hermeneutics*, trans David E. Linge (Berkeley and Los Angeles: University of California Press, 1977); David C. Hoy, *The Critical Circle: literature, history and philosophical hermeneutics* (Berkeley and Los Angeles: University of California Press, 1978); Kurt Müller-Vollmer, *The Hermeneutics Reader* (Oxford: Blackwell, 1986); Richard E. Palmer, *Hermeneutics: interpretation theory in Schleiermacher, Dilthey, Heidegger, and Gadamer* (Evanston: Northwestern University Press, 1969); Paul Ricoeur, *Hermeneutics and the Human Sciences* (Cambridge: Cambridge University Press, 1981).

11 See Note 6, above; also Habermas, *Knowledge and Human Interests*, trans. J. Shapiro (London: Heinemann, 1972).

12 Foucault, *The Use of Pleasure*, trans. Robert Hurley (New York: Pantheon, 1995); *The Care of the Self*, trans. Hurley (New York: Pantheon, 1996).

13 Rorty, *Contingency, Irony, and Solidarity* (Cambridge: Cambridge University Press, 1989).

14 See Norris, *The Truth About Postmodernism* (op. cit.); also 'Philosophy as a Kind of Narrative: Rorty on postmodern liberal culture', in *The Contest of Faculties: philosophy and theory after deconstruction* (London: Methuen, 1985), pp. 139–66.

15 Rorty, *Contingency, Irony, and Solidarity* (op. cit.); also *Objectivity, Relativism, and Truth* (Cambridge: Cambridge University Press, 1991).

16 Foucault, 'What Is Enlightenment?' (op. cit.).

17 See especially Foucault, *Power/Knowlege* (op. cit.); also Didier Eribon, *Michel Foucault*, trans. Betsy Wing (London: Faber, 1992).

18 See James Miller, *The Passion of Michel Foucault* (New York: Anchor, 1994).

19 Michael Walzer, 'The Politics of Michel Foucault', in David C. Hoy (ed.), *Foucault: a critical reader* (Oxford: Blackwell, 1986), pp. 51–68; also Walzer, *Interpretation and Social Criticism* (Cambridge, Mass.: Harvard University Press, 1987).

20 See for instance Michèle Barrett, *The Politics of Truth from Marx to Foucault* (Cambridge: Polity Press, 1992); Michael Kelly (ed.), *Critique and Power: recasting the Habermas/Foucault debate*

(Cambridge, Mass.: MIT Press, 1994); Habermas, *The Philosophical Discourse of Modernity: twelve lectures*, trans. Frederick Lawrence (Cambridge: Polity, 1987); Lois McNay, *Foucault and Feminism: power, gender and the self* (Cambridge: Polity, 1992); Barry Smart, *Foucault, Marxism and Critique* (London: Routledge & Kegan Paul, 1983).

21 Foucault, *Power/Knowledge* and *Discipline and Punish* (op. cit.).

22 Friedrich Nietzsche, *On the Genealogy of Morals*, trans. Walter Kaufmann and R.J. Hollingdale (New York: Vintage Books, 1989); *The Will to Power*, trans. Kaufmann and Hollingdale, ed. Kaufmann (New York: Vintage Books, 1968).

23 Immanuel Kant, *Critique of Pure Reason*, trans. N. Kemp Smith (London: Macmillan, 1964) and *Critique of Practical Reason*, trans. L.W. Beck (Indianapolis: Bobbs-Merrill, 1977).

24 See Barry Hindess, *Discourses of Power: from Hobbes to Foucault* (Oxford: Blackwell, 1996).

25 Eribon, *Michel Foucault* (op. cit.); also David Macey, *The Lives of Michel Foucault* (New York: Pantheon, 1993).

26 See especially Pierre Bourdieu, *The Political Ontology of Martin Heidegger*, trans. Peter Collier (Cambridge: Polity Press, 1991); Tom Rockmore, *On Heidegger's Nazism and Philosophy* (London: Harvester-Wheatsheaf, 1992); Hans Sluga, *Heidegger's Crisis: philosophy and politics in Nazi Germany* (Cambridge, Mass.: Harvard University Press, 1993); Richard Wolin, *The Politics of Being: the political thought of Martin Heidegger* (New York: Columbia University Press, 1990); Wolin (ed.), *The Heidegger Controversy: a critical reader* (Cambridge, Mass.: MIT Press, 1993).

27 Rorty, *Contingency, Irony, and Solidarity* (op. cit.).

28 See Peter Starr, *Logics of Failed Revolt: French theory after May '68* (Stanford, Ca: Stanford University Press, 1995).

29 Jean-François Lyotard, *Libidinal Economy*, trans. Iain Hamilton Grant (London: Athlone Press, 1991); also Lyotard, *Political Writings*, trans. and ed. Bill Readings and Kevin Paul Geiman (Minneapolis: University of Minnesota Press, 1993).

30 See Notes 5, 18 and 25, above.

31 See for instance – from a range of disciplinary and theoretical standpoints – Derek Attridge, Geoff Bennington and Robert Young (eds.), *Post-Structuralism and the Question of History* (Cambridge: Cambridge University Press, 1987); Jean Baudrillard, *Selected Writings*, ed. Mark Poster (Cambridge: Polity Press, 1989); Robert F. Berkhofer, *Beyond the Great Story: history as text and discourse* (Cambridge, Mass.: Harvard University Press, 1995); George W. Grace, *The Linguistic Construction of Reality* (London: Croom Helm, 1987); Bruce Gregory, *Inventing Reality: physics as language* (New York: Wiley, 1988); Keith Jenkins (ed.), *The Postmodern History Reader* (London: Routledge, 1998); John Mowitt, *Text: the genealogy of an antidisciplinary object* (Durham, NC: Duke University Press, 1993); Richard Rorty (ed.), *The Linguistic Turn* (Chicago: University of Chicago Press, 1967); Hayden White, *Tropics of Discourse* (Baltimore: Johns Hopkins University Press, 1978).

32 See Notes 5, 7 and 12, above; also Foucault, *The Archaeology of Knowledge*, trans. A. Sheridan (New York: Harper & Row, 1972).

33 Foucault, *The Order of Things* (op. cit.), p. 318.

34 Kant, *Critique of Practical Reason* (op. cit.); also *Foundations of the Metaphysics of Morals*, trans. L.W. Beck (Minneapolis: Bobbs-Merrill, 1978).

35 Walzer, 'The Politics of Michel Foucault' (op. cit.).

36 Foucault, *Discipline and Punish* (op. cit.).

37 Foucault, *The Order of Things* (op. cit.), p. 318.

38 See Note 14, above.

39 Kant, *Critique of Practical Reason* (op. cit.); also *Political Writings*, ed. Hans Reiss (Cambridge: Cambridge University Press, 1976).

40 Habermas, *The Philosophical Discourse of Modernity* (op. cit.).

Chapter 7 'The Night in which All Cows are Black': Paul de Man, 'mere reading' and indifference to philosophy

1 Rodolphe Gasché, *The Tain of the Mirror: Derrida and the philosophy of reflection* (Cambridge, Mass.: Harvard University Press, 1986).

2 Gasché, *The Wild Card of Reading: on Paul de Man* (Cambridge, Mass.: Harvard University Press, 1988). All further references given by page-number only in the text.

3   See Paul de Man, *Wartime Journalism: 1939–1943*, eds Werner Hamacher *et al.* (Lincoln: University of Nebraska Press, 1988) and *Responses: on Paul de Man's wartime journalism*, eds Hamacher *et al.* (Lincoln: University of Nebraska Press, 1989); also – among the more hostile or downright dismissive commentators – David Lehman, *Signs of the Times: deconstruction and the fall of Paul de Man* (New York: Vintage, 1991); Jon Wiener, 'Deconstructing de Man' and 'Debating de Man', in *Professors, Politics and Pop* (London: Verso, 1991), pp. 3–11 and 12–22.

4   See Note 3, above; also Jacques Derrida, 'Like the Sound of the Sea Deep Within a Shell: Paul de Man's war', trans. Peggy Kamuf, *Critical Inquiry*, Vol. 14 (Spring 1988), pp. 590–652 and Christopher Norris, 'Postscript: on de Man's early writings for *Le Soir*', in *Paul de Man: deconstruction and the critique of aesthetic ideology* (New York: Routledge, 1988), pp. 177–98.

5   See especially de Man, *The Rhetoric of Romanticism* (New York: Columbia University Press, 1984); *The Resistance to Theory* (Minneapolis: University of Minnesota Press, 1986); *Aesthetic Ideology*, ed. A. Warminsky (Minneapolis: University of Minnesota Press, 1996).

6   De Man, 'The Return to Philology', in *The Resistance to Theory* (op. cit.), pp. 21–6.

7   See especially de Man, 'Aesthetic Formalization: Kleist's *Ueber das Marionettentheater*', in *The Rhetoric of Romanticism* (op. cit.), pp. 263–90.

8   See de Man, *Allegories of Reading: figural language in Rousseau, Nietzsche, Rilke, and Proust* (New Haven: Yale University Press, 1979).

9   Johann Gottlieb Fichte, *Science of Knowledge*, ed. and trans. P. Heath and J. Lachs (New York: Meredith, 1970), p. 153, cited by Gasché, p. 40.

10 J.L. Austin, *How to Do Things with Words* (Oxford: Oxford University Press, 1963); Jacques Derrida, 'Signature Event Context', *Glyph*, Vol. 1 (1977), pp. 172–97.

11 De Man, *The Resistance to Theory* (op. cit.), p. 19.

12 See the essays collected in de Man, *Aesthetic Ideology* (op. cit.); also Stanley Corngold, 'Error in Paul de Man', *Critical Inquiry*, Vol. 8 (1982), pp. 489–507; Raymond Geuss, 'A Response to Paul de Man', *Critical Inquiry*, Vol. 10 (1983), pp. 375–82; Christopher Norris, 'Kant Disfigured: genealogy, critique and postmodern scepticism', in *The Truth About Postmodernism* (Oxford: Blackwell, 1993).

13 Ernst Robert Curtius, *European Literature and the Latin Middle Ages*, trans. W.R. Trask (Princeton: Princeton University Press, 1978).

14 See Note 3, above.

15 See de Man, *Allegories of Reading* (op. cit.); also 'Literary History and Literary Modernity', in *Blindness and Insight: essays in the rhetoric of contemporary criticism*, 2nd edn (London: Methuen, 1983), pp. 142–65.

16 De Man, *Allegories of Reading* (op. cit.), p. 285.

17 Ibid, p. 301.

18 Derrida, 'Plato's Pharmacy', in *Dissemination*, trans. Barbara Johnson (London: Athlone Press, 1981), pp. 61–171.

19 See especially Rudolf Carnap, 'The Elimination of Metaphysics through Logical Analysis of Language', in A.J. Ayer (ed.), *Logical Positivism* (New York: Free Press, 1959), pp. 60–81.

20 For a lively and informative recent account, see C.J. Misak, *Verificationism: its history and prospects* (London: Routledge, 1995).

21 W.V. Quine, 'Two Dogmas of Empiricism', in *From a Logical Point of View*, 2nd edn (Cambridge, Mass.: Harvard University Press, 1961), pp. 20–46.

22 Martin Heidegger, *Being and Time*, trans. John Macquarrie and Edward Robinson (Oxford: Blackwell, 1980).

23 See Note 19, above.

24 De Man, 'Heidegger's Exegeses of Hölderlin', in *Blindness and Insight* (op. cit.), pp. 246–66.

25 See Note 4, above.

26 Rudolf Carnap, *The Logical Structure of the World and Pseudo-Problems in Philosophy*, trans. R. George (Berkeley and Los Angeles: University of California Press, 1969).

27 See for instance – from a range of philosophical standpoints – Gareth Evans, *The Varieties of Reference*, ed. John McDowell (Oxford: Clarendon Press, 1982), Gareth Evans and John McDowell (eds), *Truth and Meaning: essays in semantics* (Oxford: Clarendon Press, 1976); Gilbert Harman and Donald Davidson (eds), *Semantics of Natural Language* (Dordrecht: D. Reidel, 1972); Mark Platts (ed.), *Reference, Truth and Reality: essays on the philosophy of language* (London: Routledge & Kegan Paul, 1980); Ernst Tugendhat, *Traditional and Analytical Philosophy: lectures on the philosophy of language* (Cambridge: Cambridge University Press, 1982).

28 De Man, 'The Resistance to Theory' (op. cit.), p. 11.

29 For further discussion, see Ora Avni, *The Resistance of Reference: linguistics, philosophy, and the literary text* (Baltimore: Johns Hopkins University Press, 1990) and Cathy Caruth and Deborah Esch (eds), *Critical Encounters: reference and responsibility in deconstructive writing* (New Brunswick, NJ: Rutgers University Press, 1994).

30 Ibid, p. 10.

31 Ferdinand de Saussure, *Course in General Linguistics*, trans. and ed. Roy Harris (London: Duckworth, 1983); also Harris, *Reading Saussure* (London: Duckworth, 1987).

32 See entries under Note 27, above; also Donald Davidson, *Inquiries into Truth and Interpretation* (Oxford: Oxford University Press, 1974).

33 See especially David Lewis, *Convention; a philosophical study* (Cambridge, Mass.: Harvard University Press, 1969); Barry Stroud, 'Conventionalism and the Indeterminacy of Translation', *Synthèse*, Vol. 19 (1968), pp. 82–96.

Chapter 8   Conflict, Compromise or Complementarity: ideas of science in modern literary theory

1 See especially Jean-François Lyotard, *The Postmodern Condition: a report on knowledge*, trans. Geoff Bennington and Brian Massumi (Manchester: Manchester University Press, 1984).

2 See Note 18, below.

3 See for instance Otto Neurath, Rudolf Carnap and Charles Morris (eds), *Foundations of the Unity of Science: towards an international encyclopedia of unified science* (Chicago: University of Chicago Press, 1955–70); also Carnap, *The Unity of Science*, ed. Max Black (Bristol: Thoemmes Press, 1995) and Robert L. Causley, *Unity of Science* (Dordrecht: D. Reidel, 1977).

4 See John Dupré, *The Disorder of Things: metaphysical foundations of the disunity of science* (Cambridge, Mass.: Harvard University Press, 1993); also Peter Gallison and David J. Stump (eds), *The Disunity of Science: boundaries, contexts, and power* (Stanford, Ca: Stanford University Press, 1996) and Joseph Margolis, *Science Without Unity: reconciling the human and natural sciences* (Oxford: Blackwell, 1987).

5 Lyotard, *The Postmodern Condition* (op. cit.).

6 See for instance Bruce Gregory, *Inventing Reality: physics as language* (New York: Wiley, 1988) and Richard Rorty, *Objectivity, Relativism, and Truth* (Cambridge: Cambridge University Press, 1991).

7 See I.A. Richards, *Principles of Literary Criticism* (London: Kegan Paul, Trench & Trubner, 1924) and *Science and Poetry* (London: Kegan Paul, Trench & Trubner, 1926); revised and expanded edn, *Sciences and Poetries* (London: Routledge and Kegan Paul, 1970).

8 See for instance Josef Bleicher, *Contemporary Hermeneutics: hermeneutics as method, philosophy and critique* (London: Routledge & Kegan Paul, 1980); David Couzens Hoy, *The Critical Circle: literature, history and philosophical hermeneutics* (Berkeley and Los Angeles: University of California Press, 1978); Kurt Müller-Vollmer, *The Hermeneutics Reader* (Oxford: Blackwell, 1986); Richard E. Palmer, *Hermeneutics: interpretation theory in Schleiermacher, Dilthey, Heidegger, and Gadamer* (Evanston: Northwestern University Press, 1969); Paul Ricoeur, *Hermeneutics and the Human Sciences* (Cambridge: Cambridge University Press, 1981); Friedrich Schleiermacher, *Hermeneutics*, ed. H. Kimmerle, trans. J. Duke and J. Forstman (Missoula, MO: Scholars Press, 1977); Peter Szondi, *Introduction to Literary Hermeneutics*, trans. Martha Woodmansee (Cambridge: Cambridge University Press, 1995).

9 See especially Lyotard, *The Postmodern Condition* (op. cit.); Rorty, *Contingency, Irony, and Solidarity* (Cambridge: Cambridge University Press, 1989), *Objectivity, Relativism, and Truth* (op. cit.), and *Essays on Heidegger and Others* (Cambridge: Cambridge University Press, 1991).

10 See Note 7, above.

11 See especially Matthew Arnold, 'The Study of Poetry', in D.J. Enright and E. de Chickera (eds), *English Critical Texts* (Oxford: Oxford University Press, 1972), pp. 260–85.

12 A.J. Ayer (ed.), *Logical Positivism* (New York: Free Press, 1959); also Friedrich Waismann, 'Verifiability', and Isaiah Berlin, 'Verification', in G.H.R. Parkinson (ed.), *The Theory of Meaning* (Oxford: Oxford University Press, 1976), pp. 15–34 and 35–60; C.J. Misak, *Verificationism: its history and prospects* (London: Routledge, 1995).

13 See especially Richards, *Principles of Literary Criticism* (op. cit.).

14 F.R. Leavis, *Two Cultures? the significance of C.P. Snow* (London: Chatto & Windus, 1962); also C.P. Snow, *The Two Cultures, and A Second Look* (Cambridge: Cambridge University Press, 1963).

15 In this connection see especially C.K. Ogden and I.A. Richards, *The Meaning of Meaning* (London: Kegan Paul, Trench & Trubner, 1923).

16 See for instance Cleanth Brooks, *Modern Poetry and the Tradition* (Chapel Hill: University of North Carolina Press, 1939) and *The Well Wrought Urn: studies in the structure of poetry* (New York: Harcourt Brace, 1947); John Crowe Ranson, *The World's Body* (New York: Scribner, 1938) and *The New Criticism* (New York: New Directions, 1941); W.K. Wimsatt, *The Verbal Icon: studies in the meaning of poetry* (Lexington, Ky: University of Kentucky Press, 1954).

17 Wimsatt, *The Verbal Icon* (op. cit.); also *The Day of the Leopards: essays in defence of poems* (New Haven: Yale University Press, 1976).

18 See entries under Note 12, above.

19 W.V. Quine, 'Two Dogmas of Empiricism', in *From a Logical Point of View*, 2nd edn (Cambridge, Mass.: Harvard University Press, 1961), pp. 20–46.

20 See for instance Barry Barnes, *T.S. Kuhn and Social Science* (Oxford: Blackwell, 1982); David Bloor, *Knowledge and Social Imagery* (London: Routledge & Kegan Paul, 1976); Derek L. Phillips, *Wittgenstein and Scientific Knowledge: a sociological perspective* (London: Macmillan, 1977); Joseph Rouse, *Knowledge and Power: toward a political philosophy of science* (Ithaca, NY: Cornell University Press, 1987); Steve Woolgar (ed.), *Knowledge and Reflexivity: new frontiers in the sociology of knowledge* (London: Sage, 1988).

21 See especially Hans Reichenbach, *Experience and Prediction* (Chicago: University of Chicago Press, 1938).

22 Thomas S. Kuhn, *The Structure of Scientific Revolutions*, 2nd edn (Chicago: University of Chicago Press, 1970).

23 See Paul Horwich (ed.), *The World Changes: Thomas Kuhn and the nature of science* (Cambridge, Mass.: MIT Press, 1993) and Paul Hoyningen-Huehne, *Reconstructing Scientific Revolutions: Thomas S. Kuhn's philosophy of science*, trans. A.T. Levine (Chicago: University of Chicago Press, 1993).

24 See Christopher Norris, *Against Relativism: philosophy of science, deconstruction and critical theory* (Oxford: Blackwell, 1997); also *New Idols of the Cave: on the limits of anti-realism* (Manchester: Manchester University Press, 1997) and *Resources of Realism: prospects for 'post-analytic' philosophy* (London: Macmillan, 1997).

25 See Notes 8 and 20, above; also Martin Heidegger, *The Question Concerning Technology and Other Essays*, trans. William Lovitt (New York: Harper & Row, 1977); Don Ihde, *Technology and the Lifeworld: from garden to earth* (Bloomington, Ind.: Indiana University Press, 1990); Stephen Mulhall, *On Being In the World: Wittgenstein and Heidegger on seeing aspects* (London: Routledge, 1990).

26 See especially Richard Rorty, 'Texts and Lumps', in *Objectivity, Relativism, and Truth* (Cambridge: Cambridge University Press, 1991), pp. 78–92.

27 See for instance Manfred Frank, *What Is Neostructuralism?*, trans. S. Wilke and R. Gray (Minneapolis: University of Minnesota Press, 1989); José V. Harari (ed.), *Textual Strategies: perspectives in post-structuralist criticism* (London: Methuen, 1980); Richard Macksey and Eugenio Donato (eds.), *The Languages of Criticism and the Sciences of Man: the structuralist controversy* (Baltimore: Johns Hopkins University Press, 1970); Thomas A. Pavel, *The Feud of Language: a history of structuralist thought* (Oxford: Blackwell, 1990); John Sturrock (ed.), *Structuralism and Since* (Oxford: Oxford University Press, 1979).

28 Ferdinand de Saussure, *Course in General Linguistics*, trans. W. Baskin (London: Fontana, 1974); also Roland Barthes, *Mythologies*, trans. A. Lavers (London: Cape, 1970); Jonathan Culler, *Structuralist Poetics* (London: Routledge & Kegan Paul, 1975); A.J. Greimas, *Structural Semiotics: an attempt at a method*, trans. D. MacDonald, R. Schleifer and A. Velie (Lincoln: University of Nebraska Press, 1983); Claude Lévi-Strauss, *Structural Anthropology*, trans. C. Jacobson and B. Grundfest (Harmondsworth: Penguin, 1968).

29 Paul Ricoeur, *The Conflict of Interpretations: essays in hermeneutics*, trans. Don Ihde (Evanston, Ill.: Northwestern University Press, 1974).

30 Roland Barthes, *S/Z*, trans. Richard Miller (London: Jonathan Cape, 1975).

31 Barthes, *Criticism and Truth*, trans. K. Pilcher Keuneman (Minneapolis: University of Minnesota Press, 1987).

32   Lyotard, *The Postmodern Condition* (op. cit.); also *The Differend: phrases in dispute*, trans. Georges van den Abbeele (Manchester: Manchester University Press, 1987).

33   See Note 21, above.

34   See Paul Feyerabend, *Against Method* (London: New Left Books, 1975) and *Science in a Free Society* (New Left Books, 1978).

35   See for instance Zygmunt Bauman, *Postmodern Ethics* (Oxford: Blackwell, 1993); Seyla Benhabib, *Situating the Self: gender, community and postmodernism in contemporary ethics* (Cambridge: Polity Press, 1992); Elizabeth Deeds Ernarth, *Sequel to History: postmodernism and the crisis of time* (Princeton, NJ: Princeton University Press, 1992); Andrew Ross, *Strange Weather: culture, science and technology in an age of limits* (London: Verso, 1991).

36   See Gaston Bachelard, *La formation de l'esprit scientifique* (Paris: Corti, 1938); *Le rationalisme appliqué* (Paris: Presses Universitaires de France, 1949); *The Philosophy of No: a philosophy of the new scientific mind* (New York: Orion Press, 1968); *The New Scientific Spirit* (Boston: Beacon Press, 1984).

37   Immanuel Kant, *Critique of Pure Reason*, trans. N. Kemp Smith (London: Macmillan, 1964).

38   Louis Althusser, *For Marx*, trans. Ben Brewster (Harmondsworth: Penguin, 1969); also Althusser and Etienne Balibar, *Reading Capital*, trans. Brewster (Lonon: New Left Books, 1970).

39   See especially Ted Benton, *The Rise and Fall of Structural Marxism* (London: New Left Books, 1974) and Gregory Elliott, *Althusser: the detour of theory* (London: Verso, 1987).

40   Michel Foucault, *The Order of Things*, trans. A. Sheridan-Smith (London: Tavistock, 1970) and *The Archaeology of Knowledge*, trans. Sheridan-Smith (London: Tavistock, 1972).

41   For some interesting commentary on these topics, see Harriett Hawkins, *Strange Attractors: literature, culture and chaos theory* (Hemel Hempstead: Harvester-Wheatsheaf, 1995) and N. Katherine Hayles, *Chaos Bound: orderly disorder in contemporary literature and science* (Ithaca, NY: Cornell University Press, 1990).

42   N. Katherine Hayles, *The Scientific Web: scientific field models and literary strategies in the twentieth century* (Ithaca, NY: Cornell University Press, 1984).

43   See Kurt Gödel, 'On Formally Undecidable Propositions of *Principia Mathematica* and Related Systems', trans. B. Meltzer (New York: Basic Books, 1962); also Ernest Nagel and James Newtman, *Gödel's Proof* (London: Routledge & Kegan Paul, 1971); S.G. Shanker (ed.), *Gödel's Theorem in Focus* (London: Routledge, 1987); David Wayne Thomas, 'Gödel's Theorem and Postmodern Theory', *PMLA*, Vol. 110, No. 2 (1995), pp. 248–61.

44   Arkady Plotnitsky, *Complementarity: anti-epistemology after Bohr and Derrida* (Durham, NC: Duke University Press, 1994); also Niels Bohr, *Atomic Theory and the Description of Nature* (Cambridge: Cambridge University Press, 1934) and *Atomic Physics and Human Knowledge* (New York: Wiley, 1958); John Honner, *The Description of Nature: Niels Bohr and the philosophy of quantum physics* (Oxford: Clarendon Press, 1987); Henry J. Folse, *The Philosophy of Niels Bohr: the framework of complementarity* (Amsterdam: North-Holland, 1985); Dugald Murdoch, *Niels Bohr's Philosophy of Physics* (Cambridge: Cambridge University Press, 1987).

45   See especially Jacques Derrida, *Of Grammatology*, trans. G.C. Spivak (Baltimore: Johns Hopkins University Press, 1974); *Writing and Difference*, trans. Alan Bass (London: Routledge, 1978); *Dissemination*, trans. Barbara Johnson (London: Athlone Press, 1981).

46   William Empson, *Seven Types of Ambiguity* (London: Chatto & Windus, 1930); I.A. Richards, *Speculative Instruments* (Chicago: University of Chicago Press, 1955) and *Complementarities: uncollected essays and reviews* (Cambridge, Mass.: Harvard University Press, 1976); Lyotard, *The Postmodern Condition* (op. cit.).

47   For a good introductory account, see Alasdair I.M. Rae, *Quantum Physics: illusion or reality?* (Cambridge: Cambridge University Press, 1986); also Paul C.W. Davies, *Other Worlds* (London: Dent, 1980); J. Polkinghorne, *The Quantum World* (Harmondsworth: Penguin, 1986); Euan Squires, *The Mystery of the Quantum World*, 2nd edn (Bristol and Philadelphia: Institute of Physics Publishing, 1994).

48   See for instance Paul C.W. Davies and J.R. Brown (eds), *The Ghost in the Atom* (Cambridge: Cambridge University Press, 1986); B. de Witt and N. Graham (eds), *The Many-Worlds Interpretation of Quantum Mechanics* (Princeton, NJ: Princeton University Press, 1973); David Deutsch, *The Fabric of Reality* (Harmondsworth: Penguin, 1997); Wheeler and Zurek (eds), *Quantum Theory and Measurement* (Princeton, NJ: Princeton University Press, 1983); E.P. Wigner, *The Scientist Speculates*, ed. I.J. Good (London: Heinemann, 1962).

49 See for instance Danah Zohar, *The Quantum Self: a revolutionary view of human nature and consciousness rooted in the new physics* (London: Bloomsbury, 1990).

50 See entries under Note 47, above; also Erwin Schrödinger, *Letters on Wave Mechanics* (New York: Philosophical Library, 1967).

51 Empson, *Seven Types of Ambiguity* (op. cit.), p. 248.

52 Ibid, p. 249.

53 Richards, *Sciences and Poetries* and *Complementarities* (Notes 7 and 46, above).

54 See Note 44, above.

55 See Notes 16 and 17, above. For Empson's generally hostile attitude to the New Criticism and its various doctrines, see the essays and reviews collected in *Argufying*, ed. John Haffenden (London: Chatto & Windus, 1987).

56 See Note 44, above.

57 Lyotard, *The Postmodern Condition* (op. cit.).

58 See for instance Jean Baudrillard, *Selected Writings*, ed. Mark Poster (Cambridge: Polity Press, 1989) and *Revenge of the Crystal: a Baudrillard reader* (London: Pluto Press, 1990); Keith Jenkins (ed.), *The Postmodern History Reader* (London: Routledge, 1998); Christopher Norris, *The Truth About Postmodernism* (Oxford: Blackwell, 1994).

59 Wesley C. Salmon, *Four Decades of Scientific Explanation* (Minneapolis: University of Minnesota Press, 1989), p. 178.

60 See Schrödinger, *Letters on Wave Mechanics* (op. cit.); also James Gribbin, *In Search of Schrödinger's Cat* (New York: Bantam Books, 1984).

61 Emmanuel Levinas, *Totality and Infinity*, trans. A. Lingis (Pittsburgh: Duquesne University Press, 1969) and *Otherwise than Being, or Beyond Essence*, trans. Lingis (The Hague: Martinus Nijhoff, 1981).

62 See Niels Bohr, 'Discussion with Einstein on Epistemological Problems in Atomic Physics', in P.A. Schilpp (ed.), *Albert Einstein: philosopher-scientist* (La Salle, Ill.: Open Court, 1969), pp. 199–241; A. Einstein, B. Podolsky and N. Rosen, 'Can Quantum-Mechanical Description of Reality be Considered Complete?', in *Physical Review*, ser. 2, Vol. XLVII (1935), pp. 777–808; also (for a generally sceptical assessment of Einstein's case) Arthur Fine, *The Shaky Game: Einstein, realism and quantum theory* (Chicago: University of Chicago Press, 1986). On the 'hidden variables' theory, see David Bohm, *Causality and Chance in Modern Physics* (London: Routledge and Kegan Paul, 1957); David Bohm and Basil J. Hiley, *The Undivided Universe: an ontological interpretation of quantum theory* (London: Routledge, 1993); also James T. Cushing, *Quantum Mechanics: historical contingency and the Copenhagen hegemony* (Chicago: University of Chicago Press, 1994) and Peter Holland, *The Quantum Theory of Motion* (Cambridge: Cambridge University Press, 1993).

63 See for instance Raymond Tallis, *Not Saussure* (London: Macmillan, 1988) and *In Defence of Realism* (London: Edward Arnold, 1988); also Valentine Cunningham, *In the Reading Gaol: postmodernity, texts and history* (Oxford: Blackwell, 1994); Raman Selden, *Criticism and Objectivity* (London: Allen & Unwin, 1984).

64 Rorty, 'Texts and Lumps' (op. cit.).

Chapter 9   Sexed Equations and Vexed Physicists: the 'two cultures' revisited

1 Alan Sokal and Jean Bricmont, *Intellectual Impostures: postmodern philosophers' abuse of science* (London: Profile Books, 1998).

2 Alan Sokal, 'Transgressing the Boundaries: toward a transformative hermeneutics of quantum gravity', *Social Text*, Vols. 46–7 (Spring–Summer 1996), pp. 217–52. See also Noretta Koertge (ed.), *A House Built on Sand: exposing postmodernist myths about science* (Oxford: Oxford University Press, 1998).

3 Alan Sokal, 'A Physicist Experiments with Cultural Studies', *Lingua Franca*, Vol. 6, No. 4 (May/June 1996), pp. 62–4.

4 Stanley Fish, 'Professor Sokal's Bad Joke', *New York Times*, 21 May 1996, p. 23.

5 C.P. Snow, *The Two Cultures, and a second look* (Cambridge: Cambridge University Press, 1963).

6 Julia Kristeva, *Semeiotike: recherches pour une sémanalyse* (Paris: Editions du Seuil, 1969).

7 Luce Irigaray, 'The "Mechanics" of Fluids', in *This Sex Which Is Not One*, trans. Catherine Porter with Carolyn Burke (Ithaca, NY: Cornell University Press, 1985).

8 Suzanne K. Damarin, 'Gender and Mathematics from a Feminist Standpoint', in W.G. Secada, E. Fennema and L.B. Adajan (eds), *New Directions for Equity in Mathematics Education* (New York: Cambridge University Press, 1995), pp. 242–57 (p. 252).

9 See for instance Michel Foucault, *Language, Counter-Memory, Practice*, trans. D.F. Bouchard and S. Simon (Oxford: Blackwell, 1977); *Power/Knowledge: selected interviews and other writings*, ed. D.F. Gordon (Brighton: Harvester, 1980); *The Foucault Reader*, ed. P. Rabinow (Harmondsworth: Penguin, 1986).

10 Jean-François Lyotard, *The Postmodern Condition: a report on knowledge*, trans. Geoff Bennington and Brian Massumi (Manchester: Manchester University Press, 1984).

11 Vaclav Havel, 'The End of the Modern Era', *New York Times*, 1 May 1992, p. 15.

12 Thomas S. Kuhn, *The Structure of Scientific Revolutions*, 2nd edn (Chicago: University of Chicago Press, 1970); W.V. Quine, 'Two Dogmas of Empiricism', in *From a Logical Point of View*, 2nd edn (Cambridge, Mass.: Harvard University Press, 1961), pp. 20–46.

13 See especially Barry Barnes, *About Science* (Oxford: Blackwell, 1985) and David Bloor, *Knowledge and Social Imagery*, 2nd edn (Chicago: University of Chicago Press, 1992); also Barry Barnes, David Bloor, and John Henry, *Scientific Knowledge: a sociological analysis* (Chicago: University of Chicago Press, 1996).

14 See for instance – from a range of philosophical standpoints – D.M. Armstrong, *What Is a Law of Nature?* (Cambridge: Cambridge University Press, 1983); Roy Bhaskar, *Scientific Realism and Human Emancipation* (London: Verso, 1986); Michael Devitt, *Realism and Truth*, 2nd edn (Oxford: Blackwell, 1986); Jarrett Leplin (ed.), *Scientific Realism* (Berkeley and Los Angeles: University of California Press, 1984); Nicholas Rescher, *Scientific Realism: a critical reappraisal* (Dordrecht: D. Reidel, 1987); Wesley Salmon, *Scientific Explanation and the Causal Structure of the World* (Princeton, NJ: Princeton University Press, 1984); Peter J. Smith, *Realism and the Progress of Science* (Cambridge: Cambridge University Press, 1981).

15 This is most famously the position adopted by Paul Feyerabend in *Against Method* (London: New Left Books, 1975) and *Science in a Free Society* (London: New Left Books, 1978).

16 See entries under Note 13, above; also Barry Barnes, *Scientific Knowledge and Sociological Theory* (London: Routledge & Kegan Paul, 1974); Barnes and Steven Shapin (eds), *Natural Order* (London: Sage, 1979); Steven Shapin, 'History of Science and its Sociological Reconstructions', *History of Science*, Vol. 20 (1982), pp. 157–210; Steve Woolgar, *Science: the very idea* (London: Tavistock, 1988); Woolgar (ed.), *Knowledge and Reflexivity: new frontiers in the sociology of knowledge* (London: Sage, 1988).

17 See Peter Winch, *The Idea of a Social Science and its Relation to Philosophy* (London: Routledge & Kegan Paul, 1958); also David Bloor, *Wittgenstein: a social theory of knowledge* (New York: Columbia University Press, 1983) and David L. Phillips, *Wittgenstein and Scientific Knowledge: a sociological perspective* (London: Macmillan, 1977).

18 Winch, *The Idea of a Social Science* (op. cit.).

19 Ludwig Wittgenstein, *Tractatus Logico-Philosophicus*, trans. D.F. Pears and B.F. McGuiness (London: Routledge & Kegan Paul, 1961).

20 Wittgenstein, *Philosophical Investigations*, trans. G.E.M. Anscombe (Oxford: Blackwell, 1958) and *On Certainty*, ed. Anscombe and G.H. von Wright (Blackwell, 1969).

21 See especially Gottlob Frege, 'On Sense and Reference', in *Translations from the Philosophical Writings of Gottlob Frege*, eds Max Black and P.T. Geach (Oxford: Blackwell, 1952), pp. 56–78 and Bertrand Russell, *An Inquiry into Meaning and Truth* (London: Allen & Unwin, 1940).

22 Wittgenstein, *Remarks on Frazer's Golden Bough*, ed. Rush Rhees, trans. A.C. Miles (Nottingham: Brynmill Press, 1979) and *Culture and Value*, ed. Rhees (Oxford: Blackwell, 1980); also Winch, *The Idea of a Social Science* (op. cit.).

23 Bertrand Russell, *A History of Western Philosophy*, 2nd edn (London: Allen & Unwin, 1961), p. 782.

24 Meera Nanda, 'The Science Wars in India', *Dissent*, Vol. XLIV, No. 1 (Winter 1997), pp. 78–83; p. 82.

25 See for instance Roy Bhaskar, *Scientific Realism and Human Emancipation* (op. cit.); Andrew Collier, *Scientific Realism and Socialist Thought* (Hemel Hempstead: Harvester, 1989) and *Critical Realism* (London: Verso, 1994); Evelyn Fox Keller, *Reflections on Gender and Science* (New Haven: Yale University Press, 1985) and *Secrets of Life, Secrets of Death: essays on language, gender and science* (New York: Routledge, 1992); Hilary Rose and Steven Rose (eds), *The Radicalization of Science: ideology of/in the natural sciences* (London: Macmillan, 1976).

26 See Note 25, above.

27 Bruno Latour, 'A Relativistic Account of Einstein's Relativity', *Social Studies of Science*, Vol. 18 (1988), pp. 3–44 (pp. 10–11).

28 Ibid, p. 15.

29 See for instance Bruno Latour, *Science in Action: how to follow scientists and engineers through society* (Milton Keynes: Open University Press, 1987); B. Latour and Steve Woolgar, *Laboratory Life: the social construction of scientific facts* (London: Sage, 1979); also – for his deep reservations with regard to strong-sociological and 'postmodern' science studies – *We Have Never Been Modern* (Cambridge, Mass.: Harvard University Press, 1993).

30 Gaston Bachelard, *La formation de l'esprit scientifique* (Paris: Corti, 1938); *Le rationalisme appliqué* (Paris: Presses Universitaires de France, 1949); *Le matérialisme rationnel* (Paris: Presses Universitaires de France, 1953); *The Philosophy of No: a philosophy of the new scientific mind* (New York: Orion Press, 1968); Georges Canguilhem, *Etudes d'histoire et de philosophie des sciences* (Paris: Vrin, 1968); *La connaissance de la vie* (Paris: Vrin, 1969); *Ideology and Rationality in the History of the Life Sciences*, trans. A. Goldhammer (Cambridge, Mass.: MIT Press, 1988); also Jacques Derrida, 'White Mythology: metaphor in the text of philosophy', in *Margins of Philosophy*, trans. Alan Bass (Chicago: University of Chicago Press, 1982), pp. 207–71.

31 See especially Louis Althusser, *'Philosophy and the Spontaneous Philosophy of the Scientists' and Other Essays*, ed. Gregory Elliott (London: Verso, 1990).

32 Wayne C. Booth, *A Rhetoric of Irony* (Chicago: University of Chicago Press, 1974).

33 Derrida, 'White Mythology' (op. cit.); also 'The Supplement of Copula: philosophy *before* linguistics', in *Margins of Philosophy* (op. cit.), pp. 175–205.

34 For further discussion see Michael Audi, *The Interpretation of Quantum Mechanics* (Chicago: University of Chicago Press, 1973); Peter Gibbins, *Particles and Paradoxes: the limits of quantum logic* (Cambridge: Cambridge University Press, 1987); Karl Popper, *Quantum Theory and the Schism in Physics* (London: Hutchinson, 1982); Alasdair I.M. Rae, *Quantum Physics: illusion or reality?* (Cambridge: Cambridge University Press, 1986); Euan Squires, *The Mystery of the Quantum World*, 2nd edn (Bristol: Institute of Physics Publishing, 1994).

35 See for instance Niels Bohr, *Atomic Theory and the Description of Nature* (Cambridge: Cambridge University Press, 1934) and *Atomic Physics and Human Knowledge* (New York: Wiley, 1958); also John Honner, *The Description of Nature: Niels Bohr and the philosophy of quantum physics* (Oxford: Clarendon Press, 1987).

36 See especially James T. Cushing, *Quantum Mechanics: historical contingency and the Copenhagen hegemony* (Chicago: University of Chicago Press, 1994).

37 See David Bohm, 'A Suggested Interpretation of the Quantum Theory in Terms of "Hidden" Variables', I and II, *Physical Review*, Vol. 85 (1952), pp. 166–79 and 180–93; *Causality and Chance in Modern Physics* (London: Routledge & Kegan Paul, 1957); D. Bohm and Basil J. Hiley, *The Undivided Universe: an ontological interpretation of quantum theory* (London: Routledge, 1993); also David Z. Albert, *Quantum Mechanics and Experience* (Cambridge, Mass.: Harvard University Press, 1993) and 'Bohm's Alternative to Quantum Physics', *Scientific American*, 270 (May 1994), pp. 58–63; Peter Holland, *The Quantum Theory of Motion: an account of the de Broglie-Bohm causal interpretation of quantum mechanics* (Cambridge: Cambridge University Press, 1993).

38 See Erwin Schrödinger, *Letters on Wave Mechanics* (New York: Philosophical Library, 1966) and – for a lively introduction to the topic – John Gribbin, *In Search of Schrödinger's Cat: quantum physics and reality* (New York: Bantam Books, 1984).

39 See for instance Paul C.W. Davies, *Other Worlds* (London: Dent, 1980); Davies and J.R. Brown (eds), *The Ghost in the Atom* (Cambridge: Cambridge University Press, 1986); David Deutsch, *The Fabric of Reality* (Harmondsworth: Penguin, 1998).

40 Cushing, *Quantum Mechanics* (op. cit.).

41 A. Einstein, B. Podolsky and N. Rosen, 'Can Quantum-Mechanical Description of Reality be Considered Complete?', *Physical Review*, ser. 2, Vol. 47 (1935), pp. 777–80; also Niels Bohr, 'Discussion with Einstein on Epistemological Problems in Atomic Physics', in P.A. Schilpp (ed.), *Albert Einstein: philosopher-scientist* (La Salle, Ill.: Open Court, 1969), pp. 199–241.

42 J.S. Bell, *Speakable and Unspeakable in Quantum Mechanics: collected papers on quantum philosophy* (Cambridge: Cambridge University Press, 1987); also James T. Cushing and Ernan McMullin (eds), *Philosophical Consequences of Quantum Theory: reflections on Bell's Theorem* (Indiana: University of Notre Dame Press, 1989); Tim Maudlin, *Quantum Nonlocality and Relativity: metaphysical*

intimations of modern science (Oxford: Blackwell, 1993); Michael Redhead, *Incompleteness, Non-locality and Realism: a prolegomenon to the philosophy of quantum mechanics* (Oxford: Clarendon Press, 1987).

43   For further discussion see entries under Note 42, above; also J.R. Lucas and P.E. Hodgson, *Spacetime and Electro-Magnetism* (Oxford: Clarendon Press, 1990).

44   David Bohm, *Wholeness and the Implicate Order* (London: Routledge & Kegan Paul, 1980).

45   Deutsch, *The Fabric of Reality* (op. cit.); David Lewis, *On the Plurality of Worlds* (Oxford: Blackwell, 1988).

46   See for instance Paul Forman, 'Weimar Culture, Causality, and Quantum Theory, 1918–1927: adaptation by German physicists and mathematicians to a hostile intellectual environment', *Historical Studies in the Physical Sciences*, Vol. 3 (1971), pp. 1–115.

47   See Abraham Pais, *Niels Bohr's Times in Physics, Philosophy, and Polity* (Oxford: Clarendon Press, 1991), pp. 301ff.

48   Gilles Deleuze and Félix Guattari, *What Is Philosophy?*, trans Hugh Tomlinson and Graham Burchell (New York: Columbia University Press, 1994), p. 129.

49   See for instance Steve Fuller, *Social Epistemology* (Bloomington, Ind.: Indiana University Press, 1988).

50   Kuhn, *The Structure of Scientific Revolutions* (op. cit.).

51   Quine, 'Two Dogmas of Empiricism' (op. cit.).

52   See for instance Nelson Goodman, *Ways of Worldmaking* (Indianapolis: Bobbs-Merrill, 1978).

53   Hilary Putnam, *The Many Faces of Realism* (La Salle: Open Court, 1987) and *Realism with a Human Face* (Cambridge, Mass.: Harvard University Press, 1990).

54   Stanley Fish, *Doing What Comes Naturally: change, rhetoric and the practice of theory in literary and legal studies* (Oxford: Clarendon Press, 1989)

Bibliography

Adorno, Theodor W., *Negative Dialectics*, trans. E.B. Ashton (London: Routledge & Kegan Paul, 1973).

Adorno, Theodor W., *Prisms*, trans. Samuel and Shierry Weber (Cambridge, Mass.: MIT Press, 1981).

Adorno, Theodor W., *Against Epistemology: A Metacritique*, trans. Willis Domingo (Oxford: Blackwell, 1982).

Adorno, Theodor W. and Horkheimer, Max, *Dialectic of Enlightenment*, trans. John Cumming (New York: Seabury Press, 1972).

Albert, David Z., *Quantum Mechanics and Experience* (Cambridge, Mass.: Harvard University Press, 1993).

Althusser, Louis, *For Marx*, trans. Ben Brewster (Harmondsworth: Penguin, 1969).

Althusser, Louis, '*Philosophy and the Spontaneous Philosophy of the Scientists' and Other Essays*, ed. Gregory Elliott (London: Verso, 1990).

Althusser, Louis and Balibar, Etienne, *Reading Capital*, trans. Brewster (London: New Left Books, 1970).

Ankersmit, F.R., *History and Tropology* (Berkeley and Los Angeles: University of California Press, 1994).

Apel, Karl-Otto, *Understanding and Explanation: a transcendental-pragmatic perspective*, trans. Georgia Warnke (Cambridge, Mass.: MIT Press, 1985).

Apel, Karl-Otto, *From a Transcendental-Semiotic Point of View*, ed. Marianna Papastephanou (Manchester: Manchester University Press, 1998).

Armstrong, D.M., *Universals and Scientific Realism* (2 vols.) (Cambridge: Cambridge University Press, 1978).

Armstrong, D.M., *What Is a Law of Nature?* (Cambridge: Cambridge University Press, 1983).

Arnold, Matthew, 'The Study of Poetry', in D.J. Enright and E. de Chickera (eds), *English Critical Texts* (Oxford: Oxford University Press, 1972), pp. 260–85.

Aronson, J., Harré, R. and Way, E., *Realism Rescued: How Scientific Progress is Possible* (London: Duckworth, 1994).

Arrington, Robert L. (ed.), *Rationalism, Realism, and Relativism: Perspectives in Contemporary Moral Epistemology* (Ithaca, NY: Cornell University Press, 1989).

Attridge, Derek, Bennington, Geoff and Young, Robert (eds), *Post-Structuralism and the Question of History* (Cambridge: Cambridge University Press, 1987).

Austin, J.L., *How to Do Things With Words* (London: Oxford University Press, 1963).

Avni, Ora, *The Resistance of Reference: Linguistics, Philosophy, and the Literary Text* (Baltimore: Johns Hopkins University Press, 1990).

Ayer, A.J., *The Foundations of Empirical Knowledge* (London: Macmillan, 1955).

Ayer, A.J. (ed.), *Logical Positivism* (New York: Free Press, 1959).

Bachelard, Gaston, *La Formation de l'Esprit Scientifique* (Paris: Corti, 1938).

Bachelard, Gaston, *Le Rationalisme Appliqué* (Paris: Presses Universitaires de France, 1949).

Bachelard, Gaston, *Le Matérialisme Rationnel* (Paris: P.U.F., 1953).

Bachelard, Gaston, *The Philosophy of No: A Philosophy of the New Scientific Mind* (New York: Orion Press, 1968).

Bachelard, Gaston, *The New Scientific Spirit* (Boston: Beacon Press, 1984).

Barnes, Barry, *T. S. Kuhn and Social Science* (Oxford: Blackwell, 1982).

Barnes, Barry, *About Science* (Oxford: Blackwell, 1985).

Barnes, Barry and Shapin, Steven (eds), *Natural Order* (London: Sage, 1979).

Barnes, Barry, Bloor, David and Henry, John, *Scientific Knowledge: A Sociological Analysis* (Chicago: University of Chicago Press, 1996).

Barrett, Michèle, *The Politics of Truth from Marx to Foucault* (Cambridge: Polity Press, 1992).

Barthes, Roland, *Mythologies*, trans. A. Lavers (London: Cape, 1970).

Barthes, Roland, *S/Z*, trans. Richard Miller (London: Jonathan Cape, 1975).

Barthes, Roland, 'The Discourse of History', in *The Rustle of Language*, trans. Richard Howard (Oxford: Blackwell, 1986), pp. 127–40.

Barthes, Roland, 'The Reality Effect', in *The Rustle of Language*, trans. Richard Howard (Oxford: Blackwell, 1986), pp. 141–8.

Barthes, Roland, *Criticism and Truth*, trans. K. Pilcher Keuneman (Minneapolis: University of Minnesota Press, 1987).

Baudrillard, Jean, *Simulations*, trans. Paul Foss, Paul Patton, and Philip Beitchman (New York: Semiotext(e), 1983).

Baudrillard, Jean, *Selected Writings*, ed. Mark Poster (Cambridge: Polity Press, 1989).

Baudrillard, Jean, *Revenge of the Crystal: A Baudrillard Reader* (London: Pluto Press, 1990).

Bauman, Zygmunt, *Postmodern Ethics* (Oxford: Blackwell, 1993).

Beiser, Frederick C., *The Fate of Reason: German Philosophy from Kant to Fichte* (Cambridge, Mass.: Harvard University Press, 1987).

Bell, J.S., *Speakable and Unspeakable in Quantum Mechanics: Collected Papers on Quantum Philosophy* (Cambridge: Cambridge University Press, 1987).

Benhabib, Seyla, *Situating the Self: Gender, Community and Postmodernism in Contemporary Ethics* (Cambridge: Polity Press, 1992).

Bennett, Jonathan, *Linguistic Behaviour* (Cambridge: Cambridge University Press, 1976).

Benton, Ted, *The Rise and Fall of Structural Marxism* (London: New Left Books, 1974).

Berkhofer, Robert F., *Beyond the Great Story: History as Text and Discourse* (Cambridge, Mass.: Harvard University Press, 1995).

Bhaskar, Roy, *A Realist Theory of Science* (Leeds: Leeds Books, 1975).

Bhaskar, Roy, *Scientific Realism and Human Emancipation* (London: Verso, 1986).

Bhaskar, Roy, *Reclaiming Reality: A Critical Introduction to Contemporary Philosophy* (London: Verso, 1989).

Bleicher, Joseph, *Contemporary Hermeneutics: Hermeneutics as Method, Philosophy and Critique* (London: Routledge & Kegan Paul, 1980).

Bloor, David, *Knowledge and Social Imagery* (London: Routledge and Kegan Paul, 1976).

Bloor, David, *Wittgenstein: A Social Theory of Knowledge* (New York: Columbia University Press, 1983).

Bohm, David, 'A Suggested Interpretation of the Quantum Theory in Terms of "Hidden" Variables', I and II, *Physical Review*, Vol. 85 (1952), pp. 166–79 and 180–93.

Bohm, David, *Causality and Chance in Modern Physics* (London: Routledge & Kegan Paul, 1957).

Bohm, David, *Wholeness and the Implicate Order* (London: Routledge & Kegan Paul, 1980).

Bohm, David and Hiley, Basil J., *The Undivided Universe: An Ontological Interpretation of Quantum Theory* (London: Routledge, 1993).

Bohr, Niels, *Atomic Theory and the Description of Nature* (Cambridge: Cambridge University Press, 1934).

Bohr, Niels, *Atomic Physics and Human Knowledge* (New York: Wiley, 1958).

Bohr, Niels, 'Discussion with Einstein on Epistemological Problems in Atomic Physics', in P.A. Schilpp (ed.), *Albert Einstein: Philosopher-Scientist* (La Salle, Ill.: Open Court, 1969), pp. 199–241.

Booth, Wayne C., *A Rhetoric of Irony* (Chicago: University of Chicago Press, 1974).

Bourdieu, Pierre, *Distinction: A Social Critique of the Judgement of Taste*, trans. R. Nice (Cambridge, Mass.: Harvard University Press, 1984).

Bourdieu, Pierre, *Language and Symbolic Power*, ed. John B. Thompson, trans. Gino Raymond and Matthew Adamson (Cambridge: Polity Press, 1991).

Bourdieu, Pierre, *The Political Ontology of Martin Heidegger*, trans. Peter Collier (Oxford: Polity Press, 1991).

Bradbury, Malcolm and McFarlane, James (eds), *Modernism* (Harmondsworth: Penguin, 1976).

Brandom, Robert, *Making It Explicit: Reasoning, Representing, and Discursive Commitment* (Cambridge, Mass.: Harvard University Press, 1994).

Brink, David O., *Moral Realism and the Foundations of Ethics* (Cambridge: Cambridge University Press, 1989).

Brooks, Cleanth, *Modern Poetry and the Tradition* (Chapel Hill: University of North Carolina Press, 1939).

Brooks, Cleanth, *The Well Wrought Urn: Studies in the Structure of Poetry* (New York: Harcourt Brace, 1947).

Canguilhem, Georges, *Etudes d'Histoire et de Philosophie des Sciences* (Paris: Vrin, 1968).

Canguilhem, Georges, *La Connaissance de la Vie* (Paris: Vrin, 1969).

Canguilhem, Georges, *Ideology and Rationality in the History of the Life Sciences*, trans. A. Goldhammer (Cambridge, Mass.: MIT Press, 1988).

Carnap, Rudolf, 'The Elimination of Metaphysics through Logical Analysis of Language', in A.J. Ayer (ed.), *Logical Positivism* (New York: Free Press, 1959), pp. 60–81.

Carnap, Rudolf, *The Logical Structure of the World and Pseudoproblems in Philosophy*, trans. R. George (Berkeley and Los Angeles: University of California Press, 1969).

Carnap, Rudolf, *The Unity of Science*, ed. Max Black (Bristol: Thoemmes Press, 1995) and Robert L. Causley, *Unity of Science* (Dordrecht: D. Reidel, 1977).

Caruth, Cathy and Esch, Deborah (eds), *Critical Encounters: Reference and Responsibility in Deconstructive Writing* (New Brunswick, NJ: Rutgers University Press, 1994).

Cavell, Stanley, *A Pitch of Philosophy: Autobiographical Exercises* (Cambridge, Mass.: Harvard University Press, 1994).

Clark, Timothy and Royle, Nicholas (eds), 'The University in Ruins', *Oxford Literary Review, Special Number*, Vol. XVII, Nos. 1 and 2 (1995).

Cohen, Sandy, *Academia and the Lustre of Capital* (Minneapolis: University of Minnesota Press, 1993).

Collier, Andrew, *Scientific Realism and Socialist Thought* (Hemel Hempstead: Harvester, 1989).

Collier, Andrew, *Critical Realism* (London: Verso, 1994).

Collins, Harry and Pinch, Trevor, *The Golem: What Everyone Should Know About Science* (Cambridge: Cambridge University Press, 1993).

Corngold, Stanley, 'Error in Paul de Man', *Critical Inquiry*, Vol. 8 (1982), pp. 489–507.

Culler, Jonathan, *Structuralist Poetics* (London: Routledge & Kegan Paul, 1975).

Culler, Jonathan, 'Convention and Meaning: Derrida and Austin', *New Literary History*, Vol. XIII (1981), pp. 15–30.

Cunningham, Valentine, *In the Reading Gaol: Postmodernity, Texts and History* (Oxford: Blackwell, 1994).

Curtius, Ernst Robert, *European Literature and the Latin Middle Ages*, trans. W.R. Trask (Princeton: Princeton University Press, 1978).

Cushing, James T. and McMullin, Ernan (eds), *Philosophical Consequences of Quantum Theory: Reflections on Bell's Theorem* (Indiana: University of Notre Dame Press, 1989).

Cushing, James T., *Quantum Mechanics: Historical Contingency and the Copenhagen Hegemony* (Chicago: University of Chicago Press, 1994).

Damarin, Suzanne K, 'Gender and Mathematics from a Feminist Standpoint', in W.G. Secada, E. Fennema and L.B. Adajan (eds), *New Directions for Equity in Mathematics Education* (New York: Cambridge University Press, 1995), pp. 242–57.

Davidson, Donald, 'Communication and Convention', in *Inquiries into Truth and Interpretation* (London: Oxford University Press, 1984), pp. 265–80.

Davidson, Donald, 'On the Very Idea of a Conceptual Scheme', in *Inquiries into Truth and Interpretation* (London: Oxford University Press, 1984), pp. 183–98.

Davidson, Donald, 'Reality Without Reference', in *Inquiries into Truth and Interpretation* (London: Oxford University Press, 1984), pp. 215–25.

Davidson, Donald, 'Thought and Talk', in *Inquiries into Truth and Interpretation* (London: Oxford University Press, 1984), pp. 155–70.

Davidson, Donald, 'A Coherence Theory of Truth and Knowledge', in Ernest Le Pore (ed.), *Truth and Interpretation: Essays on the Philosophy of Donald Davidson* (Oxford: Blackwell, 1986), pp. 307–19.

Davidson, Donald, 'The Structure and Content of Truth', *Journal of Philosophy*, Vol. 87 (1990), pp. 279–328.

Davies, Paul C.W. and Brown, J.R. (eds), *The Ghost in the Atom* (Cambridge: Cambridge University Press, 1986).

de Man, Paul, *Allegories of Reading: Figural Language in Rousseau, Nietzsche, Rilke, and Proust* (New Haven: Yale University Press, 1979).

de Man, Paul, 'Heidegger's Exegeses of Hölderlin', in *Blindness and Insight: Essays in the Rhetoric of Contemporary Criticism*, 2nd edn (London: Methuen, 1983), pp. 246–66.

de Man, Paul, 'Literary History and Literary Modernity', in *Blindness and Insight: Essays in the Rhetoric of Contemporary Criticism*, 2nd edn (London: Methuen, 1983), pp. 142–65.

de Man, Paul, *The Rhetoric of Romanticism* (New York: Columbia University Press, 1984).

de Man, Paul, 'Aesthetic Formalization: Kleist's *Ueber das Marionettentheater*', in *The Rhetoric of Romanticism* (New York: Columbia University Press, 1984), pp. 263–90.

de Man, Paul, *The Resistance to Theory* (Minneapolis: University of Minnesota Press, 1986).

de Man, Paul, 'The Return to Philology', in *The Resistance to Theory* (Minneapolis: University of Minnesota Press, 1986), pp. 21–6.

de Man, Paul, *Wartime Journalism: 1939–1943*, eds Werner Hamacher *et al.* (Lincoln: University of Nebraska Press, 1988).

de Man, Paul, *Aesthetic Ideology*, ed. A. Warminsky (Minneapolis: University of Minnesota Press, 1996).

de Saussure, Ferdinand, *Course in General Linguistics*, trans. Wade Baskin (London: Fontana, 1974).

de Witt. B. and Graham, N. (eds), *The Many-Worlds Interpretation of Quantum Mechanics* (Princeton, NJ: Princeton University Press, 1973).

DeBellis, Mark A., *Music and Conceptualization* (Cambridge: Cambridge University Press, 1995).

Deleuze, Gilles, *Kant's Critical Philosophy: The Doctrine of the Faculties*, trans. Hugh Tomlinson and Barbara Habberjam (London: Athlone Press, 1984).

Deleuze, Gilles, *Foucault*, trans. Seán Hand (Minneapolis: University of Minnesota Press, 1988).

Deleuze, Gilles and Guattari, Félix, *What Is Philosophy?*, trans Hugh Tomlinson and Graham Burchell (New York: Columbia University Press, 1994).

Derrida, Jacques, *Speech and Phenomena and Other Essays on Husserl's Theory of Signs*, trans. David B. Allison (Evanston, Ill.: Northwestern University Press, 1973).

Derrida, Jacques, *Of Grammatology*, trans. G.C. Spivak (Baltimore: Johns Hopkins University Press, 1975).

Derrida, Jacques, 'Signature Event Context', *Glyph*, Vol. 1 (Baltimore: Johns Hopkins University Press, 1977), pp. 172–97.

Derrida, Jacques, 'Limited Inc a b c', in *Glyph*, Vol. 2 (Baltimore: Johns Hopkins University Press, 1977), pp. 162–254.

Derrida, Jacques, *Writing and Difference*, trans. Alan Bass (London: Routledge, 1978).

Derrida, Jacques, ' "Genesis and Structure" and Phenomenology', in *Writing and Difference*, trans. Alan Bass (London: Routledge, 1978), pp. 154–68.

Derrida, Jacques, 'Violence and Metaphysics: an essay on Emmanuel Levinas', in *Writing and Difference*, trans. Alan Bass (London: Routlege & Kegan Paul, 1978), pp. 79–153.

Derrida, Jacques, *Dissemination*, trans. Barbara Johnson (London: Athlone Press, 1981).

Derrida, Jacques, 'Plato's Pharmacy', in *Dissemination*, trans. Barbara Johnson (London: Athlone Press, 1981), pp. 61–171.

Derrida, Jacques, 'Economimesis', *Diacritics*, Vol. XI, No. 2 (Summer 1981), pp. 3–25.

Derrida, Jacques, *Margins of Philosophy*, trans. Alan Bass (Chicago: University of Chicago Press, 1982).

Derrida, Jacques, 'The Supplement of Copula: philosophy *before* linguistics', in *Margins of Philosophy*, pp. 175–205.

Derrida, Jacques, 'White Mythology: metaphor in the text of philosophy', in *Margins of Philosophy*, pp. 207–71.

Derrida, Jacques, 'The Principle of Reason: The University in the Eyes of its Pupils', trans. Catherine Porter and Edward P. Morris, *Diacritics*, Vol. XIII, No. 3 (Fall 1983), pp. 3–20.

Derrida, Jacques, 'No Apocalypse, Not Now: Seven Missiles, Seven Missives', *Diacritics*, Vol. XX (1984), pp. 20–31.

Derrida, Jacques, 'Parergon', in *The Truth in Painting*, trans. Geoff Bennington and Ian McLeod (Chicago: University of Chicago Press, 1987), pp. 15–147.

Derrida, Jacques, 'Like the Sound of the Sea Deep Within a Shell: Paul de Man's war', trans. Peggy Kamuf, *Critical Inquiry*, Vol. 14 (Spring 1988), pp. 590–652.

Derrida, Jacques, 'Afterword: toward an ethic of conversation', in *Limited Inc*, ed. Gerald Graff (Evanston, Ill.: Northwestern University Press, 1989), pp. 111–54.

Derrida, Jacques, *Du Droit à la Philosophie* (Paris: Galilée, 1990).

Derrida, Jacques, *La Problème de la Genèse dans la Philosophie de Husserl* (Paris: Presses Universitaires de France, 1990).

Derrida, Jacques, *Institutions of Reason*, ed. Deborah Esch and Thomas Keenan (Minneapolis: University of Minneapolis Press, 1992).

Derrida, Jacques, 'Mochlos – or the conflict of the faculties', in Richard Rand (ed.), *Logomachia* (Lincoln, Nebr.: University of Nebraska Press, 1992), pp. 1–34.

Derrida, Jacques, 'Of an Apocalyptic Tone Newly Adopted in Philosophy', in Harold Coward and Toby Foshay (eds), *Derrida and Negative Theology* (Albany, NY: State University of New York Press, 1992), pp. 24–71.

Descartes, René, *Meditations on First Philosophy*, trans. J. Cottingham (Cambridge: Cambridge University Press, 1986).

Deutsch, David, *The Fabric of Reality* (Harmondsworth: Penguin, 1997).

Devitt, Michael, *Realism and Truth*, 2nd edn (Oxford: Blackwell, 1986).

Dummett, Michael, *Elements of Intuitionism* (London: Oxford University Press, 1977).

Dummett, Michael, *Truth and Other Enigmas* (London: Duckworth, 1978).

Dummett, Michael, 'Bringing About the Past' in *Truth and Other Enigmas*, pp. 333–50.

Dummett, Michael, 'The Reality of the Past', in *Truth and Other Enigmas*, pp. 358–74.

Dummett, Michael, *The Origins of Analytic Philosophy* (London: Duckworth, 1993).

Dupré, John, *The Disorder of Things: Metaphysical Foundations of the Disunity of Science* (Cambridge, Mass.: Harvard University Press, 1993).

Eagleton, Terry, *The Illusions of Postmodernism* (Oxford: Blackwell, 1996).

Einstein, Albert, Podolsky, B. and Rosen, N., 'Can Quantum-Mechanical Description of Reality be Considered Complete?', in *Physical Review*, ser. 2, Vol. XLVII (1935), pp. 777–808.

Elliott, Gregory, *Althusser: The Detour of Theory* (London: Verso, 1987).

Empson, William, *Seven Types of Ambiguity* (London: Chatto & Windus, 1930).

Empson, William, review of E.A. Burtt, *The Metaphysical Foundations of Modern Science*, in Empson, W. *Argufying: Essays on Literature and Culture*, ed. John Haffenden (London: Chatto & Windus, 1987), pp. 530–3.

Eribon, Didier, *Michel Foucault*, trans. Betsy Wing (London: Faber, 1992).

Ernarth, Elizabeth Deeds, *Sequel to History: Postmodernism and the Crisis of Time* (Princeton, NJ: Princeton University Press, 1992).

Evans, Gareth and McDowell, John (eds), *Truth and Meaning: Essays in Semantics* (Oxford: Clarendon Press, 1976).

Evans, Gareth, *The Varieties of Reference*, ed. John McDowell (Oxford: Clarendon Press, 1982).

Eze, Emmanuel Chukwudi (ed.), *Race and the Enlightenment: A Reader* (Oxford: Blackwell, 1997).

Felman, Shoshana, *The Literary Speech-Act: Don Juan with J.L. Austin, or Seduction in Two Languages*, trans. Catherine Porter (Ithaca, NY: Cornell University Press, 1983).

Feyerabend, Paul K., *Against Method* (London: New Left Books, 1975).

Feyerabend, Paul K., *Science in a Free Society* (London: New Left Books, 1978).

Feyerabend, Paul K., *Farewell to Reason* (London: Verso, 1987).

Fichte, Johann Gottlieb, *Science of Knowledge*, ed. and trans. P. Heath and J. Lachs (New York: Meredith, 1970).

Field, Hartry, 'Theory Change and the Indeterminacy of Reference', *Journal of Philosophy*, Vol. 70 (1973), pp. 462–81.

Field, Hartry, 'Quine and the Correspondence Theory', *Philosophical Review*, Vol. 83 (1974), pp. 200–28.

Field, Hartry, 'Conventionalism and Instrumentalism in Semantics', *Nous*, Vol. 9 (1975), pp. 375–405.

Fine, Arthur, *The Shaky Game: Einstein, Realism and Quantum Theory* (Chicago: University of Chicago Press, 1986).

Fish, Stanley, 'With the Compliments of the Author: reflections on Austin and Derrida', *Critical Inquiry*, Vol. VIII (1982), pp. 693–72.

Fish, Stanley, *Doing What Comes Naturally: Change, Rhetoric and the Practice of Theory in Literary and Legal Studies* (Oxford: Clarendon Press, 1989).

Fish, Stanley, 'Professor Sokal's Bad Joke', *New York Times*, 21 May 1996.

Folse, Henry J., *The Philosophy of Niels Bohr: The Framework of Complementarity* (Amsterdam: North-Holland, 1985).

Forman, Paul, 'Weimar Culture, Causality, and Quantum Theory, 1918–1927: adaptation by German physicists and mathematicians to a hostile intellectual environment', *Historical Studies in the Physical Sciences*, Vol. 3 (1971), pp. 1–115.

Foucault, Michel, *The Order of Things: An Archaeology of the Human Sciences*, trans. A. Sheridan-Smith (New York: Pantheon, 1970).

Foucault, Michel, *Madness and Civilization: A History of Insanity in the Age of Reason*, trans. Richard Howard (London: Tavistock, 1971).

Foucault, Michel, *The Archaeology of Knowledge*, trans. A. Sheridan-Smith (London: Tavistock, 1972).

Foucault, Michel, *The Birth of the Clinic*, trans. A. Sheridan-Smith (London: Tavistock, 1973).

Foucault, Michel, *Discipline and Punish: The Birth of the Prison*, trans. Sheridan (New York: Pantheon, 1977).

Foucault, Michel, *Language, Counter-Memory, Practice*, trans. and eds D.F. Bouchard and S. Weber (Oxford: Blackwell, 1977).

Foucault, Michel, *The History of Sexuality, Vol. One: An Introduction*, trans. Robert Hurley (New York: Pantheon, 1978).

Foucault, Michel, *Power/Knowledge: Selected Interviews and Other Writings* (Brighton: Harvester, 1980).

Foucault, Michel, 'What Is Enlightenment?', in Paul Rabinow (ed.), *The Foucault Reader* (Harmondsworth: Penguin, 1986), pp. 32–50.

Foucault, Michel, 'Politics and Ethics', in P. Rabinow (ed.), *The Foucault Reader*, pp. 371–80.

Foucault, Michel, *Politics, Philosophy, Culture*, ed. L.D. Kritzman (London: Routledge, 1988).

Foucault, Michel, *The Use of Pleasure*, trans. Robert Hurley (New York: Pantheon, 1995).

Foucault, Michel, *The Care of the Self*, trans. Hurley (New York: Pantheon, 1996).

Frank, Manfred, *What Is Neostructuralism?*, trans. S. Wilke and R. Gray (Minneapolis: University of Minnesota Press, 1989).

Frege, Gottlob, 'On Sense and Reference', in Peter Geach and Max Black (eds), *Translations from the Philosophical Writings of Gottlob Frege* (Oxford: Blackwell, 1952), pp. 56–78.

Frege, Gottlob, *The Frege Reader*, ed. Michael Beaney (Oxford: Blackwell, 1997).

Fuller, Steve, *Social Epistemology* (Bloomington, Ind.: Indiana University Press, 1988).

Gadamer, Hans-Georg, *Philosophical Hermeneutics*, trans David E. Linge (Berkeley and Los Angeles: University of California Press, 1977).

Gadamer, Hans-Georg, *Truth and Method*, trans. John Cumming and Garrett Barden (London: Sheed & Ward, 1979).

Gallison, Peter and Stump, David J. (eds), *The Disunity of Science: Boundaries, Contexts, and Power* (Stanford, CA: Stanford University Press, 1996).

Gardner, Martin, 'Realism and Instrumentalism in Nineteenth-Century Atomism', *Philosophy of Science*, Vol. 46, No. 1 (1979), pp. 1–34.

Gasché, Rodolphe, *The Tain of the Mirror: Derrida and the Philosophy of Reflection* (Cambridge, Mass.: Harvard University Press, 1986).

Gasché Rodolphe, *The Wild Card of Reading: On Paul de Man* (Cambridge, Mass.: Harvard University Press, 1998).

Geertz, Clifford, *The Interpretation of Cultures: Selected Essays* (New York: Basic Books, 1973).

Geuss, Raymond, 'A Response to Paul de Man', *Critical Inquiry*, Vol. 10 (1983), pp. 375–82.

Gibbins, Peter, *Particles and Paradoxes: The Limits of Quantum Logic* (Cambridge: Cambridge University Press, 1987).

Gödel, Kurt, *On Formally Undecidable Propositions of* Principia Mathematica *and Related Systems*, trans. B. Meltzer (New York: Basic Books, 1962).

Goodman, Nelson, *Ways of Worldmaking* (Indianapolis: Bobbs-Merrill, 1978).

Grace, George W., *The Linguistic Construction of Reality* (London: Croom Helm, 1987).

Grayling, A.C., *The Refutation of Scepticism* (London: Duckworth, 1985).

Gregory, Bruce, *Inventing Reality: Physics as Language* (New York: Wiley, 1988).

Greimas, A. J., *Structural Semiotics: An Attempt at a Method*, trans. D. MacDonald, R. Schleifer and A. Velie (Lincoln: University of Nebraska Press, 1983).

Gribbin, James, *In Search of Schrödinger's Cat* (New York: Bantam Books, 1984).

Guyer, Paul (ed.), *The Cambridge Companion to Kant* (Cambridge: Cambridge University Press, 1992).

Haack, Susan, *Deviant Logic: Some Philosophical Issues* (Cambridge: Cambridge University Press, 1974).

Habermas, Jürgen, *Knowledge and Human Interests*, trans. J. Shapiro (London: Heinemann, 1972).

Habermas, Jürgen, *Communication and the Evolution of Society*, trans. Thomas McCarthy (London: Heinemann, 1979).

Habermas, Jürgen, *Theory of Communicative Action*, 2 vols., trans. T. McCarthy (Boston: Beacon Press, 1984 and 1987).

Habermas, Jürgen, *The Philosophical Discourse of Modernity: twelve lectures*, trans. Frederick Lawrence (Cambridge: Polity Press, 1987).

Habermas, Jürgen, 'On Levelling the Genre Distinction Between Philosophy and Literature', in *The Philosophical Discourse of Modernity*, pp. 185–210.

Habermas, Jürgen, *Justification and Application: Remarks on Discourse Ethics*, trans. C.P. Cronin (Cambridge: Polity Press, 1993).

Hamacher, Werner *et al.* (eds), *Responses: On Paul de Man's Wartime Journalism* (Lincoln: University of Nebraska Press, 1989).

Hanfling, Oswald (ed.), *Essential Readings in Logical Positivism* (Oxford: Blackwell, 1981).

Harari, José V. (ed.), *Textual Strategies: Perspectives in Post-Structuralist Criticism* (London: Methuen, 1980).

Harding, Sandra G. (ed.), *Can Theories Be Refuted? Essays on the Duhem-Quine Thesis* (Dordrecht and Boston: D. Reidel, 1976).

Harman, Gilbert and Davidson, Donald (eds), *Semantics of Natural Language* (Dordrecht: D. Reidel, 1972).

Harris, Roy, *Reading Saussure* (London: Duckworth, 1987).

Havel, Vaclav, 'The End of the Modern Era', *New York Times*, 1 May 1992.

Hawkins, Harriet, *Strange Attractors: Literature, Culture and Chaos Theory* (Hemel Hempstead: Harvester-Wheatsheaf, 1995).

Hayles, N. Katherine, *The Scientific Web: Scientific Field Models and Literary Strategies in the Twentieth Century* (Ithaca, NY: Cornell University Press, 1984).

Hayles, N. Katherine, *Chaos Bound: Orderly Disorder in Contemporary Literature and Science* (Ithaca, NY: Cornell University Press, 1990).

Hegel, G.W.F., *The Phenomenology of Spirit*, trans. Parvis Emad and Kenneth Maly (Bloomington, Ind.: Indiana University Press, 1988).

Heidegger, Martin, *Kant and the Problem of Metaphysics*, trans. James S. Churchill (Bloomington, Ind.: Indiana University Press, 1962).

Heidegger, Martin, *The Question Concerning Technology and Other Essays*, trans. William Lovitt (New York: Harper & Row, 1977).

Heidegger, Martin, *Being and Time*, trans. John Macquarrie and Edward Robinson (Oxford: Blackwell, 1980).

Hempel, Carl G., *Fundamentals of Concept Formation in Empirical Science* (Chicago: University of Chicago Press, 1972).

Hindess, Barry, *Discourses of Power: From Hobbes to Foucault* (Oxford: Blackwell, 1996).

Holland, Peter, *The Quantum Theory of Motion: An Account of the de Broglie-Bohm Causal Interpretation of Quantum Mechanics* (Cambridge: Cambridge University Press, 1993).

Honner, John, *The Description of Nature: Niels Bohr and the Philosophy of Quantum Physics* (Oxford: Clarendon Press, 1987).

Hookway, Christopher, *Scepticism* (London: Routledge, 1992).

Horwich, Paul (ed.), *The World Changes: Thomas Kuhn and the Nature of Science* (Cambridge, Mass.: MIT Press, 1993).

Hoy, David Couzens, *The Critical Circle: Literature, History and Philosophical Hermeneutics* (Berkeley and Los Angeles: University of California Press, 1978).

Hoyningen-Huehne, Paul, *Reconstructing Scientific Revolutions: Thomas S. Kuhn's Philosophy of Science*, trans. A.T. Levine (Chicago: University of Chicago Press, 1993).

Husserl, Edmund, *Formal and Transcendental Logic*, trans. Dorian Cairns (The Hague: Martinus Nijhoff, 1969).

Husserl, Edmund, *The Crisis of European Sciences and Transcendental Phenomenology*, trans. David Carr (Evanston: Northwestern University Press, 1970).

Husserl, Edmund, *Logical Investigations*, two vols., trans. J.N. Finlay (New York: Humanities Press, 1970).

Husserl, Edmund, *Cartesian Meditations: An Introduction to Phenomenology*, trans. Dorian Cairns (The Hague: Martinus Nijhoff, 1973).

Husserl, Edmund, *Experience and Judgement: Investigations in a Genealogy of Logic*, ed. Ludwig Landgrebe, trans. J.S. Churchill and K. Ameriks (Evanston: Northwestern University Press, 1973).

Husserl, Edmund, *Ideas: General Introduction to Pure Phenomenology*, trans. W.R. Boyce Gibson (London: Collier Macmillan, 1975).

Hutcheon, Linda, *The Politics of Postmodernism* (London: Routledge, 1989).

Ihde, Don, *Technology and the Lifeworld: From Garden to Earth* (Bloomington, Ind.: Indiana University Press, 1990).
Irigaray, Luce, 'The "Mechanics" of Fluids', in *This Sex Which Is Not One*, trans. Catherine Porter with Carolyn Burke (Ithaca, NY: Cornell University Press, 1985).

Jameson, Fredric, *Late Marxism: Adorno, or the Persistence of the Dialectic* (London: Verso, 1990).
Jameson, Fredric, *Postmodernism, or, the Cultural Logic of Late Capitalism* (London: Verso, 1991).
Jenkins, Keith, *Re-Thinking History* (London: Routledge, 1991).
Jenkins, Keith, *On 'What Is History'?: from Carr and Elton to Rorty and White* (London: Routledge, 1995).
Jenkins, Keith (ed.), *The Postmodern History Reader* (London: Routledge, 1997).

Kant, Immanuel, *Religion Within the Limits of Reason Alone*, trans. Theodore M. Greene and Hoyt H. Hudson (Chicago: Open Court, 1934).
Kant, Immanuel, *On History*, ed. Lewis W. Beck (Indianapolis: Bobbs-Merrill, 1963).
Kant, Immanuel, *Critique of Pure Reason*, trans. Norman Kemp Smith (London: Macmillan, 1964).
Kant, Immanuel, *Critique of Practical Reason*, trans. Lewis White Beck (Indianapolis: Bobbs-Merrill, 1975).
Kant, Immanuel, *Political Writings*, ed. Hans Reiss (Cambridge: Cambridge University Press, 1976).
Kant, Immanuel, *Critique of Judgement*, trans. J.C. Meredith (Oxford: Clarendon Press, 1978).
Kant, Immanuel, *Foundations of the Metaphysics of Morals*, trans. L.W. Beck (Minneapolis: Bobbs-Merrill, 1978).
Kant, Immanuel, *The Conflict of the Faculties*, trans. Mary J. Gregor (New York: Abaris Books, 1979).
Keller, Evelyn Fox, *Reflections on Gender and Science* (New Haven: Yale University Press, 1985).
Keller, Evelyn Fox, *Secrets of Life, Secrets of Death: Essays on Language, Gender and Science* (New York: Routledge, 1992).
Kelly, Michael (ed.), *Critique and Power: Recasting the Habermas/Foucault Debate* (Cambridge, Mass.: MIT Press, 1994).
Kierkegaard, Søren, *Fear and Trembling* and *The Sickness Unto Death*, trans. W. Lowrie (Princeton, NJ: Princeton University Press, 1974).
Koertge, Noretta (ed.), *A House Built on Sand: Exposing Postmodernist Myths about Science* (Oxford: Oxford University Press, 1998).
Kristeva, Julia, *Semeiotike: Recherches pour une Sémanalyse* (Paris: Editions du Seuil, 1969).
Kuhn, Thomas S., *The Structure of Scientific Revolutions*, 2nd edn, revised (Chicago: University of Chicago Press, 1970).

Latour, Bruno, *Science in Action: How to Follow Scientists and Engineers through Society* (Milton Keynes: Open University Press, 1987).
Latour, Bruno, 'A Relativistic Account of Einstein's Relativity', *Social Studies of Science*, Vol. 18 (1988), pp. 3–44.
Latour, Bruno, *We Have Never Been Modern*, trans. Catherine Porter (Hemel Hempstead: Harvester-Wheatsheaf, 1993).
Latour, Bruno and Woolgar, Steve, *Laboratory Life: The Social Construction of Scientific Facts* (London: Sage, 1979).
Leavis, F.R., *Two Cultures? The Significance of C.P. Snow* (London: Chatto & Windus, 1962).
Lehman, David, *Signs of the Times: Deconstruction and the Fall of Paul de Man* (New York: Vintage, 1991).
Leplin, Jarrett (ed.), *Scientific Realism* (Berkeley and Los Angeles: University of California Press, 1984).
Levinas, Emmanuel, *Totality and Infinity*, trans. A. Lingis (Pittsburgh, Pa.: Duquesne University Press, 1969).
Levinas, Emmanuel, *Otherwise than Being, or Beyond Essence*, trans. Lingis (The Hague: Martinus Nijhoff, 1981).
Lévi-Strauss, Claude, *Structural Anthropology*, trans. C. Jacobson and B. Grundfest (Harmondsworth: Penguin, 1968).
Lewis, David, *Convention; A Philosophical Study* (Cambridge, Mass.: Harvard University Press, 1969).
Lewis, David, *On the Plurality of Worlds* (Oxford: Blackwell, 1988).
Lodge, David, *The Modes of Modern Writing: Metaphor, Metonymy and the Typology of Modern Literature* (London: Longman, 1977).

Lovejoy, A.O., 'On the Discrimination of Romanticisms', in *Essays in the History of Ideas* (Baltimore: Johns Hopkins University Press, 1948).

Lovibond, Sabina, *Realism and Imagination in Ethics* (Oxford: Blackwell, 1983).

Lucas, J.R. and Hodgson, P.E., *Spacetime and Electro-Magnetism* (Oxford: Clarendon Press, 1990).

Lyotard, Jean-François, *The Postmodern Condition: A Report on Knowledge*, trans. Geoff Bennington and Brian Massumi (Manchester: Manchester University Press, 1984).

Lyotard, Jean-François, *The Differend: Phrases in Dispute*, trans. Georges van den Abbeele (Manchester: Manchester University Press, 1988).

Lyotard, Jean-François, *Libidinal Economy*, trans. Iain Hamilton Grant (London: Athlone Press, 1991).

Lyotard, Jean-François, *Political Writings*, trans. and eds Bill Readings and Kevin Paul Geiman (Minneapolis: University of Minnesota Press, 1993).

Lyotard, Jean-François, *Lessons on the Analytic of the Sublime*, trans. Elizabeth Rottenberg (Stanford, CA: Stanford University Press., 1994).

McDowell, John, *Mind and World* (Cambridge, Mass.: Harvard University Press, 1994).

Macey, David, *The Lives of Michel Foucault* (New York: Pantheon, 1993).

Macksey, Richard and Donato, Eugenio (eds), *The Languages of Criticism and the Sciences of Man: The Structuralist Controversy* (Baltimore: Johns Hopkins University Press, 1970).

McNay, Lois, *Foucault and Feminism: Power, Gender and the Self* (Cambridge: Polity, 1992).

Margolis, Joseph, *Science Without Unity: Reconciling the Human and Natural Sciences* (Oxford: Blackwell, 1987).

Maudlin, Tim, *Quantum Nonlocality and Relativity: Metaphysical Intimations of Modern Science* (Oxford: Blackwell, 1993).

Miller, James, *The Passion of Michel Foucault* (New York: Anchor, 1994).

Misak, C.J., *Verificationism: Its History and Prospects* (London: Routledge, 1995).

Mitchell, Donald, *The Language of Modern Music* (London: Faber, 1963).

Mowitt, John, *Text: The Genealogy of an Antidisciplinary Object* (Durham, NC: Duke University Press, 1993).

Mulhall, Stephen, *On Being In the World: Wittgenstein and Heidegger on Seeing Aspects* (London: Routledge, 1990).

Müller-Vollmer, Kurt, *The Hermeneutics Reader* (Oxford: Blackwell, 1986).

Murdoch, Dugald, *Niels Bohr's Philosophy of Physics* (Cambridge: Cambridge University Press, 1987).

Naess, Arne, *Scepticism* (London: Routledge & Kegan Paul, 1970).

Nagel, Ernest and Newtman, James, *Gödel's Proof* (London: Routledge & Kegan Paul, 1971).

Nagel, Thomas, *The Last Word* (Oxford: Oxford University Press, 1997).

Nanda, Meera, 'The Science Wars in India', *Dissent*, Vol. XLIV, No. 1 (Winter 1997), pp. 78–83.

Neurath, Otto, Carnap, Rudolf and Morris, Charles (eds), *Foundations of the Unity of Science: Towards an International Encyclopedia of Unified Science* (Chicago: University of Chicago Press, 1955–70).

Nicholls, Peter, *Modernism: A Literary Guide* (London: Macmillan, 1995).

Nietzsche, Friedrich, *The Will to Power*, trans. Walter Kaufmann and R.J. Hollingdale, ed. Kaufmann (New York: Vintage Books, 1968).

Nietzsche, Friedrich, *On the Genealogy of Morals*, trans. Walter Kaufmann and R.J. Hollingdale (New York: Vintage Books, 1989).

Norris, Christopher, 'Philosophy as a Kind of Narrative: Rorty on postmodern liberal culture', in *The Contest of Faculties: Philosophy and Theory after Deconstruction* (London: Methuen, 1985), pp. 139–66.

Norris, Christopher, *Derrida* (London: Fontana, 1987).

Norris, Christopher, 'Postscript: on de Man's early writings for *Le Soir*', in *Paul de Man: Deconstruction and the Critique of Aesthetic Ideology* (New York: Routledge, 1988), pp. 177–98.

Norris, Christopher, 'Reading Donald Davidson: truth, meaning and right interpretation', in *Deconstruction and the Interests of Theory* (London: Pinter Publishers, 1988), pp. 59–83.

Norris, Christopher, *Truth and the Ethics of Criticism* (Manchester: Manchester University Press 1994).

Norris, Christopher, *The Truth About Postmodernism* (Oxford: Blackwell, 1994).

Norris, Christopher, 'Kant Disfigured: genealogy, critique and postmodern scepticism', in *The Truth About Postmodernism*, pp. 182–256.

Norris, Christopher, 'Kant Disfigured: Ethics, Deconstruction, and the Textual Sublime', in *The Truth About Postmodernism*, pp. 182–256.

Norris, Christopher, '"What Is Enlightenment": Kant according to Foucault', in Gary Gutting (ed.), *The Cambridge Companion to Foucault* (Cambridge: Cambridge University Press, 1994), pp. 159–96.

Norris, Christopher, *Reclaiming Truth: Contribution to a Critique of Cultural Relativism* (London: Lawrence & Wishart, 1996).

Norris, Christopher, *Resources of Realism: Prospects for 'Post-analytic' Philosophy* (London: Macmillan, 1997).

Norris, Christopher, *Against Relativism: Philosophy of Science, Deconstruction and Critical Theory* (Oxford: Blackwell, 1997).

Norris, Christopher, *New Idols of the Cave: On the Limits of Anti-realism* (Manchester: Manchester University Press, 1997).

Nye, Mary Jo, *Molecular Reality* (London: MacDonald, 1972).

Ogden, C.K. and Richards, I.A., *The Meaning of Meaning* (London: Kegan Paul, Trench & Trubner, 1923).

O'Neill, Onora, *Constructions of Reason: Explorations of Kant's Practical Philosophy* (Cambridge: Cambridge University Press, 1989).

Pais, Abraham, *Niels Bohr's Times in Physics, Philosophy, and Polity* (Oxford: Clarendon Press, 1991).

Palmer, Richard E., *Hermeneutics: Interpretation Theory in Schleiermacher, Dilthey, Heidegger, and Gadamer* (Evanston: Northwestern University Press, 1969).

Papineau, David, *Theory and Meaning* (London: Oxford University Press, 1979).

Papineau, David, *Philosophical Naturalism* (Oxford: Blackwell, 1993).

Pavel, Thomas A., *Fictional Worlds* (Cambridge, Mass.: Harvard University Press, 1986).

Pavel, Thomas A., *The Feud of Language: A History of Structuralist Thought* (Oxford: Blackwell, 1990).

Perrin, J., *Atoms*, trans. D.L. Hammick (New York: Van Nostrand, 1923).

Pickering, Andrew (ed.), *Science as Practice and Culture* (Chicago: University of Chicago Press, 1992).

Platts, Mark (ed.), *Reference, Truth and Reality: Essays on the Philosophy of Language* (London: Routledge & Kegan Paul, 1980).

Plotnitsky, Arkady, *Complementarity: Anti-epistemology after Bohr and Derrida* (Durham, NC: Duke University Press, 1994).

Popper, Karl, *Quantum Theory and the Schism in Physics* (London: Hutchinson, 1982).

Popper, Karl, *Realism and the Aim of Science* (London: Hutchinson, 1983).

Putnam, Hilary, *The Many Faces of Realism* (La Salle: Open Court, 1987).

Putnam, Hilary, *Realism with a Human Face* (Cambridge, Mass.: Harvard University Press, 1990).

Putnam, Hilary, *Pragmatism: An Open Question* (Oxford: Blackwell, 1995).

Quine, W.V.O., 'Two Dogmas of Empiricism', in *From a Logical Point of View*, 2nd edn (Cambridge, Mass.: Harvard University Press, 1961), pp. 20–46.

Quine, W.V.O., *Ontological Relativity and Other Essays* (New York: Columbia University Press, 1969).

Quine, W.V.O., *Philosophy of Logic* (New York: Prentice-Hall, 1970).

Rabinow, Paul (ed.), *The Foucault Reader* (Harmondsworth: Penguin, 1986).

Rae, Alastair I.M., *Quantum Physics: Illusion or Reality?* (Cambridge: Cambridge University Press, 1986).

Rand, Richard (ed.), *Logomachia: The Conflict of the Faculties* (Lincoln, Nebraska: University of Nebraska Press, 1992).

Ransom, John Crowe, *The World's Body* (New York: Scribner, 1938).

Ransom, John Crowe, *The New Criticism* (New York: New Directions, 1941).

Redhead, Michael, *Incompleteness, Nonlocality and Realism: A Prolegomenon to the Philosophy of Quantum Mechanics* (Oxford: Clarendon Press, 1987).

Reichenbach, Hans, *Experience and Prediction* (Chicago: University of Chicago Press, 1938).

Reiss, Timothy J., *The Discourse of Modernism* (Ithaca, NY: Cornell University Press, 1982).

Rescher, Nicholas, *Scientific Realism: A Critical Reappraisal* (Dordrecht: D. Reidel, 1987).

Richards, I.A., *Principles of Literary Criticism* (London: Kegan Paul, Trench & Trubner, 1924).

Richards, I.A., *Science and Poetry* (Kegan Paul, Trench & Trubner, 1926); revised and expanded edn., *Sciences and Poetries* (London: Routledge and Kegan Paul, 1970).

Richards, I.A., *Speculative Instruments* (Chicago: University of Chicago Press, 1955).

Richards, I.A., *Complementarities: Uncollected Essays and Reviews* (Cambridge, Mass.: Harvard University Press, 1976).

Ricoeur, Paul, *The Conflict of Interpretations: Essays in Hermeneutics*, trans. Don Ihde (Evanston, Ill.: Northwestern University Press, 1974).

Ricoeur, Paul, *Hermeneutics and the Human Sciences* (Cambridge: Cambridge University Press, 1981).

Rockmore, Tom, *On Heidegger's Nazism and Philosophy* (London: Harvester-Wheatsheaf, 1992).

Ronen, Ruth A., *Possible Worlds in Literary Theory* (Cambridge: Cambridge University Press, 1994).

Rorty, Richard (ed.), *The Linguistic Turn* (Chicago: University of Chicago Press, 1967).

Rorty, Richard, *Consequences of Pragmatism* (Brighton: Harvester, 1982).

Rorty, Richard, 'Philosophy as a Kind of Writing: an essay on Derrida', in *Consequences of Pragmatism*, pp. 89–109.

Rorty, Richard, 'Deconstruction and Circumvention', *Critical Inquiry*, Vol. XI (1984), pp. 1–23.

Rorty, Richard, *Contingency, Irony, and Solidarity* (Cambridge: Cambridge University Press, 1989).

Rorty, Richard, *Essays on Heidegger and Others* (Cambridge: Cambridge University Press, 1991).

Rorty, Richard, 'Moral Identity and Private Autonomy: The Case of Foucault', in *Essays on Heidegger and Others*, pp. 193–8.

Rorty, Richard, *Objectivity, Relativism, and Truth* (Cambridge: Cambridge University Press, 1991).

Rorty, Richard, 'Is Derrida a Transcendental Philosopher?', in David Wood (ed.), *Derrida: A Critical Reader* (Oxford: Blackwell, 1992), pp. 235–46.

Rorty, Richard, *Truth and Progress* (Cambridge: Cambridge University Press, 1998).

Rose, Hilary and Rose, Steven (eds), *The Radicalization of Science: Ideology of/in the Natural Sciences* (London: Macmillan, 1976).

Ross, Andrew, *Strange Weather: Culture, Science and Technology in an Age of Limits* (London: Verso, 1991).

Rouse, Joseph, *Knowledge and Power: Toward a Political Philosophy of Science* (Ithaca, NY: Cornell University Press, 1987).

Russell, Bertrand, *An Inquiry into Meaning and Truth* (London: Allen & Unwin, 1940).

Russell, Bertrand, *A History of Western Philosophy*, 2nd edn (London: Allen & Unwin, 1961).

Salmon, Wesley C., *Scientific Explanation and the Causal Structure of the World* (Princeton, NJ: Princeton University Press, 1984).

Salmon, Wesley C., *Four Decades of Scientific Explanation* (Minneapolis: University of Minnesota Press, 1989).

Sandel, Michael, *Liberalism and the Limits of Justice* (Cambridge: Cambridge University Press, 1982).

Schama, Simon, *Dead Certainties (unwarranted speculations)* (Harmondsworth: Penguin/Granta, 1992).

Schleiermacher, Friedrich, *Hermeneutics*, ed. H. Kimmerle, trans. J. Duke and J. Forstman (Missoula, MO: Scholars Press, 1977).

Schrödinger, Erwin, *Letters on Wave Mechanics* (New York: Philosophical Library, 1967).

Searle, John R., 'Reiterating the Differences', *Glyph*, Vol. 1 (Baltimore: Johns Hopkins University Press, 1977), pp. 198–208.

Searle, John R., 'The World Turned Upside Down', *New York Review of Books*, Vol. XXX, No. 16 (27 Oct. 1983), pp. 74–9.

Searle, John R., 'Literary Theory and its Discontents', *New Literary History*, Vol. XXV, No. 3 (1994), pp. 637–67.

Selden, Raman, *Criticism and Objectivity* (London: Allen & Unwin, 1984).

Shanker, S.G. (ed.), *Gödel's Theorem in Focus* (London: Routledge, 1987).

Shapin, Steven, 'History of Science and its Sociological Reconstructions', *History of Science*, Vol. 20 (1982), pp. 157–210.

Shapin, Steven, *A Social History of Truth: Civility and Science in Seventeenth-century England* (Chicago: University of Chicago Press, 1994).

Shapin, Steven and Schaffer, Simon, *Leviathan and the Air-Pump: Hobbes, Boyle, and the Experimental Life* (Princeton, NJ: Princeton University Press, 1985).

Shaw, Patrick, *Logic and its Limits*, 2nd edn, revised (Oxford: Oxford University Press, 1997).

Shaw, Patrick, 'Whatever Happened to the French Foucault? Norris on Foucault', *Journal of the British Society for Phenomenology*, Vol. 30, No. 3 (1999), pp. 275–90.

Sluga, Hans, *Heidegger's Crisis: Philosophy and Politics in Nazi Germany* (Cambridge, Mass.: Harvard University Press, 1993).

Smart, Barry, *Foucault, Marxism and Critique* (London: Routledge & Kegan Paul, 1983).

Smart, J.J.C., *Philosophy and Scientific Realism* (London: Routledge & Kegan Paul, 1963).

Smith, Peter J., *Realism and the Progress of Science* (Cambridge: Cambridge University Press, 1981).

Snow, C.P., *The Two Cultures, and A Second Look* (Cambridge: Cambridge University Press, 1963).

Sokal, Alan, 'A Physicist Experiments with Cultural Studies', *Lingua Franca*, Vol. 6, No. 4 (May/June 1996), pp. 62–4.

Sokal, Alan, 'Transgressing the Boundaries: toward a transformative hermeneutics of quantum gravity', *Social Text*, Vols. 46–7 (Spring-Summer 1996), pp. 217–52.

Sokal, Alan and Bricmont, Jean, *Intellectual Impostures: Postmodern Philosophers' Abuse of Science* (London: Profile Books, 1998).

Squires Euan, *The Mystery of the Quantum World*, 2nd edn (Bristol and Philadelphia: Institute of Physics Publishing, 1994).

Starr, Peter, *Logics of Failed Revolt: French theory after May 1968* (Stanford, CA: Stanford University Press, 1995).

Stroud, Barry, 'Conventionalism and the Indeterminacy of Translation', *Synthèse*, Vol. 19 (1968), pp. 82–96.

Sturrock, John (ed.), *Structuralism and Since* (Oxford: Oxford University Press, 1979).

Szondi, Peter, *Introduction to Literary Hermeneutics*, trans. Martha Woodmansee (Cambridge: Cambridge University Press, 1995).

Tallis, Raymond, *In Defence of Realism* (London: Edward Arnold, 1988).

Tallis, Raymond, *Not Saussure* (London: Macmillan, 1988).

Tarski, Alfred, 'The Concept of Truth in Formalized Languages', in *Logic, Semantics and Metamathematics*, trans. J.H. Woodger (Oxford: Oxford University Press, 1956), pp. 152–278.

Thomas, David Wayne, 'Gödel's Theorem and Postmodern Theory', *PMLA*, Vol. 110, No. 2 (1995), pp. 248–61.

Tugendhat, Ernst, *Traditional and Analytical Philosophy: Lectures on the Philosophy of Language* (Cambridge: Cambridge University Press, 1982).

Veeser, H. Aram (ed.), *The New Historicism Reader* (London: Routledge, 1994).

Walzer, Michael, *Spheres of Justice* (Oxford: Blackwell, 1983).

Walzer, Michael, 'The Politics of Michel Foucault', in David C. Hoy (ed.), *Foucault: A Critical Reader* (Oxford: Blackwell, 1986), pp. 51–68.

Walzer, Michael, *Interpretation and Social Criticism* (Cambridge, Mass.: Harvard University Press, 1987).

Wellmer, Albrecht, *Critical Theory of Society*, trans. John Cumming (New York: Seabury Press, 1974).

Wellmer, Albrecht, *The Persistence of Modernity: Aesthetics, Ethics and Postmodernism* (Cambridge: Polity Press, 1991).

White, Hayden, *Tropics of Discourse* (Baltimore: Johns Hopkins University Press, 1978).

White, Hayden, *The Content of the Form* (Baltimore: Johns Hopkins University Press, 1988).

Whorf, Benjamin Lee, *Language, Thought and Reality: Selected Writings*, ed. J.B. Carroll (Cambridge, Mass.: MIT Press, 1956).

Wiener, Jon, 'Deconstructing de Man' and 'Debating de Man', in *Professors, Politics and Pop* (London: Verso, 1991), pp. 3–11 and 12–22.

Wigner, E.P., *The Scientist Speculates*, ed. I.J. Good (London: Heinemann, 1962).

Williams, Bernard, *Ethics and the Limits of Philosophy* (London: Fontana, 1985).

Williams, Michael, *Unnatural Doubts: Epistemological Realism and the Basis of Scepticism* (Princeton, NJ: Princeton University Press, 1996).

Wimsatt, W.K., *The Verbal Icon: Studies in the Meaning of Poetry* (Lexington, KY: University of Kentucky Press, 1954).

Wimsatt, W.K., *The Day of the Leopards: Essays in Defence of Poems* (New Haven: Yale University Press, 1976).

Winch, Peter, *The Idea of a Social Science and its Relation to Philosophy* (London: Routledge & Kegan Paul, 1958).

Wittgenstein, Ludwig, *Philosophical Investigations*, trans. G.E.M. Anscombe (Oxford: Blackwell, 1958).

Wittgenstein, Ludwig, *Tractatus Logico-Philosophicus*, trans. D.F. Pears and B.F. McGuiness (London: Routledge & Kegan Paul, 1961).

Wittgenstein, Ludwig, *On Certainty*, ed. G.E.M. Anscombe and G.H. von Wright (Oxford: Blackwell, 1969).

Wittgenstein, Ludwig, *Remarks on Frazer's Golden Bough*, ed. Rush Rhees, trans. A.C. Miles (Nottingham: Brynmill Press, 1979).

Wittgenstein, Ludwig, *Culture and Value*, ed. Rhees (Oxford: Blackwell, 1980).

Wolin, Richard, *The Politics of Being: The Political Thought of Martin Heidegger* (New York: Columbia University Press, 1990).

Wolin, Richard (ed.), *The Heidegger Controversy: A Critical Reader* (Cambridge, Mass.: MIT Press, 1993).

Woolgar, Steve (ed.), *Knowledge and Reflexivity: New Frontiers in the Sociology of Knowledge* (London: Sage, 1988).

Woolgar, Steve, *Science: The Very Idea* (London: Tavistock, 1988).

Wright, Crispin, *Realism, Meaning and Truth* (Oxford: Blackwell, 1987).

Zohar, Danah, *The Quantum Self: A Revolutionary View of Human Nature and Consciousness Rooted in the New Physics* (London: Bloomsbury, 1990).

Index

Adorno, Theodor W. 68–9, 115, 207n, 212n
Albert, David Z. 221n
Althusser, Louis 2, 86, 166, 218n, 221n
Ankersmit, F.R. 203n
Apel, Karl-Otto 12, 44, 120, 190, 202n, 205n, 210n, 213n
Archimedes 63
Aristotle 29, 35–6, 39, 75, 77, 7–81, 84, 92–3, 95, 97, 98–102, 155, 160, 173, 208n
Armstrong, D.M. 205n, 220n
Arnold, Matthew 155, 159, 216n
Aronowitz, Stanley 194
Attridge, Derek 214n
Audi, Michael 221n
Austin, J.L. 46, 49, 55–7, 75, 95, 96, 97, 140, 207n, 215n
Avni, Ora 216n
Ayer, A.J. 204n, 216n

Bachelard, Gaston 2, 77, 81–90, 93, 94, 97, 98, 100–2, 164–6, 190, 209n, 210n, 218n, 221n
Balibar, Etienne 210n, 218n
Barnes, Barry 180–1, 205n, 209n, 217n
Barrett, Michèle 213n
Barth, John 22
Barthes, Roland 20, 22, 163, 203n, 217n
Baudelaire, Charles 119, 124, 128, 132, 133
Baudrillard, Jean 2, 23, 24, 203n, 214n, 219n
Bauman, Zygmunt 33, 204n, 218n
Beckett, Samuel 152
Beethoven, Ludwig van 66
Beiser, Frederick C. 202n, 204n
Bell, J.S. 196, 197, 221n
Bellarmine, Cardinal 110, 117
Benhabib, Seyla 218n
Bennett, Jonathan 205n, 213n
Bennington, Geoffrey 214n
Benton, Ted 210n, 218n

Berkhofer, Robert F. 203n, 214n
Bhaskar, Roy 114–6, 205n, 212n, 220n
Black, J. 83
Black, Max 80, 209n
Blanchot, Maurice 152
Bleicher, Josef 216n
Bloor, David 180–1, 205n, 209n
Bohm, David 172, 194–8, 210n 219n, 221n, 222n
Bohr, Niels 36–7, 39, 89, 90, 166–7, 169–70, 193–7, 198–200, 210n, 218n, 219n, 221n
Booth, Wayne 221n
Bourdieu, Pierre 59, 64, 67–8, 207n, 214n
Brandom, Robert 32, 204n, 211n
Bricmont, Jean 4, 175–201, 219n
Brink, David O. 203n
Brittan, Gordon G. 210n
Britten, Benjamin 66
Brooks, Cleanth 217n
Burtt, E.A. 111–14, 212n

Calvino, Italo 22
Canguilhem, Georges 2, 81–2, 83, 87, 94, 98, 101, 190, 209n, 221n
Carnap, Rudolf 148, 149, 204n, 215n, 216n
Caruth, Cathy 216n
Causley, Robert L. 216n
Cavell, Stanley 207n
Cioran, E.M. 152
Clark, Timothy 211n
Coffa, J. Alberto 90, 210n
Cohen, Sandy 211n
Coleridge, Samuel Taylor 80, 157
Collins, Harry 212n
Copernicus, N. 87
Cratylus 150
Culler, Jonathan 207n
Cunningham, Valentine 219n
Curtius, Ernst Robert 142, 215n
Cushing, James T. 195, 198, 210n, 219n, 221n

Dalton, John 36–7, 39, 89, 166
Damarin, Suzanne K. 220n
Davidson, Donald 43–4, 80, 105–8, 151, 205n, 206n, 209n, 211n
Darwin, Charles 155, 181
Davies, Paul C.W. 218n, 221n
DeBellis, Mark 65–6, 207n
de Broglie, Louis 194
Deleuze, Gilles 27–8, 52, 69, 199, 203n, 207n, 213n, 222n
de Man, Paul 3, 5, 136–52, 214n, 215n
Democritus 36
Derrida, Jacques 1, 2, 29–31, 33, 41, 45–7, 48–57, 59–74, 75–86, 89, 91–102, 137, 140–1, 144, 151, 167–8, 190, 193, 204n, 206n, 207n, 208n, 209n, 210n, 215n, 218n, 221n
Descartes, René 7, 29, 31, 76, 78, 88–9, 97, 100, 165, 202n, 210n
Deutsch, David 197, 218n, 221n, 222n
Devitt, Michael 205n, 220n
de Witt, B. 218n
Dilthey, Wilhelm 155, 161
Doctorow, E.L. 23
Dummett, Michael 20–22, 25–6, 49, 203n, 206n
Dupré, John 153–4, 216n

Eagleton, Terry 24, 203n
Einstein, Albert 36, 39, 89, 166, 172, 179, 187–9, 196, 197, 219n, 221n
Eliot, T.S. 156, 157
Elliott, Gregory P. 218n
Empson, William 80, 111–14, 168–70, 209n, 212n, 218n, 219n
Epicurus, 36, 78
Eribon, Didier 213n, 214n
Ernarth, Elizabeth Deeds 203n, 218n
Esch, Deborah 216n
Euclid 90, 98, 101, 165
Evans, Gareth 215n
Eze, Emmanuel Chukwudi 202n

Faraday, Michael 167
Faurisson, Robert 18–19, 22
Felman, Shoshana 207n
Feyerabend, Paul 37–8, 40, 43, 103, 109–11, 114–17, 164, 167, 205n, 218n, 220n
Fichte, Johann Gottlieb 32, 51, 140–1, 185, 215n
Field, Hartry M. 39, 205n

Fine, Arthur 210n, 219n
Fish, Stanley 175–6, 200–1, 207n, 219n, 222n
Folse, Henry J. 218n
Forman, Paul 198, 222n
Foucault, Michel 2, 3, 28, 40, 45, 83, 86–8, 91, 93, 103, 108, 118, 119–35, 136, 153–4, 166–7, 178, 190–1, 203n, 206n, 209n, 210n, 211n, 212n, 213n, 214n, 218n, 220n
France, Anatole 77–9, 208n
Frank, Manfred 217n
Frazer, Sir James 184
Frege, Gottlob 21, 26, 184, 203n, 220n
Freud, Sigmund 76, 88
Friedman, Michael 210n
Fuller, Steve 209n, 222n

Gadamer, Hans-Georg 83, 161, 213n
Galileo 35-6, 38, 40, 43, 89, 109–11, 117, 160
Gallison, Peter 216n
Gardner, Martin 205n
Gasché, Rodolphe 48, 137–52, 206n, 209n, 214n
Geertz, Clifford 211n
Geuss, Raymond 215n
Gibbins, Peter 210n, 221n
Glass, Philip 9
Gödel, Kurt 167, 179, 218n
Goodman, Nelson 200, 222n
Grace, George W. 214n
Graham, N. 218n
Grayling, A.C. 203n
Gregory, Bruce 214n, 216n
Greimas, A.-J. 217n
Gribbin, John 221n
Guattari, Félix 222n
Guyer, Paul 207n

Habermas, Jürgen 2, 8, 12, 41–51, 68, 84–5, 115, 118, 120–3, 135, 202n, 205n, 206n, 210n, 212n, 213n, 214n
Harman, Gilbert 215n
Harré, Rom 205n, 210n
Hartman, Geoffrey 139
Havel, Vaclav 179, 220n
Hawkins, Harriet 218n
Hayles, N. Katherine 167, 218n
Hegel, G.W.F. 10, 11, 32, 45, 51, 68, 75, 86, 95, 128, 141, 152, 185, 202n

Heidegger, Martin 32, 59, 77, 78, 83,
    124–5, 127, 147–9, 152, 161, 204n,
    207n, 209n, 215n, 217n
Heisenberg, Werner 168, 193–4, 195, 198,
    199
Hempel, Carl Gustav 204n
Hiley, Basil J. 210n, 219n, 221n
Hindess, Barry 214n
Hobbes, Thomas 124
Hobsbawm, Eric 179
Hodgson, P.E. 222n
Hölderlin, Friedrich 148, 149
Holland, Peter 219n, 221n
Hollis, Martin 209n
Homer 34, 38
Honner, John 218n, 221n
Hookway, Christopher 203n
Horkheimer, Max 115, 212n
Horwich, Paul 217n
Hoy, David C. 213n, 216n
Hoyningen-Huehne, Paul 217n
Hume, David 26
Husserl, Edmund 29, 31–3, 46, 51, 68,
    75–7, 95, 96, 100, 204n, 210n
Hutcheon, Linda 23, 203n

Irigaray, Luce 177, 186, 219n

Jameson, Fredric 8–10, 12, 202n, 207n
Jenkins, Keith 203n, 212n, 214n

Kant, Immanuel 2, 3, 7–17, 27–9, 31–4,
    40, 42–3, 45–50, 51–74, 75–7, 81,
    84–5, 87, 88, 90–1, 98, 100, 103, 104,
    108, 118, 119, 121–4, 128, 130–2,
    134–5, 136–7, 141, 154, 162, 165, 197,
    200, 202n, 204n, 207n, 213n, 218n
Keats, John 66
Keller, Evelyn Fox 187, 220n
Kepler, Johannes 112
Khomeini, Ayatollah 127
Kierkegaard, Søren 41, 205n
Kitay, Eva Feder 209n
Koertge, Noretta 219n
Kofman, Sarah 209n
Kristeva, Julia 177, 219n
Kuhn, Thomas S. 4, 35–8, 39, 40, 83, 89,
    94, 103, 107, 160, 163-6, 167, 173, 180,
    200, 204n, 209n, 210n, 217n

Lacan, Jacques 177
Lakatos, Imre 83, 209n

Latour, Bruno 112–14, 187–91, 193, 199,
    205n, 209n, 212n, 221n
Lavoisier, Antoine 37, 160, 181
Leavis, F.R. 156, 169, 217n
Lehman, David 143, 215n
Leibniz, Gottfried Wilhelm 197
Leucippus 36
Levinas, Emmanuel 29-31, 33, 37, 41–2,
    47, 172, 204n, 219n
Lévi-Strauss, Claude 217n
Lewis, David 197, 216n
Lincoln, Abraham 27
Lodge, David 202n
Lorentz, H.A. 187-8
Lovejoy, Arthur O. 6, 202n
Lovibond, Sabina 203n
Lucas, J.R. 222n
Lukes, Stephen 209n
Lyotard, Jean-François 2, 10–14, 17–19, 22,
    26–7, 32, 33, 37, 40, 41, 43, 46, 59, 70,
    83, 91, 103, 108, 127, 155, 163–4, 168,
    170, 172, 178, 202n, 204n, 207n, 208n,
    209n, 211n, 214n

Macherey, Pierre 190
Malinowski, Bronislaw 156
Mandela, Nelson 27
Mannheim, Karl 68
Margolis, Joseph 216n
Marx, Karl (and Marxism) 8-9, 10–11, 86,
    123, 127, 166, 190
Maudlin, Tim 221–2n
Maxwell, James Clark 167
McDowell, John 32, 204n, 215n
McMullin, Ernan 221n
McNay, Lois 214n
Mendeleev, D.I. 166
Michelson, A.A. 89, 210n
Miller, James 213n
Misak, C.J. 215n, 216n
Mitchell, Donald 202n
Morley, E.W. 89, 210n
Mowitt, John 214n
Mulhall, Stephen 209n
Murdoch, Dugald 218n
Musgrave, Alan 209n

Naess, Arne 203n
Nagel, Thomas 204n
Nanda, Meera 186, 220n
Neurath, Otto 216n
Newton, Isaac 36, 39, 113

Newton-Smith, William 209n
Nicholls, Peter 202n
Nietzsche, Friedrich 2, 3, 19, 32, 40, 45, 51,
    65, 77–81, 84, 88, 93, 94, 97, 103,
    119–30, 132–6, 140, 143, 164, 173,
    190–1, 208n, 214n
Norris, Christopher 204n, 205n, 206n,
    207n, 210n, 211n, 213n, 215n, 219n
Nye, Mary-Jo 205n
Nyman, Michael 9

Ogden, C.K. 217n
O'Neill, Onora 28, 204n
Orwell, George 66

Pais, Abraham 222n
Palmer, R.E. 213n, 216n
Papastephanou, Marianna 205n, 213n
Papineau, David 205n
Pärt, Arvo 9
Pavel, Thomas 203n, 217n
Peirce, C.S. 40
Perrin, Jean 205n
Picasso, Pablo 66
Pickering, Andrew 209n, 212n
Pinch, Trevor 212n
Planck, Max 172
Plato 20, 29, 31, 46, 49, 75, 76, 77, 81, 95,
    96, 144, 150
Platts, Mark 215n
Plotnitsky, Arkady 167, 218n
Podolsky, B. 219n, 221n
Polkinghorne, John 218n
Popper, Karl R. 100, 205n, 221n
Pound, Ezra 6
Priestley, Joseph 37, 83, 160, 181
Proust, Marcel 22
Putnam, Hilary 36, 200, 204n, 222n
Pynchon, Thomas 23

Quine, W.V.O. 26, 34–6, 38, 39, 91,
    107–8, 116–7, 147, 151, 158–60, 162,
    180, 200, 204n, 211n, 217n

Rabinow, Paul 205n
Rae, A.I.M. 218n, 221n
Rand, Richard 211n
Ransom, John Crowe 217n
Rawls, John 122
Redhead, Michael 210n, 221n
Reich, Steve 9
Reichenbach, Hans 204n, 212n, 217n

Reiss, Timothy J. 202n
Rescher, Nicholas 220n
Richards, I.A. 4, 80, 154–6, 157, 159, 168,
    169–70, 173, 209n, 219n, 216n, 218n
Ricoeur, Paul 162, 213n, 216n, 217n
Rockmore, Tom 214n
Ronen, Ruth 203n, 221n
Rorty, Richard 2, 41, 42, 48-50, 73, 75-8,
    83-5, 91, 94, 97, 106, 109–10, 119–23,
    125–7, 132–5, 155, 161, 164, 173, 205n,
    206n, 208n, 210n, 213n
Rose, Hilary 220n
Rose, Steven 220n
Rosen, N. 219n
Ross, Andrew 218n
Rouse, Joseph 209n, 212n
Rousseau, Jean-Jacques 46, 77, 95–7, 140,
    143, 5-4
Royle, Nicholas 211n
Russell, Bertrand 182–4, 213n, 220n
Rutherford, Ernest 36, 39, 89, 166

Salmon, Wesley C. 171, 205n, 219n, 220n
Sandel, Michael 202n
Saussure, Ferdinand de 23-4, 45, 105, 161-2,
    166, 172, 203n, 211n, 216n, 217n
Schaffer, Simon 209n, 212n
Schama, Simon 22, 23, 203n
Schelling, Friedrich Wilhelm Joseph 51
Schenker, Heinrich 64
Schiller, Friedrich 157
Schleiermacher, Friedrich Daniel Ernst 155,
    161, 216n
Schoenberg, Arnold 6
Schopenhauer, Arthur 32, 65
Schrödinger, Erwin 168, 171, 194–5, 219n,
    221n
Searle, John R. 46, 49, 50, 51, 96, 97, 206n,
    211n
Selden, Raman 219n
Shakespeare, William 64
Shapin, Steven 209n, 212n, 220n
Shaw, Patrick 3, 119–35, 212n, 213n
Sluga, Hans 214n
Smart, Barry 214n
Smart, J.J.C. 205n
Smith, Peter J. 205n, 220n
Snow, C.P. 156, 169, 176, 217n, 219n
Socrates 76, 78
Sokal, Alan 4, 175–201, 219n
Spinoza, Baruch 213n
Squires, Euan 210n, 218n, 221n

Starr, Peter 214n
Stravinsky, Igor 6
Stroud, Barry 216n
Sturrock, John 217n
Szondi, Peter 216n

Tallis, Raymond 219n
Tarski, Alfred 44
Tavener, John 9
Tennyson, Alfred 155
Tooke, Horne 150
Tugendhat, Ernst 215n

Veeser, H. Aram 203n
Vonnegut, Kurt 22, 23

Waismann, Friedrich 216n
Walzer, Michael 123, 129, 202n, 213n
Wellmer, Albrecht 44, 205n

Wheeler, John 218n
White, Hayden 19–20, 22, 202n, 214n
Whorf, Benjamin Lee 106–8, 211n
Wiener, Jon 143, 215n
Wigner, E.P. 218n
Williams, Bernard 202n
Williams, Michael 203n, 204n
Wimsatt, W.K. 157, 217n
Winch, Peter 43, 181, 205n, 220n
Wittgenstein, Ludwig 4, 21, 26, 42, 43, 83,
    161, 181–5, 201, 203n, 205n, 209n,
    220n
Wolin, Richard 214n
Woolgar, Steve 205n, 209n, 220n, 221n
Wright, Crispin 203n

Young, Robert 214n

Zohar, Danah 219n

ATHLONE CONTEMPORARY
EUROPEAN THINKERS

Aesthetic Theory
Adorno
0 485 30069 9 HB
0 485 30090 7 PB

Composing for the Films
Adorno & Eisler
0 485 11454 2 HB
0 485 12017 7 PB

Freud and Nietzsche
Assoun
0 485 11483 6 HB

Criticism and Truth
Barthes
0 485 12144 1 PB

Sollers Writer
Barthes
0 485 11337 6 PB

On Nietzsche
Bataille
0 485 30068 0 HB

Nietzsche: The Body and Culture
Blondel
0 485 11391 0 HB

Death: An Essay on Finitude
Dastur
0 485 11487 9 HB

Telling Tme: Sketch of a Phenomenological Chronology
Dastur
0 485 11520 4 HB

Proust and Signs
Deleuze
0 485 12141 7 PB

Kant's Critical Philosophy
Deleuze
0 485 12101 8 PB

Difference and Repetition
Deleuze
0 485 11360 0 HB
0 485 12102 6 PB

The Fold: Leibniz and the Baroque
Deleuze
0 485 11421 6 HB
0 485 12087 9 PB

Anti-Oedipus Capitalism and Schizophrenia
Deleuze & Guattari
Preface by Michel Foucault
0 485 30018 4 PB

A Thousand Plateaus
Deleuze & Guattari
0 485 11335 X HB
0 485 12058 4 PB

Cinema 1: The Movement-Image
Deleuze
0 485 12081 X PB

Cinema 2: The Time-Image
Deleuze
0 485 11359 7 HB
0 485 12070 4 PB

Dialogues
Deleuze & Parnet
0 485 11333 3 HB

Foucault
Deleuze
0 485 12154 9 PB

Logic of Sense
Deleuze
0 485 30063 X HB

Nietzsche and Philosophy
Deleuze
0 485 12053 4 PB

Dissemination
Derrida
0 485 12093 3 PB

Positions
Derrida
0 485 30000 1 HP
0 485 12055 0 PB

The Memory of Thought: On Heidegger and Adorno
Düttmann
0 485 11489 5 HB

The Gift of Language: Memory and Promise in Adorno, Benjamin, Heidegger and Rosenzweig
Düttmann
0 485 11488 7 HB

Nietzsche's Philosophy
Fink
0 485 11484 4 HB

Death and the Labyrinth: The World of Raymond Roussel
Foucault
0 485 11336 8 HB
0 485 12059 3 PB

Three Ecologies
Guattari
0 485 11555 7 HB

pleroma – Reading in Hegel
Hamacher
0 485 11457 7 HB

Towards the Definition of Philosophy
Heidegger
0 485 11508 5 HB

The Nature of Truth
Heidegger
0 485 11509 3 HB

On the Essence of Human Freedom
Heidegger
0 485 11516 6 HB

Phenomenology of Intuition and Expression
Heidegger
0 485 11415 8 HB

Speech is Never Neuter
Irigaray
0 485 11452 9 HB
0 485 12089 5 PB

Democracy Between Two
Irigaray
0 485 11503 4 HB
0 485 12123 9 PB

To Be Two
Irigaray
0 485 11492 5 HB
0 485 12120 4 PB

The Forgetting of Air
Irigaray
0 485 11491 7 HB
0 485 12119 0 PB

Elemental Passions
Irigaray
0 485 11409 7 HB
0 485 12079 8 PB

An Ethics of Sexual Difference
Irigaray
0 485 30067 2 HB
0 485 30070 2 PB

Nietzsche and the Vicious Circle
Klossowski
0 485 11440 2 HB

Explosion I
Kofman
0 485 11458 5 HB

Explosion II
Kofman
0 485 11459 3 HB

Camera Obscura: of Ideology
Kofman
0 485 11490 9 HB

Socrates: Fictions of a Philospher
Kofman
0 485 11460 7 HB

Nietztsche and Metaphor
Kofman
0 485 11422 4 HB
0 485 12098 4 PB

The Philosophical Imaginary
Le Doeuff
0 485 11352 X HB

Alterity & Transcendence
Levinas
0 485 11519 0 HB
0 485 12152 2 PB

Entre Nous: Essays on Thinking-of-the-Other
Levinas
0 485 11465 8 HB

Proper Names
Levinas
0 485 11466 6 HB

In the Time of the Nations
Levinas
0 485 11449 6 HB

Beyond the Verse
Levinas
0 485 11430 5 HB

Outside the Subject
Levinas
0 485 11412 7 HB
0 485 12097 6 PB

Difficult Freedom: Essays on Judaism
Levinas
0 485 11379 1 HB

Redemption and Utopia
Löwy
0 485 11406 2 HB

Sex and Existence: Simone de Beauvoir's *The Second Sex*
Lundgren-Gothlin
Preface by Toril Moi
0 485 11469 0 HB
0 485 12124 7 PB

Libidinal Economy
Lyotard
0 485 12083 6 PB

The Conflict of Interpretations: Essays in Hermeneutics I
Ricoeur
0 485 30061 3 HB

From Text to Action: Essays in Hermeneutics II
Ricouer
0 485 30064 8 PB

Hegel: Contra Sociology
Rose
0 485 12036 4 PB

Clavis Universalis
Rossi
0 485 11468 2 HB

Friedrich Nietzsche: An Introduction
Vattimo
0 485 11485 2 HB
0 485 12118 2 PB